THE LIFE OF AN AM

AND OTHER W

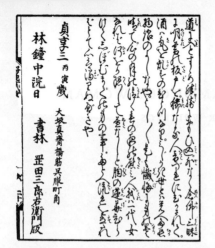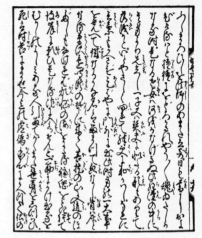

Final two pages of the first edition of *The Life of an Amorous Woman*. The text corresponds to the translation in the present book from " I fell down to the ground " on page 207 to the end of page 208, and the following colophon: *Published in the second decade of the sixth moon of the third year of the Jōkyō era, the year in which the Elder Brother of Fire is combined with the Sign of the Tiger [1686]: on the presses of Kōda Saburaemon, bookseller by the Shinsai Bridge at the corner of Gofukuchō in Osaka.*

Translation of the cover of the same edition (see overleaf); note that the poem breaks off with the implication that nothing else could have any beauty or interest: *Illustrated* / THE LIFE OF AN AMOROUS WOMAN / *Book 1.* / *Hiding his face he enters the pleasure quarters and makes his inquiries,* / *Whereupon he hears of a woman who grows more wonderful the more they tell of her.* / *In the Capital girls blossom as thick as the hills,* / *And in every province there are women to be had.* / *But even among a thousand women there is none to compare with this one,* / *So he pays two hundred gold koban towards her ransom.* / *For him who has seen the pleasure quarters of Shimabara:* / *The red leaves of autumn, the glory of the moon,* [*the women outside the quarters*]—

UNESCO COLLECTION OF REPRESENTATIVE LITERARY WORKS

THE LIFE OF AN AMOROUS WOMAN
AND OTHER WRITINGS

by IHARA SAIKAKU

Edited and translated by IVAN MORRIS

A NEW DIRECTIONS BOOK

SECOND PRINTING

TO

ARTHUR WALEY

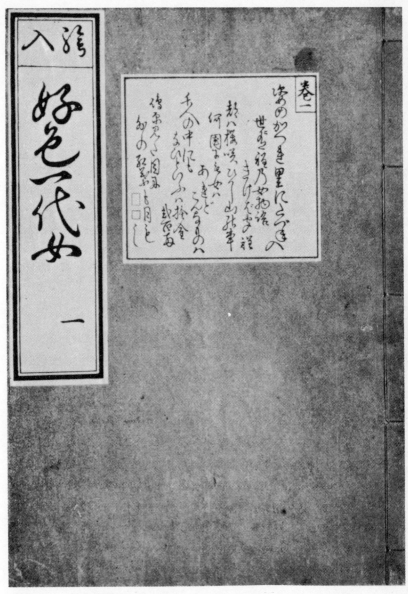

Cover of the first edition of *The Life of an Amorous Woman*, see overleaf for translation.

TABLE OF CONTENTS

LIST OF ILLUSTRATIONS

PREFACE

Saikaku was, above all, a popular writer. His books were directed not at a small intellectual coterie but at the great townsman class of seventeenth-century Japan whose members, though literate, were usually far from erudite. It may, therefore, seem incongruous that a translation of Saikaku's selected works should be burdened with a lengthy introduction, notes, appendices and index. Yet these impedimenta are, unfortunately, necessary if the selections are to be fully comprehensible to the nonspecialist Western reader. Indeed, the remoteness of pre-Meiji culture makes Saikaku's writing obscure even to most Japanese people. Although Saikaku is no more distant in time than Daniel Defoe or Molière, both the life and the literary language of Japan have changed so greatly since the seventeenth century that few educated Japanese can read the original works without the help of notes, commentaries and glosses.

In order not to mar the continuity of the text with commentaries and footnotes, all explanatory material has been placed at the beginning and at the end of the book. The introduction is designed mainly for the reader who has no special knowledge of Japan or of Japanese literature. The specialist is advised to omit the introduction, especially the first part (entitled "The Period"). Detailed information on the construction, sources and themes of the individual works translated in the present volume has been relegated to Appendix I. Appendices II and III provide factual details concerning two rather complex subjects that are important for an understanding of Saikaku's books, namely, money and the hierarchy of courtesans. The textual notes are numbered consecutively from 1 to 890 and are all placed together at the end of the volume. They are followed by an index, which includes all the important Japanese terms (and a few English words) that appear in the notes; it is hoped that, apart from providing a guide to the notes, this index will be of some use as a glossary to future students of seventeenth-century Japanese literature. The long diacritical marks are used here, in the introduction, the notes and appendices, but not in the text; on the other hand, I have occasionally provided acute accents in the text (but not in the notes) for words like Abé that might otherwise be mispronounced by readers who are unacquainted with the Japanese language. Japanese vowels are pronounced as in Spanish or Italian, with each vowel being given approximately its full value. Consonants are as in English, except that "g" is invariably hard. Names are written in the normal Japanese order, with the family name preceding the given name; it is to be noted that well-known writers in Japan are normally designated by their given names.

The decision to include extracts from four of Saikaku's works, rather than a complete translation of any one of them, may require a few words of justification. The translator's aim has been to give as wide a view of Saikaku's prose as is practical within the confines of a single volume. Saikaku is best known for his *kōshokubon* (erotic works) and his *chōnin-mono* (townsman works); the books represented in this translation are divided equally between these two classes. It is hoped that in due course a companion volume will be produced to include some of Saikaku's poetry, provincial stories, *samurai* works and tales of paederasty and of detection. The writing of Saikaku (and indeed of most pre-Meiji prose authors) is marked by a considerable laxity of construction; this applies both to collections like *Seken Munesanyō* and to the more unified works, like *Kōshoku Ichidai Onna*. As a result, these books often lend themselves to selection, to an extent that would be impossible in the case of most modern novels. Although the present book is far from providing a full conspectus of Saikaku's immensely versatile talent, it may give a better idea of his scope than would the translation of a single work.

My particular thanks are due to Professor Teruoka Yasutaka of the Literature Department of Waseda University and to Mr. Sugimoto Tsutomu of the same department. They have helped me to interpret many of the more obscure passages in the text and have painstakingly revised each page of the translation to ensure that it is as faithful to the original Japanese as the need to produce readable English will permit. I am also indebted to Professor Nishishita Keiichi of the Tokyo University of Education, who has revised my translations of some of the quoted poems that are included in the notes. Finally, I should like to thank Mr. Richard Lane for reading the manuscript and for making numerous valuable suggestions, and Miss Barbara Ruch for her meticulous work on the proofs.

TOKYO, 1958

INTRODUCTION

THE PERIOD

When Ihara Saikaku was born in Osaka in 1642, the Tokugawa Shogunate had been in power for nearly half a century and the main patterns that were to dominate Japan until the Imperial restoration some two hundred years later had taken shape.

In the middle of the seventeenth century, when feudal institutions in the West had been replaced by powerful monarchies, a centralized form of feudalism was just reaching its maturity in Japan. After almost three hundred years of political strife and intermittent civil war, the Shogunate (consisting of a series of military rulers or Shoguns, belonging to the Tokugawa family) succeeded in creating and maintaining a system that afforded the country two and a half centuries of almost complete peace.

The consistent aim of the Tokugawa government was to achieve unity under centralized power in the context of a feudal system, in which the various lords (*daimyō*) retained autonomy within their fiefs. Sovereignty remained in the hands of the Emperor and the capital was still at Kyoto. The Emperor's role, however, had become purely ceremonial; Kyoto was the centre of aristocracy, elegance and traditional artistic refinement, but not of power. Real authority was in the hands of the Tokugawa Shogun, the paramount feudal chieftain, who had his castle in Edo; and it was Edo (present-day Tokyo) that gave its name to the period which lasted from the early seventeeth to the mid-nineteenth century.

Saikaku's lifetime (1642–93) saw a steady increase in the centralized power of the feudal *bakufu* government. This government kept the country stable and peaceful for a remarkable length of time, but not without making use of spies, informers, censorship, minatory laws and

3

much of the paraphernalia that has since become familiar in modern police states. Almost every important aspect of Tokugawa policy was based on a determination to preserve the *status quo* and thus to perpetuate their power. An overthrow of the government by dissident feudal lords was the most immediate danger, but this the *bakufu* succeeded in averting by building up the strength of their own forces and by isolating and, wherever possible, weakening that of potential rivals.

A further possible source of disruption lay in the supposed ambitions of certain foreign nations to gain a foothold in Japan, particularly by means of traders or Christian missions. Already in 1623 trading with England was suspended and in 1624 the Spanish were ousted from Japan. The anti-Christian edicts, which for a time had been allowed to lapse, were rigorously enforced. The government's fear of foreign infiltration was sharpened by the Christian Rebellion of Shimabara in 1637 and thereafter the Tokugawa rulers adopted an exclusionist policy that is almost unique in history. In that year it was decreed on pain of death that no Japanese could leave the country, or, having left, return; at the same time the construction of ocean-going vessels was prohibited. Two years later the government banned all foreign trade, except that carried out by a handful of Chinese and Dutchmen who were allowed to live under strict control in a little island off Nagasaki. This was virtually to remain the extent of Japan's intercourse with foreign nations until the landing of Commodore Perry two hundred and fifteen years later. It would be hard to overestimate the effects of this exclusion policy, not only on the political and intellectual life of the Edo Period, but also on Japan's more recent history. The physical insularity of the country during the seventeeth and eighteenth centuries should be constantly kept in mind when examining the literature of Saikaku, Chikamatsu and other writers of the time.

The *status quo* was further supported by Confucian principles which were reinterpreted according to the needs of a feudal Japanese society and given official sanction by the Tokugawa rulers. The keystones of national morality were loyalty to one's superior and filial piety, with priority given to the former. Tokugawa Confucianism was a practical, conservative orthodoxy that stressed acceptance of the existing order and conformity to one's hereditary status. Scant regard was accorded to the individual and his rights; the emphasis was always on the group and, in particular, on the family. Vertical relationships, characteristic of a classic feudal society, prevailed at every level and were regulated by a code of hard-and-fast rules. People's fates were to be determined by their birth and their occupation, and every effort was made to freeze the class system in its existing form. The law was, therefore, especially harsh in its treatment of offences, such as adultery between members of different classes, or between men and women on different levels within the same class, which infringed the system. The death penalty was prescribed, for example, in cases of intercourse between a servant and his master's daughter (note 64).

Tokugawa society in theory consisted of a rigid hierarchy of four categories, namely, the *samurai* warriors, the peasants, the artisans and the merchants. The *samurai,* who formed less than eight per cent of the population and who, as peaceful times continued, became increasingly bureaucratized, had a virtual monopoly of political and administrative power. Their privileged position was clearly set forth in the putative Legacy of Ieyasu, the founder of the Tokugawa line:

The *samurai* are the masters of the four classes. Agriculturists, artizans, and merchants may not behave in a rude manner towards *samurai*. The term for a rude man is "other than expected fellow"; and a *samurai* is not to be interfered with in cutting down a fellow who has behaved to him in a manner other than is expected. [Murdoch: *A History of Japan,* Vol. III, p. 802.]

At the top of the hierarchy, then, was a nonproductive class of warriors, who monopolized the right to possess family names and crests, and who could stride through the streets with their double swords, confident in their inalienable right to cut down any offending commoner; at the

5

very bottom were the *chōnin,* the despised bourgeois money-makers, who were theoretically devoid of both power and rights. Yet, as the Tokugawa Period advanced, economic factors combined to make this hierarchy increasingly unreal.

The establishment of a stable regime had provided the conditions for the change from an agricultural to a mercantile economy. The seventeenth century saw the rapid development of commercial capitalism in Japan. Shortly after 1600, the government set up a national financial system based on gold and silver currency (to which copper was added in 1636), and metal money began rapidly to replace rice as the standard medium of exchange (App. II). Large areas of land were reclaimed and agricultural production rose considerably. Saikaku's lifetime witnessed the steady improvement of communications within Japan, a considerable increase in the total population and the expansion of the domestic market. This was accompanied by the growth of great consumer centres, like Edo and Osaka.

These conditions promoted the rise of a new independent merchant class, no longer closely tied to the interests of the provincial lords, but centred in the cities and primarily concerned with the production and free exchange of commodities. These merchant townsmen *(chōnin)* increased steadily during the seventeenth century, both in numbers and in importance. By the end of the century they had reached the apex of their power and the great city merchants had come to exceed most of the feudal lords in wealth.

The rise of the *chōnin* class was accompanied by a gradual weakening in the material position of the military, whose stipends were still paid in rice and who became more and more dependent on high-interest money loans from the merchants. At the same time, the breakdown of the rice economy aggravated the agrarian situation and steadily worsened the lot of the farmers, the second class in the theoretical hierarchy. One eventual result of this economic evolution was increasing movement between one class and another and the partial blurring of class distinctions. The

6

government attempted to halt the rise of the *chōnin* by such artificial devices as sumptuary edicts, debasement of the coinage and confiscation, but they inevitably failed to make economic realities conform to their hierarchical theory.

The immense wealth of the successful bourgeois emerges repeatedly in Saikaku's writing. In one of his books he refers to the fact that in Kyoto alone at least forty-seven merchants had the equivalent of $2,800,000 (£1,000,000 sterling) in ready cash and that thirty-six of them had double that amount (7,000 kamme of silver). The fabulous cost of visiting houses of assignation and consorting with the great courtesans is a further illustration of the merchants' wealth, for it was they who were the principal patrons of the gay quarters. A single night spent with one of the top courtesans could cost the equivalent of $420 (£150), and to become the patron of one of these ladies for a year required over $22,400 (£8,000). Not all the merchants were rich, however. During the course of the seventeenth century the divisions between poverty and wealth became immense, and some of Saikaku's later works vividly picture the miseries of the poorer townsmen in a world where, as he put it, "only money breeds money."

The prosperity of the *chōnin* class was intimately connected with the rise of the great urban centres. By the time of Saikaku's death Edo was probably the largest city in the world, having a population of almost one million. While Edo was the political heart of the nation, Osaka (Saikaku's birthplace) was the greatest commercial centre. Osaka merchants were mainly wholesalers or brokers dealing in products of the entire country. With the development of a national money economy, the role of this city became increasingly important and its population rose to some 400,000. Kyoto, the nominal capital and still the centre of traditional culture, had about half a million inhabitants.

Although in some ways the role of the Tokugawa merchants was analogous to that of their European counterparts, they failed to develop into a middle class on Western lines. The individualist spirit of free

7

enterprise and free competition made little headway and the guild or-
ganization of the *chōnin* remained almost as rigid as that of the feudal
hierarchy itself. Living in a fixed-status community based on a closed
national economy, this *bourgeoisie* was unable or unwilling to provide
the initiative for converting the mercantile economy into industrial
capitalism. Even towards the end of Saikaku's lifetime there were signs
of economic stagnation and these became increasingly evident in the
eighteenth century, when the size of the population itself became virtu-
ally static.

Another important way in which the Tokugawa merchant class dif-
fered from the rising middle classes of the West was that they failed to
convert their economic power into a struggle for political influence or
rights. Into what channels, then, did the affluent townsmen direct the
energy and strength that their economic preponderance gave them? The
expansion of business activities and the accumulation of still greater
wealth was the major focus of activity. There were, however, two other
fields, the cultural and the hedonistic, which are particularly important
for an understanding of Saikaku's literature. The townsmen's cultural
and hedonistic interests found common ground in certain areas, such as
the Kabuki theatre and the gay (or licensed) quarters, from both of
which members of the warrior class were theoretically debarred. This
was the *ukiyo*, which gave its name to the famous *ukiyoe* genre paint-
ings, as well as to Saikaku's characteristic form of prose, the *ukiyo-zōshi*.
Ukiyo had originally signified the Buddhistic "sad world" of change
and decay, but later it came to mean the "floating world" of pleasure
and fashion, whose heroes were the actor and the courtesan and whose
guiding principles were (according to a well-known saying) love and
money. In the *ukiyo* of the seventeenth century the affluent townsmen
found pleasures that were more ample and varied than any enjoyed by
commoners in Japan until then.

In view of the important role of the gay quarters in many of Saika-
ku's books, a few words should be said about this very special society.

During the early decades of the century licensed quarters were establish-
ed in various cities of Japan with the approval of the Tokugawa govern-
ment. The famous Yoshiwara in Edo was founded in 1617, the Shin-
machi in Osaka in about 1620 and the Shimabara in Kyoto in 1641; by
1679 there were over one hundred of these quarters throughout the
country and at the time when Saikaku described them they were mostly
in a flourishing condition. The Yoshiwara, for instance, consisted of
about 150 houses and contained some 3,000 courtesans, together with a
large population of attendants, dancing girls, musicians, panders, jesters
and special tradesmen.

The gay quarters—small, self-supporting "towns of pleasure" *(yūri)*
within the larger cities—were a world of their own. This world was
marked by formal etiquette, elaborate ritual and aesthetic discrimina-
tion. It had its own strict and complex hierarchy; for in a status society
like that of seventeenth-century Japan even ladies of pleasure were
rigidly stratified (App. III). In some ways the gay quarters corresponded
to the coffee-houses of eighteenth-century London as centres of elegance
and wit; but in addition they were infused with an atmosphere of gal-
lantry, glamour and sensuality. The high-ranking courtesans, many of
whom were recruited from among the daughters of unemployed *samu-
rai*, were endowed with physical beauty, magnificent dress and accoutre-
ments, artistic refinement, a knowledge of etiquette and a culture which,
though strictly circumscribed, was greater than that of most towns-
women of the period. None of this, of course, should obscure the es-
sential fact that these women were prostitutes, whose favours could in
most cases be enjoyed by any man willing and able to pay the extrava-
gant price. It is true that the qualities known as *iki* and *hari* (roughly,
"spirit" and "pride") were much respected in the courtesans and that
occasionally a high-mettled girl might turn down an unwelcome
customer or even fly the gay quarters with some indigent lover. These,
however, were rare exceptions, and the contemporary idealization of
the gay quarters, as reflected in the Kabuki and also in some of Saika-

9

ku's early works, must not draw our attention from their essentially sordid aspect, or from the harsh methods of recruiting and holding the inmates in what amounted to an elegant form of slavery.

It was the mercenary basis of value in the gay quarters that especially suited them for enjoyment by the affluent townsmen. In this world, where gold and silver ruled, the well-to-do merchant could assert himself and escape from the frustrations of outside society. For money, as Saikaku once pointed out, was the merchant's only pedigree. In the gay quarters class distinctions counted for little next to wealth, and the *samurai* who depended on his modest rice stipend, with its constantly fluctuating money value, or on loans of gold obtained from usurious merchants cut a poor figure next to the opulent and free-spending townsman. In the words of an eighteenth-century verse,

> *In the Yoshiwara*
> *The way of the warrior*
> *Cannot conquer.*

Money, it is true, was not the only key to a man's success in the gay quarters. Aesthetic taste, a form of worldly *savoir faire* known as *sui* or *tsū*, sexual prowess and a thorough knowledge of etiquette were also important qualifications. These, however, were all fields in which the merchant was the match of his theoretical superiors, and in the "nightless cities" he was able to realize a type of social equality that was impossible elsewhere.

The gay quarters also offered a ribald escape from the gloom of Buddhism, the rigid codes of official Confucianism and the draconian laws that governed sexual morality. It was a place where men could find a release from the strains of a hidebound, status-ridden feudal society by means of sensual pleasure and vicarious participation in the arts —a release that their own families, being an intimate part of that society, could usually not provide. At a time when the convivial aspect of family life was still undeveloped and when townsmen had little opportunity to participate in public activities, the "flower and willow world," as it is called, had an extremely important social function for those who could afford its pleasures. Here the merchants could resort, after a visit to the public baths or to the Kabuki theatre, and could converse in elegant surroundings and good company.

In examining the role of the gay quarters in Saikaku's books, we must remember how important these places were in vivifying the bourgeois culture of the seventeenth century. The townsmen who congregated in the fashionable houses of Shinmachi, Shimabara, Yoshiwara and elsewhere provided much of the material support and creative spirit that resulted in the remarkable artistic revival of the Genroku Period. Strictly speaking, this period lasted from 1688 to 1703, but in effect it was an entire cultural phase that reached its peak in the 1690s. Genroku art was centred in the cities and was the culmination of the expanding culture of the prosperous townsmen. As Professor Teruoka points out, this was the first time in Japanese history that the cultural leaders of the country belonged to a ruled, rather than to the ruling, class, and it may well have been the very fact that the ascendant townsmen were frustrated in so many other ways by the rigid patterns of the Tokugawa regime that led them to direct their energies to the creation and support of a new culture. Professor Teruoka regards the popularity of *haikai* poetry among members of the merchant class as a particularly important factor in promoting their wider cultural interests and in stimulating the Genroku artistic revival. Significantly, it was the great commercial city of Osaka that became the literary centre of the late seventeenth century, and it was Saikaku, a *haikai* poet and a citizen of Osaka, who brought bourgeois prose literature to its first peak in the Genroku Period.

Genroku culture did not, of course, start from scratch and owed much to the work of previous centuries. There are, however, certain salient qualities which distinguish it from classical and mediaeval culture and which apply equally to its theatre, its colour prints and its prose fiction. Among other things, Genroku culture reflected the extrava-

11

Genroku = Floating World exemplified

gance, frivolity and mundane hedonism of the Floating World. To a certain extent it can be regarded as a protest against the gloomy other-worldliness of mediaeval Buddhism and the drab severities of Tokugawa morality. The frivolous, hedonistic aspect often gave rise to bawdiness and eroticism, as seen, for example, in the "spring pictures" of the *ukiyoe* artists, in the pornographic booklets of the seventeenth and eighteenth centuries and in the general license that prevailed in the theatre. The government, ever anxious to foster the "moral nation," attempted to suppress these unseemly manifestations and also to restrict the extravagance and ostentation that were so prominent an adjunct of bourgeois culture; as a rule, however, their decrees and sumptuary regulations were of little avail. The merchants might be debarred from political influence, but they could not be prevented from enjoying the fruits of their own money and leisure.

excesses of eroticism in early theatre

govt attempted to enforce restrictions

In addition, the bourgeois culture of the Genroku Period was characterized by its relative independence. Not only was it largely unhampered by established artistic conventions, but it was remarkably free from Chinese influence. Its close association with a new, rising class also lent it a spontaneous, experimental quality that tended to be lacking in the established aristocratic culture.

These general characteristics are all found in Genroku prose fiction, the so-called "notes of the Floating World" *(ukiyo-zōshi),* of which Saikaku was the originator and greatest exponent. This was a new bourgeois literature written mainly for the amusement and instruction of townsmen in the large commercial centres and describing them and the world that they inhabited. This is not to suggest that Genroku fiction was devoid of pre-Tokugawa influences. The court romances of the eleventh century, and especially the narrative literature of the thirteenth century, frequently find an echo in the writing of Saikaku. The great prose tradition of *The Tale of Genji* had, however, been hopelessly interrupted by the centuries of internecine strife and the main influences on Saikaku were of a far more recent nature. These

12

were the "*kana*-booklets" *(kana-zōshi)*, miscellaneous, usually short, works of fiction and semi-fiction, which became popular during the early part of the seventeenth century. The *kana*-booklets were written mainly in the popular *kana* (phonetic) script and could therefore be read by the ordinary townsmen more easily than most works of the time, which contained large numbers of difficult Chinese characters. The *kana* works were also far simpler in style than those that used the traditional Sinicized grammar and syntax. The improvement of education among the merchant class and the development of inexpensive printing techniques further promoted the success of the new bourgeois literature.

Like many literary genres in Japan, the *kana-zōshi* covers an immense scope. It includes topographies, stories and anecdotes about popular actors, critiques of the leading courtesans, frivolous romances, practical books of advice or instruction, guides to letter-writing, collections of traditional stories about different localities, picaresque tales and books written in an epistolary form. The common denominator of all these works was that they were mainly written by, for and about members of the merchant class, who until then had played so negligible a part in Japanese literature.

When Saikaku was born, the *kana-zōshi* were in a very jejune state and fiction altogether was among the least respected of the arts. The standard of the *kana-zōshi* slowly improved and in particular their realistic content increased. Saikaku, however, was the first writer to shape this rather scattered and inchoate form into an important literary genre.

The *ukiyo-zōshi*, which he inaugurated in 1682 with his first work of prose fiction, *The Life of a Man Who Lived for Love,* was the culmination of the *kana-zōshi* tradition. The influence of the "courtesan critiques" *(yūjo-hyōbanki)* is very apparent and may be briefly examined as an example of how *kana-zōshi* literature evolved into the *ukiyo-zōshi.* Already in 1624 practical guides to the gay quarters were being published to help townsmen on their visits to the Yoshiwara and similar resorts. They became increasingly popular in the 1660s, and in 1680 over one hundred such guides were in circulation. Gradually the literary content of these books became greater; this trend reached its culmination in Saikaku's work *The Great Mirror of Beauties* (1684), when the literary motive in his description of the courtesans and their world largely displaces the desire to convey information.

As its name implies, the *ukiyo-zōshi* literature corresponds in a sense to the *ukiyoe* school of genre pictures. Its characteristic content is vivid, fairly realistic description of the gay, colourful life of the cities and accounts of the popular actors and courtesans who inhabited the Floating World. As in the case of the *ukiyoe*, its sensual, hedonistic aspect tends on occasion to lead to highly erotic content. The *ukiyo-zōshi* were not, however, restricted to the Floating World. In a broader sense, they were concerned with the conditions and customary ways of thought and action of the contemporary merchants and *samurai*. They thus provide us with a remarkably vivid picture of the society of the times—with the exception, that is, of the peasant class, which only figures incidentally in this literature.

Saikaku's originality, then, does not lie in having created a new genre. Both in appearance and content his *ukiyo-zōshi* belong to the established field of *kana-zōshi* writing. His achievement was to realize the full literary potentialities of an already existing genre; by infusing a new, creative approach into the *kana-zōshi* tradition, he produced a bourgeois literature of lasting artistic importance. The audience for which he wrote was far larger than that to which any previous Japanese literature had been directed. Unfortunately, we have little reliable information about the number of copies in one printing of the *ukiyo-zōshi*, or about how many copies were actually sold. We do know, however, that the books were relatively cheap; the six illustrated volumes of *The Life of an Amorous Woman*, for example, cost the equivalent of about $2.25 (16s.) in the first edition. There was also a type of lending library in most cities, from which books could inexpensively be borrowed. The potential reading public for the *ukiyo-zōshi* was far larger than at any previous period. Although the mass of the peasant population still wallowed in illiteracy, the warrior class and virtually all the townsmen were able to read. From the number of editions that appeared of many of Saikaku's works, we may judge that this was a popular literature—indeed, the first popular prose writing of literary importance in Japan.

THE AUTHOR

Considering the fame and popularity that he achieved in his own lifetime, both as a poet and as a writer of prose fiction, it is remarkable how little reliable information remains about the life of Ihara Saikaku. There are few extant records from which we can form an accurate account and, despite the recent exhaustive studies of scholars like Professor Noma, a good deal must still be based on surmise.

We cannot even be certain about the class into which Saikaku was born. The consensus is that his parents belonged to the merchant class, and in any case there is no doubt that Saikaku regarded himself as a *chōnin*. He was born in Osaka in 1642 and was thus the contemporary of some of the greatest men in Tokugawa cultural history, notably, of the *ukiyoe* artist Moronobu (1645–1715), the poet Bashō (1644–94) and the dramatist Chikamatsu (1653–1725); among outstanding European contemporaries were Molière and Defoe.

Saikaku first started to write at the age of fourteen. Although it was as an author of prose fiction that he was to make his great name, the first twenty-six years of his writing career were devoted entirely to poetry, specifically to the *haikai*. This was a form of highly condensed poetry, written in a series of alternating 17 and 14 syllables, and usually composed in series of 36, 50 or 100 verses. It owed its origins to the *renga* (linked verses) of the Muromachi Period and had been started in the sixteenth century; it was not until the seventeenth century, however, that it came to dominate Japanese poetry. The popularity of the *haikai* was particularly associated with the ·rise of the merchant-townsman class. Unlike the classical 31-syllable *tanka,* this was a form of poetry that required no special training and that could be appreciated, and even written, by anyone with a modicum of education. Furthermore, the new form permitted the use of everyday subjects and words that were barred from classical verse. The *haikai* reached its apogee in the work of Bashō. Prior to that, the most influential centres of seventeenth-century *haikai* writing had been the Teitoku School (Teimon) under Matsunaga Teitoku and the Danrin School under Nishiyama Sōin. Saikaku was originally a follower of the Teimon and by 1662 he was already fairly well known as a poet. Later he became associated with the ascendant Danrin School; in 1672 he had become the centre of a group of avant-garde Danrin poets. In 1673 this group brought out a collection of their *haikai (Ikutama Manku)*, which is generally regarded as Saikaku's first published work. During his lifetime he published about twelve volumes of poetry and of verse criticism.

In 1675 Saikaku's wife, who appears to have been a childhood friend, died of some form of influenza, leaving him with three children, one of whom was a blind daughter. Saikaku never remarried. Two years after his wife's death he took the tonsure. This was a fairly normal procedure for writers and painters of the time and meant that they intended to devote their lives to art; according to some biographers, however, Saikaku's official retirement from the world was also inspired by sorrow over the death of his wife.

The taking of Buddhist vows ushered in the era of Saikaku's greatest activity in the field of *haikai,* lasting from 1677 to 1682. This was also the period when he became famous for his *yakazu* (poetry marathons), which are discussed in the following section. In 1682 Nishiyama Sōin, the head of the Danrin School, died. Saikaku had been one of Sōin's

浪
華
西
鶴
翁

芳
一
昌
寫

Painting of Saikaku by his colleague, the *haiku* poet Haga Isshō (1643–1707). It was drawn shortly before Saikaku's death at the age of fifty-one. (Courtesy of Professor Yasutaka Teruoka of Waseda University, Tokyo.)

principal disciples and appears to have received considerable support from him; after the master's death his position among the highly competitive and faction-ridden Danrin poets evidently became difficult. It is sometimes suggested that this was one of the immediate reasons for his turn to prose. In 1682, at the age of forty, he produced his first work of prose fiction, *The Life of a Man Who Lived for Love*. This was the pioneer of the *ukiyo-zōshi* genre and appears to have had a considerable success at the time. Saikaku followed it up two years later with another prose work; at the same time he was producing *haikai* in greater volume than ever.

In 1685 Saikaku tried his hand at a *jōruri* (puppet) drama, the genre in which Chikamatsu made his great name. Saikaku's play *The Calendar (Koyomi)* coincided with a more popular work of Chikamatsu's and appears to have been a failure. For the next several years he directed his energy entirely to the field of prose. The years from 1685 to 1688 represent the high point of his career as a writer of prose fiction and most of his important works, including three out of the four translated in the present volume, were produced during this period of immense literary activity. His output of fiction reached its height in 1688, during which he published no less than five full-length works. Thereafter he wrote at a less feverish rate. This fact, as well as the more sombre tone of his subsequent writing, has prompted the belief that he fell ill towards the end of 1688. In the following year Saikaku resumed his work in *haikai* poetry. Until the end, however, he continued writing *ukiyo-zōshi*. In 1692 he produced *Reckonings That Carry Men through the World*, the last work that was to be published during his lifetime. In the same year, Saikaku's blind daughter died. His final works reflect a gathering sense of gloom, although the old vitality has certainly not disappeared.

He died in 1693 at the age of fifty-one (fifty-two in the Japanese count) and his ashes were buried in the Seigan Temple in Osaka. He left as his parting statement the words, "The life of man is fixed at fifty years and even this seems too long a span to me. How much more so . . . ," and to this he added as his final *haikai,*

> *I have gazed at it now*
> *For two years too long—*
> *The Moon of the Floating World.*

The best-known extant painting of Saikaku is by the Danrin poet Haga Isshō. It shows the writer in his later years—a small figure with a tonsured head, dressed in formal robes and seated ceremoniously on the floor. At first we are struck by the enormous ears, the staring eyes and the tiny hands; but in the end the main impression that emerges is of a clever man with strong character, a man with a sharp cynical expression, yet at the same time full of life, goodly humour and understanding.

THE WORK

Since Saikaku was first of all a *haikai* poet, and since poetry had so great an influence on his subsequent prose fiction, even a brief discussion of his work must start with a few words about the Danrin School of *haikai,* with which he was mainly associated. The Danrin School, which reached the height of its influence in the 1670s, and to which Bashō himself was attached in his early years, was the first to reveal the full modern significance of the *haikai,* the form that was to culminate in the *haiku.* Whereas the poets of the Teimon had been greatly concerned with the observation of complex poetic conventions and with elegant plays on words, the Danrin School, while retaining much of the frivolous humour of the Teimon writers, put its emphasis on the observation of real life. The typical Danrin *haikai* were poems of manners taking their material from the everyday activities of the *chōnin.*

The most skillful poet of the Danrin School was undoubtedly Saikaku himself. In his writing the various characteristics of the Danrin *haikai* were carried to their furthest point. His aim, as we may judge from his poems, was to complete the liberation of the *haikai* from the rigid conventions and restrictions that were condemning the form to sterile triviality. Saikaku's representative *haikai* are realistic poems of manners, infused with a detached sort of humour and with a vivid feeling of the life actually lived by townsmen of the time. Throughout his poetry the approach is more narrative than lyrical; the focus is on events rather than feelings, on human beings rather than nature, on the daily life of the people rather than the accepted subjects of literary aesthetics.

Saikaku's breach with poetic orthodoxy was frequently regarded askance, even by fellow-members of the relatively progressive Danrin School. By 1673 it had earned him the significant epithet of *Oranda Saikaku* (Dutch Saikaku). Holland was by that time the only non-Asian country with which Japan had any direct relations and it might be thought that this nickname referred to some exotic aspect in Saikaku's writing or to some connection with foreign studies. Saikaku, however, had no particular interest in the West. Words like *Oranda* (Holland), *Bateren* (patre, Jesuit missionary) and *kōmō* (red-haired, i.e., foreign) were widely used in the seventeenth century as epithets for something out of the ordinary or eccentric. In a rigid, conformist society like that of Tokugawa Japan this was bound to be pejorative. As Professor Teruoka points out, the term *Oranda* was at one time applied derogatively to the entire Danrin School because of its supposed unorthodoxy. Later it was applied specifically to Saikaku by his fellow Danrin poets because of his refusal to respect the canons of their school.

It is significant that, despite the contemptuous implication of the *Oranda* epithet, Saikaku should later have used it proudly about himself. For Saikaku's nonconformism was not limited to his poetry, but extended to the entire field of his writing. Just as he used the rigid form of the *haikai* to suit his own artistic purpose, so later, when he turned to prose, he was able to mould the existing genre of *kana-zōshi* into a literary form capable of expressing something entirely new. His *Oranda* background as a *haikai* poet is an essential aspect of his later development as *ukiyo-zōshi* writer.

Despite Saikaku's pre-eminence in the Danrin School, he was certainly not one of the great poets of Tokugawa Japan. With all due deference to some of his more uncritical advocates, it may safely be assumed that, if he had not later branched into prose fiction, his name as a writer would have been totally overshadowed by those of Bashō and Chikamatsu. Saikaku succeeded in freeing the *haikai* from many of its conventions and in enlarging the scope of its subject matter; but he cannot be considered to have paved the way for Bashō or for the great *haiku* masters of the following century. His outstanding qualities as a poet were speed, energy, humour, self-confidence and a remarkably logical approach to his material. In themselves these were not qualities that would make for great *haikai,* and in reading Saikaku's poetic work one is often struck by the feeling that this very restrictive genre was unsuited to his particular genius. He himself seems to have been keenly aware that his gifts were more narrative than lyrical, and his fantastic achievements in the field of *yakazu* (poetry marathons) may be regarded as one effort to escape from the trammels imposed by the laconic form of the *haikai* and to approach a more congenial genre, in which sustained narrative and a thoroughly realistic approach were possible.

The genre of *yakazu* was initiated by Saikaku himself shortly after he took the tonsure in 1677. In a period of twenty-four hours Saikaku composed a total of 1,600 linked *haikai* verses. The performance was carried out in the presence of judges, numerous fellow-poets and other witnesses; the actual writing was done by a scribe. If we allow two hours for eating and other necessities, the average time that Saikaku took to compose a single verse on this occasion was fifty seconds. The publicity that attended the feat appears to have inspired several other poets to emulate him, and the *yakazu* soon became something of a national fad. Saikaku made it clear that he did not like being outdone in this field. In 1680 he set a new record of 4,000 *haikai*, and four years later in front of the Sumiyoshi Shrine in Osaka he succeeded in composing 23,500 verses within the twenty-four-hour period, at an average rate of 3.3 seconds per verse. This remarkable feat earned Saikaku the nickname of *Nimanō* (The Old Man of the Twenty Thousand Verses), which he later adopted as a pen name. We are not surprised to hear that no one has ever attempted to beat this record.

The interest of the *yakazu* does not lie in their literary value, which was negligible. It was quantity that made for success in this field, not quality. Professor Teruoka recognizes in the popularity of the *yakazu* form the vigour and ebullient enthusiasm of the ascendant *chōnin* class. Saikaku's achievements in these poetic marathons reveal several aspects of his literary talent. In the first place, they adumbrate the immense energy of a man who during the next four years was to produce some fifteen full-length works of prose fiction. They also point to his wide knowledge, his rich imagination and his talent for association. Finally, as we have seen, his interest in *yakazu* suggests a desire to transcend the limitations of a short, essentially lyrical form; by linking thousands of *haikai* together in a more or less logical sequence, he came as close as was possible to expressing sustained narrative by means of brief, epigrammatic verses.

Two years before his climactic achievement in the field of *yakazu*, however, Saikaku had already reconciled the contradiction between form and content by branching into fiction, and from then on his main interest was turned from poetry to prose. Now at last the author was clear of the conventional restrictions of the *haikai* and could devote his energies to freely describing the life about him. In examining this turning-point in Saikaku's career, it is well to remember that he was abandoning a respected form of literature for one that was held in very low esteem. Throughout most of the Edo Period, fiction writers were ill-paid and belittled. Among the merchant class *haikai*, *haiku* and *jōruri* were the most popular literary forms and prose fiction was widely regarded as being fit only for women and children. It is all the more remarkable, therefore, that Saikaku's *ukiyo-zōshi* were able to achieve such contemporary success as they did.

Before examining Saikaku's prose works, we should take note of a theory, first advanced in 1951, according to which only one of these works, namely, *The Life of a Man Who Lived for Love,* was actually by Saikaku himself, all the remainder having been written by disciples or assistants. There has so far been little concrete evidence to support this startling hypothesis. The authorship of several of the works usually attributed to Saikaku is, however, open to question and there is still a need for considerable research, combining internal and external evidence, in this field. It is beyond the scope of an introduction to enter into this complex subject and for present purposes it will be assumed that the attributions made by Professors Ebara, Noma and Teruoka in their *Standard Edition of Saikaku's Complete Works* are substantially correct. It may be added that none of the works translated in the present volume is among those to which the problem of doubtful authorship usually applies.

Saikaku's prose fiction can be divided into three periods: (i) 1682–6, "erotic works" *(kōshokubon);* (ii) 1685–9, miscellaneous works; (iii) 1688–93, "townsman works" *(chōninmono).* These divisions are fairly arbitrary; some books fall chronologically outside the category to which they belong and, as will be seen, the periods themselves overlap. By and large, however, this division provides a useful frame of reference for briefly examining some of Saikaku's representative books and the evolution of his fiction.

The prose works of the first period are named after the untranslatable word *kōshoku,* which covers the entire range of gallantry, romantic love and sensual passion, and whose specific meaning varies with the context. The word itself figures prominently in many of the titles. In *The Life of a Man Who Lived for Love (Kōshoku Ichidai Otoko)* the emphasis of *kōshoku* is on gallantry, rakishness and straightforward sexual enjoyment. The book consists of fifty-four independent episodes in the love-life of the hero, Yonosuke, an elegant seventeenth-century rake of the townsman class. There is one episode for each year in his life, from the age of eight, when Yonosuke embarks on his amorous career (the object of his precocious attentions being a maidservant), until sixty-one, when the indefatigable hero, having experienced the love of every type of woman in Japan, sets off for a legendary island inhabited only by members of the female sex. The fifty-four episodes clearly correspond in number to the fifty-four books of the great eleventh-century novel, *The Tale of Genji,* and Yonosuke himself may be regarded as the counterpart in a bourgeois society of "Genji the Shining One," the beau ideal of an aristocratic age. The atmosphere of the book is optimistic, fresh and lively, and the focus is almost entirely on the pleasurable aspects of love. This being Saikaku's first prose work, the stylistic influence of *haikai* poetry is still extremely marked. *The Life of a Man Who Lived for Love* may be said to picture the romantic daydreams of the average *chōnin* man. This was undoubtedly one reason for its contemporary popularity. The first edition appeared in Osaka in 1682 with calligraphy and illustrations by Saikaku himself; another edition appeared in Edo two years later with illustrations by the great *ukiyoe* pioneer, Moronobu.

Although Yonosuke consorted with women of every class, the principal setting for his amours was the gay quarters, and these are depicted in the most attractive colours. This special world was also the setting for Saikaku's next two books, *The Great Mirror of Beauties* and *The Tale of Wankyū's Life. The Great Mirror of Beauties (Shoen Ōkagami),* also known as *The Life of a Man in the Second Generation Who Lived for Love (Kōshoku Nidai Otoko),* was published in 1684. It is a collection of independent stories concerning life in the "nightless cities" and is generally regarded as the culmination of the "courtesan-critique" genre of *kana-zōshi* (p. 13). *The Tale of Wankyū's Life (Wankyū Isse no Monogatari)* (1685) is based on a contemporary event and tells the story of a rich young man of the merchant class whose injudicious love for a courtesan leads to his madness and death.

In *Five Women Who Chose Love (Kōshoku Gonin Onna)* (1686) Saikaku for the first time looked outside the gay quarters for his heroines. The book consists of five independent tales, which are based on actual events of the time and each of which has for its protagonist an impetuous young girl of a non-*samurai* class. *Kōshoku* now has the sense of romantic love, rather than of gallantry, and each of the five heroines sacrifices her respectability in the pursuit of an amorous liaison. In every story except the last the results are tragic. The common theme is the conflict which was adumbrated in *The Tale of Wankyū's Life* and which was to play so great a part in Tokugawa literature (notably in Chikamatsu's tragedies)—the conflict, that is, between human passion and social realities or duty. Accordingly we find that the prevailing mood has changed entirely since Saikaku's earlier books. The characters no longer move within the insulated and slightly unreal confines of the gay quarters, but are directly confronted with the severe codes of outside feudal society, which they violate at their mortal peril.

The Life of an Amorous Woman (Kōshoku Ichidai Onna) was published in 1686, only four months after the *Five Women,* and is the culminating work of Saikaku's *kōshokubon*. Here *kōshoku* signifies pure eroticism and sensuality, utterly devoid of the romantic and sentimental aspects of love that inspired the earlier heroines. The protagonist of *The Life of an Amorous Woman* is, in blunt terms, a nymphomaniac and the book describes the steady degradation that results from her efforts to find a constant variety of sexual enjoyment, while at the same time surviving economically as a single woman in a harsh feudal society. Since, apart from her highly erotic nature, the heroine is endowed with physical beauty, her logical habitat is the gay quarters, and indeed it is here that the greater part of the action takes place. The courtesan's life, however, is no longer pictured in the rosy colours of the earlier works, but is revealed with full realism as a place where money rules the day and where sensual desire is rarely relieved by tenderness. As the heroine's beauty begins to desert her with advancing age, she sinks to the most sordid fields of commercial venery and finally becomes a common streetwalker. In this novel, then, Saikaku evokes the dark, gloomy aspect of sex and shows us the reverse side of the medal, as it were, of the *kōshoku* depicted in his first books.

In 1685 Saikaku embarked on a series of works that deal with a wide variety of subjects and which include *inter alia* local legends, tales of detection and stories about the *samurai* class. In much of the anecdotal writing belonging to this period we can detect the influence of early narrative literature, such as the famous thirteenth-century collection, the *Uji Shūi Monogatari*. The stories, however, reveal the down-to-earth, realistic approach of a modern townsman, who will frequently revise or even satirize the old legends, and who will take much of the *samurai* ethic with a grain of salt. *Saikaku's Tales from Various Provinces (Saikaku Shokoku-banashi)* (1685) and *The Pocket Inkstone (Futokoro Suzuri)* (1687) are two representative works that consist of anecdotes culled from different parts of the country, tales of the supernatural, traditional legends and modern stories. *Twenty Breaches of Filial Piety in This Land (Honchō Nijū Fukō)* (1686) is a collection of stories based partly on traditional material and partly on contemporary examples, illustrating various egregious violations of the code of filial piety. As usual, the delinquency of the present "younger generation" is contrasted with the supposed morality of an earlier age. The following year saw the publication of Saikaku's famous work on paederasty, *The Great Mirror of Manly Love (Danshoku Ōkagami)*. The book is divided into two parts, corresponding to the two areas where this practice was most prevalent—that is, *samurai* circles and the Kabuki theatre.

Although the townsmen were the chief subject of Saikaku's writing, he was also interested in the mores of the warrior class and in 1687–8 he wrote three works dealing with the *samurai*. These were *A Record of Traditions of the Warrior's Way (Budō Denraiki)* (1687), *Tales of the*

Knightly Code of Honour (Buke Giri Monogatari) (1688) and *New Records of Strange Events (Shin Kashōki)* (1688). All three were collections of independent stories, dealing mainly with the traditional themes of loyalty, honour and revenge, but presenting them in a modern, realistic way, so that we are struck not only by the noble side of the warrior's ethic, but by its futile and even pathetic aspects. In 1689 Saikaku produced one of the earliest Japanese collections of detective stories, *Judgements Made under the Cherry Blossoms in This Land (Honchō Ōin Hiji)*. Old Chinese detective stories, in which the hero was usually a shrewd examining magistrate, had been known in Japan for some time, but it was not until the 1660s that Japanese writers had tried this genre; Saikaku was the first to give it any literary significance.

The third period of Saikaku's prose fiction begins with *The Eternal Storehouse of Japan (Nippon Eitaigura)* (1688). The focus of interest is now on the practical economic life of the townsmen. The cool, objective approach of the second period, in which the author's attitude was mainly that of the impartial observer, gives way in the *chōninmono* to a sense of involvement as Saikaku concentrates on a theme with which he was deeply concerned, namely, how townsmen lived and how they should live. The didactic tone that informs many of the "townsman works" does not, however, turn them into moralistic tracts; the vivid depiction of individual character and the interest of the story itself are always paramount.

The Eternal Storehouse of Japan is a collection of thirty stories describing the varied ways in which ingenious men can accumulate money and the no less varied ways in which feckless men can lose it. The book had as its subtitle *New Lessons from the Lives of Wealthy Men,* and its practical advice on money-making appears to have made it extremely popular in the Genroku Period and during most of the eighteenth century. Its main interest for the contemporary reader, however, lies in its realistic description of various bourgeois types and in the effect that money can exert on them.

Two other collections of townsman tales were written at about this time, but not published until after Saikaku's death. *The Last Fragments of Saikaku's Cloth (Saikaku Oridome)* was published in 1694 and consists of two works written in 1688, *A Mirror of Townsmen in This Land (Honchō Chōnin Kagami)* and *The Hearts of People in This World (Yo no Hitogokoro)*. *The Myriad Letter Scraps (Yorozu no Fumi Hōgu)* (1696) belongs to the *kana-zōshi* tradition of epistolary works. It is a collection of stories dealing with bourgeois life and presented in the form of separate letters.

In *The Last Fragments of Saikaku's Cloth* a new tendency clearly emerges in Saikaku's description of the *chōnin*. His original attitude to the mercantile capitalism of his time appears to have been one of real enthusiasm. In particular, Saikaku approved of a system in which men were able to amass wealth by their own intelligence, resourcefulness and honest labours. In *The Eternal Storehouse of Japan* he shows the positive, optimistic aspects of the rise of new commercial groups, while at the same time warning his readers how easily improvidence or laziness can deprive men of the wealth that they or their fathers have accumulated. Subsequently, however, Saikaku appears to have had increasing doubts about the realities of the system. Already towards the end of the century, as we have seen, there were signs of economic stagnation and mercantile capitalism no longer seemed to offer its earlier opportunities. The more unfortunate *chōnin* families seemed to be unable to extricate themselves from their morass of poverty, however hard they worked. "Things have changed," Saikaku wrote. "Now it is only silver that can produce more silver. In these times it is not so much intelligence and ready wit that bring a man profit, but simply the fact of already possessing capital."

Saikaku's later works accordingly deal with the gloomier side of *chōnin* life. For the first time he turns his attention from the upper bourgeoisie, which has either inherited or earned wealth, to the middle and lower strata of townsman society, from the individuals who used money to those who were used by it. Saikaku provides one of the only existing records from the seventeenth century of the lives of the indigent townsmen who, far from profiting from the rise of the merchant class, were engaged in a constant struggle for the bare necessities of life.

The new approach reaches its culmination in the last of Saikaku's works to be published during his lifetime, *Reckonings That Carry Men through the World (Seken Munesanyō)* (1692). This is a collection of stories based on the theme of the year's end, that critical period for the impecunious townsmen when they were obliged to settle all their outstanding debts. Here Saikaku evokes the dark, anxious lives of the small *chōnin* and describes the various ruses by which they contrived to fob off the bill collectors. It is significant that, although Saikaku's realistic description of character is unimpaired, many of the stories in this work (for example, "The Ancient Scabbard" and "Lord Heitaro" in the present collection) use a collective method, according to which numerous anonymous individuals are presented in a group. Here Saikaku comes closer than any writer of the time to evoking the actual life of the urban masses in a period when "only money could breed money."

In both the *kōshokubon* and the *chōninmono*, then, Saikaku's realism seems to lead from a type of positive optimism in the earlier works to a growing pessimism as he focuses his attention on the gloomier and more negative aspects of love and money. In his final work, *Saikaku's Parting Present (Saikaku Oki-Miyage)* (1693), he plumbs the theme of decline and misery to its very depths. This appears to have been written during his last illness and was published shortly after his death.

This relatively sombre aspect of the later books must certainly not lead us to regard Saikaku as being in the main a gloomy or pessimistic writer. On the contrary, when we examine his prose works in general, we find that humour and a vigorous zest for life are among their outstanding qualities. Saikaku's humour takes many forms. There is the humour of parody and play on words, which derives to some extent from the *haikai* tradition and which reminds us that Saikaku's poetry is notable for its wit. Then there is the humour of hyperbole as seen, for example, in the description of the fabulous treasures that Gengobei received from his parents-in-law (pp. 117–18). It is the humour of observation, however, that travels best in time and in space, and it is in this field that Saikaku excels. Frequently his exuberant wit will emerge in a thumbnail sketch of some very minor character, such as Zetarō the Rock Leaper (pp. 93–4) or the old retainer (p. 131), who, despite his complete incapacity, derives great pleasure from lewd conversations. Saikaku was also impressed by the way in which economic need developed the cunning aspect of people's characters. *Reckonings That Carry Men through the World* gives several amusing instances of the ruses adopted by people who are better endowed in their wits than in their purses.

Some of Saikaku's most amusing descriptions are those of misers. His townsman works are full of characters for whom the accumulation of money and goods has become a devouring obsession. Like Molière, Saikaku is well aware of the tragic implications of avarice, but he never ignores its humorous aspects. Thus the old woman in *The Rat That Delivered Letters* is shown to be at the same time a wicked and a ludicrous figure. When the doctor meets her (p. 243), she is weeping profusely and from her laments he is convinced that she must have lost some close relation. What she has, in fact, lost is a small packet of money and she quickly sets the doctor right: "I may be lacking in good sense, but rest assured that I should not be grieving like this if it were merely a matter of someone dying! What afflicts me is of a more serious nature. . . ."

Saikaku's zest for life is a fascination with the material world as it actually is—the world of concrete objects, the world of living people. Sometimes this fascination will emerge in long catalogues of objects, such as the articles pawned by the tenement dwellers at New Year's (pp. 236–7), or in lists of people, such as the passengers waiting for the ferry (p. 68). But the most important aspect of Saikaku's zest for life lies in the immense range of his interests. This is reflected in both the form and the subject of his work. We have already noticed the scope and variety of Saikaku's artistic activity. *Haikai* poems, short stories, topographies, illustrations, *jōruri* drama, sketches of actors and courtesans, epistolary works, stories of detection, full-length novels—all these poured from his indefatigable brush and in many fields "Dutch Saikaku" was an innovator.

The comprehensiveness of his interests and of his experience emerges from the varied content of these works. Like his contemporary, Daniel Defoe, Saikaku was fascinated with different and distant places and he appears to have been a great traveller. His works are set not only in the well-known towns, but in the most remote provinces. These interests, of course, were circumscribed by the Tokugawa policy of exclusion (p. 4). Distances, however, must not be measured in miles but in terms of accessibility and from this point of view Saikaku's Japan was immense. The journey from Kyoto to Edo (which can now be done in seven hours by express train) took almost two months, and provinces like Ezo (Hokkaido) were almost as remote as the North Pole is for us today. In these terms the cities, too, were enormous: to travel by palanquin from the centre of Edo, for instance, to the Yoshiwara district took almost two hours. Because of its political and geographical structure, Japan (which is now becoming so uniform) was in Saikaku's time immensely varied, and when the writer arrived in some unfamiliar province it must have had all the exoticism for him that a new country has for the modern traveller.

Saikaku's interest in the different parts of Japan was not directed to their scenic aspect. His tales from the provinces are little concerned with the mountains and the lakes, the moon scenes and the blossoms, which absorbed the classical writers. On the whole it may be said that Saikaku's nature descriptions are perfunctory, stiff and conventional. It was the people who lived, or who had lived, in the places that concerned Saikaku—their customs and manners, the way in which they thought and acted, the strange things that happened to them.

31

From Saikaku's books we know that his interest extended to all manner and conditions of men. His *dramatis personae* include almost every type that inhabited the towns of seventeenth-century Japan, ranging from the stolid merchants and their families to beggars, panders, depraved priests, paederastic actors and bathhouse girls. Although several of his books are concerned with the *samurai*, his interest was naturally focused on the class to which he himself belonged and it is as the first great bourgeois writer of Japan that he is today remembered.

Just as Heian literature was dominated by the courtier and Kamakura literature by the warrior and the priest, so it was the merchant townsman who occupied the central role in the literature of the Edo Period, and Saikaku's popular success derives to a large extent from the fact that he was the first talented writer to grasp the bourgeois tenor of his age. His works were written for the townsmen of the Genroku Period and provided a penetrating analysis of their society. The *chōnin-mono* reveal an intimate knowledge of the merchant and a particular admiration for the self-confident, ingenious trader who succeeds in making a fortune by his own wits. Saikaku especially liked describing the rise of businesses that depended on the expansion of new markets. At the same time, he knew his merchants far too well to glamourize them, and there are few failings of the class that are not revealed in his stories.

As Professor Ueda points out, Saikaku and Defoe were the great exponents of the bourgeois spirit in their respective societies. In Japan, Saikaku was the first writer to give literary form to the "way of the merchant" *(chōnindō)*, which had arisen during the seventeenth century in contrast to the "way of the warrior" *(budō)*. He was, as we have seen, a great admirer of the self-confident, independent approach of the townsman and throughout his *chōnin* works we find such proud assertions as, "The townsman cares naught for family or lineage; for it is in gold and silver that he finds his pedigree." The ideal merchant in Saikaku's view was endowed, first of all, with the quality known (by verbal coincidence) as *saikaku*, a form of ready wit and ingenuity. The other essential attributes, as described in *The Eternal Storehouse of Japan,* were a good disposition, intelligence, industry, thrift and a keen head for accounts. As Professor Ueda suggests, these are the standard virtues that apply in any mercantile capitalist society and they are essentially the same as those described in Defoe's *The Compleat English Tradesman.*

Saikaku was well aware that many of these qualities could, if carried to extremes, lead to vices. Frequently he gives vivid examples of how excessive thrift can become miserliness. Similarly, resourcefulness can, if unhampered by moral scruples, turn into blatant dishonesty. We are shown a poignant instance of this in *The Ten Virtues of Tea That All Disappeared at Once,* at the end of which Saikaku gives a list of various shrewd but inacceptable ways of making money. A further danger illustrated by many of the stories (e.g., *The Wind That Destroyed the Fan Maker's Shop in the Second Generation)* is that a man's absorption in his business may utterly blind him to the world of sensual pleasure, with the result that when it finally impinges on him, he may be completely swept off his feet. Saikaku's "compleat tradesman" recognizes the strength of sensual desires and is therefore not overwhelmed by them.

The frequent "success stories" in Saikaku's townsman works are, of course, characteristic of an early stage of capitalism. His later books, as we have seen, reveal growing doubts about the realities of the system, but in *The Eternal Storehouse of Japan* Saikaku has no hesitation in advancing the theme that any man endowed with certain essential qualities can acquire great wealth, however humble his origins may be. He even prescribes a medicine for this purpose, the so-called "millionaire pills" *(chōjagan),* which the aspirant is to take regularly at morning and at night. (The *ryō* was a unit used to measure medicine.)

Early rising	5 *ryō*
Application to one's profession	20 *ryō*
Work at night	8 *ryō*
Thrift	10 *ryō*
Care of one's health	7 *ryō*
	50 *ryō* (daily total)

Money was the touchstone of the merchant's success and Saikaku's interest in writing about money was a natural extension of his sympathy with the "way of the merchant." He was probably the first author to deal in detail with the economic life of the people and many of his books can profitably be read by the student of economic history. In *The Teahouse That Knew Not of Gold Pieces* (p. 92), to take a simple example, we learn that even in the second half of the seventeenth century gold coinage had not penetrated rural areas. Saikaku was not only interested in economic processes, but appears to have been fascinated with coined money itself—with the actual gold, silver and copper which had entered into currency during the course of the century and which had come to exert so immense an effect on the lives of the people.

It is not only in the townsman works that we are struck by Saikaku's realistic treatment of money. His earlier books, too, are full of detail concerning expense—detail that would have been considered irrelevant or sordid in previous literature. This interest in expense is another point that Saikaku has in common with Defoe, and the reader may be interested to compare the passage on page 202 in which details are given concerning the cost of hiring a strumpet's clothes, with the section in *Moll Flanders* (Everyman's Library ed., pp. 140–1), where Defoe itemizes the midwife's tariff.

Money and love were, as we have seen, the two great themes of the Floating World and, significantly, love—or, more accurately, *kōshoku*—was the second main subject of Saikaku's *ukiyo-zōshi*. Here again Saikaku emerges as a representative writer of the townsman class. For his concern with love belonged to his general delight in the physical aspects of life—aspects that had to a large extent been suppressed by four centuries of civil war in which harsh military codes and the gloom of otherworldly Buddhism had turned men's minds from the potentialities of sensual pleasure. The energy and the money that the merchants of Saikaku's time devoted to their amorous pursuits can in this sense be regarded as both a reaction to the austere past and a sort of resistance to the existing rigours of military feudalism.

The rather unreal world of the pleasure quarters, which is the setting for so many of Saikaku's works, was the centre of this bourgeois hedonism. Saikaku's interest in love was not, however, limited to any single manifestation. As usual, he was fascinated by the diversity of human emotions and his early books explore gallantry, romance, lust and all the other varied aspects of kōshoku. Nor did he restrict his interest to relations between man and woman; every form of love concerned him (e.g., pp. 100–7) and, as we have seen, he devoted an entire book to the paederastic love that was so popular in his time.

His frank treatment of these subjects is one basis for the reputation that he later acquired as a lubricous writer. Saikaku wrote at a time when, as Sir George Sansom puts it, prudery had not been discovered. Pornographic works, both in literature and in art, were extremely popular among the townsmen. Many of Saikaku's imitators wrote books that were deliberately lewd and these were often attributed to Saikaku himself. His own kōshokubon, however, were never aimed at prurience. Their purpose was to describe the various effects of love on human beings (just as the chōninmono described the various effects of money); and since Saikaku lived in a nonpuritanical age when love was rarely divorced from its physical manifestations, it is not surprising that his works should often have a highly sexual content. The eroticism in the kōshokubon is not lubricity; rather, it can be regarded as an assertion of the physical potentialities of life, one aspect of the joie de vivre that informs so much of Saikaku's writing.

In his description of the townsmen and the world that they inhabit Saikaku shows them to be motivated largely by mercenary and sensual desires. Religion, except in its purely conventional aspects, plays little part in their lives. For Saikaku, as for Defoe, business preceded piety. Like so many townsmen of his time, he was an adherent of the Jōdo Sect and, as we have seen, he took the tonsure at the age of thirty-five. Whatever his religious feelings may have been, however, they had relatively little effect on his writing.

Buddhist observances, like those of Shinto, were an accepted part of everyday social life, but for Saikaku's townsmen they had largely lost the religious motive that originally inspired them. It is true that the underlying Buddhist conception of life had deeply penetrated the national consciousness. Saikaku's characters (and no doubt the author himself) accepted the standard Buddhist notions of karma, retribution, reincarnation and also the possibility of automatic salvation by Amida Buddha. It would not appear, however, that these ideas were a great inspiring force in their lives. When Onatsu in *Five Women Who Chose Love* or the heroine of *The Life of an Amorous Woman* abandons the world for the religious cell, it is not primarily from any desire to attain salvation, but because the world no longer has anything to offer them.

So far as Buddhist institutions themselves were concerned, Sir George Sansom points out that the church was to a large extent disliked among commoners and despised among men of learning. In Saikaku's time the Buddhist priesthood was largely sunk into lethargy and uncreativeness and had ceased to be an inspiring force in the artistic or intellectual life of the country. Its main function, indeed, was to minister to the dead; the aura of the crematory hung heavily over the temples (pp. 150–1). The priests themselves were frequently corrupt and cynically unmindful of their vows. Comfortably ensconced in their "worldly temples" (*seken-dera*), many of them not only partook of flesh, but violated their vows of celibacy by secretly indulging themselves with boys or women. It is certainly not suggested that *namagusa-bozu* (priests smelling of fish and meat), as they were popularly called, constituted the majority of the clergy. They were, however, sufficiently numerous to colour Saikaku's view of the church; and the priests that figure in his books are no idealistic ascetics, but mercenary, lustful and all-too-human men of this world. Seen in this light, they were, of course, a perfect butt for Saikaku's humour, and in his disrespectful treatment of the clergy we are frequent-

36

ly reminded of such European writers as Boccaccio, Rabelais and Balzac.

So far as Tokugawa morality was concerned, thought and behaviour were regulated, not by Buddhist doctrine, but by an official form of Confucianism, based on the doctrines of loyalty and service (pp. 4–5). On the whole, it would appear that Saikaku accepted the standard code of Tokugawa ethics. When the characters in his book violate it, they almost invariably come to a bad end. The heroes and heroines who allow individual emotion to precede social duty are likely to finish their days in the shambles of the execution ground, the loneliness of a hermit's cell or the horrors of madness. This is not to imply that Saikaku was a moralizer. The didactic element was always secondary to his interest in the reality of human emotions. In comparing *The Life of an Amorous Woman* with *Moll Flanders,* for example, we find that, although Saikaku ends his book on a moral note, he is in fact far less concerned than Defoe with "the penitent part"; whereas Defoe repeatedly justifies the licentious aspects of his story by pointing to its moral intent, Saikaku seems to consider that the significance of his heroine's debauched life is in itself sufficient justification for telling the tale.

Saikaku's acceptance of the conventional Tokugawa code does not appear to be so much a matter of strong moral conviction as part of his general approach to the realities of his time, an approach that is based essentially on moderation and common sense. For better or for worse, Saikaku seems to say, these are the rules of our society and we should adapt ourselves to them as best we can. This eminently practical outlook, however, is frequently tempered with a certain warmth and sympathy as Saikaku describes those people who, for one reason or another, cannot obey the code and who suffer accordingly. There is little doubt that Saikaku's sympathies are with the *daimyō's* daughter in *Tales from Various Provinces* who elopes with a menial retainer and is condemned to death, and with the heroine of *The Life of an Amorous Woman,* whose own rebellious nature leads to her downfall in the pleasure quarters. His later works, also, reveal an increasing sympathy for people (such as the impecunious couple in *The Man Who Turned into Gold Coins While He Slept*) whose lives are rendered unbearable by the economic system.

All this has led some observers to believe that Saikaku was profoundly opposed to the harsh social and economic conditions of his time and in particular to the lack of respect given to the individual. The tendency to regard Saikaku as being a reformist writer and many of his works as being attacks on the inequities of the socio-economic *status quo* has been especially pronounced since 1945. It belongs to a form of postwar criticism according to which *The Tale of Genji,* for example, is an exposé of the corruption and decay of the Heian Court and much of the Kabuki a protest against military despotism. In the view of such observers, Saikaku differed from his contemporaries in his profound respect for the individual and in his opposition to the inhumanity of the feudal system. Sometimes the argument is carried even further and Saikaku emerges as a precursor of modern democracy and egalitarianism.

Various aspects of Saikaku's approach tend, it is true, to give his works a vaguely "modern" air. His interest in the pursuit of individual happiness, his assertion of the physical joys of life, his advocacy of the "way of the merchant," his statement that only the double sword makes the *samurai* different from other men—all this may lead us to view Saikaku as a precursor of a more liberal age. In the opinion of the present writer, however, there is little justification for regarding him as a great humanist, or his *ukiyo-zōshi* as a literature of protest. As Professor Nakamura Yukihiko points out, we must avoid assuming that Saikaku reacted to the contemporary cruelties and illogicalities reflected in his books in the same way that we do. He was no doubt out of sympathy with some of the harsher aspects of the code and frequently he reveals his compassion for the people who are buffeted by the social and economic realities of the time. Our evidence, however, does not suggest that Saikaku was opposed to the code itself or that he wished to reform it. The first four stories of *Five Women Who Chose Love,* for example, may

38

imply a certain criticism of the rigid cruelties of Tokugawa law; yet this is never central to the theme and it would be sheer anachronism to view the book as being an indirect attack on the social system. Like Dickens, Saikaku frequently described the injustices and inhumanities of his time; to regard him as a social reformer, however, or as a prophet of humanism is surely to misconstrue the tenor of his work.

THE STYLE

An outstanding aspect of Saikaku's writing that will have emerged from the above discussion is its realism. In this respect his work belongs to a tradition that had already been established in the eleventh century with the great masterpiece of Japanese realistic fiction, *The Tale of Genji*. As we have seen, however, the main literary influences on Saikaku were of a far more recent nature.

What, then, was the quality of Saikaku's realism? In the first place, it involved a rejection of elements of the supernatural and the fantastic. This is not to say that ghosts, spirits and magic are completely excluded from Saikaku's works. In *The Ten Virtues of Tea That All Disappeared at Once*, for example, Risuké's spirit wanders about after his death demanding the debts that are due to him (p. 229). Such touches, however, are extremely rare and, except in some of the legendary tales, they are never central to the story. More important than this is Saikaku's avoidance of implausible happenings. It is only in the most exceptional cases (such as Osan's seduction while she is asleep pp. 86–7) that he allows something improbable to intrude into his narrative.

Saikaku's realism was an attempt to describe clearly and honestly the society that he knew and the living people whom he saw about him. For the modern reader one of the most valuable aspects of his work is its social realism. The *kōshokubon* and the *chōninmono* provide us with the same vivid view of Japanese bourgeois society in the second half of the seventeenth century that Defoe's works give of the English middle classes under Queen Anne. This realism emerges particularly in Saikaku's treatment of the twin themes of love and money that were central both in the Floating World and in the motivation of his fellow-townsmen. In his earlier writing, as we have seen, there is still a certain tendency to idealize the gay quarters and the lives of the merchants, but this becomes increasingly rare as the author turns his attention to the less gay side of the "gay" quarters and to the struggles of those townsmen who were not blessed by the possession of capital; the later works give a remarkably unadorned picture of conditions as they actually were for the majority of Saikaku's townsmen contemporaries.

Saikaku's writing also shows a marked development in point of psychological realism. Compared to the work of many modern writers, Saikaku's books are, of course, lacking in depth of characterization and in detail of psychological analysis. On the whole he depicts his characters in broad strokes and by placing emphasis on their peculiarities and eccentricities. Despite this "pre-modern" aspect of Saikaku's realism, his knowledge of human nature and his powers of observation were such that most of his main characters and not a few of the minor figures impress even the modern Western reader as being convincing and alive.

It is perhaps only natural that this author of the merchant class should have had considerable insight into the minds of his fellow-townsmen. What is perhaps more striking is his ability to penetrate the psychology of women. *The Life of an Amorous Woman,* in particular, provides an extraordinary example of the range of Saikaku's psychological realism. Here the author enters completely into the mind of a woman and there is hardly a false note throughout the book. In spite of her rather obsessed nature, the heroine emerges as a well-rounded and singularly real character.

A further aspect of Saikaku's realism is his insistence upon physical detail. Sometimes these details seem quite gratuitous (as in the description of the objects left by Osan and Moemon before their pretended suicide—p. 89), but on the whole their cumulative effect is to build up an atmosphere of reality. Saikaku's fascination with physical objects was, as we have observed, part of his zest for the real and sensual world. He was especially interested in details of dress and hairstyle. In the Genroku Period, as Sir George Sansom points out, costume itself had become one of the fine arts, and Saikaku rarely misses an opportunity to tell us what his characters were wearing. Minute depictions of feminine dress are unfortunately not designed to entrance most Western readers; indeed, few modern readers, either Western or Japanese, can derive any great delight from such prolix accounts as we find in *The Inspections of Beauties* (pp. 78–82). It should be remembered, however, that for most of Saikaku's contemporaries these elaborate descriptions of costume must have served not only to produce considerable aesthetic pleasure, but to enhance the reality of the characters and of the general scene in which they move.

The main weakness of Saikaku's style lies in his poor plot construction. This is especially evident in his longer works. As Professor Hisamatsu indicates, Saikaku's "novels" lack the rigid construction that we have come to expect in the modern novel and are often closer to collections of stories or sketches. Here we can clearly see the influence of the mediaeval narrative tradition that had so great an influence on *kana-zōshi* literature. While most of Saikaku's works have a certain unity of theme, the individual chapters or sections are as a rule structurally independent. Of the four books translated in the present volume, only *The Life of an Amorous Woman* remotely approaches the form of a novel, and even here it is the character of the heroine alone that binds the various episodes together. Saikaku's construction is further weakened by his tendency to wander from the point in long irrelevant passages.

We must, of course, avoid judging Saikaku's books by the standards of the modern novel. He wrote at a time when the genre was extremely undeveloped, and in comparison with their precursors in the *kana-zōshi* field his works represent a great improvement in construction. In examining the structural weaknesses in Saikaku's books, we must also remember the fantastic speed at which he wrote. During the last eleven years of his life the "Old Man of the Twenty Thousand Verses" produced no less than twenty-five full-length volumes of prose fiction—over two books a year, not taking into account the large quantity of poetry that he also wrote at this time. This inevitably lent a rough, uneven quality to much of his work. Writing with such feverish speed, Saikaku could hardly give his books the polished construction that a slower and more methodical author might have achieved.

The haste with which Saikaku's brush must have moved down the page also emerges from the numerous grammatical and orthographical mistakes and other careless errors that occur throughout the text. A good part of these can probably be attributed to the errors of copyists; many, however, were no doubt Saikaku's own, and they suggest that he allotted little time to revising his manuscripts.

The outright grammatical errors in Saikaku's work must not be confused with the many stylistic idiosyncrasies, such as his deliberate use of final verb forms where we would expect the attributive. In numerous ways Saikaku made his own grammar. His writing contains an unusual mixture of classical and colloquial style. Saikaku's frequent use of seventeenth-century colloquialisms is one of the things that make his books difficult for the modern reader. This reveals the influence of the Danrin school of *haikai*; at the same time, it is one aspect of Saikaku's aim to give a realistic depiction of the contemporary townsman class. Colloquial forms occur in both the dialogue and the narrative, and a further difficulty arises from the fact that it is frequently very hard to distinguish between the two.

In almost every respect Saikaku's language is highly individual. The sentences, which are unusually long (sometimes running for a page or more), are as a rule composed of uniformly short phrases. Here again we see the influence of the *haikai*; for the various phrases within the sentence are linked together, much like the consecutive *haikai* within a series. The outstanding characteristic of the language is its terse, elliptical quality, known in Japan as the *shōryaku* (abbreviated) style. Not only will Saikaku omit all unnecessary words from within the sentence (and frequently some that seem very necessary), but he will very rarely provide transitional words or phrases between one sentence and the next. Another speciality of Saikaku's is to break his sentence with some indeclinable word like a noun, thus leaving it up to the reader to decide the logical connection between the different parts. The remarkable economy of words, combined with the length and complexity of the sentences, makes much of Saikaku's writing hard to understand. Yet, difficult as the sentences are, the general effect is one of speed, especially when the works are read aloud. In the words of the modern novelist Kōda Rohan, "Saikaku's style is a boat that carries the reader along a swiftly flowing stream."

Saikaku's style is further characterized by its use of allusion and imagery, often of a rather stereotyped nature. This frequently appears in the form of conventional elements, such as pivot words, associate words and quotations. Much of this derives from classical Japanese literature. Here again, however, we must remember the effect on Saikaku of *haikai* poetry, in which paronomasia was so important. These conventional devices are especially frequent in the early works, such as *The Life of a Man Who Lived for Love,* when the poetic influence was greatest. In Saikaku's later works, word plays and allusions become less frequent, and in the *chōninmono* their place is often taken by proverbs and aphorisms.

The artistic effect of *kakekotoba, engo, makura-kotoba, michiyuki* and similar conventional adornments is, of course, lost in translation, where they inevitably become the subject of academic footnotes. Furthermore, it may safely be said that few modern Japanese readers derive much enjoyment from this form of ornate embellishment. At the time when Saikaku wrote, however, such devices as literary allusion were regarded as the height of stylistic refinement, and the way in which Saikaku used his wide (though not always accurate) knowledge of the classics to enrich his narration, and sometimes to enliven it by means of parody, was undoubtedly one reason for his contemporary success.

The Illustrations

All Saikaku's prose works are profusely illustrated with black-and-white drawings. The inclusion of such drawings is far from being original with Saikaku. Illustrations are a standard ingredient in *kana-zōshi* books and reflect the close link between literature, painting and calligraphy that we find already in books of the Heian period such as *The Tales of Ise* and *The Tale of Genji*. Many of the finest Japanese scroll paintings, notably the magnificent twelfth-century *Genji Mono-gatari Emaki,* were produced as illustrations of romances or novels. In addition, several of the great calligraphers lent their talents to copying the relevant portions of the texts on elaborately decorated sheets of coloured paper; here again the Genji scrolls provide an impressive example.

This traditional relationship between the three arts continued in the Tokugawa period, where it finds its main expression in the close bond between *ukiyo-zōshi* and *ukiyoe,* the latter of course being the woodblock prints of the Floating World that caused such a stir when they were first introduced into Europe late in the nineteenth century. Professor Hibbett has pointed out that the *ukiyoe,* which reached their apex in the eighteenth-century colour prints of Harunobu, Sukenobu, Utamaro, Kiyonaga and the other great masters, were a direct outcome of the development of popular book illustrations such as those in Saikaku's works. Many of the finest colour-print artists (including those mentioned above) produced illustrations for books in addition to their independent works. So close was the connection between writing and painting that it is virtually impossible to find fictional works of this period that do not include illustrations. They were regarded not as an extraneous decoration but as an integral part of the work.

The calligraphy in which the texts were presented also played an important part in the total enjoyment. To read a Tokugawa author like Saikaku in the original cursive "grass writing" *(sōsho)* with its idiosyncrasies and its sweeping style points up the individuality and verve of his writing; much of this is inevitably attenuated (though clarity is certainly gained) in modern printed texts.

The dichotomy between writing and painting that we take for granted in the West is of course far less marked in the Far East. This can largely be attributed to the role of calligraphy as an intermediary art between the other two. An author versed in the technique of *sōsho* and accustomed to presenting his manuscripts in skilled calligraphy was already at least half way to being a competent draughtsman. An effective calligraphic style was regarded as an important aspect of the writer's talent— hardly less important, indeed, than his ability to use the grammatical equipment of his native language or to make apt references to classical literature. In a country where calligraphy had for centuries been regarded as the art *par excellence* writers were thus obliged to recognize visual and even pictorial effects in a way that would scarcely be necessary for their counterparts in the West.

In the case of Saikaku this keen visual sense not only had an important effect on his prose style but encouraged him to add drawing to his other accomplishments. He found time to illustrate a number of his own works, including *The Life of a Man Who Lived for Love* and *Saikaku's Tales from the Provinces*. These drawings do not as a rule show any great professional skill, but many of them have a pleasing freshness and wit. It is interesting, too, to have a more or less authentic pictorial record of how Saikaku imagined the scenes and characters that he described in his prose.

The most famous artist to produce illustrations for Saikaku's works was his great contemporary Hishikawa Moronobu, whose influence on the development of the wood-block print was at least as great as that of Saikaku on Tokugawa fiction. In his time Moronobu was known mainly as an illustrator and print maker, and a large part of his output consisted of illustrations for contemporary works of fiction. Among these are his drawings for the pirated Edo edition of the first *ukiyo-zōshi*, Saikaku's *The Life of a Man Who Lived for Love*.

The principal Saikaku illustrator, however, was Yoshida Hambei, who flourished in the Osaka-Kyoto region during the period from about 1665 to 1690. He wrote and illustrated two books about the perennial *ukiyo* subject, the pleasure quarters; in addition he illustrated half of Saikaku's *ukiyo-zōshi*, about twenty in all. Some of his most effective drawings were done for *The Life of an Amorous Woman*. Although today Hambei's name would hardly be remembered but for his connection with Saikaku, his contemporary fame in the western part of Japan equalled that of Moronobu in Edo. It is hard to see exactly why he should have established such a reputation: there is a pleasant clarity about Hambei's drawings, but his work lacks the forcefulness and originality that made Moronobu one of the great names in Japanese art. Since all except one of the illustrations in the present volume are by Hambei, the reader will be able to make his own judgement about this particular artist's talent. The other Saikaku illustrator whose work is represented in this book, on page 241, is Makieshi Genzaburō, a younger and less gifted contemporary of Yoshida Hambei.

Illustrations in the *kana-zōshi* and *ukiyo-zōshi* had various functions. On the simplest level they provided information for such unfortunate readers as might be ignorant of the settings described in the text, notably the Floating World of the pleasure quarters and the theatre. This function has become a very useful one so far as the modern reader, particularly the modern Western reader, is concerned; by examining the illustrations we can often find explanations for obscurities, as well as concrete details about a world that is so distant from ours in both time and space. The drawing on pages 140–1, for example, helps us to imagine a street scene in the Kyoto brothel quarter some three centuries ago; the picture of the five hundred disciples on page 205 clarifies a description that from the text alone might have been obscure.

For the contemporary reader the illustrations often served to bring out specific points in the story that might otherwise have been missed. They also provided certain descriptive details, not to be found in the text, which might enhance the enjoyment of the narrative. It should be remembered that the illustrators frequently made use of conventional symbols (the pine tree symbolizing New Year, for example, on page 241) which would be immediately understood by readers of the time but which nowadays may easily be overlooked. Owing to the loose construction and scattered narrative that characterize so much of Saikaku's writing, the illustrations served a useful explanatory function that would not be needed in a more coherent type of prose. Sometimes several scattered aspects of a particular narrative sequence will be included in a single illustration, as for example on pages 196-7.

A brief glance at the Saikaku illustrations will suggest that they are not purely representational or informative. Admittedly, few if any of the drawings could stand on their own as works of art, and in this respect they differ completely from early scrolls like the *Genji Emaki,* which are masterpieces in their own right, quite apart from the works of literature that they illustrate. The fact remains that many of Saikaku's own drawings, as well as Hambei's, serve to enrich our vision of the author's imaginative world. In particular they add to the comic mood that we have examined earlier as an outstanding aspect of Saikaku's writing. Often, as we have seen, there is a distorted, slightly bizarre quality about Saikaku's characters and situations. At times we are reminded of the grotesqueries in Charles Dickens; and as with the Boz illustrations, which have become so integral a part of our conception of Dickens' world, the drawings in Saikaku (such as that on page 219) point up his characteristic type of humorous distortion.

The Saikaku illustrations, like the text itself, were reproduced by the

47

wood-block process; colour was not normally used in seventeenth-century prints. Most of the drawings show a single scene spread across two pages. In the case of Hambei's work each side measures about six and a half by eight and a half inches; Makieshi Genzaburō's are a few inches smaller. The total numbers of illustrations are as follows: *Five Women Who Chose Love*—16 double-page and 8 single-page; *The Life of an Amorous Woman*—21 double-page and 3 single-page; *The Eternal Storehouse of Japan*—21 double-page and 10 single-page; *Reckonings That Carry Men through the World*—12 double-page and 8 single-page.

Saikaku's *kōshokubon* might well have lent themselves to the type of erotic prints that were so popular in his time and which were produced by most of the great artists like Moronobu. In fact, none of the illustrations show any erotic details, though the situations that they depict are frequently suggestive. In the illustration on pages 64–5, for instance, we see Onatsu and Seijūrō just after they have retired into their enclosure; the drawing does not hint at their subsequent behaviour, nor does it show the woodcutter who so enthusiastically observes them, which would have been ideal material for an erotic print. Similarly we are shown Seijūrō's party (page 56 of the text) as it looked *before* the girls have taken off their clothes. Again, the amorous woman is depicted on page 155 writing a letter for the young man, but we are not shown what she does to him afterwards. If Saikaku's underlying intentions were in fact as lascivious as is widely believed, we may be sure that this would have been reflected in at least some of the illustrations.

Of the conventional devices in the Saikaku illustrations the most striking is one that derives from the earliest *yamatoe* traditions and which is already conspicuous in the Genji scrolls. This is the so-called *fukinuke yatai* (roofless houses) whereby we are shown indoor scenes from above at an angle of about forty-five degrees, with the roof and other obstructions conveniently removed. Another traditional convention is to be found in the tufts of cloud or haze which improbably wrap themselves round the characters and which will even chase them indoors, no doubt aided by the absence of a roof or solid walls. A final device is the disregard of perspective and proportion; frequently the illustrator will draw a character on a disproportionately large scale in order to focus the reader's atttention on him and thus to emphasize some aspect of the narrative. Here again the Saikaku drawings belong to a time-honoured tradition.

SAIKAKU'S PLACE IN LITERATURE

It is only quite recently that Saikaku's place in Japanese letters has become firmly established. Although he appears to have achieved considerable popularity during his lifetime and although he had numerous imitators, Saikaku had no important successor in the field of prose fiction until Ueda Akinari almost a century later—and Akinari, with his interest in the supernatural, was a very different type of author indeed. During most of the eighteenth and nineteenth centuries Saikaku was completely overshadowed by the two other great writers of the period, Chikamatsu, the playright, and Bashō, the poet. He was generally scorned in literary circles as not having been a real man of letters. The comment of the famous Edo novelist, Bakin, is typical: "[Saikaku] does not have an atom [literally, a character] of literature in his belly." It was not only his supposed lack of erudition that earned him the disdain of intellectual circles. The failure of "Dutch Saikaku" to respect literary conventions (in both his poetry and his prose), his interest in plebeian subjects and the supposedly immoral content of his work all militated against his reputation.

The low esteem in which he was held during the Tokugawa Period continued during the first half of the Meiji Era. One result was the delay in research and the paucity of material concerning his life. Although numerous books were produced about his contemporary Bashō nothing was written on Saikaku until about 1887; the first serious work concern-

49

ing the author was an article by Kōda Rohan published in 1890, and the first full-length study appeared in 1897.

The "rediscovery" of Saikaku towards the end of the nineteenth century was largely inspired by the realistic quality of his writing. This was bound to have an appeal to such writers as Ozaki Kōyō and Kōda Rohan, who were trying to reintroduce a form of realism into Japanese literature. Later, Saikaku was taken up by authors of the naturalist school, like Tayama Katai, who, as Professor Kunitomo points out, recognized in this early Edo writer the same vigorous realism that they had found in the French naturalists of the nineteenth century.

Although work on Saikaku progressed steadily during the first decades of this century, it was not until 1945 that it was possible to publish complete editions of his works. During the 1930s the government, and especially the military, looked askance at Saikaku because of his supposedly lubricous inclinations. All his works that had the remotest erotic content were bowdlerized and, as so often happens in such cases, the censor's eye detected prurience in some of the most innocuous passages. The resultant blanks that disfigure many of the pages of the pre-war texts were frequently filled in by students, who (it need hardly be added) usually supplied passages that were considerably more lubricous than anything in the original. One inevitable effect of this censorship was to make the general public imagine that Saikaku's works were far more erotic than they actually are.

The removal of literary censorship in 1945 paved the way for a spate of Saikaku research, which continues until this day and which is rapidly making up for past delays. The publication of the *Standard Edition of Saikaku's Complete Works (Teihon Saikaku Zenshū)* is the most important event in postwar Saikaku scholarship and will undoubtedly provide the basis for further detailed research on the author and his works. This unexpurgated, annotated and highly authoritative edition (on which the present translation is based) is the work of the three outstanding scholars in the field of Saikaku studies, the late Professor Ebara, Professor Teruoka and Professor Noma. The new edition includes not only all Saikaku's prose works, many of which have hitherto been unavailable, but the entire range of his poetry and also his *jōruri* drama. The first volume appeared in 1949 and there is to be a total of fifteen volumes.

Among the factors that added to the renewed interest in Saikaku was the realistic trend in postwar fiction. The fact that his works were mainly concerned with the *bourgeoisie* (as opposed, for example, to those of Chikamatsu, which dealt chiefly with the *samurai*) further helped to establish his reputation in a period when democracy had once more become fashionable; the rather exaggerated tendency to regard Saikaku as an anti-feudal and egalitarian writer has already been noticed.

Although Saikaku is now widely recognized as one of the great writers of prose fiction, ranking in the same general class as the authors of *The Tale of Genji* and *The Tales of the Heike*, the fact remains that his work is still little known by the great majority of literate Japanese. This is partly because of the extraordinary difficulty of his language and partly because of the continued preoccupation of most Japanese intellectuals with European literature. Though no statistics are available on the subject, the statement may safely be ventured that far more people in Japan are acquainted with the great Russian and French novelists of the nineteenth century than with their own master in the field of realistic fiction.

With the steady increase in knowledge concerning Saikaku and his work, it appears likely that his reputation will increase, not only in Japan, but in other countries as well. As the first full-scale bourgeois literature in Japan, his prose fiction occupies a role analogous to that of Defoe's in England. At the same time, as will have been gathered, there are numerous aspects of his writing that remind one of Rabelais, Boccaccio and Fielding. Though Saikaku belonged to a remote and fantastically isolated country, and though he was very much a child of his times, there is a scope and universality about his work that far transcends any barriers of space or time.

FIVE WOMEN WHO CHOSE LOVE

1. *Love Is Darkness, But in the Land of Love the Darkest Night Is*   2
Bright as Noon.

The town of Murotsu is a great bustling harbour and here, in the   3
peaceful springtime waves, rest the ships with their heavy cargoes of   4
treasure. In this town dwelt one Izumi Seizaemon, a brewer of sakè.
His was a flourishing house which lacked in nothing. Furthermore
this merchant was blessed with a son, Seijuro, who in natural beauty
excelled even the depictions of the hero of old.   5

The graces of this lad could not but find favour with women.
From the autumn of his thirteenth year Seijuro had embarked on
the path of love and by now there was not one among Murotsu's
eighty-seven courtesans whose charms he had not tasted. The writ-
ten pledges of fidelity from his mistresses might be piled up to the   6
very ceiling; the fingernails that they had sent him as marks of their
attachment would more than fill a casket; and from their raven
tresses he could have woven a rope stout enough to bind the most   7
jealous of women. Every day brought him a veritable mountain of
tender missives and so many gifts of crested silk garments that with-
out even trying them on, he would cast them aside on a heap—a
heap of clothing massive enough to still the avarice of the old wom-
an at the River of the Three Ways, and beyond the purses of even   8
the secondhand-clothes dealers at the Korai Bridge. All these things   9
young Seijuro piled up in a storeroom and on its door he wrote the
words, "Storehouse of the Floating World."   10

How could such foolishness bear profit? Observing Seijuro's

extravagances, people grieved and remarked, "If you go on like
11 this, you will soon end up by being publicly disowned." Yet, this
path, once trod, is not so easily forsaken.

12 At this time the young man was attached to a girl of pleasure
named Minakawa. This was a real love, strongly bound by pledges
of lifelong devotion, and in its pursuit Seijuro cared neither for the
calumny of onlookers nor for the idle gossip of the world.

13 A lantern on a moonlit night is extravagance indeed, but Seijuro
far surpassed this by burning lights during the very brightness of the
noonday sun. When visiting Minakawa in the gay quarters, he direct-
ed that all the doors and paper screens be shut, and thus he made of
the room a kingdom of eternal night, where they might disport
themselves without any thought of the passing hours. Here he in-
14 vited a company of the most facile drum-holders. He had some of
them imitate the sound of the town watchmen's wooden clappers
15 and others the screeching of bats, while aged procuresses were set to
16 warming ceremonial tea and intoning Buddhist chants. Then, in
mock mourning of the manservant Kyugoro, who, be it added,
was by no means dead, a Holy Shelf was set up, so that they might
celebrate the Buddhist mass for the departed; but when it came to
17 lighting the Sacred Bonfire to speed the spirit of the dead, they
burned tooth sticks in place of the usual hemp reeds, and by their
glow indulged in the full range of nocturnal diversions.

18 Next, Seijuro's fancy turning to that "Isle of Nakedness" which
he had seen on maps of the world, he bade all the courtesans in the
room disrobe. Much as they were loath to obey and shamed to
display their nudity, each and every girl was constrained to re-
19,20 move her kimono. Among them was a courtesan named Yoshizaki,
who for many years had contrived to conceal the white macula that
she bore on her hip. Now this blemish was exposed to the whole
21 company, who, seeing it, exclaimed, "The Goddess Benzai in the
very flesh!" and so saying, did her mock reverence. Thereupon the

men's enthusiasm cooled, for as they looked about at the assembled women, they saw that there was not one but suffered from some imperfection. Gradually, a chill fell over the company and their revels seemed to lose their savour.

It was at this moment that Seijuro's father, highly incensed, burst into the house of pleasure like a sudden tornado. There was no time for the young man to save anything from the oncoming blast; he could only plead, "Forgive me, sir, for I will this very day abandon my evil ways."

"Be that as it may," replied his sire, "begone out of my sight and take yourself where you will!"

So saying, he bade the assembled company adieu and left the house.

First Minakawa, then all the other girls, burst into tears and were utterly distraught at the knowledge of Seijuro's ruin. One of the company, however, a drum-holder named Jisuké of the Dark Night, showed not the least alarm, but turning to their young host, said, "Be not dismayed, Seijuro. A man stripped stark naked is yet, they $\quad$ 22 say, worth a hundred *kammon*. So long as you have a loincloth about you, you'll get along in this world!" Thus, in the midst of their gloom, this drum-holder was able to find cheer; and the others, hearing his words, used them as a relish with which to enjoy more sakè, and so contrived to forget their sadness.

The proprietors of the house, however, lost little time in show- $\quad$ 23 ing that things were no longer as before. When Seijuro clapped his hands, no one answered his call; when the time came for the evening broth, none was brought; and when he ordered tea, the servant appeared with one cup in each hand and on the way out stopped $\quad$ 24 to turn down the wick of the lamp. One by one the girls were called from the room. Alas, in houses of pleasure it is fickleness that rules the day and human warmth lasts but so long as a man has gold in his $\quad$ 25 purse.

Minakawa alone stayed behind in the room. Seeing the sorrowful girl sunk in tears, Seijuro could only mutter the words, "Alas the day." In this one phrase he had discovered his intention to end the present misfortunes by death, and sensing that the girl would insist that she too must take this course, he was overcome with grief.

His mistress had indeed understood his plan, but her words were far from what the young man had thought to hear.

"That you should aim to take your life," said she, "is the very essence of folly. Yet, such being your intention, would that I could
26   offer to accompany you! However, I have attachments to the world and, in this work of mine, to change one's affections from one man to another is but the normal course. So let us look on our love as a thing of the past. Farewell." With these words, she too left the room.

Thoroughly cast down by Minakawa's fickleness, Seijuro reflected that even for a strumpet so callous a rupture of a tender bond was passing cruel. Shedding bitter tears, he was about to leave the room when Minakawa, attired all in white, came running back and clinging to her lover, cried, "What! Were you going to leave this place and not die after all? Come, if we are to kill ourselves, now
27   is the time!" So saying, she pulled out a pair of razors.

"Ah!" exclaimed Seijuro, much pleased at this proof of the girl's constancy. Yet before he could say more, the people of the house burst into the room and separated the two lovers.

28   First they took Minakawa back to her employer's house; then, surrounding Seijuro, they led him off to the Eiko-In, his family temple, where he might make amends to his father by taking the
29   tonsure. He was but eighteen years of age —pitifully young, indeed, for one to aspire at renouncing the world.

2. The Letters That a Sash Revealed

"Alas, what a fearful thing! Call a surgeon! Quick, the smelling salts!"

"What's happened?" asked someone, hearing all the clamour.

"It's Minakawa. She's gone and killed herself," was the doleful reply.

"Is it too late? Can nothing be done?"

But even as they stammered out the question, her pulse beat its last. Alas, how transient the way of the world!

For more than ten days the tragedy was concealed from Seijuro and thus it was that he did not follow Minakawa in death. Sadly thwarted is the life of man!

Because of a note received from his mother, Seijuro resolved to drag out his existence, unwanted though it was. Stealing out of the temple one day, he left secretly for the town of Himéji in the same *30* province. On his arrival, he visited an acquaintance, and he, mindful of their past friendship, did not begrudge his help.

After some time had elapsed, it came about that Kuemon, the merchant who owned the Tajima-ya, was looking for a clerk to manage his shop.

"This would be a splendid opportunity for you to get on in the world," Seijuro's friend told him. Through his good offices, he obtained the post and thus for the first time in his life took service under a master.

Seijuro, with his good breeding, his kindly disposition and his keen intelligence, could not but find favour with all whom he encountered. Though by his looks he was bound to attract the fair sex, he had in the course of things abandoned all attentions to his personal appearance and wholly lost interest in the world of love. Thus he was able to devote himself steadily to his work. His master entrusted him with everything and, seeing how the gold and silver accumulated in the till, he rejoiced greatly and came more and more to count on the young man for his plans of the future.

Now this master had a younger sister, Onatsu by name, who was in her fifteenth year. So far as men were concerned, this young girl was of the greatest fastidiousness and as yet no partner had been *31* chosen for her. Onatsu was endowed with excellent beauty, the like of which one would not find, outside the ranks of professional courtesans, in the capital itself, let alone in country districts. Those of Kyoto said that she even surpassed in comeliness that famed courtesan of Shimabara whose crest displayed the side view of a huge butterfly. As such was the report, it would be idle indeed to catalogue her various charms. Suffice it that we compare her beauty with that of the great courtesan and add that in her feelings too she was no less passionate.

It happened that one day Seijuro called for the maidservant Kamé and, handing her the thick silk sash that he was wont to wear, said, "This is too wide for my taste. Pray sew it narrower."

Kamé promptly unstitched the sash and in it she found a bundle of letters, relics of the young man's past adventures. She and the other maids, joined now by Onatsu, lost no time in reading the jumbled notes, of which there were some dozen or more, all addressed to "Master Kiyo," but with a variety of senders' names—Hanacho, Ukifuné, Kodayu, Akashi, Unoha, Chikuzen, Senju, Choshu, Ichinojo, Koyoshi, Matsuyama, Kozaémon, Dewa, Miyoshi—each that of a girl from Murotsu's haunts of pleasure.

Examining the letters now one by one, they read that these girls had each been deeply enamoured of Seijuro and had set their affections on him at the greatest risk. Nor were these merely the idle conceits common among women of pleasure, for every sentence rang true. Courtesans capable of such deep feelings could be no mean creatures. Besides, so far as this youth was concerned, it was evident, reflected Onatsu, that he had not spent his hours in the gay quarters for nothing. Was it not clear that apart from his handsome exterior he must be endowed with many creditable qualities of a more hidden nature? Surely none but a man of the most consummate charms could inspire love in all these women. And so, without even knowing it, Onatsu herself became enamoured of Seijuro.

Day and night she was consumed with her love for him until her very soul had deserted her and lodged itself in Seijuro's breast. She lived in a sort of haze where she was not even sensible of her own words, where the bright springtime flowers seemed shrouded in darkness and the moonlit night no different from the day, where the snow at dawn was no longer white and the sweet sound of the evening cuckoo no longer echoed in her ears, where she marked neither the Feast of the Dead nor the New Year's celebrations. Later *37* she seemed to lose all consciousness of herself, for every look betrayed her secret and every word her passion.

Seeing this infatuation, her maids could not but grieve for their mistress. " Such things," said they among themselves, "are apt to happen in this world. Would that in some way we could help bring this to a happy issue!" Nor were they themselves immune to the young man's charms. The sewing woman pierced her finger with a needle and, squeezing out the blood, wrote to Seijuro of her inmost feelings. One of the maids, an untutored girl, had recourse to a manservant who was able to write, and thus it was that she thrust into Seijuro's sleeve a declaration of love penned in a masculine hand. The parlourmaid went to special pains to bring the *38* young man his tea in the shop where he was working. On the pretext of having Seijuro admire the baby of the house, the nurse one day approached the youth and handed him the infant, who thereupon passed water over his lap.

"You, too, should be quick to have a little one like this," said the nurse. "I had a pretty little child myself, before I took service in this house as wet nurse. That man of mine, though, he was a ne'er-do-well if ever there was one! Now he's taken himself off to Kumamoto in Higo Province and gone into service there. When we parted, I got myself a proper writ of separation. So now I'm on my own and fancy free! I'm naturally on the plump side, you know. My mouth is small and my hair quite curly." *39*

It was droll indeed to hear her ramble on in her sugary tone.

The scullery maid, too, tried in her way to win favour with the young man; for, when it came to ladling out the fish stew, she would always see to it that the choicest morsels were reserved for his plate —attentions which he could not but find vexatious.

For Seijuro to be thus the cynosure of admiration was in one way pleasing, to be sure, but at the same time it was irksome. As he was obliged to answer all the tender missives that he received, his work in the shop began to suffer. In time these diversions became odious and he abandoned them, as though awaking himself from a dream.

Albeit, Onatsu continued by means of an intermediary to convey one loving letter after another to the young man, until in the end his own feelings were inflamed and he yielded his heart to her. It was a busy house, however, and afforded them no chance of a secret *40* tryst. Consumed with the flames of fleshly lust, tortured by unsated passion, their bodies were both gradually emaciated; as the days and months passed in bootless waiting, their beauty, alas, assumed a gaunt appearance. It was with difficulty that they contrived the means of hearing each other's voices, and even this they looked forward to with the keenest joy.

41 Yet while there is life, there is hope—hope in the case of Onatsu and Seijuro that one day the love which each bore for the other would find union, as two blades of grass that sway in each other's direction. In the path of such fulfilment Onatsu's sister-in-law placed a special barrier; for each night, in fear of fire, she would without fail secure the partition that separated the main house, where Onatsu slept, from the shop, where the young man lay. As the lovers heard the sliding door clang shut, it echoed in their ears more fearful than the roar of thunder.

3. *The Lion Dance to the Sound of the Tabor*

When the cherries come into blossom, men's wives set out for
Onoé, some to flaunt their own beauty, others to display their come- *42*
ly daughters. Not to admire the blossoms, but to be themselves
admired—such are the ambitions of our modern ladies. Females,
indeed, are witches, who would ensorcell the very demon fox who *43*
dwells in the tower of Himéji Castle.

The women of the Tajima-ya household, too, thought that this
would be a fitting time for a country expedition, and so it was that
they all set out one day in their open palanquins, with Seijuro follow-
ing behind to superintend the arrangements.

In Takasago and Soné the pines were showing forth their bright
green shoots, and the sight of the sandy beach was lovely beyond
compare.

The village children, each wielding a rake, were forking aside the
thickly strewn pine needles, so that they might discover spring
truffles, while others picked violets and reeds. All this caught the
fancy of the ladies and soon they joined in plucking all manner of
spring sprouts; then, finding a spot where the young grass grew
sparsely, they spread out their flower mats and carpets.

With the calm waters of the ocean in the background, the red of
the ladies' sleeves vied in beauty with the crimson evening sun, and
drew the gaze of the other flower viewers from the wistaria and
the wild roses. Soon all attention was concentrated on the curtain of
silken garments behind which the ladies sat. Abandoning thoughts of
departure, the men opened their sakè casks and cried cheerfully that
drunkenness was a great joy, reserved for humans alone. Casting
aside cares, they decided that the sight of these fair maidens would
serve as relish for the day's carousal.

In the meanwhile, the women in their silken enclosure were also
enjoying themselves over cups of sakè. Of their male companions
only Seijuro remained. The palanquin bearers, having quaffed sakè

The ever-popular lion dance is in full swing. On the right the gaudy lion is performing his gyrations to the accompaniment of three tabors, a flute and a pair of clappers (played by a long-nosed clown). On the left the young lovers are taking advantage of the excitement to meet in secret and consummate their passion.

from large bowls to their hearts' content, a memorable delight indeed, found themselves no less dazed than that figure of old who
44 in his dreams became a butterfly; in their fuddled minds the very
45 field appeared as their private domain, and, with much rejoicing, they lapsed into an utter stupor.

It was at this point that people began gathering in a clearing to
46 observe a company of pantomime dancers who had made their appearance to the beat of a tabor. The players, seeing the flower viewers assembled, began to perform the lion dance. The movements of the lion's head were skilfully executed indeed, and all the merrymakers flocked forward to observe the dancers' art.

Only Onatsu paid no heed to the dances. Instead, she complained of an aching tooth and remained behind the enclosure with an air of distress. In a dishevelled state she lay there with her head resting on one arm, and made no effort to tie her sash, which had come unfastened. Screened by a pile of spare silk garments, she emitted an occasional drowsy snore in simulation of sleep. Altogether her disor-
47 dered posture was not without a certain charm. Outside the company of courtesans there can be few girls so versed in the ways of the world that at a time like this they should conceive the desire of bringing to prompt consummation a tender bond. Such, however, were Onatsu's thoughts.

Seijuro, perceiving that Onatsu alone had remained behind, now made his way by a circuitous route through the thick undergrowth and, in response to the girl's invitation, joined her in the enclosure. Little did they care for the disorder of her headdress as, without a
48 word, the two young lovers came together. Soon they were gasping with passion and the heavy beating of their hearts bespoke their joy.

Even in the midst of these delights they kept their eyes on an opening in the curtain, fearful lest they be discovered by Onatsu's sister-in-law. Thus they paid no heed to the back of the enclosure, and it was not until they arose that they espied a woodcutter who stood there observing the young couple with an air of surprise mingled with pleasure. The fellow had placed his load on the ground and, while one hand still grasped a sickle, the other was busy at his loin- *49* cloth. That the lovers should have been oblivious of his presence was truly a case of "hiding one's head while revealing one's but- *50* tocks."

When Seijuro emerged from the enclosure, the lion-dancers, seeing him, stopped at the very height of their performance. This greatly dismayed the onlookers, for the players' repertory was still far from exhausted.

Now the evening mist wreathed the mountains and the sun was slanting to the west. Putting their things in order, the company set out on the return for Himéji. It may be mere fancy, but already *51* Onatsu's gait seemed to have acquired a new ease.

Seijuro fell behind the others and addressing the lion-dancers, said, "Thanks for your services today, good friends." Had they heard his words, even the gods in all their wisdom would hardly have realized that the recent pantomime had been an artfully contrived ruse.

How then could Onatsu's addle-brained sister-in-law have scented the young man's stratagem?

4. *The Man Who Left His Dispatch Box at the Inn*
Now that they had set about it, there was no turning back and *52* that very evening Seijuro departed with Onatsu in great haste so that they might embark from Shikamazu before nightfall. The *53* young lovers had resolved to journey to the area of the capital and *54* there to make a life together, even though it might mean enduring long years of poverty. No sooner had they reached their decision than they had prepared their travelling clothes and now already they were sitting in a mean hut close by the pier awaiting the de- parture of the boat.

Here also was a group of fellow-voyagers, each with the luggage that betokened his business—a pilgrim bound for the Grand Shrine of Isé, an ironmonger from Osaka, an armourer from Nara, an itinerant priest from the Monastery at Daigo, a maker of tea whisks from Takayama, a pedlar of mosquito curtains from Tamba, a draper from Kyoto and a fortune-teller from the Shrine at Kashima. "Ten men—ten provinces" is a true saying, and travel by ferryboat is indeed fraught with interest.

Now the boatman appeared and calling out in a loud voice, "All aboard, we're weighing anchor! Pray make your offerings in honour of the Gods at Sumiyoshi," he flourished a scooper in which to collect the donations. Then, counting the number of passengers, he assessed upon each of them seven coppers for food and drink, regardless of whether or not they wanted sakè. In the absence of a proper heating pan, the sakè was ladled cold from a small bucket; as an accompaniment, strips of dried flying fish were served in a stew bowl. The passengers downed their sakè in three quick draughts, whereat the captain shouted, "May the Gods give us speed, for the wind is due astern!" Then, boarding the boat, they put on all sails and were soon some two miles out to sea.

It was at this point that one of the passengers, a courier from the Province of Bizen, clapped his hands and exclaimed, "O heavens, I've gone and forgotten it! I strapped that box to my sword and left it at the inn." And gazing in the direction of the shore, he continued his lament: "Oh dear, I remember now—I leaned it up against the wall in the corner of that room with the holy image!"

At these wailings the other passengers turned to him and shouted, "Do you really think the innkeeper can hear you from this distance? Look here, fellow, are you sure you haven't left your balls behind too?"

After careful scrutiny, the messenger replied, "Yes, quite sure. I've got them here—both of them."

The passengers all laughed heartily. Then, addressing the captain, they said, "What with all this, there's nothing for it. We'll just have to go back."

The captain, then, turned full rudder and they headed back for port.

"We've got off to a fine start!" They all muttered angrily.

When at length their vessel reached shore, the men who had been dispatched from Himéji in pursuit of the couple and who were now bustling about the harbour, searching high and low for the fugitives, said, "Perchance they are aboard this boat."

Thereupon they set to searching the vessel. There was no way for Onatsu and Seijuro to hide themselves and they could only exclaim, "Alas, alas!"

Their lament fell on stony ears. Onatsu was placed in a closely-guarded conveyance, while Seijuro was secured with ropes, and thus they returned to Himéji. Seeing the two young lovers in their unexampled grief, none could help but be moved.

From that day forward, Seijuro was confined to a room. Yet even in his present dire straits he set his own woes at naught and thought only of Onatsu.

"Onatsu, Onatsu!" he babbled forth. "Oh, if only that wretch had not left his dispatch box behind, we should by now have safely reached Osaka. We could have rented lodgings in some back street in the environs of Kozu with just an old woman to look after us. *58* For the first fifty days we should have lain in each other's arms, caring not whether it was day or night, for so we did agree in secret. But, alas, those are all empty dreams of the past. Oh, will no one end my misery by killing me? Long indeed are the days and wearisome this life of mine!"

So saying, time after time he would bite his tongue and firmly shut his eyes. Yet, because of Onatsu, he could not rid himself of all attachment to the world.

The ferry is on its way through the Inland Sea with the fugitive lovers aboard. The scatter-brained courier stands at the bow lamenting the loss of his dispatch box. The other passengers (priest, fortune-teller, pedlar, etc.) are absorbed in their own affairs and show little sympathy.

"Would that but once more I could cast my eyes on her lovely form and bid her a last farewell," he said, and, caring nought for shame or for the censure of onlookers, he wept bitter tears. This, forsooth, is what people signify when they speak of being utterly unmanned.

Seeing him thus distraught, even his guards felt sorry, and as the days passed, they tried in one way or another to cheer his spirits.

Onatsu for her part was no less disheartened and for seven days she would touch no food. Then she wrote a petition begging that Seijuro's life be spared, and this she presented to the Mount Myoshin Shrine at Murotsu. Strange to relate, there appeared by her bedside at about the middle of that very night an old man who imparted to her ears a wondrous message: "Heed well what I say. The people of this world, when they find themselves in distress, are wont to make such utterly unreasonable requests that even I, the deity of Mount Myoshin, do not find it in my power to grant them. Some pray for sudden prosperity, or again, that they may enjoy a secret tryst with some other man's wife. Some pray that their enemy may be haunted to death, others that a rainy day may turn to fine weather, still others that the short nose with which they were born may grow longer. One after another they come with these selfish requests which cannot possibly be realized, and by praying to the Gods and Buddhas who can in no wise serve them, they only make thorough nuisances of themselves. At the last festival I was visited by eighteen thousand and sixteen worshippers, but of this great company there was not one but prayed for his own selfish ends. It was odd indeed to hear them. Yet the offerings which they threw into the box were pleasing to me, and, as such is the duty of a God, I listened to their prayers. Among all these visitors there was but one who showed real piety—a servant from a charcoal dealer's in Takasago. 'I have no special favour to ask,' said she, bowing to

59

72

me. 'Just let me continue in good health. I shall come here again
to worship you.' She left, but had not gone more than a few yards
when she returned and addressing me again, said, 'Grant also that
I get myself a handsome man.'

"'Kindly address such requests to the Gods at the Great Shrine   60
of Izumo,' I answered. 'These matters are not in my province.'
Thereupon she left the precincts, unable, of course, to hear me.

"Now in your case, if you had but taken a husband in accordance
with your elder brother's wishes, all would have been well. But   61
since you were so fastidious in love, you landed yourself in this   62
present plight. You, Onatsu, will drag out the life which you no
longer value. But Seijuro, who still has some attachment to his
life, will shortly lose it."

When the girl awoke from this dismal vision, which she had
most vividly dreamt, she was thoroughly cast down and wept until
the break of day.

As foreseen, Seijuro was in due course summoned before the
Tribunal, and there he met with an unexpected charge. For seven
hundred gold *koban* had disappeared from the metal safe where   63
they had lain in the indoor storehouse of the Tajima-ya. It was
noised about that Seijuro had set Onatsu on to stealing this money
and that, taking it, he had then fled with her. Things now looked
dark indeed for the young man and the new charge was hard to
answer.

And so, alas, it came about that on the eighteenth day of the
Fourth Moon he met his end, being then in the twenty-fourth   64
year of his life. Of those who witnessed the execution, there was not
one but lamented for him. "Fleeting, indeed, is this world of men"
—so they murmured and the tears wetted their sleeves as though
they had been drenched by a sudden evening shower.

It happened thereafter, at the beginning of the Sixth Moon, that,   65
in carrying out a thorough airing of the house, it was found that

the seven hundred gold coins had been moved from their original place and stored away in the great trundle chest.

"It shows that you can never be too careful," muttered a sensible old man, when the error was bruited in the neighbourhood.

66 *5. The Seven Hundred Gold Pieces That Should Have Been Found While Life Yet Lasted*

67 To know nothing is to enjoy the peace of Buddha, and for some time thereafter Onatsu remained in ignorance of her lover's death.

Then one day, as she sat sunk in thought, she heard the words sung by a band of children from the neighbourhood who passed outside her window:

"If you put Seijuro to death,
68   Kill Onatsu too!"

Thereat Onatsu was seized with misgivings and questioned her old governess, who, unable to reply, fell to weeping.

"So it's true!" cried Onatsu, going into a frenzy. "Rather than live on like this, thinking of him that I love, better were it to die." So saying, she joined the group of children in the street and led them in their singing.

Seeing this, everyone lamented and tried in various ways to restrain the girl, but she was not to be stopped. Letting fall a shower of tears, she sang:

"That man who passes there—
Is he not Seijuro?
That sedge hat he wears
Is just like Seijuro's.
69   Yahan ha ha!"

And she cackled with laughter.

In time her beautiful body was ravaged with madness and she became utterly distraught.

74

On one occasion she made her way to a mountain village. When dusk fell, she lay down to sleep, with the grass of the field as her pillow. The serving women who had accompanied her there each of her own accord became as crazed as their mistress and later they all turned utterly insane.

A group of men who had for many years been intimates of Seijuro's agreed that they should at least lay his remains to rest. Thus resolved, they went to his place of execution and, having washed clean the blood which stained the surrounding weeds and rubbish, buried the corpse. To mark the spot, they planted a pine tree and an oak, and named the place the Mound of Seijuro. Sad happenings, indeed, even for this grief-laden world of ours! *70*

Every night Onatsu repaired to this place and mourned for her dead lover. At these times Seijuro would appear vividly before her eyes exactly as he had been while still alive.

So the weeks passed, until on the hundredth day after the execution Onatsu seated herself on the dew-drenched grass before the grave and pulled out her dagger. Her attendants, however, perceived her purpose and managed after much effort to restrain her, saying, "What would it avail you, madam, to end your life now? If your heart is indeed sincere, take the tonsure and spend long years praying for the repose of him who died. Such is the Way of Salvation. And we too have it in mind to renounce the world." *71*

Hearing these words, Onatsu entered into the feelings of her companions and her spirits were quieted.

"So be it," she answered. "I shall not disregard your counsel."

Thus it was that she betook herself to the Shokaku Temple, and, having made her requests to the Superior, was admitted to holy orders and changed her light-coloured clothes to vestments of a sombre hue, being then in the summer of her fifteenth year.

Thenceforth she devoted herself to piety. In the mornings she went down to the valley to fetch water and in the evenings she

would pluck flowers at the mountaintop to decorate the altar. Dur-
72 ing the summer period of retirement she would each night make
a lantern of her hand; nor was she negligent in her recital of the
Great Sutra. Thus she became a worthy nun indeed.

Seeing this, people marvelled at her devotion and declared that
73 she must be a reincarnation of Princess Chujo of legendary fame. In
the presence of her hermit's cell, it is said that even the owner of the
Tajima-ya felt moved to seek his salvation, and offering the same
seven hundred *koban* of gold that had helped bring Seijuro to his
doom, he ordered masses to be held for the repose of the dead
man's soul.

At about this time the story of Onatsu and Seijuro was made
74 into a play which was performed in the area of the capital, and it
was not long before their names had floated far and wide, even to
the remotest hamlet in the land. For the tender bond between these
two was launched forth into the world aboard a boat, to drift along
the New River of Love; yet whither such love was bound, none
indeed could tell in this poor world of ours where life is no more
75 certain than a bubble on the river's surface!

THE ALMANAC MAKER'S TALE IN THE
76 ## MIDDLE PART

77 I. *The Inspection of Beauties*
78 Thus is it written in the almanac for the second year of Tenna:
79 "The first day of the First Moon: New Year's Writing, an auspicious
80 day for all things. The second day: men first lie with women."

As to this latter practice, it has from the age of the Gods been
81 taught by the wagtail; since those ancient times dalliance between
men and women has never ceased.

Now there lived in Kyoto a woman known as the Beautiful

Wife of the Almanac Maker. Her fame had spread far and wide, and   *82*
by her beauty she had stirred up a mountain of love in the capital.
Her eyebrows, delicately shaped like a new moon, rivalled in love-   *83*
liness the crescent float displayed through the streets at the time of   *84*
the Gion Festival; her figure was fresh like the early cherry blossoms
at the Kiyomizu Temple when gradually they begin to unfold;
and the beauty of her lips appeared no less than that of the maples
in Takao at the height of their crimson glory. She dwelt in Muro-   *85*
machi-dori and in her attire she displayed the latest tastes. She was
indeed the very acme of fashion; nor was there any woman to
equal her in the entire capital.

It was full spring, the season that gladdens the hearts of men, and
the wistaria blossoms in the Eastern Hills by Yasui were at their   *86*
loveliest. Billowing out like clouds of purple, they robbed even   *87*
the pine trees of their colour. As dusk fell, the crowds began to return
to the city from their flower viewing, and as the fair women flocked
down the slopes of the Eastern Hills, they made them into veritable
hills of beauty.

There was in Kyoto at that time a band of young pleasure seek-
ers, famous under the name of the Four Heavenly Kings, who stood   *88*
out from the common ruck of men by the handsomeness of their
features. Relying on their fathers' generosity, these men gave them-
selves over to enjoyment, and from one New Year's Day to the
next New Year's Eve they did not let a single day pass without
engaging in some amorous delight.

On the preceding night they had visited the gay quarters of Shima-
bara and indulged themselves until dawn with the courtesans Moro-   *89*
koshi, Hanasaki, Kaoru and Takahashi; today they had repaired to
Shijogawara, there to practice another form of love with men like   *90*
Takenaka Kichisaburo, Karamatsu Kasen, Fujita Kichisaburo and
Mitsusé Sakon. Now, having engrossed themselves both in the love

of men and in the love of women, without regard for day or night, they had exhausted the full range of their diversions; and in the 91 evening, after the theatre had finished, they repaired to the tea- 92 house called Matsuya and sat down side by side.

"Outside the company of courtesans," one of them remarked, "it is rare indeed to see so many pretty women as one can today. I wonder whether we may find one now who really dazzles us with her beauty."

And so, choosing a discerning actor in their group as judge, they prepared for their evening inspection of the beauties who were now returning from the Eastern Hills. Here was a new diversion for the Heavenly Kings!

To their dismay, most of the ladies were riding in closed palan- quins and remained therefore invisible. Presently, however, a group of women came by on foot, all passably attractive, though none strikingly so.

"At all events," said one of the young men, "let us record only those who are truly beautiful."

Then, calling for inkstone and paper, they embarked on a cata- logue of the passing beauties.

First came a woman of some thirty-three years. Slender was the nape of her neck, and there was ardour in her eyes. The line of the hair on her brow was of a natural beauty, and though her nose stood rather high, this was not sufficient to mar her other charms. This lady's undergarment was of white satin, above which she wore a kimono of pale blue and, over this, one of reddish yellow, all these being lined with the same fine silk. On her left sleeve, painted in clas- 93 sical style, was a likeness of the bonze Yoshida, above the words, "To sit alone in the lamplight with a book spread out before you . . ." Clearly this was a woman of ingenious fancies. Her sash was of woven velvet with a chequered pattern, and gracefully draped over her kimono was a cloak of the fashion favoured by court ladies. Her feet, encased in a pair of light-mauve socks and shod with sandals of three-coloured braids, glided noiselessly over the street. Struck by her natural elegance, they could not help exclaiming, "Lucky devil —that husband of hers!" But at that very moment the lady opened her mouth to speak to an attendant, and they became aware of a missing lower tooth. And at that their ardour instantly cooled.

Following close behind her, came a maiden of not more than about fourteen, accompanied on one side by a woman who may have been her mother and on the other by a black-gowned nun. 94 In close attendance were a number of serving women and lackeys. For a girl to be thus carefully escorted, thought the young men, she must be still unmarried; but then it struck them that her teeth were 95 blackened and her eyebrows shaved. Her face was round and well-favoured; her eyes shone with intelligence; her ears elegantly framed the pretty head. The men also observed her slender fingers, smooth-skinned and white. Her style of dress was of the most matchless elegance. Underneath she wore a yellow garment lined with the same rich silk, above this a purple robe of fully dappled design, and over it all a kimono of grey satin sewn onto which was the design of many sparrows. Her sash, of single thickness, was dyed 96 with multicoloured stripes. She walked along with splendid bearing, her dress slightly opened at the top. The cords fastened to her well-lined lacquered sedge hat were plaited with twists of paper. 97 A beauty indeed—or so they thought at first sight; but a second look revealed an inch-long blemish upon her face. This could be no ordinary birthmark, thought the young blades. "How she must detest that nurse of hers!" said one of them, and they all laughed as 98 she passed them by.

Then came a girl of some twenty years, wearing a striped garment of hand-woven cotton. So threadbare was it that when the wind blew it back, one could see that even the lining was covered with patches and her shame was exposed to all. Her sash appeared to have

been made from left-over pieces of a coat and was pitifully thin.
99 On her feet she wore purple leather-soled socks, evidently the only
type at her disposal, and an unmatched pair of Nara sandals. An old
cloth kerchief covered her head. The hair escaping underneath had
clearly seen no comb for many a long day, and its dishevelment was
hardly relieved by an artless effort to tie it into a knot. With utter
lack of coquetry she walked along, quite self-contained, it seemed,
and caring nothing for what people thought. Now when they turned
their eyes on her, they saw that her features lacked none of the
requisites of beauty, and the young men were all enchanted to find a
girl so uniquely endowed with natural charms.

"Were she but attired in proper clothes," said one of them, "she
would surely capture some man's heart. But there's no help for
poverty!"

They were all touched by the poor girl, and after she had gone her
way, they had someone follow her in secret to make inquiries. Thus
they learned that she lived at the end of the Seiganji-dori, where she
worked at chopping tobacco leaves. The young bucks felt heavy-
100 hearted at this report. Here indeed was food for smoke!

Next to catch their eye was a woman of about twenty-seven,
decked in the greatest elegance. Her triple-layered garments were of
rich black silk; their hems were trimmed with crimson. The outer
101 kimono was adorned with an informal crest in gold. All this was
secured with a wide Yorishima sash, woven of Nishijin brocade in
102 Chinese style and knotted in front. Her hair, adorned with a pair
103 of combs, was tied with a wide paper cord in a Shimada coiffure, so
shaped that it fell down in the back; round it was draped a kerchief
104 decorated with a delicately dyed pattern; and over this a Kichiya-
style sedge hat, enlivened with four-coloured braid, rested on her
head—but lightly, so as not to conceal the fair looks of which she
105 was so obviously proud. Seeing her move towards them with soft-
footed gait, her hips voluptuously swaying, the young men ex-

claimed, "Here, here, here she is—the woman we've been waiting for! Peace, so that we may observe her closely!"

They waited for her to approach, then perceived that the three maids who accompanied her each held a child in her arms. Small children they were, to boot, probably born within the space of three short years. The young blades were amused.

"Mamma, Mamma!" cried the children from behind, but the lady walked on, feigning not to hear them.

"Though they be her children," remarked one of the men, "she assuredly finds their presence now most vexing. The flower of a woman's beauty ill survives her motherhood!"

At these words they all laughed boisterously, hearing which the lady would fain have been quit of this fleeting world.

Next, attended in lordly manner by lackeys carrying a palanquin, came a girl barely thirteen years of age. Her long hair was combed out in back, turned slightly up at the ends and secured with a scarlet band. Her forelock stood out and was parted like a young boy's, the *106* coiffure being tied with a paper cord of gold and decorated with a half-inch comb of immaculate beauty—all of which displayed such perfect grace that it would be idle to catalogue her charms one by one. Her under-kimono was of white satin relieved with a black-and-white design; the outer garment was a silken veil of Chinese lace, elegantly contrived so that beneath it one could perceive the iridescent satin of the middle kimono, on which had been sewn a peacock pattern. All this was fastened with an unpadded sash of many colours. Her bare feet were encased in a pair of sandals with paper braids and one of her attendants carried her stylish sedge hat. In her hands she held high a rich spray of trailing wistaria and her expression seemed to say that this was "for those who had not *107* seen the blossoms."

Of all the lovely women they had singled out, she was the very nonpareil. When the young men fondly inquired of one of her

81

attendants what the lady's name might be, he replied over his
shoulder, "She is the daughter of our master in Muromachi. And she
108 is called the Present-Day Komachi."
109   They knew that evening that hers was the beauteous "colour of the
flowers." Only later were they to understand that hers too was a sin-
gular wantonness of spirit.

2. *The Pillow Dream That Was Thrust upon a Lady*

Jolly though a bachelor's house may be, when evenings come,
a home without a wife can be a dismal place indeed. A certain alma-
nac maker in these parts had for the past many years lived in un-
married state. This man aspired after a wife of such excellent beauty
that even in the capital with all its colourful women his ideal was
hard to realize. Yet so forlorn he was that he recommended himself
110 "like a floating weed" to the good offices of his acquaintances; and
thus it was that he was led to gaze fondly on the Present-Day
Komachi, she who on that springtime day had carried in her hand
111 the spray of wistaria and whose "fragile loveliness" had shone so
brightly during the inspection at the Shijogawara barrier.
    Most odd it was to see how this inveterate bachelor now let noth-
ing stand in the way of speeding his betrothal. At the time there was
112 a woman, known for the fluency of her tongue as the Glib Arranger,
113 who dwelt above Karasumaru off Shimo-tachiuri Street, and who
practised the trade of go-between. The almanac maker called on her,
earnestly requesting that she arrange the match, and forthwith he
114 sent the two-handled keg of sakè so that the betrothal might be
115 sealed. His suit having been favourably answered and an auspicious
day picked out, Osan—for such was this young beauty's name—
was welcomed to his house as wife.
    For full three years they lived together in connubial bliss. He was
so steeped in the beauty of his spouse that he never cast his eyes
afield, caring neither for the flower-fragrant evenings, nor for the

early moonlit dawns. Osan, for her part, day and night faithfully carried out her wifely duties: for which end she took especial pains to exercise economy in the preparation of her husband's attire, herself assiduously plaiting strands of red ochre thread by hand and supervising her maids in the task of weaving the pongee silk; in the kitchen, too, she was frugal in her use of fuel, and made all entries in her housewife's cash book with the utmost care: here indeed was a wife that any townsman would covet for himself.

By and by the household came to flourish and the master's joy knew no bounds. It happened then that he was obliged to journey to the Eastern provinces on business. It grieved him sorely to leave the capital, but there was no help for it. Harsh indeed are the calls of a man's livelihood!

Having at length resolved on his departure, he had his travelling clothes made ready. Before leaving, he visited Muromachi and called on his wife's father to inform him of the circumstances. This gentleman was much concerned at how his daughter would manage all the duties that her husband's absence would entail—concern, indeed, that any parent would be bound to feel.

"If we could but find some clever fellow," he said, "who could take charge of things while you are gone—someone who might look after the shop and help Osan with the household bookkeeping." Then he bethought himself of Moémon, a clerk who had served him well for many years, and, summoning this man, he dispatched him to his son-in-law's house.

Now this Moémon was of that honest breed of men of whom it is said that their head is the seat of God—though, be it added, in the 116 styling of the hair upon his head he took not the slightest interest, leaving such fripperies to others; he let it grow at will, thus giving his brow a narrow look. The sleeves of his kimono measured barely 117 more than seven inches at the wrist; he took scant care of the ap- 118 pearance of his sword; and so far as the lighter diversions were con-

119   cerned, not once since the Ceremony of Boyhood had he donned a
120   sedge hat. Instead, he lived all day only for making money, and at
      night he placed an abacus under his pillow, so that in his dreams he
      might conceive some profitable scheme.

      It was now the autumn season, when storms blow harshly at night,
      and Moémon bethought himself with concern of the coming
      winter months. Resolving for the sake of his health to undergo
121,122 cauterization, and hearing that the parlourmaid Rin was adept at
      laying on the moxa, he requested her help. Several twists of the
      herb were then prepared and a striped cotton quilt spread over
      Rin's mirror stand, against which Moémon might lean. The first
      few applications of the burning herb were almost more than he
      could bear, and those about him—the nurse, the housemaid and
123   even the scullery maid Také—pressed the afflicted regions to alle-
      viate the pain; at the same time, they could not forbear laughing as
      they saw the patient twist his face in agony.

      After the treatment had continued for some time, the moxa was
124   smoking violently and Moémon could hardly wait for the final
      application of salt. It was then that a pellet of the burning herb by
      ill luck slipped down his spine, puckering up the skin over which
      it passed. The pain was of no short duration, but out of regard for
      the girl who had treated him, Moémon merely closed his eyes and
      clenched his teeth. For all the patient's fortitude, Rin was moved
      with pity for his suffering as she crushed out the embers on his body.
      It was from having thus touched his skin that she suddenly con-
      ceived an infatuation for Moémon. At first she kept her longing for
      him secret, but it did not take long for her feelings to become known
      and to reach the ears of her mistress, Osan. Yet even then she could
      not quench her fondness.

      It was a source of special grief to the poor maid that, being of
      the meanest education and unversed in putting words to paper,
      she was unable to express her love in writing. She looked with

envy at the manservant Kyushichi, who could at least contrive to   *125*
scribble down his thoughts with clumsy strokes. Secretly she
besought his help; whereat he conceived the desire—a most odious
one for Rin—to taste her charms himself before she could bestow
them on Moémon.

Vainly the days flowed by, and soon it was the beginning of the   *126*
Tenth Moon—that season of winter rains and deception. One day,   *127*
after Osan had finished writing a letter to her husband in Edo, she
said, "Now let us compose a love-letter for Rin." Quickly her
brush ran along the paper; then folding the note into a wish-knot,
she simply wrote on the outside, "To Mister Moémon—from my-
self," and handed it to the girl. The latter received it with joy, and
was eagerly awaiting a favourable moment for its delivery when
from within the shop came the cry, "Some fire to light my tobacco!"
Using this as a pretext and taking advantage of the fact that no one
else was in the kitchen, she went into the shop and personally handed   *128*
the note to Moémon. He, for his part, had not the remotest idea
that the writing was in fact Osan's. Having read the message, he
could only think that this Rin was truly a girl of some charm. He
therefore penned a suitable reply and had it delivered to the girl.
Rin, hard put to read Moémon's words herself, sought out an oc-
casion when her mistress was in good humour to show the missive
to her.

"That you should have cast your tender thoughts on me," it read,
"was unexpected news indeed. I too am still in my youthful years and
matters such as these are far from odious. Yet when our attachment
deepens, it may forsooth bear fruit and we shall be faced with all
the trouble of calling on a midwife. For all that, if you will take
upon yourself the expenses of the clothing, the baths and all the
rest, I shall accede to your desires despite my doubts."

"Well, really!" exclaimed Osan, after reading these blunt words.
"What a hateful man he is! Does he fancy that there is a dearth of

males in the world? Rin is no such ill-favoured girl and I'll warrant she could find herself a man as good as this Moémon any day."

So saying, she resolved that in letter after letter she would sue the young man for pity and, having finally won him over, serve him a fine trick. With this design, she now used every means to snare his heart by tender missives; to such effect, indeed, that before long Moémon's feelings were aroused, and regretting his earlier asperity, he dispatched this earnest note: "The fourteenth night of the Fifth
129 Moon is fixed for the Vigil. Let us use that night as the occasion for our tryst."

Seeing this, Osan and her maid held their sides with laughter. "Rather than enjoy a night of love," said she, "that evening he'll become good sport for all of us!"

On the appointed night, then, Osan changed places with Rin, and, disguising herself in an unlined cotton dress, lay down in the bed where the girl was wont to sleep. Here she waited until close to dawn, when she could not help falling into a pleasant doze. Meanwhile the various maids had been standing ready here and there with cudgels, staves and candlesticks, waiting to rush out in a body at the agreed word of command from their mistress; but, being weary from the excitement of the previous evening, they too were soon emitting drowsy snores.

130 It was after the seven bells had sounded that Moémon made his
131 way stealthily through the darkness, undoing his loincloth as he went. Reaching Rin's chamber, he stripped himself naked and slipped in between the bedclothes, his heart pounding with excitement. In his eagerness for enjoyment, he dispensed with all verbal preliminaries and soon he had acquitted himself to his manly credit.

As Moémon replaced the covers and left the room on tiptoe, he was aware of the elegant scent that lingered on the lady's clothing.

"Odd indeed," he pondered to himself, "and brazen the ways of this Floating World! I should scarcely have thought that this Rin would already have known a man's love. Yet someone has surely been here ahead of me and done the deed!" And, apprehensive of discovery, he resolved to return to the charge no more.

Later when Osan awoke of her own accord, she found to her sur- 132
prise that the pillow was out of place and in disorder, while her 133
sash too was undone and not at hand. Then she saw paper handker- 134
chiefs scattered about the bed and was overcome with shame at the knowledge that Moémon had taken his pleasure with her while she slept.

"What has been done," she reflected, "cannot possibly remain secret, and now that it has come to such a pass, I can but continue on this course and throw away my life. For the remainder of my days, 135
this amour of mine will be the gossip of the world, until at last I tread the paths of Hades in company with Moémon." 136

She disclosed this firm intention to the young man, who realized now the unforeseen mistake that he had made that night. Dismissing, then, "the horse he once had rid" for her whom he now "so 137
dearly craved," he took to visiting Osan each night, and cared naught for the censure of reproving tongues.

Thus having both wandered astray in their own fashion, Osan and Moémon gave themselves over to the consequences of their error, and soon they were braving a most perilous toss of the coin between life and death.

3. *The Lake That Took People In* 138
"That which in this world lies quite past our control is the way of love"—so it is recorded in *The Tale of Genji*. 139

At this time there was being performed at the Ishiyama Temple the Ceremony of Exhibiting the Holy Image, and people were 140
thronging to see it, having quite put out of their minds the cherries that blossomed in the Eastern Hills. Yet, as one observed them, hav-

141 ing crossed the Osaka Barrier, with its "people leaving the capital and others returning," it appeared that not one of all these women in their fashionable attire was bent on visiting that temple to seek her salvation in the world to come; instead, each had on her face a self-admiring look produced by the elegance of her own apparel. Gazing into their hearts, even the Goddess Kannon could hardly have forborne from laughter.

It was at this season that Osan herself visited the temple, with Moémon in attendance. Seeing the flowers in bloom, they likened them to their own lives; for who could tell when they too would fall? Little knowing whether this might not be the last time that they would set their eyes on these fair bays and hills, they hired a dragnet fishing boat in Seta, so that this day might remain as a happy memory in their minds. As they rowed off, they saw the

142 Long Bridge of Seta and wished that it might bode them well. And yet they knew that this joy of theirs was bound to be short-lived.

143 Floating past Mount Toko, they made the rippling waves serve as the

144 pillow of their couch, and soon the disorder of Osan's hair bespoke

145 the nature of their pleasure. Later, as they drifted by Kagami Mountain, their pensive expression must have been mirrored on its slopes

146 and caused it to be overcast with tears. Nearing Cape Wani, they bethought themselves that to escape their fate would be as hard as to be delivered from a crocodile's mouth, and when they heard

147 someone hailing a boat from Katada, their spirits froze at the idea that these might be pursuers who had come after them from Kyoto.

148 Now Mount Nagara came into view, calling to the lovers' minds the

149 brevity of their own lives; and gazing into the distance at the Fuji of the Capital, which, if one were to compare it to that other Fuji, must be "piled up twenty-fold," time after time they wet their sleeves with tears, thinking that "if there be snow," it presently must melt.

150 Seeing the town of Shiga, they recalled that people spoke of how it had flourished in ancient times as a capital; just so were they fated to be spoken of after they were dead and gone. At this thought they fell into still deeper gloom.

When evening came and the lanterns of the Dragon God were lit, *151* they betook themselves to the Shirahigé Shrine; yet as the lovers offered up their prayers, the evanescence of their lives became ever clearer in their minds.

"Come what may," said Osan, "the longer we linger in this world, the more bitter will be our hardships. Should we not throw ourselves into this lake and in the Land of Buddha plight our lasting troth?"

"I don't cling to this life of mine," replied Moémon. "Yet, being ignorant of what may come hereafter, I have bethought myself of a plan. Let us both leave messages of farewell for those in the capital, and have it reported that we are drowned. Meanwhile we can quit this spot, betake ourselves to some place in the country—it matters not where—and spend our years together."

Hearing these words, Osan rejoiced and said, "Even such was my intention from the time I left my home—and for this purpose I brought along in this box five hundred gold *koban.*" *152,153*

"That will indeed provide us with our livelihood," said Moémon. "So let us now escape and go into hiding."

They each then set to preparing notes. "Having succumbed," they wrote, "to evil inclinations and indulged in adulterous pleasure, we cannot escape the doom of Heaven, nor is there any place for us in this world. On this day of the present month we take our leave of the Floating World." *154*

In addition they each arranged to leave behind various tokens that people would clearly recognize as having belonged to them. Osan added a few strands of her black hair to the two-inch image of the Buddha that she was wont to wear next to her skin as an amulet, while Moémon left the twenty-inch sword that he carried by his side, with its iron guard of coiled-dragon design wrought by the swordsmith Seki-no-Izumi-no-Kami. They even carried their *155*

precautions to the point of placing their coats, Osan's straw slippers and Moémon's leather-soled sandals under a willow tree by the water's edge. Next they secretly engaged two fishermen from those shores, who, being skilful divers, were in the habit of displaying
156 Rock Leaps. Handing them money, they explained their circumstances to the men, and the latter gladly undertook the task. Then the two lovers waited for the onset of darkness.

The time having come and all their preparations being made, Osan and Moémon left open the bamboo gate of their lodging, then
157 went to shake the attendants out of their sleep.

"For reasons of our own we are resolved to die forthwith!" So saying, they rushed out of doors.

A moment later from the height of the craggy cliffs the sound
158 could be faintly heard of voices invoking the Sacred Name of Buddha. Then two bodies hurtled down through space, ending in a splash of water; whereat the people in the house put up a great wailing. Meanwhile Moémon, carrying Osan on his shoulders, was making his way through the undergrowth at the foot of the mountains, where he took refuge in a dense grove of pine trees. The fishermen, for their part, had dived under the waves, to reappear at some other point along the beach.

Osan's companions clapped their hands in lamentation. With the help of the villagers, they searched high and low, but to no avail. When dawn broke, however, they discovered the keepsakes; these they collected, weeping bitterly the while, and returned with them to Kyoto. When they related what had befallen, the people of the household, fearful of the family's reputation, directed them to keep these matters secret. But in our world of prying eyes precautions of this kind are bootless, and soon the gossip spread far and wide, being a fine topic for springtime tattle. Such was the outcome of this wanton couple's deed; and none could deflect them from their folly.

4. *The Teahouse Which Knew Not of Gold Pieces*   159

Now these two lovers had entered the ranks of those who fly   160
across the hills to Tamba. Moémon held Osan's hand as they made
their own path across the trackless heath. Finally they dragged
themselves to the top of a steep hill. From here the way ahead looked
even more foreboding and, thinking of their plight, it seemed as
though, while still alive, they had already joined the dead. All this,
to be sure, proceeded from their own free choice, yet that did not
make it one jot less grievous.

Pursuing their course, they came to a place so desolate that not
even the mark of woodcutters' footsteps could be seen. Now they
truly knew to their cost the sorrows of losing one's way. Osan with
her woman's frailty could no longer continue the journey. Seeing
the girl in this suffering state, her breath now coming but weakly,
and all colour gone from her face, Moémon was sorely moved. He
gathered on a leaf the drops of water that had trickled on a rock and
poured them in her mouth. In various other ways he sought to nurse
her, but for all his cares she gradually lost strength and the beating
of her pulse grew faint. It seemed as if the end was not far off, and,
having nothing at hand to use as medicine, they could but wait for
the final breath. It was then that Moémon approached his mistress
and murmured dolefully in her ear, "If you could but have gone a
little farther! In a village that lies ahead I have acquaintances. There
we could forget these present hardships, rest to our hearts' content
and, lying side by side, engage in the most intimate converse."

"What happy words!" Osan replied. "You are indeed a man
for whom one would gladly pay one's life." And forthwith her
spirits revived.

Seeing this girl, so prepossessed with lust that all else had been cast   161
out in its favour, Moémon could not forbear from being moved. He
lifted her again upon his shoulders, and they had not gone far before
they reached the fences of a little village.

Through this village ran the highway to the capital and along the
mountain edge a road wide enough for two horses to pass each
other. Here they came upon a straw-thatched hut, from whose eaves
162 hung a sheaf of cedar leaves and on a sign the inscription, "First-
Grade Sakè." Entering this place, they saw a tray of rice cakes
adorned with the dust of many days and quite lacking in their pris-
tine whiteness. In the corner of the shop, however, were displayed
163 for sale tea whisks, clay dolls, bean drums and other such objects,
which, being quite familiar to the young couple and savouring of
the capital, served to heighten their spirits. They stayed there and
rested for a while, after which, being in a contented frame of mind,
they handed the old shopkeeper a gold *koban*. But this was to show
164 an umbrella to a cat, and the man, seeing it, made a wry face and
said, "Please pay me for the tea you drank."

Thoroughly amused by the thought that a place like this, not even
forty miles from the capital, should be unfamiliar with gold coins,
they set forth for the village of Kayabara. Here Moémon visited the
house of his mother's sister. It was many years since they had last
had tidings of each other, and neither knew how the other had
fared. Moémon spoke to her of the past, and she, mindful of their
connection, gave him no cold welcome, but regaled him with talk
of his father, Mosuké. Thus, with tears in their eyes, Moémon and
his aunt spent the night in fond recollections of their family.

When dawn broke, however, his aunt, growing suspicious of the
fair young lady who had journeyed in his company, inquired, "And
who may she be?"

Not having prepared himself for such a question, Moémon was
taken off his guard. "She is a younger sister of mine," he replied,
"who for many years held service in the household of a court of-
ficial. But growing indisposed and wearying of the formality of life
in the capital, she thought that if she could find a suitable match in
some peaceful mountain village such as this, she would gladly lower

92

her status and in some rustic field pursue the humble work of country folk. For this reason I have brought her here with me. She brings a dowry of some two hundred gold *koban*."   *165*

Thus he blurted out his makeshift story. But this is a world where avarice holds sway in every corner, and his aunt promptly marked the mention of a dowry.

"A happy circumstance indeed!" said she. "My only son is yet un-betrothed and as you are my very flesh and blood, let us make this   *166* girl his wife."

Hearing her plead in this manner, the young couple was more troubled than ever, and Osan secretly shed bitter tears.

"How will this end?" she was lamenting to herself, when the son himself returned home, the night being now well advanced. And what a fearful sight he was! Towering above the common run of men, he stood there, his hair ruffled like a lion's mane, his beard like a shaggy bear's, his eyes bloodshot and strangely gleaming, his limbs knotted with sinews like a very pine tree. The fellow's clothes were sewn together from old rags and his sash was made of a twisted rope of wistaria vines. A bunch of matchlocks hung from his rifle and in his straw bag were thrust the bodies of rabbits and badgers, all of which proclaimed that he made his living as a hunter. His name was Zetaro the Rock Leaper, and he was known in the whole village as a notorious ruffian.

Hearing his mother say that he was to be married to a city girl, the young stalwart was much elated. "Strike while the iron's hot!"   *167* said he. "Let's have the ceremony this very evening." Bringing out his pocket mirror, he set to examining his face—pretty doings for such a churl!

His mother meantime produced a salted fish stew and a sakè bottle with a broken spout—all in readiness, as she said, for the coming nuptials. To serve as bridal chamber, she enclosed a small corner of the room, using straw matting for a screen. Here she placed two wooden pillows, two thin mats and striped bedding. Then she burned some kindling in the brazier. That night she was indeed in the very height of spirits.

Not so Osan and Moémon, the one of whom was sunk in sorrow, the other in perplexity.

"This is what comes of my heedless words," said Moémon. "And how vexing it is to know that all this is the inescapable consequence of my own folly! So once again we have come to grief. After all, the Gods will not forgive us for living on, when we should have died beneath the waters of that lake in Omi."

He lay hold of his sword and stood up. But Osan restrained him, saying, "So hasty-spirited, Moémon! But stop, for I have many thoughts. Tomorrow at daybreak we must quit this place. Leave all to me." Thus did she calm his spirits.

That evening, after she and her intended spouse had cheerfully exchanged their nuptial cups, Osan announced, "I was born under that

168 sign that men most abhor—the Fiery Horse."

"It wouldn't worry me in the least," answered Zetaro, "if you were born in the year of the Fiery Cat or the Fiery Wolf! I'm a

169 fellow who even eats blue lizards—likes them, for that matter— and I've managed to survive. In fact, in all my twenty-seven years I've never once had as much as the slightest bellyache. You should try and take after me, Moémon my lad! Now, when it comes to wiving, I can tell you I wouldn't myself have chosen any soft,

170 city-bred wench for my mate. But since we're related, I'll just have to put up with you!"

With these words he lay his head on Osan's lap and lolled there comfortably. Even in the midst of their distress, Osan and Moémon could not but be amused at his uncouth demeanour.

They waited impatiently for Zetaro to fall asleep, then stole out of the house and once more hid themselves in the depths of Tamba.

171 Slowly the days passed and they reached the Tango Way. One eve-

ning they kept vigil in the Monju Temple at Kirédo. It appeared to   *172*
be the middle of the night when Osan, having dozed off, was
confronted with a miraculous vision of the guardian God, who ad-
dressed them in these words: "Ye have displayed an unexampled
wantonness, and fly where'er ye will, ye shall ne'er escape the
adversity that followeth on such deeds. Nor can ye in any way
contrive to redeem the past. Yet if thou, Osan, shouldst hereafter
abandon the ways of the Floating World, cut off those black tresses   *173*
that thou dost value so, join the Holy Priesthood, live forever apart
from this man that thou lovest, cleanse thy heart of all evil designs
and enter the Way of Salvation, then it may be that men will
spare thy life."

Hearing these gracious words as in a trance, Osan replied, "Do
not concern yourself, I pray you, for what may befall me in the
future. I like what I am doing and should gladly give my life for the
illicit love that I now enjoy. You may indeed, Lord Monju, under-
stand love between men, but so far as womanly passion is concerned,   *174*
you cannot have the slightest knowledge."

No sooner had she spoken than she awoke from her unpleasant
dream. The wind was soughing in the pines at Hashidaté. Hearing it,   *175*
Osan bethought herself of "this fragile world of dust which the very
wind can blow away"; and still more she gave herself over to her
aberrant passion.

5.   *The Eavesdropper Who Heard about Himself*
Men know only too well the bad things that befall them and seek
to hide these from their neighbours. Thus it is that the gambler is
silent about his losses, that the man who has been cozened by a trol-
lop assumes a knowing look as if nothing untoward has happened,
that the brawler who has been worsted in a fight keeps it a secret and
that the merchant who has suffered loss in some speculation con-
ceals the knowledge from the world. All these are cases of "a dog's   *176*

dung in the darkness." But among the several misfortunes that can befall a man, none is so cruel as to have a wanton wife.

"Osan is dead and nothing can be done to change the past." Thus accepting the report of her drowning, the almanac maker put up a good front to the world. As his thoughts went back to the happy years that they had spent together, he could not but feel bitter at the outcome. Yet, summoning a priest, he would direct that masses be read for the repose of his dead wife's soul. Most pitiably, Osan's colourful silk garments were offered to the family temple, where, having been made into banners and baldachins, 177 they fluttered in the uncertain wind of death, thus to become a further source of grief.

Now in this wide world there is nothing so intrepid as man. Moémon, who had at first exercised such prudence that he durst not issue abroad even under the cover of darkness, had now in the course of time quite lost himself in the desire to see the capital again. One day, then, he dressed himself in humble attire, and, pulling his 178 sedge hat down to hide his face, set forth on a "useless journey to the capital," commending Osan to the care of the people in the village.

Walking along the road, more fearful even than one who dreads the onslaught of his enemy, Moémon presently approached the Hi-179 rosawa Pond as dusk was gathering. He gazed at the double image of the moon that shimmered on the waters, and, bethinking himself of Osan, wet his sleeves with doleful tears—tears that fell onto the stone and broke like pearls; like scattered pearls, too, glittered the drops of water on the rocks of Mount Narutaki, which Moémon now left behind him as he hastened through the familiar quarters of Omuro and Kitano. Entering the city itself, he was overcome with a vague sense of apprehension, and every now and then was chilled with terror at the sight of his own shadow reflected in the light of the seventeen-day-old moon. At length, then, he came near to the house of Osan's father, the place where he himself had dwelt so long. Approaching the shop, he crouched down out of sight and eavesdropped, so that he might learn the recent state of things. One group of men was talking of the delay in the arrival of silver payment from the branch shop at Edo. Some of the clerks had gathered to discuss the various ways of styling hair and were exchanging critical remarks about the workmanship of each other's cotton clothes and other matters of manly fashion; all this proceeded from the wish to appear pleasing to women and thus to satisfy their own lust. Having listened to them discuss these various topics, Moémon heard their conversation turn, much as expected, to himself.

"Well indeed," said one of the clerks, "that fellow Moémon made off with a beauty whose equal one could hardly find in this wide world. Worth paying for with one's life, in troth! I'll warrant he counted himself a lucky man even though he had to die for it."

"Ay, to be sure," said another, "to have had a girl like that would be the memory of a lifetime for any man!"

Then up spake one of the other clerks with a knowing look: "That Moémon was a scurvy rogue and fouled the very air we breathed! What wretch in this world would have tricked both master and husband as he has done?"

Overhearing the censure of this man, for whom chill reason was unrelieved with any human warmth, Moémon muttered to himself, "Assuredly that was the voice of Kisuké from the Daimonji Shop. Unfeeling wretch that he is with all his hateful talk! To think that he borrowed eighty *mommé* of silver from me and that I even have his bond of loan! I'd like to wring his neck to pay him for those callous words of his."

180

Grinding his teeth with anger, Moémon rose to his feet. But those who are hiding from the world must bear such hurts in silence, and Moémon restrained himself despite his rage. Just then his blood froze as one of the men said, "Moémon is no more dead than me or you! They say he's hiding somewhere in the region of Isé with Mistress Osan—and having a fine time with her, I'll be bound!"

Overhearing these words, Moémon started to tremble. He left the place with rapid steps and made his way to the Hatago Inn by

181 the Third Avenue, where he rented a room, and, without so much as taking a bath, lay down to rest.

182 It being the seventeenth night of the month, the Begging Proxies were abroad, and, calling one of them, Moémon wrapped up twelve coppers and gave them to him, commending to the Gods his earnest prayer that he might for many years make good his hiding. Yet how could even the God of Atago Shrine redeem him from his errant ways when he continued to enjoy the fruits thereof?

On the following day, thinking to have a final look at the capital, Moémon stole down the Eastern Hills and visited the Shijogawara district. Here he was met by a crier who announced, "See the actor

183 Fujita appear in a modern drama. The three-part programme will presently begin!"

Moémon did not know what this drama might be, but he resolved to visit the theatre, considering that Osan might on his return enjoy a description of the play. Accordingly he rented a round cushion and took his place with the other spectators, peering about nervously the while, for fear that someone there might recognize him. Looking at the stage, he was seized with a vague apprehension as he saw that the play dealt with the story of a man whose daughter was abducted. This, however, was as nothing to his horror when he noticed that at the end of his very row sat none other than Osan's

184 husband. He felt as though one foot were dangling over the chasm of Hell; his blood ran cold and beads of sweat broke out over his body. Rushing for the entrance, he left the theatre, and hardly slowed his pace until he had reached his village in Tango. From that day forth Kyoto to him spelled naught but fear.

185 The Chrysanthemum Festival was now at hand, and, as was his yearly wont, a chestnut vendor from Tamba called at the almanac maker's house. After he had rambled over sundry topics, he asked, "By the bye, how fares the mistress of this house?" A strained air fell over the company and no one answered him, until the almanac maker with a bitter look said, "She is dead."

Hearing this, the chestnut vendor continued, "Strange indeed how people can resemble each other in this world! Not far from Kirédo in Tango I came across a lady who does not differ from your wife in the smallest particle, and a young fellow who was the living image of the clerk who worked here." So saying, he took his leave.

Now the husband, who had listened attentively to his words, sent a man to observe the couple. Having ascertained that they were indeed Osan and Moémon, he assembled a large company of his retainers and arrested the fugitives.

There was no escaping the consequences of their offence, and, after the inquest had been concluded, the two lovers, together with *186* the girl who had acted as their confidante, were led together through the street and at the Execution Grounds of Awataguchi their lives vanished as the morning dew on the grass. Thus on the *187* twenty-second day of the Ninth Moon their end came smoothly like an evanescent dream at dawn; nor was there aught ignoble in the way of their departing. The tale of how these two finished their lives was handed down to posterity; and Osan bequeathed her name of love to the world, so that even now men seem to see the image of the pale-blue silk she wore that morning. *188*

THE TALE OF GENGOBEI, THE MOUNTAIN
OF LOVE

I. *How Sorrowfully Ends the Concert of the Flutes*

189   Gengobei—he of whom they sing in the ballads—hailed from
Kagoshima in the Province of Satsuma, but for a native of so out-
landish a place he displayed in his taste a most unusual fastidious-
190   ness. He shaved his hair, according to the fashion of that region, so
that his sidelocks fell down at the back, and he wore his topknot
short. The long sword that he carried by his side was most striking,
191   but, this too being a custom of these parts, none thought to reprove
him.

Day and night this Gengobei devoted himself to the love of men;
nor had he once in the twenty-six springs of his life dallied with the
frail and long-haired sex. For many years now he had been enam-
oured of a young boy by the name of Nakamura Hachijuro, to
whom he had from the outset bound himself by the deepest vows
of lifelong loyalty. Hachijuro was a youth of the greatest beauty,
like in purity to a single-petalled cherry whose blossoms are yet but
192   half opened. His indeed was the flavour of a flower endowed with
the gift of human speech.

One evening as the rain fell gloomily outside, the two young men
immured themselves in the little room where Gengobei was wont
to stay, and played their flutes in concert. The sound of the music
echoed quietly in the dark, adding to the night's gentle melancholy.
The wind that blew in through the window carried with it the
fragrance of plum blossoms, scenting therewith the loose sleeves
of the young men's dress; outside, the birds at roost were startled by
the rustling of the black bamboo, and the sound of their wings as
they fluttered to and fro had a mournful note.

Gengobei and his young paramour play their flutes together for the last time. Outside it is raining and the sound of their music adds to the gentle melancholy of the night.

As the lamp gradually grew dim, Gengobei and his companion stopped their music. On this evening Hachijuro seemed more affectionate than ever. His fair form was utterly yielding, and the love-charged phrases that he uttered each carried a novel fascination. In the presence of all this grace Gengobei was quite overcome with yearning and he conceived a desire that ill befits this Floating World—the desire that this boy's beauty might never tarnish, that he might forever wear the forelock of a lad.

They shared the same pillow and soon their disorder bespoke the passion that they felt. As dawn approached, Gengobei fell into a sleep. Then Hachijuro, overcome with pain, awakened him, saying, "Alas, will you thus waste the night in idle dreams?"

Drowsy and confused, Gengobei listened as the boy continued: "In case you have aught to tell me, Gengobei, tonight is your final chance. Have you no message to bequeath me ere we part?"

Though still half asleep, Gengobei was much dismayed and said, "You may speak in jest, Hachijuro, yet you give me great concern. If I failed to see you even for a single day, your vision would haunt me like a phantom till we met. Though it be merely that you wish to ruffle me with your talk of present leave-taking, desist, I pray you."

They took each other by the hand and Hachijuro smiled wanly. "Evanescent," he said, "is this Floating World and uncertain the life of man." The words were not out of his mouth when his pulse suddenly ceased its beating and the talk of parting that had seemed to be in jest proved to have been all too earnest.

"What now?" exclaimed Gengobei, and, quite forgetting that his love was of a secret nature, he set up a great wailing and shed bitter tears. Startled by his cries, people hastened to the room. Various medicaments were administered to the boy, but all to no avail. Most grievous to relate, Hachijuro had irretrievably departed this world.

When his parents were informed, their sorrow knew no bounds. Yet, so far as the circumstances of his death were concerned, they were resigned.

"These two," they said, "were close to each other for many a long year. We have no grounds for suspicion about Hachijuro's end. Things have come to pass as they must and naught we can do will change them."

It was time now to see the boy laid in his last place of rest. His body, lovely as when it still held life, was placed in an urn and buried in a field near where the grass was sprouting forth its springtime verdure. Gengobei prostrated himself before the grave and lamented most grievously. But tears brought no relief and the only course he could conceive was to cast away his own life. After much deep thought he came to his resolve: "Alas and alack, Hachijuro, how frail you were! For just three years will I linger on and mourn over your remains. Then on this same month and day will I come once more to this place and put a term to my dewlike life." *193*

Forthwith, in front of the grave, he cut off his topknot. Thence he repaired to the Saien Temple, where he addressed himself to the Father Superior, explaining to him the circumstances, and then himself took the earnest vows of priesthood.

Each day during the summer period of retirement he culled flowers for Hachijuro's grave, burned incense and said mass for the repose of the dead boy's soul. Thus the time passed as in a dream and soon the autumn season was at hand. The morning glories that flowered on the hedgerows, only to fade at night, brought to Gengobei's mind the impermanence of the world. Even the dew that sparkled on these fragile blossoms seemed to him less fleeting than the life of man. So thinking, he recalled the past and the death that could never be revoked. As now it was the very eve of that season at which the spirits of the dead return, Gengobei set to preparing a *194* welcome. He cut some branches of purple clover to spread upon

the holy shelf, thereon quaintly adding cucumbers, eggplants, dried
195 green soybeans and other offerings. By the dim light of the square
196 lantern he busily recited sutras for the dead, and in front of the
197 houses the hempen reeds burned away in the sacred bonfires.

However, in the gathering dusk of the fourteenth day, the
198 peaceful air was rent with the clamours of the bill collectors; for
even temples are not spared their debts. Meanwhile the sound of
199 drums beating the Bon dances resounded outside the temple gates.
For one who had retired here like Gengobei to fly the tumult of the
world all this was nothing short of odious, and he resolved forth-
200 with to make a pilgrimage to Mount Koya. Accordingly, on the
201 following day, the fifteenth of the Poem Month, he set forth from
his native place. His black vestments, it is said, were bleached with
tears and the sleeves thereof quite worn away from all his weeping.

2. *Frail as the Life of the Birds He Catches Is the Life of the Bird-Catcher*

In the mountain village, preparations for the winter were well
afoot. Bush cover and brushwood had been cut and stored, snow
guards erected in anticipation of the heavy drifts, and the northern
windows firmly boarded. The sound of clothes being beaten on the
fuller's block echoed loudly in the winter air.

By a field not far from this same village a lad was taking careful
aim at the little birds that fluttered among the red-tinged foliage
fighting for a nesting place. From seeing the boy one would have
judged him to be fourteen, or at the most fifteen, years of age. He
wore a hempen kimono, lined with the same light-blue material and
secured with a purple sash of medium width. The short sword that
202 hung by his side was embellished with a gilded guard. His long hair
203 was artlessly secured in a whisk style, and he had about him a volup-
tuous, feminine beauty.

This stripling held his lime stick in the middle and, as the birds of
passage fluttered overhead, he tried time after time to catch them.

Yet he did not succeed in ensnaring a single one, and a look of dismay settled on his face. Gengobei stood there, feasting his eyes upon the scene. "To think that there exists in the world a lad of such exquisite beauty!" he murmured to himself. "In years he hardly differs from Hachijuro when yet he lived. But in beauty he far excels him!"

All Gengobei's pious resolutions were forgotten as he stood gazing in rapture on the boy. As dusk fell, he approached his side. "Though I be a priest," he said, "I am not unskilled in catching birds. Pray lend me your stick."

Setting about his task, Gengobei first addressed himself to the birds. "You fowls above," said he, "why should you begrudge your lives at the hands of this fair youth? Come, come, you inelegant creatures, have you no feeling for such boyish charms?"

In no time at all Gengobei had caught a goodly number of the birds and presented them to the lad. The latter was overcome with joy.

"Pray tell me how you came to take your vows?" he said. Thereat Gengobei gave himself over to relating the story of his life. The boy listened with such distress that he was moved to tears.

"To renounce the world for such a cause seems to me especially worthy," said he. "Come with me, I pray you, and spend this night in my poor dwelling."

So saying, he led Gengobei in most friendly fashion to a splendid manor house set in the midst of a dense forest. Horses neighed in the stables and armour shone on the walls. Passing through the great hall, they emerged on a veranda, whence a long gallery led to the garden. Here, striped bamboos grew luxuriantly and in the back stood a great aviary, where various sorts of birds—white and golden pheasants, Chinese pigeons and the like—joined their voices in song. 204

On a balcony a little to the side was a room which commanded a view in all directions. The walls were worthily lined with bookshelves, this being the youth's habitual place of study. After they had seated themselves here, the boy called for the servants. "This travelling priest," he said, "is to be my reading master. See that he wants for nothing."

The evening passed in many pleasant entertainments. When darkness fell, the two of them held intimate converse and soon had pledged their fervent vows. Retiring, then, to bed, they exhausted
205 their ingenuity in making this into "a thousand nights."

On the following morning, they were much loath to part from each other.

"I know that you must make your pilgrimage to Koya," said the boy, "but on your return voyage pray do not fail to come and see me here."

They exchanged solemn promises, weeping the while at the thought of their separation. Then Gengobei left the manor, unbeknown to any other members of the household. Reaching the
206 village, he made inquiries. "The master of that manor is the Governor of these parts," people informed him, and told him also about the Governor's handsome son.

"Well indeed," thought Gengobei, much pleased at the status of his new-found love, and he begrudged each step that took him to
207 the capital. Plunged alternately in memories of the departed Hachijuro and in fond thoughts of his successor, he had scant room in his mind for the Holy Way of Buddha.

208 Finally he reached the sacred mountain of Saint Kobo. He spent one day in a visitor's lodging in the Southern Valley; then, without so much as paying his respects at the Saint's tomb, he set forth on his return journey.

He proceeded, as promised, to the house of his young friend, and the latter, not changed one jot since when they last conversed, came forth to greet him. Together they entered a certain chamber, and here exchanged news of all that had happened since their parting;

during which time, Gengobei, much wearied by his travels, fell into a sleep.

When dawn broke, the boy's father came into the room. Seeing a strange priest, his suspicions were aroused and he awakened Gengobei. The latter was taken by surprise and straightway blurted out in frankest detail all that had befallen him, from the time when he took the tonsure until the very present. Hearing this, the master of the house clapped his hands in amazement. "Passing strange!" he exclaimed. "Though it ill becomes a father's modesty, I could not but feel proud of that boy's beauty. Yet in this world of ours all is transitory and mortal. Some twenty days ago he died most unexpectedly. Until the very last moment he called out the words: 'The priest! The priest!' At the time I fancied that these were but feverish rantings. . . . So it was you for whom he called?" So saying, the gentleman fell into the most grievous lamentation.

Hearing these words, Gengobei felt, more strongly than ever before, that his life was a thing of utter worthlessness. Why should he not throw it away here and now—this existence that meant so little to him? Yet in this world of ours the life of man is not so easily cast off.

Thus in a pitifully brief space of time Fate had robbed Gengobei of two young men, and bitter indeed it was to linger on himself. Yet perhaps in these very deaths lay a rare karma: perhaps, these youths had died so that he might learn the sorrows of this world. And sorrows they truly were.

3. *A Lover of Men Has the Flowers Scattered from Both Hands*   209

Naught is as abject and unfeeling as the heart of man. Looking about us in the world, we see that when great sorrows strike—when parents lose a child at the very height of their devotion, or again, when a man's wife, to whom he has sworn vows of eternal loyalty, is brought to an early grave—though our first thoughts be to put an end to our own lives, yet, before our tears have even dried, desire once more regains its sway and griefs are callously forgot.

Thus a woman whose husband has barely drawn his final breath will, either from desire for worldly wealth or from some whim of the moment, lend willing ear to talk of finding a new spouse. Sometimes she will choose her husband's younger brother as successor to the dead man's rights; or again, she may put heart and soul into the task of picking some suitable man from among the family, who will

210 marry her and take her name. In either case she will dismiss from her mind all thought of her departed lord. She will, to be sure, recite prayers, burn incense and offer flowers at his grave, but all this from mere sense of duty and in order to be seen by others. Impatiently she

211 awaits the ending of the mourning period, and five weeks have hardly passed before she embellishes her face discreetly with light powder, tastefully oils her hair, though leaving it in studied disarray,

212 and beneath her uncrested silk garment dons an under-kimono of brilliant hue. Thereby she gives herself an unobtrusive air; yet the effect is all the more alluring.

Another woman may at her husband's death perceive the frailty of human life; moved by various sorrowful tales she will with her own hands cut off her tresses, as she prepares to spend her days in some rustic convent, there to make offerings of dew-drenched flowers to him who lies beneath the sod. Scattering her fine garments on the floor—some embroidered, others of dappled silk— she says, "Such things as these no longer are of any use to me. They shall go to the Temple, there to become banners, baldachins and altar cloths." Yet, even as she speaks the words, she is moved in

213 her heart with grief to see that the sleeves are slightly short.

Naught in this world is as fearsome as women. Should anyone try to restrain them from their fickle ways, he will be faced with a great show of womanly tears. Thus there are two creatures we shall never meet with in this world of ours—one is a ghost, the other a widow who remains faithful to her husband's memory.

Since such, then, is the way of women when their husbands die, what chance is there that men will be reproved when, having lost three, four or even five wives, they set forth in search of yet another? Yet our bonze was of a different metal. Having now twice undergone the grief of seeing the young men he loved reach a pitiful end, Gengobei retired to a distant mountain hermitage, full of the sincere intent to seek salvation in a future life and to banish all thought of earthly lust. Praiseworthy resolves indeed, and rarely to be met with in this fickle world!

Now at this time there dwelt in Hama of Satsuma a certain man, *214* the proprietor of the Ryukyu-ya, who had a daughter named Oman. She was fifteen years of age and so well favoured by nature that even the moon in its mid-month glory regarded her with *215* envy. She was of warm disposition and now at the very height of her beauty, so that no man looked at her without being struck by her charms.

Since spring of the previous year, Oman had been consumed with yearning for Gengobei, that flower of manly beauty. She poured forth her longings in letter after letter, and had these delivered secretly to Gengobei. But he, having turned his back on the love of women, made not the slightest effort to reply. This was grievous indeed for Oman, who spent both day and night in love-lorn pining.

Offers were made for her hand from all quarters, but these she dismissed as odious and would invent the most preposterous illnesses and belabour the people about her with the most offensive ravings, until they thought she must in truth be mad. She remained in ignorance of Gengobei's retirement from the world, until one day she happened to hear mention made of it.

"Lamentable indeed!" was her immediate thought. She had always consoled herself with the idea that at some time, she knew not when, her longings would be satisfied. But now, alas, it was too late! How hateful they were to her, those black vestments that Gengobei had donned! Come what may, resolved Oman, she must pay him a visit and chide him with his cruelty to her.

Thus resolved, she stealthily made her preparations, thinking forever to renounce her present life. With her own hands she fitly cut her hair and shaved her head in the fashion favoured by young boys. Then, having changed into clothes which she had set aside for this purpose, and which artfully transformed her into a boyish paramour, she left her home in secret.

From the moment that Oman "set forth up the Mountain of Love," she had to brush away the dew that clung to her clothes from the ground-bamboo; and for all the deceptions of the Godless Month, her woman's heart was chilled by the perils of the journey that lay ahead. After much walking she passed a village and entered a grove of cedars of which she had been told. Behind her, great boulders were piled in fearsome array, and to one side there opened up a yawning cavern, into which she gazed forlornly, feeling that into its depth her very heart might sink. Next, her path led her across a fearful bridge wrought of a few unstable logs of rotten wood, beneath which the rapid waters of a mountain stream thrashed against the banks, seeming at the same time to thrash her spirits with their awful roar.

Coming at last to a small stretch of level ground, Oman perceived a hermit's cell with sloping roof and overgrown with vines and creepers. Drops of water trickled from the sodden eaves—so steadily, indeed, that one might have thought it was a local shower. On the south side of the hut a dormer window opened up, and, peering through it, Oman saw a type of humble kitchen range often to be found in rustic hovels, in which a fire of pine needles had been left to burn. A pair of tea bowls completed the hermit's chattels, which did not include so much as a soup ladle. To such a wretched state had Gengobei come!

"He who inhabits such a place," thought Oman, "must indeed find favour with Buddha himself."

Looking round about, she ascertained to her dismay that the master of the cell was absent. There was none here of whom she might inquire his whereabouts—only the pine trees that stood by silently to watch her pine as she waited now for Gengobei's return. 218

Fortunately the door was open, and the girl entered the hut. On a lectern Oman noticed a book. This seemed admirable indeed in such a humble place, but when she came to examine the title, she saw that it was *Both Sleeves Wet with Tears from Waiting for His Lover,* a volume that set forth the mysteries of manly love.

"So this passion is one thing that even now he has not relinquished," thought Oman, as she began her tedious wait for Gengobei's return.

Soon dusk gathered, and, there being no way for Oman to light the lamp, it grew hard for her to read the characters in the book. As time passed, she felt ever more desolate, and thus she kept solitary watch through the long night hours. All this she could endure for the sake of love. 219

It must have been about the middle of the night when the bonze Gengobei made his way back to the hut by the dim light of a pine torch. Seeing him, Oman was overcome with delight; but then she noticed two elegant young boys emerging from a clump of withered reeds. They seemed to be equal in age and no less close in beauty; for one was like a springtime blossom, the other like a maple leaf in all its glory. Each was competing for amorous attention, the one with resentful pouting, the other with tearful wailing; here was a veritable battle for manly love. Gengobei was one, his lovers two— and seeing him dragged, now one way, now the other, tormented by the importunities of his boyish lovers and a troubled look of sorrow on his face, Oman was overcome with pity. At the same time she could not but experience distaste at the damping scene before her. "Well, well," she thought, "here is a fickle man indeed."

Howbeit, she had set her heart on this love and could not leave things in their present state. If nothing else, she must briefly unbosom herself of the secret that consumed her. So resolved, she stepped forth from the hut. Startled by her sudden appearance, the two young paramours disappeared into thin air, much to Oman's bewilderment.

"What now?" she thought.

Gengobei, no less surprised, addressed himself to her.

"Pray, what manner of young boy are you?" he said.

"As you see, sir," answered Oman, "I am one who has embarked on the way of manly love. For some time past, I have heard speak of you, Sir Priest, and thus it was that I risked all to steal hither to your mountain fastness. Little did I know, alas, how inconstant a man you were, and now I perceive that I have set my heart on you in vain! A grievous disappointment in truth."

There was bitterness in Oman's tone, but, hearing these words, Gengobei clapped his hands with joy.

"Your aim in coming here is gratifying indeed!" said he, and once again his fickle feelings were aroused. He told Oman, then, of how his two earlier lovers had already departed this world and of how the boys outside the hut were merely their phantoms. At this piteous narration, they both shed tears in unison.

"They have gone," said Oman, "but do not, I pray, abandon me."

"No," said Gengobei, with deep emotion, "I shall never give you up. Nor, priest though I be, can I give up the form of love I have espoused." And even as he spoke, he set to wantoning with his young visitor. To know nothing is to enjoy the peace of Buddha; and even Buddha would surely have pardoned Gengobei, who little knew that this was a maiden in his hermit's cell.

4. *Love Turns Topsy-turvy*

"When first I took my vows," continued Gengobei, "I swore to Buddha that I would once and for all abjure the love of women. Yet fair boys with their forelocks—they were a thing that I could ill banish from my heart. Ever since that time, I have prayed to all the Buddhas that this form of love at least may be vouchsafed me, and I feel sure that none will now reproach me for my bent. You, my young friend, were moved to pity me in my bereavement and have even gone so far as to visit me in this lonely place. Having shown yourself to be of so compassionate a nature, never, I pray you, forsake me." So saying, he pursued his amorous dalliance.

Oman was much tickled by all this, and, to stifle her mirth, she pinched her thighs and held her breast.

"Pray listen, sir, to what I say," quoth she, "and give heed to my meaning. I loved you as you were before, and, seeing you now in priestly guise, I love you all the more. How greatly you have troubled my spirits, you may judge yourself from my having come here, from my having risked life itself for the sake of the love I bear you. Since such, then, are my feelings, you must banish from your mind all thoughts of making tender vows to other boys. If I may have your written oath that henceforth you will do as I say, even if at times it may not suit your wishes, I will pledge you my heart—ay, and my body, too—in this world and the world to come." 221

Hearing this, the bonze Gengobei most imprudently inscribed the oath. "For a boy like you," said he, "I could do anything—even renounce the cloth." The words were hardly out of his mouth before he began to pant with passion, and slipping his hand up 222 Oman's sleeve, he set to feeling her naked body. Finding that she wore no loincloth, he showed a puzzled look, which once again amused the girl.

Reaching into his bag, Gengobei put something in his mouth, 223 which he then began to crunch.

"Pray, Sir Priest, what are you doing?" asked Oman. But Gen-
gobei merely blushed and hid the object. It was no doubt that root
called mandioc, so often used in manly love, and Oman's fancy was
further tickled at the thought. She turned away in bed from her
companion. At this, Gengobei threw off his vestments, thrusting
them with his foot into the corner of the room. Now he set in earnest
about the task of love-making, an absorbing one indeed whoever
we may be. He untied her medium-width sash, which was knotted
in the back.

"This is not like towns or villages," he murmured. "Night winds
blow fiercely in these desolate parts." So saying, he covered Oman's
body with a wide-sleeved cotton kimono.

"Pray rest your head here," he said ecstatically, putting out his
arm as a pillow for his paramour. Even before stretching himself
out beside Oman, the priest was half senseless with excitement. Nerv-
ously he passed his hand over her back.

"Not so much as a single blemish," he said. "Seemingly you
have yet to undergo the moxa."

As his hand began to move about below her hips, Oman could
not but feel uneasy. Now that things had reached this point, she
bethought herself of feigning sleep. But the impetuous priest was not
to be put off, and next began toying with her ear. Oman threw one
leg over him but as she did so, revealed part of her red silk underskirt.
Gengobei was stunned and, now that he took notice, he perceived in
his companion a softness of feature that bespoke a woman. Struck
dumb with amazement, he arose from the bed. But Oman, restrain-
ing him, said, "According to your recent promise, Gengobei, you
are pledged to do just as I say. Can you so soon have forgotten
your solemn vows? Know, then, that I am Oman of the Ryukyu-
ya. Since last year, I have written you letter after letter telling of my
love, but you, most cruel, did not so much as deign to answer.
Bitter indeed was your cold indifference, but I was helplessly bound

by my love for you, and thus came to disguise myself as a boy and visited you here. Surely you cannot hate me for my pains."

Hearing Oman as she thus urged him with heart and soul, Gengobei at once was overcome. "What difference does it make— the love of men or the love of women?" he said, and, growing shamefully enraptured at the fair prospect that lay before him, he displayed once more the fickleness of the human heart.

In this world Gengobei is not alone in having out of mere caprice   *225* espoused a pious life. Far from it, indeed, and rare it is that piety drives out wordly lust. When we consider the matter, may it not be that Buddha himself let one foot slip into a trap whose depths are far from unpleasing?

5.   *Even Riches Are a Burden When Piled Up in Excess*

A tonsured pate can be overgrown with hair within a year, and once a man's priestly vestments are cast off, naught will distinguish him from his earlier self. Thus Gengobei resumed his former name,   *226* idled away his time by the plum calendar of the mountains and in   *227* the First Moon no longer lived on maigre diet. At the beginning of   *228* the Second Moon, he removed to a remote country place in Kago- shima, where, having old acquaintances, he was able to rent a poor cottage with shingled roof in which he could dwell secretly with Oman.

Not having the slightest means of livelihood, he visited his family's house, only to find that it had changed hands. No longer could one hear the tinkling of the scales in the money broker's shop; instead, a   *229* sign hanging from the eaves announced the sale of bean-paste. Overcome with dismay, Gengobei stood for some time gazing at the house. Then he approached a stranger, and addressed him: "Pray tell me, sir, what may have happened to one Gengoémon, who used to dwell hereabouts?"

The man related to him what he had heard from others. "This

Gengoémon of whom you ask," he said, "was at first a man of ample means. But he had a son, by name Gengobei—as handsome and as lustful a youth as ever you would chance to meet in this province. This youth managed in the course of eight years to do

230 away with close upon seventy-five hundredweight of silver, which, alas, caused his father to come down sadly in the world. As for

231 Gengobei himself, they say he went and became a priest because of some love trouble. To think that there are such fools in the world! I wouldn't mind setting my eyes once on that rascal's face. It would certainly prove a good topic of conversation in days to come!"

"You have that very face before you now," thought Gengobei in shame, and, pulling his sedge hat far down over his head, he returned to his cottage.

Here all was poverty and gloom. In the evenings they had no oil to burn in their lamp and in the mornings no firewood for their stove. Much is said of the joys of love and of love-making, but they last only so long as does prosperity.

At night Gengobei and Oman lay down side by side, but no sweet

232 lovers' talk passed between them. The next morning was the third day of the Third Moon. Children went about serving mugwort rice cakes; cock fights were arranged and various other diversions set afoot. But in the shingled cottage sadness reigned. They had their

233 tray for the Gods, but not so much as a dried sardine to lay thereon. Their celebrations were limited to breaking off a spray of plum blossoms and placing it in their empty sakè bottle. Thus the day drew to a close and on the fourth things looked even more forlorn.

Then it was that Gengobei, having pondered with Oman over how they might make their living, bethought himself of the plays that he had witnessed in the capital. Thinking to turn these memories to account, he lost no time in making up his face and painting on a beard. Thus Gengobei, who in his life had been a bondman to

234 love, came to copy the role of bondman on the stage, and, in

so doing, bore a striking resemblance to Arashi Sanémon himself.   235

"Yakkono, Yakkono!" he intoned, but his trembling legs be-   236
trayed his inexperience.

Then he would start singing:
  "Gengobei, Gengobei, whither are you bound?   237
  To the hills of Satsuma you go
  With your three-penny scabbard   238
  Your two-penny sword knot
  And in it your sword of rough-hewn cypress!"

Hearing his rough voice, the children of the villages through   239
which he passed were much delighted.

Oman, for her part, performed Cloth Bleaching posture dances,   240
and so they eked out their meager livelihood.

When we think about this couple, we can see that those who
become slaves to love lose all sense of shame. Gradually they wasted   241
away, wholly losing their former beauty; yet this is a harsh world
and there was none to take pity on them. As helpless, then, as the
wistaria's purple blossoms, that are doomed to fade away and die,   242
they sank ever lower in fortune and, receiving no help from any
quarter, could but think with rancour of their former friends. Bit-
terly they bemoaned their fate, until it seemed that their final day
had come.

Then it was that Oman's parents, who had been wearily search-
ing for their daughter's whereabouts, finally discovered them—and
great was their rejoicing. "Since this is after all the man she loves,"
said they, "let us unite the two in marriage and then convey this
house to them!" Forthwith they dispatched a number of their
retainers to fetch the young couple home, where, when they arrived,
there was much jubilation on every side.

To Gengobei they handed the various keys of the house—three
hundred and eighty-three in all. Then, an auspicious day having
been determined, they set about a Storehouse Opening. First they   243

244 inspected six hundred and fifty chests, each marked "Two Hundred
245 Great Gold Pieces," and eight hundred others, each containing one
246 thousand gold *koban*. The ten-*kan* boxes of silver, which they next
247 examined, were mildewed from disuse and a fearful groaning
248 seemed to come from those beneath. In the corner of the Ox and
249 Tiger stood seven great jars, filled to bursting with rectangular
gold pieces, which sparkled as when they had issued from the mint;
and copper coins lay scattered about like grains of sand.

250   Proceeding now to the outside storehouse, they found treasures
galore: fabrics brought over from China in olden days were piled up
to the very rafters; next to them precious agalloch lay stacked like
so much firewood; of flawless coral gems, from ninety grains to
over one pound in weight, there were one thousand two hundred
251 and thirty-five; there was an endless profusion of granulated shark
skin and of the finest willow-green porcelain; all this, together
with the Asukagawa tea canister and other such precious ware, had
been left there pell-mell with utter disregard for the damage that
might befall it. Other wonders too were in that storehouse: a mer-
maid pickled in salt, a pail wrought of pure agate, the wooden rice
252,253 pestle that Lu Sheng used before his wondrous dream, Urashima's
254 carving-knife box, the hanging purse worn in front by the Goddess
255,256 Benzai, the razor of the God of Riches and Longevity, the javelin
257 of the Guardian God of Treasure, a winnow of the God of Wealth,
the petty-cash book of God Ebisu and so many more that memory
cannot hold them all.

258   Here, indeed, were the treasures of the world in full array, and,
seeing them, Gengobei was happy and sorrowful in turn. For,
259 thought he, with riches such as these, not only could he buy up all
the great courtesans of Edo, Kyoto and Osaka, but he could invest
260 money in the theatres so long as he lived and yet not exhaust his
boundless means. In vain he searched for ways to squander all his
new-found wealth. And how, indeed, can he have managed?

THE LIFE OF AN AMOROUS WOMAN

chaps of two novellas

style both have melancholy opening

by in form of prologue

An 1st para

Confusing, Saikaku introduces the story sets the stage warns of the
dangers of too much love   + then introduces the woman who tells
Saikaku   but. warns reader in the beginning that
one can die from amorous pursuits — quite a different
warning than one would normally expect of say about
morals.

AN OLD WOMAN'S HERMITAGE

is amate according to ancients cuts If life is an axe.

A beautiful woman—so the ancients say—is an axe that cuts off a   261
man's very life. The blossoms scatter, the trees wither away, and
when evening comes all are thrown into the hearth and burned.
Even so is it with the flower of the human heart; for death is the fate   *heart last sentence of book.*
that no one can escape. Yet most foolish it is to abandon oneself to
wordly lust and cut short one's life by reckless dissipation, like a   *fate of some of her lovers?*
flower that offers its petals to a sudden morning storm. Howbeit,
such foolishness lacks no instances in this world of ours.

It was on the Day of Man that I set forth on an errand to Saga in   262
the western purlieus of the capital. By the banks of Mumézu River   263
the plum trees were beginning to display their blossoms, as if to tell
me, "Spring is here!" As I crossed the river, I met a dapper young   264
man. He was of fashionable mien, yet so languid, wan and gaunt   *fate of too much love*
from love that his survival seemed precarious and one could but
judge that he would soon depart this world, young as he was, and
leave his parents as his heirs.

Now this young man, turning to his companion, declared his great-
est wish as follows: "Hitherto I have lacked for nothing in this
world. Yet, were I now to express a hope, it would be that the
pledging liquid might gush forth unceasingly like this river that   265
flows beneath us."

His companion wondered at these words and said, "For my part,
I should wish to find a country without women. There I should
retire and live in perfect peace of mind, long to enjoy my cherished
life, as I observed the world and all its divers changes."

Though these two men differed greatly in their wishes, yet they were alike in pursuing dreams that never could be realized in this world where all is fated. Thus they stumbled along the river bank in their dishevelled state, half asleep and half awake, muttering their nonsense as they went, and heedlessly crushing underfoot the shrubs and thistles that sprouted on their path. At length they made their way into the recesses of the northern hills, far from any human habitation. My curiosity was vaguely awakened and I followed their footsteps, until they reached a place deep in the hills, where the red pine trees grew in clusters. Here stood a sparse hedge of withered clover; a gate, fashioned of bamboo grass, had fallen into ruin, and a dog's track led through the undergrowth. A little beyond this I saw a peaceful dwelling, whose rough sloping roof was nothing but the upper part of a rocky cave. The eaves were overgrown with hare's-foot fern, and the dried ivy still remained from last year's autumn. By a willow tree to one side I could hear the refreshing sound of water as it passed through a bamboo conduit.

I was wondering what priest might inhabit this hermitage, when I perceived to my surprise that the owner was an old lady of noble visage. She was bent double with age—age that had frosted her hair and made her eyes dim as the waning moon. The lady's sky-blue silk kimono was of an ancient style, splashed with a dappled crest of double chrysanthemums; her sash, knotted in front, was of medium width and decorated with an elegant water-chestnut pattern. Being so finely arrayed, she seemed immune to the ravages of her years.

A tablet, wrought of a piece of bleached wood, hung from the lintel of the chamber where she evidently slept at night, and on it appeared the device, "The Cell of Love." A lingering aroma hovered in the air; I judged it to be that incense called "First Music" of which I had heard people speak.

For some time I stood there, gazing at that hermitage, and grew so curious about its occupant that I felt that my very heart would fly in through the window. Then the two men whom I had followed entered the hut. They were, it seemed, familiar with the place, for they did not so much as announce themselves when they stepped inside. The old lady, seeing them, smiled and said, "So you have come today to visit me once more. Surely the world is full of alluring girls with whom young gentlemen like you might dally! Why, then, does the fresh wind blow on this withered tree? I have of late become hard of hearing, nor can I any longer express myself with ease. Seven years it is since the world became irksome to me and I retired here to live by the plum calendar. When the blossoms appear, I know that spring has come; when the white snow hides the green of the mountains, I know that it is winter. Scarcely ever do I see a human face. Why, good sirs, do you come to visit me?"   *268*

Hearing her words, one of the young men made reply: "My companion is plagued by the tender passion and I too have many afflictions. We are both hard put to understand love in all its divers aspects. Having heard, madam, of your great repute, we have come here to learn these mysteries from you. Pray tell us afresh of your own rich past."

So saying, the young man poured some sakè into a goblet and pressed it on the lady. The latter drank, and soon had become quite merry. For a while she strummed upon her *koto* and sang a love   *269* song; then, entering into the mood of the moment, she started, as though she were talking in a dream, to recount the story of her life with all its wanton doings.   *270*

I did not begin life in my present humble state. My mother, it is true, was not of noble lineage, but my father was the scion of a gentleman who once enjoyed high rank in the court of the cloistered Emperor Hanazono the Second. As is the way in this changing   *271* world of ours, my father fell into decline—to such a point that life no longer seemed worth the living. By good fortune I was well

favoured in my looks and was able to take service at court in at-
tendance on a most excellent lady. In due course I became accus-
tomed to the elegance of palace life, and had things continued as
they were, I doubt not but that I should after some years have risen
in the world. But from the beginning of my tenth summer I fell
prey to wanton feelings. No longer was I content to leave the
styling of my hair to others; instead I was guided by my own fasti-
dious taste. Having carefully examined the various fashions, I
adopted a Shimada coiffure, without a chignon and so shaped that
it fell down at the back; this I secured with a hidden paper cord after
the fashion of the time. During this period I devoted myself as-
siduously to the practice of Court Dyeing and I may say that this art
owes its later popularity to my efforts at that time.

Now life for those at court, whether they be reading poems or
engaged in a game of *kemari,* is ever flavoured with the spice of love.
Day and night my eyes were intoxicated with the vision of that
one thing alone and my ears palpitated with the sound of it. It is
but natural that all this should have called forth my own amorous
inclinations and indeed that I should have come to regard love as
the most important thing in life. It was about this time that I began
to receive tender missives from every quarter, all suing ardently for
my affection—and all equally disconsolate. In the end I was hard put
to find place to store them. Addressing myself, then, to a soldier of
the Guards—a man of few words—I had him make these letters
into ephemeral wisps of smoke; strange to relate, those parts in
which the writers had affirmed their love by invoking the names
of the myriad Gods did not burn, but were carried away by the
wind and blown to the Yoshida Shrine.

There is naught in this world so strange as love. The several men
who had set their affections on me were both fashionable and hand-
some; yet none of them aroused any tender feelings in me. Now
there was a humble warrior in the service of a certain courtier. The

fellow was low in rank and of a type that most women would
regard askance. Yet from the first letter that he wrote me his
sentences were charged with a passion powerful enough to slay
one. In note after note he set forth his ardent feelings, until, without
realizing it, I myself began to be troubled in my heart. It was hard
for us to meet, but with some cunning I managed to arrange a tryst
and thus it was that I gave my body to him.

Our amour was bound to become the gossip of the court and one
dawn it "emerged into the light." In punishment I was banished to
the neighbourhood of Uji Bridge. My lover, most grievous to
relate, was put to death. For some days thereafter, as I lay tossing
on my bed, half asleep, half awake, his silent form would appear
terrifyingly before me. In my agony I thought that I must needs
take my own life; yet, after some days had passed, I completely
forgot about him. From this one may truly judge that nothing in
this world is as base and fickle as a woman's heart.

Because I was only twelve years old at the time, people were
disposed to pass over my fault; indeed they could hardly believe
such an intrigue possible for one of my tender years. I myself could
not help being amused at their feelings. To be sure, young girls have
changed greatly. In former times, when a girl was about to set off
for her marriage, she would weep bitterly at the thought of leaving
her parents' roof. But our present-day young lady is cleverer by far.
She frets and chafes until the go-between appears at the door, quick-
ly slips into her finest clothes, waits impatiently for the arrival of
the palanquin and when it comes jumps into it hurry-scurry. Her
joy shows on her face up to the very tip of her nose. How different
things used to be! Until some forty years ago a girl would play on
her bamboo hobbyhorse by the gate of her house until she was
seventeen or eighteen, while a boy would wait until he was twenty-
four to celebrate the coming-of-age ceremony.

But I myself embarked on the way of love when I was yet a mere

283 flower bud, and, having first muddied myself in the Rapids of the Yellow Rose, found ruin in dissipation, until in the end I came to purify myself by dwelling here.

284 ## THE PLEASURES OF THE MAIDEN DANCE

285 It has been said by some discerning man that the Upper City and the Lower City differ from each other in every respect. Consider, for
286 example, the season when the blue "colour of the flowers" has begun to fade from the summer robes, and when the girls, with
287 their long hanging sleeves and their hair tied in the *agémaki* style,
288 dance to the beat of the tabor. As far down as the Fourth Avenue, the city is quiet and serene, and reveals the august air befitting a great capital. But how different it all is when we pass below the Fourth Avenue! Here we have nothing but loud voices and the clatter of busy feet.

289 Now, to play the tabor well is no mean art. The hand that beats the drum must needs keep perfect time, and someone who excels
290 may truly be called a man among men. In the Manji Period there was a blind minstrel, by name Shuraku, who hailed from the
291 neighbourhood of Abékawa in the Province of Suruga. This man proceeded to Edo, where he performed for the entertainment of knights and their households. He would enter behind a paper net
292 and there render the Music of the Eight Parts. Later he made his way up to the capital and further spread his art abroad. It was here that he devised an especially elegant form of dance, which he taught to many people. Hearing of this, a group of maidens in the capital studied this art with a view to making a living from it.

293 This new dance differed from Women's Kabuki; for, unlike the latter, it involved the training of comely young girls, who would
294 then display their skill before the wives of the great lords, performing one night in one mansion, the next in another. In general their

form of dress was well determined. Over a red under-kimono lined with silk of the same colour, each girl wore a garment of white padded silk with a pattern embossed in gold and silver foil and a black detachable collar. The sash, which she tied in the back, was of three-coloured cords plaited to the left. By her side the girl would carry *295* a short gilt sword, and she also wore a medicine box and a money *296* pouch. The girls shaved their hair in the middle, so that the forelock was erect like a lad's, and their coiffure stood out in the back; each *297* one, indeed, was the very image of a handsome young man. Thus attired, they sang, danced and did the honours of pouring sakè; later they took the habit of bringing along a broth for the refreshment of the guests.

When people in the capital invited out their guests—warriors *298* from other provinces or elderly gentlemen—they would often take them to the Eastern Hills and summon five or six of these maidens *299* to add to the evening's entertainment. To watch the elegant attendance of the girls was a matchless pleasure indeed; but, being so very young, they tended to make dull companions for gentlemen in their prime. As fee they each received one rectangular gold piece; *300* so altogether one may say that this was an inexpensive diversion.

As time passed, these girls became thoroughly versed in their calling, accustomed to the society of the capital and adept at humouring their customers' whims. Indeed, though none of them was more than twelve years old, they were more artful by far than the young ap- *301* prentices employed in the pleasure houses of Naniwa. Nor did they lose much time in growing up. By the time that she was thirteen or fourteen, a girl of this company would rarely take leave of her guest before he had acquitted himself of his virile duty. This is not to say that she would force her attentions on the man. Rather, she would nestle close to her companion during the evening's entertainment in as lascivious a manner as he could wish. Then at the crucial moment she would turn away from him, and, when

he was quite beside himself with excitement, would murmur,
302 "If I am to your liking, sir, pray come alone and in secret to my em-
ployer's house, so that we may bring things to an agreeable con-
clusion. We can both pretend that we are drunk with sakè and
utterly bemused. Then, just before we lie down, you might give our
young musicians a small gratuity and they will surely humour us
303 with some noisy airs. Under cover of this, sir, you and I can put our
time to excellent use."

With talk such as this, our girl rouses her companion to even
greater interest. And in fact these dancing girls can by their various
ruses squeeze large sums of money out of visitors from distant prov-
inces. Those who are not of the profession ignore these things,
but the fact is that every one of our dancing girls will freely disport
304 herself with men. Even highly reputed *maiko* have the price of
305 their favours set at one piece of silver coin.

In my young days I had no intention of entering on this path.
Howbeit, I took a fancy to the manners of these young girls and
used to go all the way from Uji to study their fashionable art. I found
that I had a natural talent for dancing, and soon I was being praised
by all and sundry; this made me yet more interested, and I paid no
heed to those who bade me abandon these diversions. In time I
became well skilled in the Maiden Dance and was summoned on
occasion to appear at lavish entertainments. Yet, as my mother
always attended me on these occasions, I did not indulge one jot in
the wanton habits of the other girls. Among my customers many
were sorely afflicted because they could not have their way with
me and might well have died with unsatisfied yearning.

306 At about this time a lady arrived in the capital from the West
307 Country and rented a villa on the Kawaramachi, where she might
308 recruit her health. There she remained from the warm season until
309 the days when the snow covered the northern hills. She was not
especially ill and every day she would issue forth luxuriously in

her palanquin. From the first time that this lady espied me near the Takasé River, she looked on me with favour. Using an intermediary, *310* she had me summoned to her house, and there I came to reside.

From morning till night she and her husband used me with the utmost kindness. Finding nothing to reproach in my manner, they even said that they would not scruple to accept me as wife for their only son, who was then living in their native place. Thus it was determined that I should become affianced to this young man and I was assured of an auspicious future.

Now this lady was of an ugliness that one would be unlikely to meet with in the rustic wilds, even less so in the capital; her husband, on the other hand, was of such handsome mien that it would have been hard to find his match among the gentlemen of the court. This good couple, seeing in me a mere child whose appetites must as yet be unawakened, had me couch between them where they slept. *311* As I lay there, a witness to their amorous intercourse, I was beset by strange feelings. "It is now three years since I myself was initiated into these joys," I thought, and gnashed my teeth in silence.

One night while I lay in lonely wakefulness, the gentleman's leg touched my body. All other thoughts now left my head as I listened with pricked ears for the sound of the lady's snores. Being assured, then, that she slept, I crept under her husband's bedclothes and set about seducing him. Soon we were both transported with our single-minded lust.

It was not long before these relations came to light. The couple was much amused at my precocity.

"Well indeed," said they, "this capital is a place where one can ill be negligent. At home in the country, girls of her age are still playing outside their houses on bamboo hobbyhorses!" So saying, they laughed loudly and dismissed me from their service. Thus was I once again sent back to my parents' home.

313,314 In the auspicious days of this Reign, when even the winds that blow
through the pine trees do not disturb the peace of Edo, the lady of
315 a certain lord who was serving in the Eastern provinces died with-
out leaving issue. The clansmen, sorely grieved at the lack of an heir,
selected more than forty comely girls, all of fine lineage, and,
316 through the contrivance of the housekeeper, found a propitious
time when their master was in good humour, and had the girls
approach him severally in his bedchamber, where they set about
engaging him in amorous discourse. Now these maidens were
fresh as the newest cherry buds and would, it seemed, open up in
317 all their glory when once they were bedewed with rain; nor could
one ever tire of looking at them. Yet, much to the distress of the
household, not one of the girls found favour with their lord.

In this regard be it said that the common girls brought up in the
eastern provinces are mostly of an ungainly aspect—flat-footed,
thick-necked and tough-skinned. They may be yielding in spirit, yet
they have little allurement for men; for they do not know the mean-
ing of lust and show none of the timidity that this knowledge
brings: though they be true in heart, girls such as these can never be
interesting partners in the ways of love.

When it comes to women, search as you will in every province
of the land, you will never find any to excel those of Kyoto. These
latter are endowed with divers graces. One of their special points is
the charming way in which they speak their words. This manner of
speech, I may add, is not something that can be purposely learned,
but is a tradition handed down from ancient times in the Imperial
Palace; in proof whereof we may note that, though the men and
318 women of Izumo speak in slurred tones, those of the nearby Oki
Islands, rustic though they may appear, can boast the accent of the
capital. Nor is it in speech only that their elegance appears; for the

women of these islands enjoy playing the harp and the game of *go*, 319
and are also adept at versification and the art of incense. All this may 320
be accounted for by the fact that the Emperor—he who was the 321
second son of an Emperor—was banished to these regions, and
that these noble customs have lasted since his day.

Thinking, then, that in Kyoto they might find someone to their
lord's taste, his clansmen dispatched thither an aged retainer, who 322
had for long years held service in the household. This man was
now past his seventieth year. He could see nothing without the
aid of glasses; as most of his front teeth were missing, he had long 323
since forgotten the relish of octopus and could now eat nothing but 324
finely grated pickles; his days were all equally barren of pleasure.

So far as the ways of love were concerned, his incapacity was
even more hopeless, and, though he sported a man's loincloth, he
was in fact little better than a woman. The most that he could
manage was to engage in lewd discourse, which he did to his heart's
content. Having been born in knightly estate, he could appear in 325
ceremonial dress, yet as for wearing the double swords, it was held 326
that this could ill be permitted a mere carpet knight whose task it
was to keep the household keys. To assign a man like this to journey 327
up to Kyoto and pass judgement on its women was to place a stone 328
Buddha before a cat; for the very prettiest woman might be put 329
next to this greybeard without causing him the least concern. And,
be it added, the wares that he was now to judge were such as one
would not have entrusted even to the Buddha in his younger days.

Reaching the Heavenly City, the old man repaired to a certain 330
elegant draper's shop, named the Sasaya, in the Muromachi quarter. 331

"I come this time on business," he said as he entered, "business of
a kind that I can entrust to none of your young clerks. Pray let me
address myself in private to the retired master and mistress of this 332
house."

Hearing this, the old couple waited anxiously for what he might tell them. With an air of great circumspection he began, "I have come to find a concubine for my lord."

"Well, to be sure," said the old master of the shop, "that is no such rare thing for a lord. And what type of girl may you be looking for?"

The old retainer then opened a scroll box of straight-grained paulownia and from it extracted the painting of a woman.

"I should like you to find someone," he said, "who by and large resembles this."

Hearing this commission, they looked at the picture and saw a girl, some sixteen years of age, with a face well-rounded in the modern style. Her complexion had the delicate tint of a single-
333 petalled cherry blossom and her four features were of flawless beauty. Her eyes were of perfect width and above them the thick eyebrows were widely spaced, giving her face a tranquil air. Her
334 nose was high-bridged and finely tapered, her mouth small, her teeth even and sparkling white. Her ears, which were delicately shaped and of just the right length, stood out a little from her head and were of so fine a texture that one could see through them up to their very roots. The hairline on her brow was of perfect natural beauty, her neck was long and slender; no unruly wisps of hair marred the perfect elegance of her back.

Next they looked at her hands and observed the long, delicate
335 fingers with their translucent nails. Her feet were scarcely eight
336 inches in length; the big toes were bent back, the arches elegantly
337 raised. The trunk of her body was unusually long. Her hips were firm, and, though the girl was by no means plump, the soft curve of her buttocks could be seen through her clothing. Her deportment and her style of dress left naught to be desired, and her entire form revealed the metal of her breed.

As though all this were not enough, the old man added that the girl must be of a gentle disposition, must excel in every womanly art and must not have a single mole on her body. Hearing which, the master of the establishment said, "Though the capital is a large place and abounds in women, to find one that suits these exacting tastes will be no mean task. Howbeit, since this is the demand of the great lord you serve, and since expense need not be our concern, I shall find the girl for you, if only there be such a one in this world." He then explained the circumstances to an agent named Hanaya *338* Tsunoémon of Takéya-cho, who was well versed in matters of this kind.

Now those who follow the calling of agent for their livelihood will as a rule ask one hundred *koban* of gold as an advance payment; *339* out of this sum, they take exactly ten *koban* and, having exchanged these into silver coin, give ten *mommé* to their errand woman. *340,341*

As for the girls who aspire to the role of concubine, those who do not have the proper clothes can rent them freely. For a daily rental of twenty *mommé* of silver they can have the following: a kimono of white silk or figured black satin, a wide sash of Nishijin brocade in the Chinese style, a petticoat of scarlet silk crepe, a cloak of the fashion worn at court; the fee even includes a quilt to spread inside the palanquin. If the girl is accepted into service, the agent receives one piece of silver coin as his payment. *342*

In case the girl is of humble provenance, she may have recourse to a substitute-parent—some townsman who at least has a small house *343* to his name, and who can present her as his own daughter. This man will receive a gratuity from the girl's employer, and later, if she should provide her master with a son and heir, her substitute- *344* parent will also receive part of her rice allowance.

Needless to say, the girls are eager to obtain as good a position as they can, and the audience is a trying thing indeed. Sometimes a girl must spend as much as twenty *mommé* on the hire of her kimo- no; then she may pay three and a half *mommé* for the hire of a palan- quin borne by two men, though, to be sure, for such a fee she may

be conveyed anywhere in the city that she pleases; finally, she must
have a young girl and a woman to attend her, the former receiving
345 six *fun* and the latter eight, and both being paid for their morning
and evening meals. Thus it is that, if after all these preparations the
audience turns out fruitlessly, the girl has lost no less than twenty-
four *mommé* and nine-tenths. Yes, to be a professional concubine is
indeed a hard way to make one's living in the world!

Nor is this the only trouble that these girls can have. On occasion,
346 merchants from Osaka or Sakai may, between their jaunts to Shima-
bara and Shijogawara, be inspired by some new desire for fun.
They will then summon a few of these town girls who aspire to the
role of concubine and use them for their entertainment, making out
347 the while that the bald-pated drum-holders in their company are in
fact wealthy gentlemen from the West Country. If one of the girls
348 should take their fancy, they will speak secretly to the proprietor
and ask him to arrange some sport for the passing hour. When the
girl discovers what is afoot, she will protest that she has never
dreamed of such a thing, and, much vexed, she will start to leave the
chamber. But her companion will talk her down, and before long,
being herself impelled by base desire, the girl will share a temporary
349 pillow with the man. As fee for this entertainment, the girl will
350 receive but two small pieces of gold. To sell one's body in this way
351 is futile work indeed! Such things, I may add, only happen to girls
of poorer families.

Now the agent, Tsunoémon, picked out more than one hundred
and seventy young beauties and showed them to the old man; but,
alas, not one of them was to his satisfaction. In the meantime, he
happened to hear of me, and, through the intermediary of a villager
in the hamlet of Kobata, visited me in my retired dwelling at Uji;
and, having seen me, he brought me with him to the capital. Al-
though I appeared before the old gentleman just as I was, without
having embellished myself in any way, he took one look at me and

declared that I surpassed in beauty the girl in the picture that he had
brought along from Edo. Accordingly he gave over further search
and settled the terms with me just as I wished. Thus it was that I
became a so-called noblewoman of the provinces.   352

In the company of the old retainer I made the great journey to   353
the Province of Musashi. On arrival I was installed in a villa at   354
Asakusa, where both day and night I passed my time in great felic-
ity. In the daytime I feasted my eyes on flowers as beautiful as if
a second Yoshino had been transported thither from Cathay with   355
all its wondrous blossoms; when evening came, actors were invited
from the Sakai-cho and I spent the night in merry talk. It was in-   356
deed a life of such splendour that one could aspire after nothing
more.

Yet we women are base creatures and hard put to banish from our
minds that other thing. The satisfaction of these last wants was no   357
such easy matter. For a warrior's household is bound by the strict-
est rules, and the women who dwell there never so much as set
their eyes on a man, not to speak of enjoying the scent of a loin-   358
cloth.

One day, as I was examining a fascinating depiction by Hishikawa   359
of an erotic scene, I was stirred despite myself to the most intense
excitement. I sought, then, to quench my amorous flames, now
with my heel, now with the middle finger of my hand. These were   360
cold and insensible tools indeed for stilling my wanton lust, and   361
soon I was overcome with desire for a more solid form of love.

Great lords, in general, spend much time at their official duties
and often they become attached to the young lads with their fore-
locks who attend them closely from morning till night. Their feel-
ing for these boys is deeper than that which they have for a woman;
in many instances they begin to neglect their own wives. When
I come to think of it, is this not precisely because a nobleman's
wife may not, like common women, experience jealousy? Nothing   362

in this world is so fearful as a woman's jealousy, be she high-born or of low estate.

The part of a concubine may be a hapless one, yet the lord into whose household I was now received showed me a fondness that was far from shallow and we shared a happy pillow. Yet in the end it came to naught. Though he was still a young man, he already 363 had recourse to invigorating herbs. Indeed, it turned out that he was utterly impotent; which was a source of the greatest sorrow to me. I mentioned the matter to no one, but lamented about it myself both day and night.

In the meantime my master gradually grew haggard and uncomely; whereat I became the object of a most unlooked-for suspicion on the part of the people in his household, who now began to mutter among themselves, "It is all the fault of that woman from the capital, who has enfeebled our lord with her lustful ways."

The chief retainers—people who knew nothing whatever of the ways of love—then took it upon themselves to discharge me out of hand, and once more I was sent back to my native place.

Looking about us, we can truly say that a man whose appetite for love is weak is a sorry thing for the women of this world.

A BEAUTY OF EASY VIRTUE

364   By the West Gate of the Kiyomizu Temple a woman sat strumming on her *samisen*. And as she played, I heard her sing these words:

365   "Bitter is the Floating World
              And pitiful this frame of mine!
              Would that I could alter into dew
              My life that I prize so little."

Her voice was gentle. She was a beggar woman.

Wretched indeed was her appearance! One could imagine that in the summer she must wear heavy padded clothes, and that in the winter, when the mountain winds blow fiercely from all directions, she would have nothing to protect her but an unlined summer dress. Seeing her in this present condition, I inquired what manner of person she had been in the past, and was told that, in the days when the gay quarters had been at the Sixth Avenue, this woman had flourished as one of the great courtesans, being known as Katsuragi the Second. Since then she had fallen on bad days, as indeed is the way of this world, and finally reached her present state. In the autumn, when I went to view the cherry trees in their russet tints, I and the others of my party pointed at this woman and laughed. Little do we know what fate has prepared for us!

At about this time my parents fell into sorrowful adversity; they had unthinkingly become surety at the request of a certain man, who had then disappeared without a trace, leaving my parents much embarrassed over how they might obtain the money for which they were now held answerable. Finding no other means to extricate themselves, they sold me to the Kambayashi in Shimabara for fifty gold *koban,* and thus it was that I unexpectedly found myself in this profession. I was now just fifteen years old and, being in the fullness of my beauty, was—or so my new employer said as she looked with rejoicing to the future—unequalled in the Moon Capital.

As a rule, the floating trade is one that a girl learns, by means of observation and without any special lessons, from the time that she is first employed as apprentice in a house of pleasure. But I, being a "midway starter," had to learn the new fashions all at once. These, I may say, differ in every respect from the ways of ordinary townsfolk. A courtesan shaves her eyebrows, paints heavily above her forehead and eyes with an ink stick, wears her hair in a great Shimada without inserting any wooden support; she secures her

366
367
368

369
370
371
372

373
374
375
376

coiffure with a single hidden paper cord, decorating it outside with a wide band that she has folded into a narrow strip, and, forbidding even one stray wisp, she plucks her hair carefully from the back of her neck. Her long hanging sleeves are cut in the modern fashion, measuring two and a half feet at the bottom; no padding is used at the hips, and the bottom of her skirt is wide. The courtesan's buttocks should look flat as an open fan. A wide, unpadded sash is tied loosely about her and artlessly secures her three layers of clothing. Underneath she wears a petticoat of triple width, tying it rather higher than do women who are not of the profession.

A courtesan, also, has many special ways of walking. When she 377 sallies forth, she usually wears no socks and adopts a floating walk; 378 on reaching the house of assignation, she trips in nimbly; in the parlour she uses the soft-footed gait; this is followed by a hasty gait as she goes up the stairs. When it comes to leaving, she lets the servant arrange her sandals for her and slips them on without even looking; in the street she walks with her head held high and does not step aside for anyone.

There are many ways of winning a man's favour. The "amorous gaze," as they call it, consists of looking at some man, even though he be a complete stranger, in such a fashion as to make him believe that one finds him most attractive. Again, when evening comes at the house of assignation, one may go out on the front veranda and, if one sees some man of one's acquaintance on the street, one can throw him a distant glance; thereafter one sits down casually and, being sure that the man does not notice, gives one's 379 hand to the town drum-holder who has accompanied him on his jaunt; one praises the crest on the drum-holder's coat, or again his hair style, his modish fan or any other mark of elegance that may catch one's attention.

"'You're a fellow to capture any woman's heart! From whom, 380 pray tell me, did you learn that style of hair?" So saying, one strikes him smartly on the back and returns into the house. However much experienced this drum-holder may be in the ways of the world, he is bound to succumb to such flattery from a woman; he now feels sure that, if he woos her at the proper opportunity, he will have her for himself. In anticipation he casts aside all desire for selfish gain: he sings her praises in the company of great men, and, should some bad rumour be noised abroad about her, he will put his own name in pawn to see her cleared.

One way to cause pleasure to a man is to tear up some letter that one does not need, crumple it into a ball and throw it at him. The *381* method is simple and requires no special material; yet there is many a dull-witted courtesan who cannot even manage this.

There were girls, I remember, who, though they were every jot as comely as the others, had no customer on the appointed day of *382* payment and were bidden to make their personal offerings to the *383* house. Such a courtesan will try to have the others think that she does in fact have an appointed lover, for whom she is now waiting; but her pretence is to no effect and everyone in the house treats the unwanted girl with disdain. She sits alone in a corner of the room, without even a proper table, munching her cold rice and her egg-plant pickles flavoured with raw soy sauce. So long as no one sees her, she can bear the humiliation; yet it is all most painful. When she returns to her abode and sees her employer's expression, she *384* assumes a timid air and softly asks the maid to heat the water. *385* There are indeed many painful sides to a courtesan's life; but we can have no sympathy with those foolish women who slight a money-spending customer because he is not exactly to their taste, and who pass their time in idleness. Such women bring trouble on their masters and disregard their own standing in the world. Nor should a courtesan, when she is entertaining a customer at sakè, lard her conversation with over-clever repartee and display her parts with much ingenious talk. Such tactics may avail if her

A street in the gay quarters of seventeenth-century Kyoto. The "amorous woman" sits on the veranda flirting with a professional male entertainer. Three small gentlemen enter on the right followed by a servant; a couple of women glance back at them seductively. Near the veranda a courtesan is unfolding a letter (presumably from some admirer) while her procuress looks on; she is accompanied by a young apprentice courtesan.

companion is a real gallant and well versed in the ways of the world;
386 but, if he is an inexperienced man who has only dabbled in these
paths, he will be abashed by such a show and will acquit himself
387 ill with the woman. When they retire to bed, he may be gasping
with excitement; yet he will be too overawed to perform the proper
motions; his occasional remarks will be uttered in a quivering voice;
and, though he should by rights be enjoying what he has bought
with his own money, yet he finds it all most trying. He is just like
a man who knows nothing about the art of the tea ceremony, yet
388 finds himself thrust into the seat of honour.

All this is not to say that a courtesan should turn down such a
man because he is not to her liking; there are other ways to handle
389 him. Since he has chosen from the beginning to give himself the
airs of a man of the world, the woman should use him with the
greatest decorum. When they reach the bedchamber, she is most
390 polite in her bearing to the customer; but she does not undo her
sash, and soon she pretends to fall asleep. Seeing this, the man will
as a rule move closer to her and lay his leg on hers. The courte-
san still lies there quietly, waiting to see what may happen next.
Her customer starts to tremble with nervousness and breaks into a
sweat.

Then he pricks up his ears to listen to the happenings in the next-
door room. Here things are advancing far more smoothly, perhaps
because the customer next door is already intimate with his courte-
san, or perhaps again, because he is an experienced man, who even
at their first meeting has caused her to throw off all restraint.
Listening in the dark, he hears the woman say, "Your naked body
feels plumper than I had expected from seeing you in your clothes."
Next comes the sound of amorous embraces. The man's actions be-
come more vehement, and in his onset he pays little heed to the
pillow or to the surrounding screen. The woman lets out a cry of
heart-felt delight. In her spontaneous joy she throws aside the

pillow and there is the sound of the ornamental comb in her hair as it snaps in two.

Meantime, from the floor above comes the voice, "Ah, ah, what bliss that was!" followed by the rustling of paper handkerchiefs. *391* And in yet another room a man who has been pleasantly asleep is tickled awake by his partner, who says to him, "Already it is growing light outside. Will you not leave me one more remembrance of this night?" Hearing this, the man, still half asleep, says, "Pray forgive me, but I cannot do another thing!" One wonders whether it can be that he has drunk too much sakè the night before; but then one hears the sound of his loincloth being undone. This hussy is clearly of a more sensual nature than most. Is it not truly a blessing for a courtesan to be endowed with a hearty appetite for love?

With all these pleasant diversions afoot in the nearby rooms the unsuccessful customer cannot catch a wink of sleep. In the end he awakens his companion and says, "The Festival of the Ninth Moon *392* will soon be with us. May I inquire whether you have any special friend who will visit you on that day?"

Such words are a cheering tonic for a courtesan. But his purpose is too transparent for her and brusquely she replies, "I shall be taken care of in the Ninth Moon—and in the First Moon, too."

Now the man is at a loss for anything to say that might bring him closer to her; and, alas, the time has come when she must get up and leave, like all the other courtesans. Then she is greeted with a comical sight as her customer unties his hair and secures it loosely into a whisk, and also redoes his sash—all this to make others be- *393* lieve that his night has been crowned with the joys of intimacy.

As a rule a customer who has been used in such a heartless fashion will regard this courtesan with bitterness. On his next visit to the house he may call for another girl and spend five or even seven days there, indulging in lavish entertainment, thus causing the most lively regret to the courtesan who treated him so coldly. Or again, he may for once and all renounce these quarters and determine henceforth to consort for his pleasure with young actors. As he leaves the house, he will call flurriedly for the friend who accompanied him here, and, paying no heed to the latter's reluctance at being dragged at dawn from the arms of his fair companion, he will say, "Come, let us quit this place and hasten our return!" With no further ado he takes leave of his disobliging courtesan.

But there are also ways to prevent this. One may, for instance, tweak the man's ear in the presence of his friends and, while smoothing his ruffled side-locks, whisper to him: "What a heartless rogue you are to leave like this with no regard for a woman's true feelings —ay, without even having bidden her undo her sash!" So saying, one strikes him on the back before hurrying back into the house. His companions, having taken note, will say to him, "You lucky dog! How do you manage to enravish a woman at the very first meeting?"

Delighted, the man replies, "Ah yes, I'm her lover and I'll warrant she'd give her life for me now! The attentions she showered on me last night were amazing. She even insisted on rubbing my shoulder that has been so stiff these past few days. Frankly, I can't understand why she was so taken with me. Surely you spoke to her in my favour and told her I was a man of property?"

"No indeed," his friends answer him. "No courtesan will use a man with so much warmth out of mere avarice. You'll have a hard time ridding yourself of her now!"

Thus they flatter him, and in due course the woman's stratagem has effect. If things can turn out well even after such an inauspicious start, how much better if she uses her client with true regard from the outset! Aye, he will be ready to give his very life for her!

If some undistinguished customer asks a courtesan to spend the night with him, she should not turn him down just because this is their first meeting. However, a man may be overawed in the presence of a high-ranking courtesan like herself and at the crucial moment he may let slip his opportunity. Should this happen, he will get up and leave, the amorous spell having been broken.

A woman of the floating trade should not let herself be drawn to a man because of his handsome looks. So long as he is of high standing in the capital, she should willingly accept him, even if he be a greybeard or a priest. A young man who is liberal with his gifts and to boot boasts of a handsome appearance is a courtesan's natural ideal. But where is one to find a customer equipped only with such excellent attributes? *397*

The appearance that an up-to-date courtesan favours in a man is as follows: his kimono, of which both the outside and the lining are of the same yellow silk, is dyed with fine stripes; over this he wears a short black crested jacket of Habutaé silk. His sash is wrought of light yellowish-brown Ryumon, and his short coat is of reddish-brown Hachijo pongee, lined at the bottom with the same material. His bare feet are shod in a pair of straw sandals, and he dons a new pair each time that he goes out. In the parlour he bears himself with dignity. The short sword by his side protrudes slightly from its scabbard; he wields his fan so that the air is blown inside his hanging sleeves. *398*

Though the stone basin may already be full of water, he has it filled afresh; then he washes his hands in a leisurely fashion, gargles softly and performs his other ablutions with like elegance. Having completed his toilet, he bids one of the girl assistants fetch his tobacco, which his attendant has brought along wrapped in white Hosho paper. After a few puffs he lays a handkerchief of Nobé paper by his knees, uses it with artless elegance and throws it away. *399* *400*

Next he summons an assistant courtesan, and, telling her that he would fain borrow her hand for a moment, he has her slip it up his sleeve to scratch the moxa that has been applied for the cramp *401*

402 in his shoulder muscles. Now he calls upon a drum courtesan to
403 perform the Kaga Air, though paying but little attention to her
as she strums on her samisen and sings; instead, in the middle of the
404 tune, he turns to the jester who is in attendance and says, "In yester-
405 day's performance of *The Seaweed Gatherer,* the supporting actor
truly put Takayasu to shame with his skill." Or again, he may re-
406 mark, "When I inquired of the Chief Councillor about that old
verse I was mentioning the other day, he confirmed that it was
407 indeed the work of Ariwara no Motokata."

In the presence of a customer who—without giving himself airs—
starts out with some elegant conversation of this kind, and who in
all things shows an attitude of perfect dignity and composure,
even a top-ranking courtesan is overawed and inspired with a new
spirit of modesty. Everything that the man does seems to her ad-
mirable and she looks on him with awe; the result is that she quite
throws off her usual haughty air and comes to humour his every
whim.

The pride displayed by courtesans of high rank is always due to
their having been pampered by customers. In the palmy days of the
408 gay quarters at Edo there was a connoisseur of fashion named
Sakakura who grew intimate with the great courtesan Chitosé.
This woman was much given to drinking saké; as a side dish she rel-
ished the so-called flower crabs, to be found in the Mogami River
in the East, and these she had pickled in salt for her enjoyment.
409 Knowing this, Sakakura commissioned a painter of the Kano
410 School to execute her bamboo crest in powdered gold on the tiny
411 shells of these crabs; he fixed the price of each painted shell at one
rectangular piece of gold, and presented them to Chitosé through-
out the year, so that she never lacked for them.

Again, in Kyoto there was a connoisseur called Ishiko. This man
412 was much smitten with the high-ranking courtesan Nokazé, for
whom he would purchase the most rare and fashionable wares,

hastening to do so before anyone else could acquire them. On one occasion, Nokazé received a wadded autumn kimono dyed with pale scarlet; the silk was of fully dappled design and in the centre of each dapple a hole had been burned with a taper, so that one could see through the surface of the dress into the scarlet-tinted wadding. This material was of matchless elegance, and the single kimono was said to have cost close upon twenty-five pounds of *413* silver.

In Osaka, too, there was a man, since deceased, who called himself Nisan, and who had made Dewa of the Nagasaki House into *414,415* his private courtesan. During one gloomy autumn he made show *416,417* of his great compassion by paying for numerous courtesans in the Kuken-cho who were not in demand by other customers; this merciful usage of her colleagues afforded much comfort to Dewa. On another occasion, when the clover bloomed profusely outside the house, Dewa noticed that some of the water which had been sprinkled in the garden had come to rest on the leaf tips; it sparkled just like early morning dew, and Dewa was deeply moved by its beauty.

"I have heard," she said to Nisan, "that loving couples of deer are wont to lie behind clover bushes. How I should like to see this in real life! Surely these animals cannot be dangerous, for all they are equipped with horns."

Hearing this, her lover is said to have replied that nothing could be simpler than to grant her wish; he then—so the story has it—ordered the back part of her parlour to be demolished and had numerous clover bushes planted there, thus making the room into a veritable field; next he sent word during the night to people in the mountains of Tamba and had them round up wild deer of both sexes, who were dispatched to the house. On the following day he was able to show them to Dewa; after which he had the parlour restored to its former state. Surely Heaven will someday punish men like *418* these, who, though endowed with little virtue, permit themselves luxury that even noblemen can ill afford!

Now, concerning my own career as a top courtesan, though I sold my body to men who were not to my taste, yet I never yielded myself to them. Indeed, I used these men harshly, so that they came to regard me as a cold-hearted woman and to turn their backs on me. Day after day the number of my customers diminished; I was thus inevitably eclipsed by the other courtesans of my rank, and I began fondly to remember my past glory.

Truly, a courtesan can only afford to dislike a man while she herself is in great favour; for once she is no longer in demand, any customer will be welcome, not excepting servants, mendicant priests, cripples and men with harelips. When one comes to think of it, there is no calling in the world so sad as this one.

419   A BONZE'S WIFE IN A WORLDLY TEMPLE

420   A woman who opens up her sleeves when once they have been sewn, and who thus returns to her pristine purity, is known as a Female
421   T'ieh Kai. To accomplish this, it is well to be of small build.
422   Now this period was the very "noonday of Buddhism"—and indeed even at noon the priests disported themselves with their
423   temple pages. Repressing my shyness, then, I shaved my head in the centre to look like a young man's, simulated a male voice and committed to memory the general bearing of a man; when I came
424   to put on a man's loincloth, I was amazed how well I could resem-
425   ble the other sex. I also changed my sash for an ordinary one of narrow width, and thrust a pair of swords by my side. These made me unsteady in my gait, and, though I covered myself in a coat and a sedge hat, I could not but feel strange.

Thus attired, I set out, accompanied by a well-versed drum-
426   holder and by a servant with a specially painted beard, who carried

my straw sandals. Having heard of an affluent Worldly Temple, I
made my way thither. On arrival, I pretended to admire the cher-
ries that blossomed in the temple garden; then I entered the pre-
cincts through a gate in the wall. The drum-holder went to the
private apartment of the priest, and, finding him at leisure, whis-
pered in his ear. Thereupon I was invited into the guest chamber
and introduced by the drum-holder in the following terms: "This
young man is an unattached warrior. Until such time as he finds   427
himself suitable service, he may on occasion visit this place for his
enjoyment. May I request your good offices on his behalf?"

As he listened, the bonze was already beside himself with joy.
Turning to me, he blurted out, "I learned last night how to concoct
an abortifacient that women like yourself might find most useful."
But then he firmly shut his mouth, comically embarrassed at what   428
he had said.

Thereafter we all became fuddled with sakè, while from the
kitchen was wafted the aroma of fish and meat. The fee for my   429
services was fixed at two rectangular gold pieces a night.   430

In the course of time I urged this one religion on temples of all 431
the eight sects, and I may say that I never found a single priest
who was not ready to slash his rosary. Later it happened that the
bonze of another temple became infatuated with me. It was agreed
that I should be paid twenty-five pounds of silver for a three years' 432
period of service, and thus I assumed the role of a bonze's wife.

Dwelling there day after day, I came to understand the strange
ways of a Temple of the Floating World. In earlier times it used to 433
happen that a group of priests who were on friendly terms would
live together in a temple. These men would mark the Six Days of   434
Fasting in the month, and, so long as these did not fall on the an-
niversaries of the various Buddhas or of the founders of their temple,
they would regard them as the occasions when they might freely
break their holy vows; at the same time, they would swear to respect

these vows during the remainder of the month. On the appointed days they would partake of fish and fowl, visit the gay quarters, consort with trollops on the Third Avenue and give themselves over to other such license. Yet, since their normal conduct was befitting to the cloth, no harm was done, and even Buddha would surely understand and forgive them their lapses.

In recent years, however, with the growing prosperity of the temples, the priests have become ever more licentious. In the daytime they wear their vestments, but at night they sally forth dressed in short coats. Furthermore, they install women in their temples. For this purpose the priest will have a deep recess built in the corner of his private apartment; this is provided with a narrow skylight, so designed as to be invisible from the outside. In order that no sound of voices may escape, he has his apartment built to a considerable depth, with earth piled heavily on the roof, and the walls a foot in thickness.

It was in such a place that I was now immured each day; only at night I would emerge to visit the priest's bedchamber. This was indeed a constrained existence, and it was grievous to think that it was not love that had brought me to it, but the need to gain a livelihood.

The priest to whom I had entrusted myself was a disagreeable man. He indulged ceaselessly in fornication, until all my interest in these matters stopped and all my pleasure died away. Gradually I became wasted and thin from overmuch indulgence. Yet the bonze had not the slightest mercy on me, and would regard me with a baleful look, as though to say, "If you die, I shall simply bury you in the precincts of this temple."

Howbeit, even this form of life is tolerable when once a woman has grown accustomed to it. Finally it came about that when my priest returned late at night from a death watch, I would wait impatiently for him, and that when he set out at dawn to gather the

435

436
437

ashes, I would be plunged in sorrow at the parting. The flavour of incense from his white vestments was conveyed to my own person and became a lingering scent that grew dear to me. In the end I forgot my forlorn feelings; even the sound of the gong and cymbals, at which formerly I had stopped my ears, now became familiar and served to beguile the hours; no longer was I conscious of the reek of burning bodies; and, when people died one after another in the neighbourhood, I thought happily of the profit that would accrue to the temple.

In the evenings a vendor came with various relishes. I would then prepare a dinner of stuffed teal or swellfish broth, or fish baked on splints of cedar. Lest I attract attention by the smell of cooking, I would place a cover over the charcoal brazier. But in due course I learned of the temple's slovenly ways, and found that even the acolytes would wrap dried sardines in old scraps of paper, on which they had scribbled the Sutra of the Names; they would hide these packages in the sleeves of their vestments and later bake the fish. It was just because they indulged day and night in such pursuits that the inmates of the temple were lustrous and fleshy in appearance and apt for the performance of their offices. How different they looked from those men who, renouncing the world, retire to mountain groves to live on the berries of the trees, or again, from those priests who, being poor, cannot do other than observe religious abstinence! One can recognize this latter sort at once, for they come to look like dried-up bits of wood.

Now my service in this temple continued from spring until about the beginning of autumn. At first my priest regarded me with deep suspicion, and never left without first locking the door. But, as time passed, he relaxed his guard: he allowed people to visit him in his quarters, and even when parishioners called at the temple, he no longer made haste to conceal me.

One evening, as the wind whistled in the branches and soughed through the leaves of the plantains, I lay by myself on the bamboo veranda, resting my head on my arm and drearily thinking of this world in which all is doomed to change. While I lay dozing, an old woman appeared before me like a ghost. There was not a single black hair on her head, her face was furrowed as though with waves, and her limbs were as thin as a set of fire-irons. She tottered up to me, and in a thin, pathetic voice addressed me as follows:

"I lived in this temple for many a long year with the priest whom you know, and had people believe that I was his mother. I myself am not of such humble origin, but on purpose I made myself seem unsightly. Being twenty years older than the priest, I felt my position to be a shaming one. Yet this was a way to gain my livelihood and I gave myself to him with no reserve. As an outcome of our deep intimacy, we exchanged the most tender vows. Yet in the end the priest renounced these, telling me that, since age had made me as I was, he no longer had use for me.

"He has thus thrust me aside to live on the offerings of rice that people make to Buddha, and he looks reproachfully at me when yet I fail to die. You may regard all this as brutal usage; but it is not the worst. What really makes me pass my days in bitter thought is— you. You do not know it, but every night I listen as you and the priest lie in bed engaged in your intimate converse. Even though age has withered my body, the path of love is a hard one to forsake. Finally I have resolved that the only way to calm my spirits is to get my hands on you—and so I will do this very night!"

The old woman's words hit home, and I realized that it was boot-less for me to stay in this place any longer. I adopted a droll way to make my departure from the temple. In the front underfold of my everyday kimono I stuffed some wadding. Then, feigning a cumbrous gait, I approached the priest and told him. "I have managed to hide things until now. But the months of my pregnancy have piled up and soon my time will come."

Hearing this, the priest was much distraught and said, "Go home with all haste, I pray you, and return here when all is well again."

He then collected the alms that had accumulated in the collection box and gave them to me, together with various warnings regarding my confinement. Some unhappy couple in the parish had lost their child and, being unable to bear the sight of the infant's tear-stained clothes, had offered them to the temple. These the priest now gave me to use for swaddling clothes. Finally, he held a service in celebration of the expected birth, assigning the name Ishichiyo to the unborn child.   *439*

I had become utterly weary of this temple, and, although my period of service was not yet elapsed, I did not return. Unfortunately for my bonze, he could enter no action against me.   *440*

THE WOMAN'S SECRET MANUAL
OF ETIQUETTE   *441*

"Time and again have I feasted my eyes on the splendid iris that you were so good as to send me. . . ."

To teach people to write letters in this style is known in Kyoto as imparting the "woman's secret manual." Court ladies, who have learned the forms of etiquette followed by people of quality during the several seasons, will often on retiring from service put this knowledge to use in making their livelihood; such ladies will hang up a sign calling on young girls of gentle breeding who wish to receive training in these arts to visit them where they live.

Since I had in the past enjoyed the honour of serving a great lady at court, I now took advantage of this connection to open a school of penmanship for young girls. To the gatepost I affixed a sign with the inscription, "Penmanship Lessons for Ladies." I neatly arranged a small parlour, hired a rustic maidservant and settled down happily to living in my own home.

Since I now had charge of young girls from outside families, I was aware that I could not conduct things in any haphazard fashion. Each day I would diligently draw anew the practice characters and would teach the girls such rules of decorum as they required.

I had cast aside all wanton ways and was living in perfect innocence when one day I received a visit from a young gentleman, who was then at the height of his virile charms. This man asked me to compose some tender missives for him. Now, having myself followed the calling of courtesan, I knew the principles that would serve to ensnare such a bird and bring these two to flutter together through the sky on the same wing; for I could couch his appeal in letters that would move her to the very vitals of her being. Again, if it should be a young girl who was not of the profession, I could see into her heart too; or if it was a well-versed woman of the Floating World, I knew of fitting tricks to win her favours. In short, there was no one of my sex whom I could not bring to yield.

To convey one's true feelings, nothing is of such avail as a letter. For one can make one's brush set all one's thoughts on paper and then transmit them to people, even in the most distant parts. Should the letter be imbued with falsehood, this will appear of itself, however much it be tricked out in wordy phrases; the reader's interest will soon flag and the letter will be thrown aside with no regret. But when the brush writes true, the message will engrave itself on the reader's mind, and it will seem as though the writer were there in very person.

When I held employ in the gay quarters, there was one among my many customers of whom I was especially fond. When I met this man, I never thought of myself as a courtesan; instead, I cast off all reserve and unbosomed myself with utter frankness. He for his part kept faithful to me, until, alas, it came about that he fell into embarrassment and we could no longer meet. Each day, then, he had letters secretly delivered in which he informed me of his

In an effort to regain her long-lost respectability the heroine has taken to teaching letter-writing and etiquette. One of her customers is a handsome young man, whom later she almost kills by her physical demands. Here she is depicted writing a love letter for the man; she holds the thick folded paper in one hand and her brush in the other. Her customer and she are seated in formal style with the writing equipment and inkstone in front of them. The maid brings in a cup of tea. The heroine's room is discreetly furnished in traditional Kyoto style. The instrument leaning against the screen in the background is a *koto*, an ancient type of harp.

tidings. As I read them, I felt that I was truly in the presence of my lover. Having perused each letter several times, I would place it next to my body when I retired alone to bed. I would fall into a slumber and dream that this letter had assumed my very own form and was talking through the night—much to the surprise of those who slept nearby!

Later, when this man became clear of his encumbrance and could once more consort with me as before, I related to him what had passed in his absence. It turned out, then, that my thoughts during that time had been exactly conveyed to him through my letters. This, indeed, is just as it should be; for when one is writing a letter, one must needs forget all outside things; and those feelings on which one concentrates with one's very soul will surely find their mark.

Having, therefore, been asked to write tender missives for the young man, I put my heart into the task and told him, "However insensible your partner may be, I can assure you that, since you have now called on me to write for you, things will go as you wish." In the meantime, however, I myself came by gradual degrees to look fondly on this man.

One day as I was sitting beside him with a writing brush in my hand, I paused for a moment and a pensive look came to my face. Throwing aside all shame, I spoke to him as follows: "To cause a young gentleman like you to languish in this fashion by refusing to bow to his desires bespeaks a coldness of heart that must be unequalled among the women of this world. Rather than pursue this slow-paced course, why will you not turn your thoughts to me? This, sir, could be settled here and now. I shall leave aside the question of our respective merits as women. But surely for the time being it is no small advantage that I am kindly disposed and that the love which I would grant can be consummated forthwith."

Hearing this, the young man was much amazed and for a moment made no reply. But, being ignorant of his lady's true feelings, and deeming that what I had to offer might be better in the short run; having, in particular, noticed that my hair was curly, 443 my big toes bent back and my mouth small, he answered me: "Let me be frank with you, madam. My affairs are such that, if money is required, I cannot afford to embark on an amour, even were it one advanced from my own side. I cannot offer you so much as a single sash. And if, after our intimacy has deepened, you should, for instance, ask me whether I know of a good draper's, I shall not be able to offer you a roll of silk or even half a piece of red cloth. 444 It is best that these things be said from the very outset, lest there be disagreements later on."

To have proposed so pleasant a thing as I had done, and then to be answered with such harsh conditions, struck me as both hateful and wretched. In this great city of Kyoto there was no dearth of men, and I had decided that I might do well to look in other quarters when an early summer drizzle began to fall and a bush sparrow flew in through the window, extinguishing the lamp. Taking advantage of the darkness, the man caught me tightly in his arms. A moment later he was panting with excitement; then 445 he placed a small Sugiwara paper handkerchief next to the pillow, and, slapping me gently on the buttocks, said, "You until a hun- 446 dred!"

"Very funny!" thought I to myself. "So you, my foolhardy fellow, expect to live till you are ninety-nine! By what you said to me earlier, you stung me to the quick; and before a year is out I shall have you with fallen chaps and hobbling along on a stick. Thus will I see you dismissed from the Floating World!"

Thereupon I set to disporting myself with him constantly, making no distinction between day and night. When be began to weaken, I fed him on loach broth, eggs and mountain potatoes. As I had foreseen, the man was gradually subjugated; and, most

447
448 pathetic to relate, when it came to the Sun-Flower Month of the
following year, though all other people were busy with Clothes-
Changing, this man still wore his thickly padded cotton clothes.
One by one the doctors abandoned him. His hair became shaggy,
his nails long. And when in his presence the conversation turned to
delightful women, though he listened with his hand cupped be-
hind his ear, he would shake his head with a bitter look.

449,450 ## A TOWNSMAN'S PARLOURMAID

451 It was during the great summer heat of nineteen days, when the
weather was unbearably hot and people vainly muttered among
themselves, "Oh, for a land without summer! Oh, for some place
where one need not sweat!"—it was, I say, on such a day that
a funeral procession came into sight, to the accompaniment of
gongs and cymbals. The men who carried the bier did not seem
especially grief-stricken and, looking about, I could see no one
among them who might be the heir of the deceased. The towns-
452 folk in the procession were wearing ceremonial dress—though,
as I judged, merely from a sense of duty—and they carried rosaries
in their hands. As they walked, they were discussing sundry mat-
ters—suits that were being brought to law over money disputes,
or the condition of the rice market, or again, the incident of the
453 Three-Foot Goblin.

The young men of the party had fallen behind the procession
and were talking about what was to be had at the various tea-
houses where they resorted for their pleasure, and already they
were making their plans for going directly from the place of
burial to the gay quarters. Far behind them came some men who
454 looked like house tenants, and who were dressed in the oddest
455 garbs: one wore a pair of hempen trousers over a lined robe, the
next had ceremonial socks yet no sword by his side, and still a

third wore a padded coat over a hand-woven summer garment. In a chorus of loud voices they pronounced judgement on the light afforded by whale oil and talked about picture puzzles painted   *456* on round fans. It is wretched indeed to overhear such things wherever it may be, and one is moved to ask such people, "Can you not give a little heed to the calls of human sorrow?"

Now I had a general idea as to who this company might be; for it seemed to me that some of them dwelt by the road that goes up   *457* from Gokomachi to the Seigan Temple. The dead person could then be none other than the proprietor of the Tachibanaya on the west side of that street. Now the wife of this man was, I remembered, a woman of uncommon beauty; I had heard many an amusing tale about people going into the shop to buy heavy paper   *458* of which they had not the slightest need, merely in order to look at her.

"A wife is someone on whom one gazes all one's life; yet it is just as well if she be not too beautiful"—so spake Jinta of the Gion.   *459* This may be the flippant saying of a go-between, but it is not to be dismissed too lightly; for indeed a beautiful wife occasions her husband naught but solicitude. When a man marries in order that he may have someone to look after his house in his absence, what need is there for such fair looks in his partner? Besides, it is with beautiful women as with beautiful views: if one is forever looking at them, one soon tires of their charm. This I can judge from my own experience. One year I went to Matsushima, and, though at   *460* first I was moved by the beauty of the place and clapped my hands with admiration, saying to myself, "Oh, if only I could bring some poet here to show him this great wonder!"—yet, after I had been gazing at the scene from morning until night, the myriad islands began to smell unpleasantly of seaweed, the waves that beat on Matsuyama Point became obstreperous; before I knew it I had let all the cherry blossoms at Shiogama scatter; in the morning I overslept and missed the dawn snow on Mount Kinka; nor was I much impressed by the evening moon at Nagané or Oshima; and in the end I picked up a few white and black pebbles on the *461* cove and became engrossed in a game of Six Musashi with some children.

A man who lives in Naniwa will, when he comes to the capital, resort to the Eastern Hills; whereas he who comes from Kyoto *462* will be eager to gaze on the seashore and, when he does so, will find everything there most wonderful. Even so it is that a wife will in the beginning pay the greatest heed to her appearance out of deference to her spouse; but later, alas, such cares are abandoned. Then she dresses her hair hurriedly, strips herself naked to the waist, letting her husband see the birthmark on her side that she has hitherto concealed; and when she walks in his presence she no longer cares about her gait, so that for the first time he perceives that her left leg is a little longer than the other. What with all this negligence, he comes to feel that she is not endowed with so much as a single virtue; and after she has given birth to a child his affection for her diminishes still further.

When we come to think of it, indeed, a man's state is better without a wife. Howbeit, in order to live in this world, he cannot *463* go without one. Once I went into the mountain recesses of Yoshino, far beyond where the flowers bloom, to a place so remote that *464* not a soul was to be seen but for an occasional pilgrim who had *465* climbed the peak by the Regular Entry. On a distant precipice I found a hut with a sloping roof. Here dwelt a man whose diversions were limited to listening to the stormy winds blow through the cedars during the day and to gazing into the light of a pine fire at night. "Why in this wide world of ours," I asked him, "should you have chosen a place like this for your abode, and not the capital?" Hearing this, the rustic fellow laughed and said, "I am not lonely here. For I have my wife to keep me company."

And so it needs must be: the solace of having a partner is one thing that a man can ill forego.

Nor, be it said, does it afford a woman any comfort to live alone. And so it was that at about this time I stopped giving my penmanship lessons to young girls and took service as a parlourmaid in an elegant draper's, the Daimonji-ya by name. It used to be deemed   *466* that the ages from eleven to fourteen were best suited for becoming a parlourmaid. In recent times, however, people have, on economic grounds, come to employ women of middle age; for a woman   *467* between the ages of eighteen and twenty-four is adept at putting   *468* up and laying down the bedclothes, and is also said to cut a pleasing figure when she walks in attendance in front of the palanquin or behind.

Much as I disliked having to tie my sash in the back, I now   *469* changed into the garb that fitted my new role. I made up a narrow sash of dark orange tinged with black and embellished with a medium-sized pattern scored with a fine zigzag design. My hair I arranged in a medium Shimada with a low, flat chignon, and in my coiffure I wore paper cords that I could throw away each time after I had used them. In every respect I made myself look like an innocent young girl.

Addressing the old housekeeper, I would ask her such questions as, "Whence do all those snowflakes come that fall so heavily outside?"

"What an artless girl you are," she would say, "to ask such questions at your age! I'll warrant that you've been tied to your mother's apron strings all your life!" Thereafter the old woman was completely off her guard with me.

In other ways too I deluded the people of the house, to such effect that no one even vaguely suspected that I had formerly been a woman of the town. If any man tried to take my hand, I would flush with embarrassment; if someone touched my sleeve, I would make a great show of being shocked; and if I was told a joke, I would let out a girlish squeal. Finally it came about that I was no longer called by my proper name; instead, though I was still in the 470 bloom of my beauty, I was spoken of as "the wild monkey from the treetops."

Comical it is in truth to see what fools the people of this world really are! I had already, I confess with shame, undergone eight abortions; yet no one had an inkling of all this and now I was placed in close attendance on the master of the house himself.

While serving him in this office, I each night overheard him as he disported himself with his wife. Now this gentleman was endowed with the greatest vigour; in his amorous onslaughts he cared for no one, but, roughly pushing aside the pillows and the screen, caused even the sliding doors to rattle.

As I was listening to this one night, I could no longer contain myself. Being off duty, I got up and went to look in the kitchen. Alas, there was not a proper man in sight—only an old fellow, long since in the service of this family, who was now crouched on the wooden floor, where he had been posted to keep watch over the fish boxes.

"Well," thought I, "at least I can give this creature something pleasant to think back on."

With this in mind, I stepped purposely on his ribs.

471 "Hail, merciful Buddha! Hail, merciful Buddha!" he exclaimed. "The lamp is lit, is it not? Why must you trouble an old man like this?"

"I stepped on you by mistake," I answered. "If you cannot pardon my fault, pray use me as you will. The blame attaches to this foot of mine."

So saying, I slipped the foot onto the old man's chest. He ducked his head in amazement, and rapidly began to mutter, "Hail, Goddess of Mercy! Deliver me, I beseech Thee, from this peril!" Seeing that there was nothing to be gained in this quarter, I gave the old fellow

a cuff on the ear and, trembling all over, returned to my bed and
impatiently waited for the night to end.

Finally the Twenty-Eighth Day dawned. The stars were still
glimmering in the sky when the master of the house began to
bustle about, giving instructions for the altar to be put in order and
the like. My mistress was still abed, wearied from the exertions of
the previous night. Her vigorous husband broke the ice in the basin
and washed his face. Then, clad in nothing but his ceremonial robe,
he came up to me, with the Holy Writings in his hand, and asked,
"Have you made the rice offerings to the Buddha?"

"Pray pardon me, sir," said I, "but do those writings you carry
set forth in general terms the way of love?"

This question did not seem to please my master and he made no
reply.

Laughing softly, I said, "There's no one here to disturb us, sir.
The others are all in the front." Then, with a hazy sensual air, I
languidly began to untie my sash. Thereat my master, without so
much as removing his ceremonial robe, set to taking his pleasure
with me. In his violent onset he made the statue of Amida Buddha
shake and upset the crane-and-tortoise candlestick. Thus did I banish
religion from his mind.

Thereafter, I secretly brought him under my power and myself
grew ever more proud in my demeanour, until in the end I did not
give a fig's end for my mistress' commands. My next aim was to
have him divorce her, and even I am appalled at the design that I
adopted to this end. For I resorted to a certain mountain priest and
had him put a curse on my master's wife. It proved of no avail, but
by now I was burning like a very demon, and ever more my fury
grew in violence. I blackened my teeth, thrust solid bamboo tooth
sticks in my mouth—and prayed. But still the curse had no effect.
Indeed, my machinations recoiled upon myself, and I blurted out

the secret; by revealing my deceits and my full shame, I exposed my master to grievous scandal. Truly, to disclose at a stroke all the wantonness of one's past months and years is a thing that anyone in this world must guard against.

Thereafter I became quite mad. One day I roamed in Murasaki-no; on the morrow I showed my face on the Bridge of the Fifth Avenue. I was carried away as though in a dream.

"I want a man! I want a man!" I repeated, and sang the ancient
482 words of a Komachi Dance, as though the past had been rendered into the present—and I only sang the words that bore on love.

"Here is the wreck of a maid who was too well versed in the love of men!" said people when they saw me.

With my dance-fan fluttering in the wind, I came near to the
483 archway of the Inari Shrine in the shadow of the cedar grove, and here it was that I finally perceived my own nakedness and returned to my senses. Casting off all evil thoughts, I was overcome with the knowledge of my own baseness. Now I understood that the reward for cursing others was to have had the curse recoil on my own head. Thus chastened, I made my confession and left the precincts of the shrine.

There is nothing in the world so wretched as a woman. Aye, this is indeed a fearful world!

THE EVIL WROUGHT BY A GORGEOUS LADY

484 *Kemari* was originally a game for men, but when I was in charge of
485,486 the Front Service in the household of a certain great lord, I learned
487 that women also play it. One day I accompanied my lady to her villa
488 in Asakusa. In the great park the Kirishima azaleas had come into
489 bloom, and all the fields and hills were decked in crimson; crimson too were the trousers that the ladies-in-waiting wore as they moved
490 about softly on their *kemari* shoes, indulging in divers pretty plays

like Cherry-Piling and Mountain-Crossing. They had hung their
robes on the bamboo hedge and the wide sleeves were fluttering in
the breeze. It was the first time that I had ever seen this, and, al-
though the players were of my own sex, I gazed on them in wonder.

In the capital, ladies of the court were wont to amuse themselves
by practising archery with the small bow. This too seemed strange
to me, but as the sport is said to have been started by Yang Kuei Fei,   *491*
it is even now held to be a suitable diversion for women. *Kemari,* on
the other hand, was originated by Crown Prince Shotoku and it is   *492*
unheard of that it should thus be played by women. Howbeit, the
wife of the lord whom I served was free to disport herself in any
merry way she chose.

When dusk gathered, the wind began to blow fiercely through
the trees. The ball no longer went as the players intended and soon
their interest flagged. My lady was taking off her *kemari* costume and
throwing it aside when something seemed to cross her mind. Sud-
denly her mien grew fierce and there was no humouring her; her
attendants lapsed into silence, and their movements and demeanour
became subdued. Thereat one of the ladies, Kasai by name, who had
been in the service of this house for many a long year, approached
her mistress with a flippant, servile air, shaking her head the while   *493,494*
and joggling her knees.

"Would Madam be pleased," said she, "to hold a Jealousy Meet-   *495*
ing again this evening, until the candle burns itself out?"

Hearing this, my lady instantly recovered her good humour.

"Yes indeed, yes indeed!" said she in high spirits.

Thereupon Yoshioka, the head attendant in charge of the ladies-
in-waiting, went to the corridor and pulled a bell rope, which was
decorated with a Chinese tassel. Some three dozen women, in-   *496*
cluding kitchen maids and serving girls, answered the summons and
seated themselves without ceremony in a great circle. I also joined
the company. As I was wondering what might happen next, the

The ladies-in-waiting at the *daimyo's* mansion where the heroine is now employed enjoy a game of court football. Later the *daimyo's* wife and her attendants (on the left) participate in a "jealousy meeting"; using a life-size doll as a scapegoat, they give vent to their pent-up spite against men.

lady-in-waiting Yoshioka addressed us severally in these terms: "Each of you may speak without reserve and confess your troubles openly. If you thwart the love of other women by pouring forth your hate, if you revile men with your bitter jealousy, if you tell of loves that went awry—all this will be to the greater relish of the lady whom we serve."

Here was an exceptional pastime indeed, but, since it was all at the orders of my mistress, it did not behoove me to laugh. The Lady Yoshioka opened a lid wrought of cedar and cypress and decorated with the drawing of a weeping willow. From beneath she extracted a female doll, which was the very image of a living person. I know not whose work it was, but, as I now observed its grace of form and its face, which was the very counterfeit of a fair flower in bloom, even I, woman though I am, could not but be captivated by its beauty.

Thereat the women began to speak in turn of what lay on their minds. First came a lady-in-waiting named Iwahashi, whose

497 countenance was such as to court disaster. She was indeed of inexpressible ugliness; far from aspiring to enjoy love in the daytime,

498 she had long since abandoned the idea of "even a night pledge," and she never so much as set her eyes on a man. Now she pushed herself ahead of all the other women and spoke as follows.

499 "I was born in the town of Tochi in Yamato, and duly pledged my troth in marriage. But that rascally husband of mine went to

500 the city of Nara and met the daughter of a priest at the Kasuga Shrine. She was a girl of outstanding beauty and he began to visit her. One day I followed him secretly. My heart was pounding as I eavesdropped by her house. I saw the girl open the side door to let

501 my husband in. 'My eyebrows were itching all this evening,' said she, 'and so I knew that something agreeable would befall me.' Then, without the slightest sign of shame, she drew her body close

to him. 'Oh no,' said I at this, 'that man is mine!' And opening my tooth-blackened mouth, I fastened my teeth on her."

So saying, the Lady Iwahashi fastened herself onto the beautiful doll that stood before us. Boundlessly terrifying it was, and I can remember her appearance at that moment as though she were before me now.

This was the beginning of the Jealousy Meeting. Next another lady-in-waiting squirmed her way forward, quite beside herself with spiteful rage. How wretched a thing is a woman's heart that it can express itself like this!

"In my young days," she began, "I lived in Akashi in the Province of Harima. I had a niece of marriageable age, and a husband was chosen for her, who married into the family and took her name. Now this rascal was endowed with the most outrageous vigour. Even the lowest serving girl in the household was not spared his attentions, and he set at the various maids with such an appetite that they were always half asleep during the day. My niece took all this quite well and let things follow their course; yet at heart she was chafing under these constant infidelities. Seeing this, I took to going myself each night to the door of their bedchamber and would carefully secure the hinge from the outside so that it could not be opened. Having thus locked up my niece and her husband and constrained them to spend the night together, I would leave. Before long my niece grew emaciated and even the sight of a man's face became odious to her. 'If things continue in this way,' she said, trembling, 'I fear I shall not be long for this world.' The girl was born in the year of the Fiery Horse. Yet this was of no avail; for instead it was her husband who finished her, and she fell into a decline. . . . Oh, that I could but put that insatiable rogue up against this doll and kill him here and now!" So saying, she knocked down the doll and wildly roared abuse.

502

503

504

There was also a lady-in-waiting called Sodégakidono, who
505 hailed from Kuwana in the province of Isé. Even as a girl she had
been deeply jealous by nature—so much so, indeed, that she had
stopped even the scullery maids from dressing themselves properly,
had made them arrange their hair without the use of mirrors and
had not let them embellish themselves with powder. By such means
she had made the women in her service appear unsightly, even
though many of them were by no means of coarse extraction. This
conduct of hers had been noised abroad and people had come to
avoid her, until in the end she had been constrained to come down
506 here as virgin as on the day when she was born. Looking now at
the doll, she started to shower it with rebukes, as though it were
507 to blame for her misfortune: "That chit of a girl has far too much
good sense," she cried. "Even if her husband were to spend the
whole night out, she'd take it calmly!"

Although each of the women thus pushed herself forward to
vent her spite, their jealousy did not seem to appease my lady.
When it came to my turn, I abruptly turned the doll face down-
wards and, having climbed on top of it, spoke as follows: "You
wretched creature! You came here in the part of concubine, and,
having found favour with our lord, made him set his true wife
508 at naught and did not scruple to share a bolster with him every
night! But you shall smart for what you've done, you hussy!"

So saying, I glared at the doll, gnashing my teeth and acting as
though rancour had pierced the marrow of my bones. My words
had hit the very core of my lady's concern, and, when I had finished,
she said:

"That's it, that's it! It was not for nothing that I had them
fashion that doll! Though I be ever at my lord's disposal, he is
pleased to treat me as though I were not there. Instead he has
summoned that beautiful woman from his fief and clings to her
both day and night. Such is the sad lot of our sex that I cannot ex-

press my bitter feelings to my lord. But at least I have been able to have a likeness made of that woman and thus I can revile her at my will."

No sooner had she spoken than, most strange to relate, the doll opened its eyes, stretched out both hands and looked round at the company. It appeared to be on the point of standing up; but none of the ladies waited to observe further and all rushed helter-skelter from the place. The doll clung to the hem of my lady's outer skirt, till she finally managed to throw it off and succeeded in making her escape without misadventure.

Yet thereafter, no doubt as a consequence of this affair, my lady fell ill and started to babble away in a most distressing fashion. Her attendants, surmising that this distemper might be due to the spite of the doll, took counsel together.

"If we leave things as they are," they said, "that doll will pursue its implacable course hereafter. It were better to consign it to the flames."

Having thus agreed, they carried the doll to the corner of the mansion and burned it, taking care to bury the ashes so that nothing might remain above ground. Yet they themselves soon became fearful of the place where the ashes lay; every night the wailing tones of a woman's voice proceeded unmistakably from that grave. This was bruited abroad and earned the scorn of the world for the women of our household.

The report found its way to the middle residence, and greatly astonished my lord. In order that he might inquire into the circumstances, he was pleased to summon the woman in charge of the Front Service. There was no avoiding my duty, and I had the honour of appearing in his presence, where, being unable to hide anything from my lord, I told him the tale of the doll exactly as it happened. All those who were in attendance clapped their hands with wonder, and my lord was pleased to observe, "Noth-

ing in this world is so odious as a woman's mind. If things are
510 like this, my mistress will not fail to lose her life before long, owing
to my wife's single-minded spite. Apprise the girl of these things
and have her return to our fief."

Now this concubine of his was a most graceful creature, and,
as she knelt down to implore her lord, she far surpassed the doll
in comeliness. I was not a little proud of my own fair looks, but
here was a woman who could dazzle even one of her own sex.
Lovely as this woman was, my lady had, in her spite, tried to curse
her to death through her Jealousy Meetings.

My lord now came to regard all women as truly fearful beings,
and thereafter he did not deign to set foot in the women's quarters.
He took a lifelong parting from his spouse, and she was obliged
to assume the state of a widow. Seeing this, I was inspired with
a repugnance against my present service, and, having received
511 permission to end it, I returned to the capital, half inclined to take
the vows. Truly, jealousy is a thing to be eschewed, and we women
must ever guard ourselves against it.

512 ## A PAPER SPRING CORD OF GILT

A lady's dressing room is really something to be seen, with its
combings of jet-black hair scattered on the floor, its boxes of
513 cosmetic preparations and its pairs of shining mirrors.

Among all the aspects of their appearance women consider
the beauty of their hair to be the most important. At some time
during my career I had practised myself in the art of attending
514 to women's adornment. Now I adopted a Low Shimada, secured
a kerchief on both sides of my coiffure and took service with a
certain lady as her hairdresser.

The styling of hair changes with the times. Nowadays the
515 Hyogo style has become old-fashioned and the Five-Stage style is

considered unsightly. In former times, howbeit, to do one's hair in such a careful fashion was known as Wifely Decency. Our modern young wives have truly lost all gentleness of manner. They are forever striving to learn the styles favoured by courtesans and by actors of the Kabuki; in the width of their sleeves they copy the foppish young men of the town; they walk along, swaying their hips loosely and kicking out their feet. No longer can a young woman feel at ease; for she is ever concerned with the impression that she may be making on others. If she happens to have been born with a birthmark on her face, she is at the greatest pains to hide it; if her ankles are on the thick side, she conceals them by wearing the bottom of her kimono long; if her mouth is large, she loses no time in puckering it; nor does she give her speech free rein.

Indeed, the hardships that young ladies have to endure these days are quite beyond our imagination! If only their consorts would forbear and look with indulgence at their flaws, women might reconcile themselves, realizing that in this Floating World we cannot have everything as we wish. But when a man can choose between two women, it is always the fairer who will win. It has come about—since when I know not—that men not only expect their partners to be passing fair, but look for a dowry in the bargain. Now it is rare indeed for a woman to be well equipped in all the nine points, and nothing could be more bootless than to demand so much from a single person. Would it not be more reasonable that the man himself should pay the dowry, depending on the beauty of his future wife?

Having taken service, then, I received my clothes for the four seasons, and was assured of a salary of eighty *mommé* of silver a year. My term started on the second day of the Clothes-Lining Month, and I betook myself early at dawn to the residence of my new employers. My mistress was having her morning bath when I arrived. After I had waited for some time, she summoned me

516
517

518

519

520
521

173

522   to a private room in the back of the house for my audience. She was a graceful young lady, hardly nineteen years of age, and boasted a most elegant demeanour.

"Can there really be such fine ladies in this world?" I thought enviously, and, though she was of my own sex, I gazed on her with fascination.

My mistress spoke to me freely of sundry matters. "Excuse me," she then said, "for a request that may seem strange in these modern days, but pray take an oath, inscribing the names of the myriad Gods of Japan, that you will in no way disclose the secret that I shall now impart."

I had no idea of what might follow, but, now that I looked on this lady as my mistress and had committed myself to her service, it was not my place to gainsay her. I therefore took a brush and inscribed an oath of secrecy exactly as she required. But even as I wrote the characters, I was secretly praying in this fashion: "Since my heart is now fixed on no particular man, may the Buddhas and the Gods forgive me should I play the wanton!"

"Now that you have sworn," said my mistress, "I can freely disclose to you what is on my mind. Though I may match other women in my looks, my hair, alas, is scanty and only grows in scattered tufts. Pray you look at this!"

So saying, she undid her coiffure, whereat numerous locks of false hair fell to the floor.

523   "Of real hair," said she, "I can boast but ten strands. The Wight of the Ten Strands, one might call me!"

At this she was choked with bitter tears.

"It is now four years," she continued, "since I became attached to my lord. On occasion he will return home late at night. When this happens, I know that he has not spent his time out for nothing. Being nettled at this, I place my pillow at some distance from his and pretend to be asleep. Although I can afford a mild tiff of this

174

sort, I dare not risk anything more violent. For in a heated quarrel my hair might come undone and my husband's love for me would vanish utterly. Bitter indeed it is when one thinks of it! How hard it has been to hide this flaw from him all these years! Do your best, I pray you, to see that he never discovers it. We women must help each other, must we not?"

With these words, she gave me the fully figured silk robe that 524 she was wearing. Seeing the lady so overcome with shame, I felt all the more sorry for her. Thereafter, I attended her closely and helped her to keep up appearances.

Yet, as time passed, she began to evince a most unreasonable jealousy over the fact that my own hair was by nature long and beautiful. In the end she ordered me to cut it. Much as this grieved me, there was no help for it, inasmuch as these were my mistress' orders, and I cut my hair so short as to be unsightly. But even now my mistress was not satisfied. "You may have cut your hair," said she, "but it will soon grow back to its former state. Pluck it out, till the line of the hair on your brow becomes thin!"

At this cruel bidding, I asked my mistress to release me from her service. But even this she would not allow and she now set to tormenting me from morning until night. I grew haggard and most bitter in consequence, and began to plot some evil scheme.

It was my aim to acquaint the master in some way or other with the truth about his lady's hair, and thus to turn him against her. With this in mind I won the affection of the pet cat in the house and had him toy with my hair all night long. In the end he came every evening to nestle on my shoulder.

One night, when it was raining forlornly outside, the master, being in a pleasant humour, sat with the women of the house from early in the evening and played the *koto* in concert with his wife. 525 It was then that I set the cat on her. The animal clawed her hair relentlessly and the ornamental hairpin and wooden support fell out; thus was a love of five years destroyed in a single moment. My mistress, her fair countenance utterly transformed, rushed into her chamber and hid her head under the bedclothes. Thereafter she was plunged in gloom. The lady's intercourse with her husband became infrequent; they drifted apart from one another, and in the end he found some pretext to have her return to her home place.

After that I searched for a way to win this man for myself. One rainy evening I found my master sleeping soundly in the parlour, with his head resting on the edge of the alcove; on his face was a melancholy look. There was no one else about, and I realized that, if I were to embark on an amour with him, this was the time.

"Aye, sir, I am coming," I said, for all he had not called me. I then approached him where he lay and woke him with the words, "Aye, sir. If you please, sir."

"You called for me, sir," I said, when he started to stir. "What is your good wish?"

"I did not call," he answered.

"Well, sir, I must have heard wrong," said I. But, instead of leaving, I stood by him with a languid, sensual air. Then I brought him a pillow and covered his legs with a quilt.

"Is there no one else about?" he asked.

"No, sir, just today there happens to be no one."

Hearing this, he took me by the hand; after that, I got him into my hands and made him my own creature.

THE DRAWING FOUND IN A WANTON ROBE

The way to sew women's clothes was first laid down during the reign of our forty-sixth sovereign, Empress Koken, since which time the styles worn in the land of Yamato have become ever more elegant. When silk garments are being sewn for the nobility, one

526
527

begins by counting the exact number of needles in one's case, and when the job is finished, one counts the needles once again. The greatest care must be taken in all respects; one's body must be especially purified, and women who are suffering from their monthly malady should not be admitted to the room.

At some time in my career I had become proficient in the art of sewing, and I now took employment as a seamstress. In this capacity I led a calm and virtuous life. My mind was free from care and untroubled by any thoughts of lust. Instead, I found my pleasure in looking out of the southern window or in feasting my eyes on the beauty of the rushes growing in the landscape tray. By combining our store of money my fellow-seamstresses and I were able to regale ourselves with Abé tea and with Tsuruya   528
bean-jam buns from Iidamachi. As our days were spent in the company of none but our own sex, they were innocent of sin, and the cloudless moon could sink behind the hills without troubling   529
our spirits: this must verily be akin to that state of true Buddhahood in which are comprised Eternity, Bliss, Real Self and Purity.   530

I was living in this serene condition when one day I happened upon a drawing in the lining of a young lord's white silk under-robe   531
that had been consigned to me for sewing. The artist, whoever he may have been, had with consummate skill depicted a man and a woman consorting together in amorous sport. I was dazzled simply from observing their naked flesh and admiring the beauty of the woman's body as she lay there, exposing herself without re- serve, her heels held high and her toes bent back. Scarcely could   532
I believe that these were mere figures drawn in ink; I even seemed to hear sweet lovers' talk proceeding from their motionless lips. My senses were befogged, and I leaned against my workbox, overcome with dizziness. Then the desire for a man arose within   533
me—so powerfully, indeed, that all thoughts of sewing vanished and I could no longer put my hand to thimble or bobbin.

Later, as I lay in bed sunk in reverie, it occurred to me that to sleep alone as I now did was a sorry thing indeed. "Oh for those nights I used to have!" thought I, as one by one I called to mind my experiences of the past; and I was overcome by gloom.

It may well have been that when I wept in those palmier days of mine I had wept true, and that when I laughed I had laughed falsely. Yet, true or false, it had all been for the sake of men—of men whom I loved so dearly. Being endowed as I was with far too passionate a nature, I had caused these men to plunge themselves into food and sakè and love; I had made them repeat their tender vows time after time—so much so that on occasion I had constrained them to take early leave of this Floating World. Most grievous it was, as I now recalled it!

The men whom I could remember having enjoyed as partners were more than I could count on my fingers. And when I now bethought me that in this world there existed women who in their entire lives consorted with but a single man, women who, even if their husbands left them, did not look for a future partner, or who, if their husbands died, took holy vows and, by thus resigning themselves to a life of chastity, showed that they knew what it meant to suffer at parting from a man one loves—when, I say, I bethought me that there were such women, I could not look into my own heart without bitter remorse. Then and there I resolved that, whereas in the past I had enjoyed the knowledge of countless men, henceforth I would at all costs subdue my wanton nature.

Meanwhile the night was gradually turning into dawn. My fellow seamstresses who had been sleeping next to me got up, folded their bedclothes and put them away on the shelves. I waited impatiently for my single *go* of rice. Having finished it, I searched in the brazier for some glowing embers, lit my tobacco and puffed away. Knowing that no man would see it, I tied up my dishevelled black hair in haste, and, quite heedless of the fact that my chignon was awry,

Once again the heroine tries to break away from her downward path, this time by becoming a seamstress. Again she is foiled: in the lining of a young man's silk under-robe she discovers an erotic drawing which fires her amorous nature and makes her give up sewing for more solid pleasures. The seamstresses in the foreground are putting together a formal kimono.

secured it with an old paper cord. Then, meaning to throw away
538 the hair water that remained, I glanced through the dark bamboo
slats of the window.

A man was standing there. From his looks I judged him to be a
539 lackey in the service of a warrior lodging in one of the long-houses.
Apparently he had gone out for his morning purchases, and he car-
540 ried some Shiba fish in his basket. In the same hand he held a bottle
of vinegar and some spills; with the other hand he now pulled up
541 the skirt of his plain dark-blue clothes and, believing that he was
unobserved, pointed his weapon downwards and performed his
542 needs. It was as powerful as the Waterfall of Otowa, and as it tum-
543 bled in cascades, dislodging the very stones in the ditch, the thought
impressed itself upon my mind that this man could make an abyss in
the solid earth.

"Alas, you poor fellow!" thought I, as I looked at him. "That fine
544 spear of yours will never be turned to any account in the Kyoto
battlefield of Shimabara."

The idea that it would simply become old and rusty, without ever
having been used for any noble exploit, rued me sorely. Of a sudden
545 I could no longer stand it. It was irksome to continue my present
service, and, without even waiting for the end of my term, I feigned
some illness and took leave of my employer.

I now moved into a house in a rear alley of the Sixth District in
546 Hongo. On a pillar at the entrance to the alley I posted a placard
with the inscription, "Seamstress in this alley will perform any type
547 of sewing." Then I held myself free for that one thing alone, fully
intending to avail myself of any man who came to my house.
But, alas, I received visits only from useless women, who belaboured
me with tedious talk about modern styles of sewing. When they
gave me orders, I stitched their clothes for them in the most slovenly
fashion. Ay, it was outrageous behaviour when I think back on it.

Both day and night I was plagued with wanton thoughts, but it

was hard for me to speak openly of this matter. One day an idea occurred to me, and I set out for Motomachi, accompanied by a *548*
maid to carry my bag. On arrival I visited a draper's by the name of Echigo-ya, whose clerks were in the habit of calling at the house *549*
where I had formerly held employ.

"I have given up my service," I said, "and now live by myself. *550*
I don't have so much as a cat in the house. My neighbours on one side are always out; on the other side lives an old crone in her seventies, deaf in the bargain. There is not a soul opposite my house —only an *ukogi* hedge. If any of you gentlemen happen to have *551*
business in that part of the city, pray do not fail to call on me and take your rest."

So saying, I selected half a roll of the finest quality Kaga silk woven with organzine, a red silk kimono and a sash of Ryumon, and left the premises. There was a firm rule in the Echigo-ya against selling retail wares on credit, but the young men in the shop were so overcome by my presence that they could not gainsay me; they let me go without paying.

Soon the eighth day of the Ninth Moon had come, and the *552*
master of the shop bade his men collect the payment for the purchase. There were some fifteen clerks in the shop, but they all now vied in avoiding this task. There was one elderly clerk, however, who knew naught of either love or tender feelings, who even in his sleep dreamed of the abacus and in his waking hours was evermindful of the tier box. The proprietor in Kyoto called him a white *553,554*
rat; and indeed this clerk was an exceptionally clever man, who, *555*
even as he leaned at ease against a pillar, was in his mind shrewdly criticizing those about him. Having now listened impatiently to the other men, he said. "Leave the matter of that woman's bill to me! If she won't pay her debt, I'll pull off her head and bring it back with me."

There was no holding him back and he set off instantly for my house. On arrival he abused me in the roughest terms, but I listened calmly and said, "Forgive me, sir, for having made you come all this way for such a trifling matter."

At once I stripped myself of my light pink kimono, saying, "As you see, sir, this is dyed in the most elegant fashion. It has only been next to my skin twice—yesterday and today. And here is my sash. I am sorry, sir, to incommode you," I continued, handing my clothes to him, "but as for the present I have no money, pray you take these."

My eyes were glistening with tears, as I now stood before him, quite naked but for my crimson petticoat. When he saw my lovely, milk-white body, fleshy without being fat, and free from a single moxa scar, even this hardy man began to tremble like an aspen leaf.

"Do you really expect me to deprive you of these clothes?" said he. "You will take cold for sure."

Thereat he bade me put on the kimono once again. I now had him fairly in hand.

"You are indeed a warm-hearted man," I said, leaning my body against him.

556
557
558

Quite overcome, he called for his young attendant, Kyuroku, and, bidding him open his box, took out a small silver coin weighing about five and a half *mommé*.

"I am giving you this," he said to the lad, "so that you can go to Shitaya-dori and have a look at the Yoshiwara. You needn't hurry back."

At this the boy's breast heaved with excitement and his face flushed. He could ill believe that it was true, and for some time he had trouble in replying. Finally, he understood. Ah yes, he thought, while he indulges himself with this woman, I'd be in the way. At the same time he perceived a rare chance for extracting some more lucre from his close-fisted master.

"But, sir," said he, "whatever happens, I cannot very well visit the gay quarters in a mere cotton loincloth."

"To be sure," said his master, and gave him a goodly length of wide Hino silk. Without even waiting to have the hem stitched, the lad tied the material about his loins and hurried away as his fancy guided him.

After he had left I secured the latch on the door and covered the window with a sedge hat. Then, without applying to any go-between for help, we concluded a bond of union.

Having once succumbed, my clerk banished all greed for profit from his mind and utterly lost himself in his infatuation. This could hardly be excused as the folly of youthful ardour. His work in the Edo branch of the shop fell into complete confusion, and soon he was dismissed and ordered up to Kyoto.

From this time forward I was seamstress in name only. I took my pleasure here and there, having set my fee at one rectangular   559
gold piece a day. Though I had the maid carry my workbox when I went out on my visits, it was by another form of work that I contrived to make my living; for, as one might say, the thread with which I now so loosely sewed would not serve for binding   560
buttocks.

HE WHO LOOKED FOR FUTURE SPLENDOUR   561

To wander about the country taking service, now in one place, now in another, is a most entertaining practice even for women. For some time I had thus been going between Edo, Kyoto and Osaka, but now I tired of these places and at the Autumn Change I   562
made my way to Sakai in the province of Izumi. This town, I   563
thought, might afford some new experiences of interest. On arrival I repaired to Nishiki-no-cho to the west of Nakahama. Here dwelt an agent named Zenkuro, whom I now asked to find me

564 a post. While waiting for employment, I was constrained to pay six *fun* a day for my board and lodging.

Before long, however, an old woman came and applied for
565 someone to take service with—as I understood it—a certain retired gentleman who dwelt on the Great Road. The rank would be that of housemaid, serving close by the bedchamber, and the only duties
566 would be those of putting up and laying down the bedclothes. As soon as this woman saw me, she said, "You are of the right age and, so far as appearance goes, you are perfect to the very tips of your fingernails. Your bearing leaves nothing to be desired and I am sure that you will find favour in my employer's eyes." The old woman herself had been long employed in this household and now she cheerfully conducted me thither without haggling in the slightest about the terms of my advance payment.

On the way she imparted various pieces of information that might stand me in good stead. The old woman had a fearful face, but she seemed to be good at heart. It made me glad to think that
567 there were indeed "no devils in this world," and I listened attentively to what she might tell me.

568 "In the first place," she began, "you must know that the mistress is deeply jealous, and she takes it most amiss if any of the women servants converse with the clerks in the shop. Far from tolerating talk about love affairs, she even pretends not to notice when the
569 birds are engaged in amorous sport! Next, be warned that she belongs to the Lotus Sect, and never dream of invoking the Sacred Name in her presence! Also, she has a pet white cat with a collar. This is her special treasure and you must never chase it away, even if it tries to steal the fish.

570 "As to the wife of the young master in the main house, she is
571 forever lending herself airs, but don't you give a fig's end for what she says, however arrogantly she may hold forth! She entered the

184

household as a chit of a parlourmaid called Shun and was employed by the young master's former wife. I don't know what came over the master, but, when his wife died of influenza, he went and married this maid. It isn't even as though she were especially well favoured in her looks! Well, once she was married, she began to behave like a typical upstart. She insists on having her own way in everything. Even when she goes out in her palanquin, she has the cushions piled up luxuriously. It's a wonder the Gods haven't broken her hipbone for her, arrogant creature that she is!"

Thus the old woman poured forth her harsh denunciations. Having ears, I could not forbear from hearing; and, I confess, it was not without some amusement that I listened to her screed.

"When it comes to their morning and evening meals," she continued, "though most families manage with red rice, in this house nothing will do but Tenshu rice from Banshu. When they need bean-paste, they get it from the grocer's shop that belongs to their son-in-law. They have a bath heated every day of the week, but usually they're too lazy even to wash themselves and it's an utter waste. At New Year's they get gifts from all the members of their family—rice cakes, fish and what not. Sakai is a large place, but from the Osho Way down to the very south of the city there's not a single person who hasn't borrowed money from them at one time or another. Only a few hundred yards from here, in the devil's corner, stands a house belonging to one of their former clerks whom they've set up in business.

"I don't suppose you've ever been to the Sumiyoshi Festival. Well, it won't be with us again for many a month, but when the time comes, you'll see that on the eve of the festival the whole household gathers together and sets forth in a group. Before that, though, we'll be having the wistaria-viewing at the Harbour, when we all go out with our great wooden boxes lined with Nanten leaves and filled with mountains of red rice. When all is said and done, if one's going to be in service, one's lucky to work in a house like this.

"Now you, my dear, should serve out your period here faithfully and, when the time comes for you to leave, they'll arrange a good match for you. The only important thing for you is to please our retired employer. On no account must you go against orders, and you must never breathe a word to the others about any private matters. To be sure, our employer is well advanced in years and is inclined to be short-tempered. But this is no more than a spurt of water; it springs up quickly, but leaves no unpleasant aftermath. Do your best to please our employer. You won't regret it, I can tell you. The others do not know it, but the fact is that our
576 employer has put aside a considerable sum of money for retirement funds. If death were to come tomorrow, who knows where the wheel of Fortune might not turn? Already our employer is over seventy, covered all over with wrinkles and, if I be any judge of the matter, not long for this world. When a person reaches that age,
577 though the spirit may be willing enough, the flesh is weak! We aren't intimate friends, you and I, but you seem to be an amiable young woman, and that is why I've told you all these things."

I had followed these disclosures in a general fashion, and now I felt myself to be well apprised of the situation. It would, I thought, be no such hard task to handle this aged employer of mine as I wished. I should remain with him until my years of service had accumulated. To satisfy my nether appetites, I could no doubt strike up an attachment on the side with some younger man. If my belly should by any chance show the effects of this bond, I could easily fob off the child on my old master. In due course I should have him write a testament in which he would bequeath his wealth to me. Thus would I assure myself of a fair livelihood for many a long year to come.

As I walked along, with this scheme taking shape in my mind, my companion said, "Well, here we are. Pray you come in." So saying, she led the way into the house.

When I reached the middle door, I removed my sandals and 578 walked across the wooden floor of the kitchen. I had just sat down when there came towards me an old woman who, I at once realized, was my new employer. Though in her seventies, she looked decidedly robust. This old lady fixed me with her gaze, as though she meant to bore a hole in me. "Splendid!" said she. "There's nothing wrong with this girl."

Things had turned out differently from my expectations! I bethought me ruefully that, if I had known my employer was a woman, I certainly should not have come. Howbeit, she was kindly in her manner of address, and, considering that six months' service would soon be finished, I resolved to "tread the salt" of these 579 shores.

The shop itself was no different from the ones I had known in Kyoto, but in the rear things were much more agitated; here the men were busy with the hulling mortar, the women were plying their needles without surcease and each servant was carrying out the duties for which he had been strictly trained. There were half a dozen maids in the house and every one of them was assigned her own task. Only I was free to wear a look of leisure on my face.

As I was observing these matters, night began to fall and I was ordered to lay down the bedclothes. This was as I had foreseen, but the next order put me to a nonplus: "You are to sleep in the same bed as your mistress," I was told.

Since this was a command, I could not gainsay it. Having joined my mistress in bed, then, I expected that she would tell me to scratch her hip, or something of the sort. But once more I was to be surprised: for now I was bidden to take the woman's part, while my mistress assumed that of a man and thus disported herself with me during the entire night. I had indeed been reduced to a sorry pass! The Floating World is wide and I had worked in many different places; but never before had I been used like this.

"When I am reborn in the next world, I will be a man. Then I shall be free to do what really gives me pleasure!" Thus did my new mistress voice her fondest wish.

580   MYSTERY WOMEN WHO SING DITTIES

581   What can be called for six *mommé* of silver a night is a call-bird, in other words, a mystery woman. When people are "perplexed" and ask why these women are thus named, one can reply that it is for the same reason that bath attendants are known as "monkeys."

So far as their temper and their customs are concerned, bathhouse women are much the same wherever one may go. Since washing the body is their speciality, they bathe themselves every 582   day. They wear their hair in a great Shimada with the chignon bound in the back, tie a wide, flat paper cord into a diamond shape, bending its ends round tightly, and complete their coiffure by thrusting in a comb whose ridge is as wide as a trencher's, being more than half an inch across.

583   Once the evening begins, it is their aim to ensnare customers by their fair looks; they therefore take care to conceal such blemishes as they may have with thick white powder, and they are unsparing in their use of lipstick. Their undersash is fashioned of Kaga silk and often has turned light grey from much use; they secure it tightly, wearing the hem of their underskirt short. Over this they don an unlined cotton garment, long enough to cover their heels and decorated according to their fancy; some women will have a willow-and-ball pattern dyed in five different places by a special process of squeezing the material; others will have their sleeves dyed with a chequered pattern. They wear a sash of Ryumon silk twice

folded over double and tied in the back; their sleeves are always   *584*
short. Thus attired, they take turns in going to the washing place,
there to carry out their duties.

As soon as a customer enters the bathhouse, the attendants will
call out, "Welcome, sir!" and night after night will assume the
same alluring air. When the customer steps out of the water and
seats himself on his bath cloth, one of the women will approach   *585*
him and, regardless of whether or not they may be on intimate
terms, will address him with some such remark as, "Will you be
visiting the theatre on your way home this evening, sir, or will
you perchance call at the gay quarters?"

The woman speaks so that others in the room can overhear her   *586*
words, and thus she tries to curry favour with her customer. A
certain type of young man, however, will respond to this by
taking a courtesan's letter out of his bag with an absurd flourish,   *587*
and will then flaunt it before the bathhouse woman, murmuring,
"I wonder wherein lies the special charm in the writing of a great
courtesan."

Now this woman knows nothing whatsoever of the writing of
such courtesans as Ogino, Yoshida, Fujiyama, Itsutsu, Musashi,   *588*
Kayoiji, Nagahashi, Sanshu, Kodayu or again of Mikasa, Tomoé,
Sumunoé, Toyoura, Yamato, Kasen, Kiyohara, Tamakazura, Yaé-
giri, Kiyohashi, Komurasaki or Shiga. Even to show her a letter
written by the strumpet Yoshino would be to place the finest scent   *589*
of aloeswood before a dog, and all the man's pretensions are lost   *590*
on her.

A young fellow like this will often carry on his person the crested
comb of some high or medium courtesan whom he has not so much   *591*
as set eyes on. This is shaming behaviour indeed. Howbeit, when a
man is young, he is ever pressed for money and, much as he would
like to indulge in luxury, he can ill afford to do so. These preten-
sions, then, are such as anyone might affect.

Now, for a young man like this to resort to a bathhouse is a
592 pleasant enough diversion. He will arrive unaccompanied, make
a great show of his new loincloth and have his favourite attendant
fetch the cotton robe that he keeps here for his special use. All this is
most delightful and also in accord with his humble means.

When the customer leaves the bath, one places a tobacco tray
593 next to him and gives him an infusion. He cuts a remarkably fine
figure as he sits there, being cooled by a fan, on which is executed
594 the copy of a painting by Yuzen. Then one sits by his back, ap-
plies a new plaster to the scar left by his moxa burn and smoothes
down his rumpled sidelocks.

When it comes to a chance visitor to the bathhouse, one treats
him in a more casual fashion and omits such special attentions.
Though these attentions may be of no great consequence, the visi-
tor can but look enviously on those customers who receive them.

When a customer inquires about an inn where he may enjoy an
amorous encounter and calls one of the bathhouse girls for this
595 purpose, she will herself enter the final bath, wash herself thorough-
ly and attend to her toilet. Meanwhile, a meal of boiled rice and
tea is being prepared for her. After she has laid down her chop-
sticks, she will hastily throw on her rented clothes and hurry pit-a-pat
596 out of the front door, attended by the servant Kyuroku, who car-
ries the lantern. Although in the evening she has worn a kerchief
of floss silk, she does not bother to cover her head now that it is
night. The sound of her footsteps echoes softly as she trips through
the dark. Reaching the inn, she enters unabashedly and joins her
customer in the visitor's room.

"Excuse me," says she, as she sits down, "but I'm weighed down
597 with three layers of clothes. It's far too hot for comfort."

With no further ado, she pulls off the top part of her dress and
only keeps on her under-kimono.

598 "Have them bring me a glass of clear water, will you, dear?" she says. "I've never known such a sultry night. It's terrible when there's no chimney, isn't it?"

Thus she casts off all reserve, acts according to her whims and comports herself with utter ease. For all one may expect scant ceremony from a bathhouse girl, she really seems to be carrying her indecorum too far.

Nonetheless, she refrains from stretching out her hand for the sweetmeats and she has also learned to hold her sakè cup aslant. *599* Moreover, although there are various side dishes, raw shellfish and baked eggs on the table, she neglects these and instead directs her chopsticks to the seasoned beans, the pepper skins and similar light condiments. By such a show of refinement, she tries to make her customer believe that she has studied the elegant ways of the gay quarters.

"Won't you have another drop?" she says, each time that she pours the sakè, or else, "Allow me to pour you a trifle more." The phrases are mere commonplaces, and, if one were to call a hundred different women of this type, each one would comport herself in the self-same fashion. Yet the customer should forbear, regarding all this as but a temporary expedient to tide him over while he is short of funds. A man who lives in Naniwa and is accustomed to feasting on sea bream from the Front may, when he goes to Kumano, be *600* invited even in the Ninth Moon to eat spiked mackerel from the Bon Festival; yet, considering the rustic circumstances, he finds it most enjoyable. Just so, a customer who is in the company of a bathhouse girl must forget that he has ever seen a proper courtesan; he must regard his present doings as a mere diversion, aimed at washing off the filth of evil passions and letting it vanish in the *601* water's flow.

While the bathhouse girl is thus seated with her customer at the inn, a group of her colleagues is engaged in eager chat, each trying to outspeak the other. At the sound of the midnight bell, one of them says, "Let us now go to bed! We work hard night after night and our bodies aren't made of iron. I don't even want any supper."

"I shouldn't mind a bowl of vermicelli," says one of the others, and a moment later there is a clatter as the women bring out their trays. Then they go to bed. For three women there is but one set of bedding and two suits of wadded nightclothes; even wooden pillows are in short supply in this poor house where they live. As they lie in bed, love does not enter into their minds; instead, they

602   talk about the digging of the new canal, or about their own home places; and later their conversation will invariably turn to actors.

Meanwhile the couple in the inn has retired for the night. The

603   man touches the girl's body. Perhaps it is merely his fancy, but her hands and feet seem cold. Raucous snores escape her lips.

Later in the night she commits her body to the man. Was it not a promiscuous bedchamber scene like this that the poet had in mind

604   when he wrote the words: "Carnal pleasure between man and woman is but the mutual embrace of stinking bones"?

605   I, too, became such a woman and thus did I defile the water of my heart.

SONG FOR A WOMAN OF THE STREETS

By now I had tried every possible form of employment, and, being

606   furrowed with the waves of age, I took to roving about the gay quarters of Shinmachi, or, as one might call it, Settsu's "sea of love." I was familiar with this place from past years and through the good offices of some acquaintances was able to take service here as a

607   procuress. So it was that I, who had myself once been a courtesan, assumed the role of supervising other courtesans; for which purpose I adopted the shameful and unmistakable habit that befitted one of my new calling. I wore a light-mauve apron and a sash of medium width, tied on the left side. Thus attired, I shuffled along

stealthily with my keys of office, my hands hidden in the folds of my dress, my skirt pulled up slightly at the back and a towel wrapped about my head by way of kerchief. My face was usually fixed in a scowl, and soon I found that people feared me even more than I had expected.

In training the courtesans who were in my charge I was able to make even the most weak-spirited girl into an adept practitioner. I instructed them so that they knew exactly how to humour every customer and never had to spend a single idle night. Thus I was able to turn them to the profit of their employers. Yet, because I was so well acquainted with the true circumstances of a courtesan's life, I was forever finding fault with these girls and reproving them for their secret trysts. Not only did I come to be feared by my charges themselves, but their customers, as well, found me irksome. Without waiting for the fixed days of payment, they would give me my two rectangular gold pieces in advance, feeling, as they did so, that the devil himself was fleecing them of their Six Coppers for the Way.

Such heartless behaviour can never continue unpunished in this world. Soon I found myself disliked by everyone, and it was hard for me to go on living in my present abode. Accordingly I removed to the suburb called Tamazukuri. In this forlorn place there were no shops, but only small houses, and even at noontime the bats fluttered through the streets. Having taken lodgings in a house on a rear alley, I settled down to a life of seclusion.

I had put by no money for my livelihood, and I was now constrained to sell my last proper clothes. When I needed kindling wood in the morning, I had to break the shelves in my room and burn them. For my evening meal I drank a cup of plain hot water, and for nourishment I could only nibble at a handful of dried beans. On stormy nights, when most people lie in fear of the thunder, I would beg the elements, "If you have any compassion for human

608

609
610

611

suffering, cast your bolts down here and crush me to death!" For I held my life at naught and was utterly weary of the Floating World.

Although I had lived sixty-four years, people who saw me still took me for a woman in her forties. This I owed to the circumstances that my skin was fine-grained and that I was of small build. Nevertheless, in my present frame of mind such matters afforded me no great joy.

One night, as I lay gazing into the past through the window of my heart, calling to mind my various wanton doings, I seemed to see a procession of some ninety-five different childlike figures, each
612   child wearing a hat in the form of a lotus leaf and each one stained with blood from his waist down. Standing before me, they spoke
613   in slurred and weeping tones: "Carry me on your back! Oh, carry me!"

These, I thought, must be like women who had died in childbirth; for I had heard it said that they returned to earth in the form of spirits. But as I gave heed, I heard each of the small figures cry bitterly, "Oh, cruel mother that you were!"

Then I perceived to my grief that these were the children whom I had conceived out of wedlock and disposed of by abortion. If, instead, I had brought them up safely, I should now be living
614   worthily with a family larger than that of Wada himself! I looked back wistfully on the past. After a time the children vanished without a trace. This vision, I felt sure, must signify that my days were finally drawing to an end. Yet dawn came, and I was still alive. Alas, thought I, to rid oneself of this life is no such easy matter!

615   I took to observing my neighbours in the lodging house. In the room next to mine three women were living together, all apparently in their fifties. These women slept the entire forenoon, and I could not imagine what they might do for their livelihood. My

curiosity was aroused and I observed them carefully. I found that both at noon and in the evening they regaled themselves with food that seemed far too luxurious for people of their quality; they feasted on small fish caught off the shores of Sakai and quaffed pints of sakè, as though all this were the most natural thing in the *616* world. Their conversation, too, was not such as one would expect. Instead of exchanging the usual talk about how hard it was to make a living, these women made such remarks as, "My next New Year's dress will be of light-yellow silk, decorated with informal *617* crests of sailboats and Chinese fans. I shall have a sash that can be clearly seen at night. The base will be grey and it will be dyed with lines of five colours slanted backwards." New Year's was still far off, and these women must have been affluent indeed to indulge in such talk.

When they had finished their evening meal, they started to make their toilet. First they applied layer after layer of cheap face powder; then they used black dye from an inkstone to emphasize their hairlines; next they rouged their lips until they sparkled, embellished the napes of their necks and powdered their bodies up to their nipples, covering every wrinkle with a thick white coating. Each woman eked out her scanty hair by adding a number of false locks, twisted three hidden paper cords on a bound Shimada and above *618,619* these fastened a wide cord of folded Takénaga. Round a loose- *620* sleeved kimono of dark blue, they wore white cotton sashes, tied at the back. Their feet were shod in roughly sewn socks and straw sandals; and, in place of braided cords for their under-kimono, they used ordinary breastbands. Then, having equipped themselves with refabricated paper handkerchiefs, they awaited the con- *621* cealing cloak of evening.

Before long, three sturdy young men appeared in their room. They wore short coats, headbands and cheek towels, and had long *622* hoods pulled down over their eyes. Drawers, gaiters and straw

The heroine, now deserted by her youth, lives in lonely squalor. One night she has a hideous vision of all the children to whom she should have given birth, "each wearing a hat in the form of a lotus leaf and each one stained with blood from the waist down." On the right we see her neighbours, three elderly, bedizened harlots; they are having a drink of salted hot water to fortify themselves after the night's exertions.

sandals completed their attire. Each man carried a stout staff and
623   a long, narrow roll of matting.

"The time has come," said one of them, and they accompanied
the women into the street.

My attention now turned to my neighbours on the other side.
These were a man and wife who made their living by planing the
624,625 clasps for rain capes. Yet this woman, too, had to embellish herself
and issue out of doors. Before leaving their room, the couple gave
some rice cakes to their little girl, who was about four years of age.

"Father and Mother have to go out," they informed the child.
"While we are away, you must look after things for us!"

Then, while the father held their little one-year-old baby in his
arms, the mother put on an old hemp coat and opened the door.
After looking nervously in both directions, as though in fear of the
neighbours, they hurried out of the house. Once again I was at a
loss to gather what was happening.

When morning came, my three women neighbours returned to
the lodging house—but how different they looked from when I had
seen them on the previous evening! Their clothes were rumpled;
they tottered about, as though their legs could hardly support them;
626   and their breath came in short gasps. I watched them as they poured
salt into hot water and gulped it down. Then, after a hurried bowl
of rice gruel, they stepped into their tub and sat there for some time
to calm their ruffled spirits. When this was finished, their male com-
627   panions took some odd coppers from their sleeves, and, having by
628   rough calculation kept five coppers for themselves out of each ten,
they left.

The women then gathered together and embarked on a con-
fession of the night's doings.

"Alas," said one of them, "last night I did not come across a single
629   man who had his own paper handkerchiefs! Besides, the men I met
were all in the hot vigour of their youth. By the time I came to my

forty-sixth customer for the night, I was gasping for breath. 'This is the end of my tether!' I thought to myself, as I stood there, utterly spent. But this is one thing in life to which there seems to be no limit! For even then I took advantage of the fact that some more men came along to have another seven or eight before returning home."

Meanwhile one of the other women was chuckling to herself.

"What is it? " they asked her.

"Never in my life," said she, "have I had such an irksome time as last night! After I left here I set out on my usual route in Temma, 630 heading for the farmers' boats from Kawachi. Then I noticed a boy, who looked like the younger son of some village headman. He could hardly have been more than sixteen years of age and he had not yet so much as shaved the sides of his forelock. A trim country 631 lad he was, with quite an endearing figure in the bargain. From the looks of it, he was not very familiar with women. He had a companion with him—some peasant from the same village, I judged, —who kept peering about in all directions. 'The price of these women may be fixed at ten coppers,' I heard this fellow say, 'but there's always a chance of finding a good pennyworth if one looks carefully enough.' But the lad appeared to be impatient, and, having caught sight of me, he said, 'I like this girl.'

"With these words, he took me in tow and brought me to an uncovered boat, where we made the waves of the river our pillow and 632 indulged in one amorous bout after another. When this was finished, he pleasantly stroked my thigh with his soft young hand and asked me how old I was. This struck me in a sore spot and put me greatly out of countenance. But I managed to affect a sugary voice as I replied, 'I am just sixteen.' My companion was delighted. 'In that case,' said he, 'you and I are the same age.'

"Fortunately it was dark and he could not see me in my true form. But since I am, in fact, fifty-eight, I had told him a lie of forty-two years! When I reach the next world, I shall surely be censured by the devil and even have my tongue pulled out for my deceit. I only hope that he may forgive me by taking into account that this is my only way to earn a living.

"After that, I strolled round by the Nagamachi and was summoned into a pilgrims' inn. A small group of pilgrims was sitting there in a row, as though engaged in a ceremony of invoking the Sacred Name. Since the lamp in the room was shining brightly, I held my face to the side when I entered. Yet, as soon as the men set eyes on me, their enthusiasm cooled and no one spoke a word. Even simple country folk balk when they see a woman like me. This rebuff wounded me deeply, but there was no help for it, and turning to the pilgrims, I said, 'Is there no one among you gentlemen who wishes to distract himself with me? If I'm going to spend the night with any of you, that's all right. But, if it's just a matter of a short meeting, there's no time to be wasted.'

"When they heard my voice, the pilgrims were more repelled than ever and each of them seemed to shrink into himself. Among them there was an old man with a knowing look, who now pressed three fingers of each hand to the floor before him and said, 'Woman, pray do not take it to heart that these young men should be so appalled at the sight of you. The fact is that only this evening they happened to be talking to each other about the cat demon who assumes the form of an old woman. When they saw you, they were reminded of this and became frightened. They are all on a tour of the Thirty-Three Holy Places in the pious hope of assuring their salvation in the world to come. But, being at the height of their youthful vigour, they let their minds wander to lustful thoughts and sent someone to call a woman to their lodgings. You, it would seem, were a punishment visited on us by the Goddess Kannon. I neither like nor loathe you, woman, but pray make haste and quit this place!'

"I was much nettled at these words. 'To leave empty-handed,' thought I, 'is a sheer loss.' As I went out, then, I looked about the entrance and noticed a Kaga sedge hat lying close at hand. This would surely make a suitable gage for ten coppers, and I took it 637 with me when I left the inn."

"Yes, to be sure," said one of the women, having listened to this narration, "things are usually best when one is young. Of course, there are all kinds in our profession. One finds some quite pretty girls—even some who could pass for middle-ranking courtesans. Yet 638 this is a wretched condition for any woman to reach. There's no top, middle or bottom rank for us; it's fixed at ten coppers a time, whatever a woman may look like. In fact, the prettier she is, the greater is her loss. What we want in our profession is a land without moonlight!"

I was much amused by their conversation, and, as I listened, I realized that these must be the women known as *soka* of whom I 639 had heard reports. No doubt they were obliged to act as they did in order to make a livelihood. Yet I could not help smiling scornfully when I thought of them. There was even something frightening about women behaving thus at their age. In my own case, I thought, I should prefer to die and have done with it. But life, alas, however little one may cling to it, is hard to throw away!

In the rear of my lodging house dwelt an old woman who was now in her seventies. She was living in sorry straits and forever lamenting the fact that her legs would no longer support her. One day she remonstrated with me, "With a body like yours, it is foolish to waste your time as you do. Why don't you go out at night and earn some money like the others?"

"What man is going to accept me at my age?" I asked her.

At this the old woman flushed with indignation.

"If only these legs of mine would carry me," she said, "even I, old as I am, would add some false locks to my white hair, deck myself out to look like a widow and fob myself off on any man I could find. Alas, I can no longer use my body as I wish! But there's nothing to stop you. Go ahead, go ahead!"

In the end I was won over by her urging and came to feel that what she proposed would at least be better than dying of starvation.

"I shall do it," I said. "But, dressed as I am, I can hardly hope for much success."

"There's a way to put that right directly," she said, and hurried out, to return almost instantly with an elderly man of no mean appearance. On seeing me this man fully guessed the state of affairs.

"Yes indeed," said he, "there's money to be made in the dark!"

He then returned to his lodgings and had a parcel delivered to me. In it were a long-sleeved kimono, one sash, one petticoat, one pair of cotton socks. These clothes had all been especially made for rental and their prices were fixed as follows:

640
For 1 set of wadded cotton clothes	3 *fun* per night
For 1 sash	1 *fun* 5 *rin*
For 1 petticoat	1 *fun*
For 1 pair of socks	1 *fun*
For 1 umbrella (in case of rain)	12 coppers
For 1 pair of lacquered wooden shoes	5 coppers

Indeed, everything that was needed for this profession could be had by rental.

Forthwith I transformed myself to look like a *soka,* and, having
641 by now observed the ways of this calling, I tried to sing the tune, "In Your Nightdress." But there was something strange about my voice,
642 and, when the time came, I had the pimp sing it for me as I set forth across the bridges in the frosty night air. Although it was the dire need to make a living that had brought me to this pass, my new condition grieved me sorely.

In these days people have become so canny that, though it be only a matter of ten coppers, they exercise more care in their choice of a harlot from the streets than does a rich man in selecting a high-class courtesan. Sometimes they will wait until a passer-by appears with a torch, sometimes they will conduct the woman to the lantern of a guard box—in either case they scrutinize her closely, and nowadays, even when it is only a matter of hasty diversion, a woman who is old or ugly is promptly turned down. "For a thousand men who see, there are a thousand blind." So the saying goes; but on that night, alas, I did not meet a single one who was blind!   643

Finally dawn began to appear: first the eight bells rang out,   644
then seven. Aroused by their sound, the pack-horse drivers set forth with a clatter in the early-morning light. Yet I persisted in walking the streets, until the hour when the blacksmith and the bean-curd dealer opened their shutters. But no doubt my appearance and demeanour were not suited to this calling, for during the entire time not a single man solicited my favours. I resolved, then, that this would be my last effort in the Floating World at plying the lustful trade, and I gave it up for once and all.

THE FIVE HUNDRED DISCIPLES WHO   645
FOUND A PLACE IN MY HEART

When the evening of the year arrives, the myriad trees on the hills fall asleep and the branches of the cherry trees are laden with snow. Yet all these can look forward to the dawn of spring. Only human beings are such that once they are beset with age, they can no longer hope for any pleasure. Especially barren was my own old age, laden as I was with a shameful past. To pray for my salvation in the next world was the only true path that I could follow, so once more I returned to the capital. Approaching the city, I was inspired by the worthy notion of paying my respects at the Daiun   646
Temple, the paradise of this present world.

It was just at the season when people perform the Recitation of   647 the Holy Names, and I, too, joined in the chanting. On leaving the main temple, I found myself in the Hall of the Five Hundred Disciples, and I stopped there to examine the holy images. I do not know who the sculptor may have been, but he had so skilfully fashioned the Buddhas that each one looked different from the others. I had heard it said that among this great throng of statues one was bound to come across some that reminded one of acquaintances. Aye, thought I, that seemed most probable, and I began to observe them carefully.

It was then that I perceived that all these statues were perfect images of men with whom I had shared a pillow in my palmy days.
That Buddha over there was like Yoshi-sama from Chojamachi, who had a hidden tattoo on his arm. I was thinking fondly of how, in my days as a courtesan, he and I had exchanged the tenderest pledges of affection; at that moment I noticed that a Buddha ensconced behind one of the rocks was the very image of the master whom I had served as parlourmaid in the Kamigyo district and with whom I had shared all manner of unforgettable intimacy.

Then on the other side I saw an image that did not differ one jot from that gentleman called Gobei with whom I had once lived: even the arched nose was the same as his. Ours had been a troth that kept us together for many a long moon, and it was with especial nostalgia that I gazed at this image.

Closer at hand was a plump figure, clad in a pale-blue robe that fell off one shoulder. He reminded me vaguely of someone, but who could it be? Ah yes, of course, there could be no mistaking him! It was Dampei of Kojimachi, who, when I was working in Edo, had enjoyed regular assignations with me each month on the Six Days of Fasting. Then on one of the rocks in the back I noticed a pale-faced Buddha. This called to mind a certain handsome man who had been an actor in Shijogawara. I had come to know him when I was employed in a teahouse, and it was thanks to me that

The heroine stands in the Daiun Temple outside Kyoto and looks at the statues of the Five Hundred Disciples surrounding the Amida Buddha. One by one she is reminded of all the men to whom she has given herself during her long career.

this young man first became acquainted with the love of women. In my company he had exhausted all the various postures, until before long his days were folded up; he was snuffed out like the candle in a folded paper lantern and, at the age of twenty-three, was consigned to Toribéno. Ay, with that thin chin and those sunken eyes, there could be no doubt that it was he.

My eyes lighted on a moustachioed Buddha with a bald head and a ruddy face. Were it not for the moustache, one would instantly have recognized him as that priest with whom I had lived as a temple wife and at whose hands I had suffered such cruel usage. Accustomed as I was to amorous sport, there was as a rule no limit to my capacity; but this priest had so pressed himself on me both day and night that in the end I had contracted some form of consumption. Yet there is a limit for every human being, and even this vigorous gentleman had ended in smoke.

Then under a withered tree I beheld an intelligent-looking Buddha with a projecting forehead, who seemed to be in the act of shaving his head. So lifelike was this figure that its limbs seemed to move as I watched, and the only thing it did not do was utter human speech. The more I looked, the more it came to remind me of someone. Ah yes, this was the warehouse clerk from the West Country whom I had known during my time as a singing nun! Although I had consorted with different men every day, he had stood out among them all through his devotion. He would have sacrificed his very life on my behalf! No, this was someone I could never forget, for both the happy and unhappy moments we had shared. He had bestowed on me that which the people of this world so greatly prize, and had even exerted himself to defray my manager's fee.

As I stood there gazing calmly at these five hundred Buddhas, I found that every single one reminded me of some man with whom in the past I had been intimate. I thought back incident by incident on all my years in the sad floating trade, and felt that nothing in the world is so terrible as a woman who practises this calling. The men I had met numbered more than ten thousand, yet my body was only one. Shameful and wretched it was that only thus had I lingered in this world! My breast seemed to roar like the chariot of fire and tears welled up in my eyes like bubbles of boiling water. I was overcome by a delirium of grief, and quite forgetting that I was in a temple, I fell down to the ground.   *666*

As I lay there, a great company of priests entered the hall. "It will soon be dark," said one of them, and they began to ring the bell for vespers. As I came to my senses, I heard a priest say, "What can have brought this old woman to such a state of sorrow?" Turning to me, he continued, "Does one of these Buddhas remind you of some dead child of yours, or your husband? Is that why you weep so?"

To be addressed in such a kindly fashion made me feel even more ashamed, and, without so much as replying, I hurried out of the temple gates.

It was then that I reached my great decision; for I perceived the truth of the poet's words, "One's name remains in the world; but *667* one's body, having lost its every feature, is cast at the bottom of the pine-clad hill. The bones thereof are transformed into dust and scattered by the pond among the weeds."

I made my way to the foot of Mount Narutaki. Now I was bound by no fetters, and could freely enter the mountain of enlightenment; aye, now I could release the ship of the Sacred Law *668* from her moorings and, having crossed the sea of evil passions, *669* could aspire to reach the other shore. All this I could achieve by consigning my body to the waters of that pond! I started running *670* thither, filled with this most earnest resolve, but on the way was stopped by an old acquaintance, who provided me with this thatched hut where I now dwell.

"Leave death to its own season!" said this good counsellor.

"Turn your back on the falsehood in which you have lived, regain your purity of heart and enter the path of Buddhahood!"

671 Convinced that this was a worthy course to follow, I thereafter gave myself up wholeheartedly to invoking the Sacred Name from morning until night. But today, having received unwonted visitors at this rude wooden door, and being bemused with sakè, I have been led to trouble you needlessly with a story far too long for this short life of ours.

672 By this confession of my sins I have cleared away the clouds of my own delusion, and I feel that the moon of my heart is shining forth. For you young gentlemen, who came here especially to visit me, I have tried to provide diversion befitting this spring night. As I am but a single woman, it seemed bootless to hide anything. I have revealed my whole life to you, from the day when the lotus of my heart first opened, until its petals withered. I may have lived in this world by selling my body, but is my heart itself polluted?

THE ETERNAL STOREHOUSE OF JAPAN

New Lessons from the Lives of Wealthy Men

THE WIND THAT DESTROYED THE FAN
MAKER'S SHOP IN THE SECOND
GENERATION

The plum, the cherry, the pine and the maple—these are what 673
people like having in their houses. But more than this, in truth,
they want gold, silver, rice and coppers!

There was a man who considered that the prospect of his garden 674
storehouse was more pleasing by far than any hillock which might
adorn his garden, and that the pleasure of stocking this storehouse
with the various goods that he had bought up in the course of the 675
year was in no wise inferior to the joys of Kiken Castle. This man 676
dwelt in the present licentious city of Kyoto. Yet never once in his
life had he crossed the Bridge of the Fourth Avenue to the east, or 677
ventured west from Omiyadori to Tambaguchi. Nor did he sum-
mon priests from the surrounding hills, or consort with *ronin*. 678,679
When he had a slight cold or a stomach-ache, he used whatever
medicine he might have on hand.

All day long he worked hard at his business; when evening came,
he stayed at home and, for his own distraction, sang the *No* songs 680
that he had learned in his youth, reciting them in a natural voice, so 681
that he might not disturb his neighbours. He always sang from
memory without using a text, and thus managed to save the cost of
oil for the lamp. Indeed, he never indulged in a single needless ex-
pense. Not once in his entire life did he step on the cords of his san-
dals and break them; not once did he catch his sleeve on a nail and
tear it. He exercised care in all that he did and, in the course of the
years, amassed a fortune of one hundred and fifty hundredweight of 682

silver. When he reached the age of eighty-seven, people regarded him with envy, and, aspiring to take after this worthy elder, asked
683 him to carve them a strickle.

684 Nevertheless, there comes a limit to every man's life, and when the autumn rains began to fall that year, distressing clouds of ill health gathered about him. Before they knew it, the old man was dead. His only son was standing by his deathbed. He inherited his father's entire fortune, and thus at the age of twenty, without any
685 exertion on his own part, became a man of great wealth.

For this young man economy was even more important than it had been for his sire. When it came to distributing keepsakes to the numerous relatives, he would not give so much as a single chopstick.
686 As soon as the ceremonies of the seven days were finished, he opened the shutters and the front door of his shop and began to devote himself single-mindedly to business. He thought constantly of ways to save money. When he went to pay a visit of condolence to people who had suffered loss in a fire, he walked slowly, lest he should needlessly stimulate his appetite.

Thus the year drew to an end, and before long it was the anniversary of his father's death. On this occasion the young man visited the family temple to pay his respects. On his return home he was plunged in memories of the past, and the tears flowed over the sleeves of his kimono.

"Father used to wear these very clothes," he muttered to himself. "Well I remember how he used to say that this hand-woven chequered pongee was the most durable material. Ah yes, life is indeed a
687 precious thing! If he had but lived another twenty-two years, he
688 would have been a full hundred. It is truly a loss to die as young as he did!" So it was that even in matters of living and dying, avarice came first for this young man.

689 As he passed the bamboo hedge of the Imperial Botanical Gardens in the neighbourhood of Murasakino, the servant girl who accom-

panied him noticed a sealed letter lying on the ground. She was carrying the empty bag for offertory rice in one hand; with her free hand she picked up the letter. Her master took it from her and read the inscription, "For Hanakawa from Nisan." The letter had been closed with rice paste, and carefully impressed with a seal, over which were clearly written the characters, *"The Five Great Bodhisattvas."*

"Hanakawa—that is surely the name of some great nobleman of whom I have not heard," said the fan maker, and when he returned home, he made inquiries of his assistant.

"This must have been addressed to some strumpet in the Shimabara," he said at a glance, and handed the letter back to him.

"Well," said the young man, "at least I have profited by acquiring one sheet of good Sugihara paper. I don't come out the loser."

So saying, he calmly broke the seal, whereupon one rectangular gold piece dropped out of the letter.

"Good heavens!" he cried in utter amazement, and lost no time in testing the coin with his touchstone. Having made sure that it was solid gold, he placed it on the upper scale of his weighing machine and found to his delight that it weighed precisely one *mommé* and two *fun*. Calming his throbbing breast, he admonished his servants to keep silence.

"This was an unforeseen stroke of luck," he said. "Do not breathe a word about it to anyone outside!"

The fan maker then looked at the letter, and found that it was a sensible piece of writing, in which everything was clearly set forth in businesslike form:

"I am well aware that this is the season for requests, but the fact is that I, too, am pressed for money. However, because of my great devotion to you, I have drawn in advance on my spring stipend and am able to send you the enclosed coin. Pray use two *mommé* out of this to defray the various entertainment expenses that I have incurred. All the rest I bestow on you, so that you can pay off any debts that may have accumulated during the past year.

"The gifts that people give should always be attuned to their standing in the world. Thus it is that a certain great merrymaker from the West Country could give three hundred gold coins to Nokazé of the Ozakaya, telling her, 'This is to see you through the Chrysanthemum Festival.' Now when I send you this one humble coin, my intention is no less than his. If I had more to give, you may be sure that I should not begrudge anything on your behalf.."

Thus was the letter charged with feeling, and, as he read it, the fan maker felt more and more sorry for the unknown couple. "Whatever happens," he thought, "I cannot keep this money for myself. That would be a terrible thing to do to a man who shows such devotion. But since I don't know his address, how can I return the letter? My only proper course is to go to Shimabara, whose whereabouts I know, to ask for Hanakawa and to deliver the coin to her myself."

With this resolve in mind, he smoothed down his side-locks and left the house. On his way it occurred to him that it was a shame to return the coin free of charge, and time after time he almost changed his mind and retraced his steps. Nevertheless he soon reached the gate of the gay quarters.

He hesitated before entering, and, while he stood there, a man came out of a house of assignation to fetch some sakè. The fan maker approached him and said, "Pray, sir, may I inquire whether it is all right for me to enter this gate without advance notice?"

The man did not deign to reply, but simply nodded his head.

"Well, I suppose it's all right," thought the fan maker, and removing his sedge hat, he entered the gay quarters, crouching timidly as he walked. He soon passed in front of the teahouses and reached the streets where the ladies of pleasure lived. Here he approached the great courtesan, known as the Present-Day Morokoshi of the Ichimonjiya, who was just then setting forth in full style to join a customer at a house of assignation.

"Where might I find the lady called Madam Hanakawa?" he asked her. The courtesan did not answer him directly, but simply turned to the procuress by her side and said, "I do not know." The procuress pointed to a shop with blue curtains, saying, "You'd *708* better ask someone over there." Meanwhile, the manservant who was following the courtesan glared angrily at the fan maker and shouted, "Bring that doxy of yours over here and let's have a look at her!"

"I am calling on her for my own business," replied the fan maker, "and don't require any help from you." So saying, he stepped aside and let them pass.

After numerous inquiries he finally discovered the correct house. On his arrival someone hurriedly informed him that Hanakawa was a trollop whose price was fixed at two *mommé* of silver. For the *709* past few days, however, she had been unwell and confined to her bed.

Now as the fan maker set forth on his return journey, with the letter still undelivered, he was overcome by an unwonted mood of wantonness. "In actual fact," he told himself, "this gold coin does not belong to me. Why don't I enjoy myself here, just to the extent that this money will permit? I could make this day serve as a memory for my entire life, something to talk about in my old age."

So resolved, he made inquiries at a teahouse (a proper house of assignation being far too expensive for his taste) and arranged to visit the second storey of the Fujiya Hikoémon. Here he summoned *710* a courtesan at nine *mommé* of silver for the day period. Being un- *711* accustomed to sakè, it was not long before he found himself utterly bemused.

Thereafter the fan maker set his hand to these new pursuits.

He began to exchange love letters with various women of the quarter, and gradually moved up in the hierarchy from low to high-ranking courtesans, until in the end he had bought the favours of every single top courtesan in Shimabara.

712   At the time there was a group of jesters in the capital known as the Four Heavenly Kings—Gansai, Kagura, Omu and Rashu. He was flattered and goaded on by these men, and in time became most adept in the ways of the world, so that the fops of the city began to copy their fashions from his. People called him "Mr. Love-Wind of the Fan Shop"; and truly he blew his money away like so much chaff.

    There is no telling a man's destiny in this world. In the case of the
713 young fan maker we find that after a few years not a speck of dust or ash remained from his great fortune of one hundred and fifty
714 hundredweight of silver. He did not even have the strength to blow the embers of the fire, and all that was left him was an old fan, a reminder, as it were, of the great fan shop that had once been his. Having sunk to the state of a beggar, he lived from hand to mouth and went about singing the words of the old ballad, which now
715 so aptly described his own fate: "Once in prosperity, later in adversity."

    Observing this example, a certain strait-laced gentleman who
716 owned the Kamadaya told the story to his children. "In these days when money is so hard to make," said he, "imagine having squandered it all like that!"

717   THE DAIKOKU WHO WORE READY WIT
                IN HIS SEDGE HAT

718 When we survey the two-storeyed houses packed with bales of rice and the three-storeyed warehouses, we find among their owners
719 a certain man of wealth who was the proprietor of the shop in

Kyoto known as the Daikokuya. This man's greatest wish had been
to live in affluence, and when the Bridge of the Fifth Avenue was   *720*
being rebuilt in stone, he had bought the third plank from the west   *721*
end of the bridge and had it carved into an image of Daikoku, the
God of Wealth. Truly there is profit in faith; for thereafter he in-   *722*
creased steadily in prosperity. He called his shop the Daikokuya
Shimbei; and there was no one in the capital who did not know
him.

In bringing up his three sons he exerted the greatest care, and to
his delight, they all turned out to be clever lads. He was looking for-
ward to fully enjoying the consolations of old age and was making
plans for presently retiring from active life when his eldest son,
Shinroku, suddenly embarked on a reckless course of libertinism.
He spent money like water and, before half a year had elapsed,
twelve hundredweight of silver in ready cash were missing from   *723*
the accounts in the ledger of receipts. The clerks examined the
matter, but could find no easy way to set it arights. They therefore
consulted with Shinroku himself and finally contrived to adjust the
accounts so that it looked as if the missing money had in fact been
used to lay in stock. Thus they helped him through the eve of the   *724*
Seventh Moon.

"Henceforth, sir," they pleaded with him, "give up your
extravagant ways!"

But Shinroku paid not the slightest heed to their counsel, and at
the end of that year the accounts were out of balance by a further
one thousand seven hundredweight of silver. This time the matter   *725*
came to light and the young man was obliged to flee the parental   *726*
roof and to take refuge with an acquaintance of his who dwelt hard
by the Inari Shrine.

His upright sire was greatly incensed and, although various pleas
were advanced on the young man's behalf, he would not be rec-
onciled. He had the town members don their ceremonial skirts and,   *727*

217

728 having submitted a bill of disownment, he cast Shinroku out alone into the world. His was truly a wrathful nature that he could become thus utterly estranged from his own son.

Shinroku now saw that there was no help for it, and, unable to
729 remain any longer in his temporary lodgings, he set out for the East. Realizing that he could not afford to buy even a pair of sandals for the journey, he was plunged in lonely sorrow. However, lamentations were of no avail.

On the evening of the twenty-eighth day of the Twelfth Moon Shinroku was having his bath when the cry rang out, "Your father's here!" Terrified at this news, the young man threw some wadded clothes over his wet body and, without even bothering about his loincloth, grabbed his sash and fled the place. As he now set forth
730 on his journey, he was much distraught at not even being able to tuck up his clothes.

On the following day the sky was unsettled. The scattered flakes of snow settled heavily on the pine groves of Fujinomori. Shinroku did not even have the protection of a sedge hat and the moisture dripped down his neck, while the mournful sound of the temple bell announcing the vespers echoed in his heart. At Okamédani and Kanjuji he was attracted by the sight of the teahouses, where steam issued pleasantly from the kettles. Here he might have found refuge from the unbearable cold; but he did not have a single copper to his name and had to give up all thought of resting. A constant stream of palanquins stopped at the inns on their way to Otsu and Fushimi, and in the bustle of the crowds Shinroku managed to enter one of the places and to quench his thirst with a cup of water. On leaving he took along a piece of Teshima matting that someone had hung up on entering the teahouse. Having thus for the first time been inspired by the idea of theft, he made his way to the village of Ono.

Under a bare persimmon tree a group of children had gathered,

The spendthrift Shinroku is surprised by his irate father and has to make a quick escape from his bath. Three bathhouse girls excitedly watch the scene; at the bottom left a servant holds the young man's clothes.

and Shinroku heard them lamenting, "Alas, Benkei is dead!" Benkei turned out to be a great black dog, the size of a prize bull. Shinroku went up to the children and obtained the body from them. He wrapped it in his piece of matting, and, when he reached the foot of Mount Otowa, beckoned to a man who was ploughing the fields.

731   "This dog," said he, "will make a wondrous cure for inflammation of the brain. For three years I have been feeding him on various medicines and now I am going to char the body."

"Aye, to be sure," said the man, "this will be of great benefit to our people."

Shinroku gathered brushwood and dried bamboo grass from round about, and, taking out his flint bag, set fire to the dog. He gave some of the charred ashes to the villager and wrapped the remainder in his matting, which he flung over his shoulder. Thereafter Shinroku went from place to place peddling the ashes. "Charred wolf for sale!" he cried in a strange voice, aping the dialect of the mountain folk.

732   He crosssed the Osaka Barrier, where people leaving the capital pass those who return, and thrust his wares "on people who knew
733   each other and those who were strangers." Even sharp needle pedlars and men who sold writing brushes, accustomed though they were to the wiles of itinerant salesmen, were tricked by Shin-
734,735 roku's deception. From Oiwaké to Hatcho he received five hundred and eighty coppers, thus for the first time earning the title of a man of ready wit.

"If only I had hit on this scheme while I was still in Kyoto, I should not have had to venture all the way to Edo!" he thought, and, as he walked along, he was plunged into alternate moods of sorrow and of joy.

736   Crossing the Long Bridge of Seta, he wished that it might bode him well. He welcomed the New Year at a travellers' inn in Kusatsu

near Mount Kagami, and, as he munched the Uba rice cakes, he called   737
to mind the Kagami rice cakes that he had eaten in past years.

When he saw the village of Sakurayama, where the cherry trees
were almost in bloom, the flower of his heart, too, began to blos-
som forth and he regained his spirits.

"I am still in the bloom of my youth," he told himself, "and
have lost neither the colour nor the fragrance of my young years.
The God of Poverty is not so fleet of foot that he can catch up with   738
true diligence. Indeed, he is but a tottering old man."

While he was thinking in this way, he noticed the sacred straw
festoons in the Forest of Oiso and was put in mind of the approach-
ing spring. This must be a pleasant place for seeing the moon in the   739
autumn, reflected Shinroku as he continued on his journey. He
advanced steadily day after day, crossed the Fuwa Barrier, followed
the Mino Highway into Owari, passed the several stages of the
Tokaido and on the sixty-second day after leaving the capital   740
arrived at Shinagawa.   741

The sale of the dog medicine had so far provided him with his
subsistence and he still had two *kan* and three hundred *mon* of copper   742
in reserve. He now threw what remained of the charred animal into
the waves of the sea and hastened his entry into Edo. As it was be-
coming dark, and as he had no particular destination in mind, he de-
cided to spend his first night before the gate of the Tokai Temple.   743

Hard by the temple gates lay a small group of outcasts clad in   744
rush matting. Even in springtime the wind blows violently from the
bay, and it is noisy for those whose pillows are close to the waves of   745
the seashore. Unable to sleep, the outcasts lay there into the depth of
the night, telling each other their life stories. As he listened to them,
Shinroku discovered that they were all men who, like himself,
had been cut off from their families.   746

One of them came from the village of Tatsuta in Yamato. "I used
to have a small sakè brewery," he said, "and was easily able to

support my fair-sized family on the proceeds. But as my savings accumulated and reached the sum of one hundred gold *koban,* I decided that business in that place was too sluggish for my taste. I gave up everything and came down to Edo. My entire family and my close friends tried to stop me with all sorts of arguments, but I

747 let recklessness rule the day and rented a vintner's provision shop on Gofukucho.

"My new place was on a street with several sakè shops that displayed signs advertising 'Finest Quality Sakè Made of Pure White Rice and Yeast.' Yet it was hard for us to compete with such well-established manufacturers as Konoiké, Itami, Ikéda and Nanto, whose sakè bore the fine aroma of their cedar casks. Finally, it came about that I had wasted all my capital in vain. I was destitute and had nothing to wear but a piece of rush matting that had formerly been used to wrap round a sixteen-gallon cask. I do not care about

748 wearing red-tinged brocade. If only I had a new suit of wadded cotton clothes, I should return to my home-place of Tatsuta, but alas . . ." His words were lost in bitter tears.

"This should teach one," he continued after a while, "not to give up the business for which one has been reared."

But it was impossible for him now to profit from this lesson; for when wisdom comes to a man, it is already too late.

Another of the outcasts hailed from Sakai in the province of Izumi. He had been a most versatile young man who had come down to Edo full of confidence in his own artistic talents. Here he studied calligraphy under Hirano Chuan, the tea ceremony under Kanamori Sowa, Chinese poetry under Gensei of Fukakusa, linked

749,750 verses and *haikai* under Nishiyama Soin, *No* dancing under the fan of Kobataké and the hand drum under Shoda Yoémon. In the morn-

751 ings he listened to the Way, as expounded by Ito Genkichi; in the evenings he learned the art of *kemari* from Asukai-dono; in the daytime he participated in the *go* meetings of Gensai; at night, he took

222

lessons in the *koto* from Yatsuhashi Kengo. For the small flute he   752,753
became a disciple of Sosan; for the *joruri* he studied the songs of   754
Uji Kadayu; for dancing, he was trained by Jimbei of the Yamato-
ya. The top-ranking courtesan, Takahashi of the Shimabara, trained
him in the ways of the gay quarters, and Suzuki Heihachi taught him   755
how to consort with young boys: before long, the drum-holders of
both the gay quarters came to regard him as a true man of the   756
world in matters of merrymaking. Thus this man succeeded in
learning each art from the outstanding expert in the field, and he
was confident that he could acquit himself with distinction in
whatever company he might find himself.

Yet when it comes to making a living, artistic versatility is of
little use, and soon the young man was to regret that he could not
manipulate the abacus or the weighing scales. Knowing nothing of
the warrior's life, he took service as a merchant's apprentice, but was
dismissed on grounds of negligence. Thus finally he had sunk to his
present state. As he recalled all these circumstances, he was moved
with rancour against his parents. "Why could they not teach me
how to make a living," he said, "instead of all those artistic skills?"

Another man who lay there was a native-born inhabitant of Edo,
his family being indigenous to the city. He had owned a great
mansion on Toricho and enjoyed a fixed income of six hundred
gold *koban* a year from his property. But since he could not grasp
the sense of the two syllables "frugal," he had ended by having to
sell even his own house. The young man did not know what to
do with himself, and finally he fled the heart-consuming mansion   757
of anguish and became an unregistered beggar under Kuruma Zen-   758,759
shichi.

As Shinroku listened to these tales, he realized that all these men
had suffered the same fate as himself. He was deeply moved with
sympathy for them, and, approaching them, said, "I am a man of
Kyoto. Having been disowned, I came down here to try my luck in

Edo. But now that I have heard each of you tell his story, my future seems less hopeful." He then told them without reserve of his own circumstances.

Having heard his story, the outcasts said with one accord, "Have
760 you no way of making your apologies? Have you no aunt who could intercede for you? On no account should you have come down to Edo."

"All that belongs to a past to which there is no return," replied Shinroku. "Now I must make my plans for the future. Each of you who lies here is a clever man, and it seems strange that you should all have sunk to such a sorry state. If you had settled on some form of work, whatever it might be, surely you would have found what you wanted."

"Far from it," said the outcasts. "This is a great castle town, to be sure, but it is also the gathering place for the shrewdest people from all Japan and they won't let one come by even a couple of
761 coppers for nothing. When all is said and done, people who have money in this world think only of piling up more money."

"Yet surely," said Shinroku, "while you have been looking about the place, you must have hit upon some new shift for making money."

"Indeed," they replied. "You can pick up the shells that are al-
762 ways being thrown away in great quantities, take them to Reigan Island and make them into lime by burning. Also, since trade is so lively in this city, you can prepare shredded seaweed or the shavings of dried bonito and go about the streets hawking it by the measure. You can also buy lengths of cotton and cut them into towels which can be sold by the piece. But apart from that, you won't find any simple way of making money in these parts."

Shinroku thereupon conceived his plan. As soon as dawn broke, he took leave of the outcasts, first bestowing three hundred coppers upon the three men to whom he had spoken. They were beside themselves with joy.

"Your luck will be sure to turn," they said, "and before long your wealth will be piled as high as Mount Fuji itself!"

Having left Shinagawa, Shinroku went to call on an acquaintance of his who had a draper's shop on Temmacho. He told him of his present circumstances and received a sympathetic response.

"This is a good city for a man to work," the draper told him. "I shall help you."

Shinroku was much enlivened by these words. As he had planned, he now bought some lengths of cotton and cut them into towels. Then on the twenty-fifth day of the Third Moon he pro- 763 ceeded to the Tenjin Shrine at Shitaya and started selling the towels by the water stand. Those who had come to pay their respects at the shrine bought his wares, saying, "Luck to the buyer," and by the 764 evening Shinroku had cleared a good profit.

Every day thereafter he thought of some new device for making money, and before ten years had elapsed, he had become the cynosure of admiration for his ready wit, and was noted as a man 765 of wealth worth no less than five thousand *koban*. The townsmen came to him for guidance and he was now the very treasure of the people in that place. He had his shop curtains dyed with a painting of the god Daikoku wearing a sedge hat, and people therefore called his shop the Sedge-Hat Daikoku. 766

Eighth, he had access to the residences of the various *samurai;* 767 ninth, he invested his wealth in gold *koban;* tenth, he had the good 768 fortune to live in no other period than this peaceful and auspicious 769 reign.

THE TEN VIRTUES OF TEA THAT ALL
DISAPPEARED AT ONCE

Numerous are the ships that call at the harbour of Tsuruga in the province of Echizen. The daily keelage is said to average one great gold piece—no less, indeed, than what is collected from all the boats that ply the Yodo River. Every manner of wholesale merchant flourishes in this place. Things are especially lively when autumn comes; the markets bustle with activity, numerous temporary buildings are put up for business and it is as though one had the capital itself before one's eyes. Nor is it only a world of men; for the women whom one sees are handsome and of good disposition. Truly, this can be called the Kyoto of the North.

Strolling players make their way to this town, and it is also a favourite resort for pickpockets. The inhabitants, therefore, have learned to be careful; they never carry their medicine boxes hanging from their sashes, and they even tuck their bags under their clothes where no one can reach them. It is impossible to get so much as a single copper from these people for nothing, and even when robbers speak of this town they sigh and say, "What a difficult world we live in!" Yet, difficult though it may be, he who goes about his trade diligently and with an honest head, who treats even his casual customers with respect and who is ever ready to welcome buyers in his shop will never be hard put to make his livelihood.

Now in the suburbs of this town there lived a man of ready wit called Risuké of Kobashi, who, having neither wife nor children, was obliged to support himself. For this end, he had equipped himself in fine fashion with a portable tea stall. He tied back his sleeves with a spruce sash, smartly tucked up the bottom of his trousers and wore an Ebisu headgear with most comic effect. Thus attired, he would set out early in the morning before anyone else was about and walk through the market streets, calling out, "Ebisu morning tea for sale!" Hearing this cry, the merchants, who were ever looking out for something new, would buy his tea, even though they might not be thirsty, and as a rule would throw twelve coppers into his cup.   778

Every day Risuké made more money, and before long he had accumulated a goodly capital. He used this to start a large tea shop; later he began to employ numerous clerks and became one of the great wholesale merchants of the town. By dint of hard work he grew to be a man of wealth and basked in the sun of universal admiration. Many notable families in the area were desirous of having   779 him for a son-in-law, but he invariably replied, "I shall not marry until my fortune has grown to ten thousand *koban*. Even if I should have to wait until I am forty, it won't be too late." He calculated every expenditure with the minutest care, and thus one lonely year followed another, with the accumulation of money as his only pleasure.

In the course of time Risuké was inspired to indulge in some base trickery, and he dispatched one of his clerks to Etchu and to Echigo to buy up discarded tea grounds. He gave out that these were to be used for dyeing material in Kyoto, but in fact he mixed the grounds with the tea leaves in his shop and sold them to unsuspecting customers. For a time this practice bore fruit and his business flourished more than ever. But it would seem that Heaven wished to rebuke him; for thereafter Risuké suddenly went mad and himself began to spread abroad an account of his own misdeeds.

"Tea grounds, tea grounds!" he prated, until people began to mutter among themselves, "Ah, so it was by such knavish practices that he acquired all that wealth!" and they would have no more to do with him. Risuké summoned a physician, but none would answer his call. Gradually he became so weak that he could not even swallow a glass of water. As his end was not far off, Risuké tear-

227

fully addressed his attendants, saying, "This is the last request of my life. Pray bring me a cup of tea."

They brought him tea, but his evil karma seemed to have formed a barrier in his throat and he could not swallow a drop. His final breath was approaching when he bade his attendants bring forth the money from his indoor storehouse. He spread it out by his feet and next to his pillow, muttering, "When I am dead, who will get all this money? Alas, alas, how grievous it all is!"

With these words he clung to his money and gnashed his teeth. *780* The tears gushed from his eyes like scarlet streaks of blood and his expression was that of a hornless blue devil. Next he began to run round the room like some sort of phantom. When he collapsed, his attendants held him. Again and again he revived, and each time he insisted on examining his money to make sure that it was all there.

Finally, the servants became disaffected and regarded their master with terror, so that none of them would remain in his room. They all gathered in the kitchen, each one holding a club in his hand for protection. When a few days had passed with no sound from Risuké, several of the servants went to the door of the sickroom. They peered into the room over each other's shoulders and saw their dead master lying there, with his money still clasped to his breast, his eyes wide open. At this sight they came near to fainting with horror. With no further ado they packed Risuké into a palanquin just as he was, and set off for the place of cremation.

It was a balmy spring day when they left the house; but suddenly the sky was covered with black clouds and drops of rain as large as carriage wheels began to pour down, soon becoming a great torrent *781* that flowed through the fields. The wind roared in the trees, breaking off the dead branches, and here and there one could see the glitter of fires that had been caused by lightning. It seemed to the attendants that the devil himself was going to carry off Risuké's body before it was turned into smoke, and that they would be left there with an empty palanquin. Now indeed the men found themselves face to face with the burning mansion of anguish, and each of them fled *782* home, overcome with a devout desire to compass his salvation.

After Risuké's death his distant relatives were invited to a distribution of his property; but they, having heard the story of his end, were overcome with fear and would not accept so much as a single chopstick. Consequently they summoned Risuké's servants, saying, "You may share this property among yourselves." But the servants replied, "We desire no part or parcel of it," and they all left the house, not taking along so much as the livery that they had received during their service. Thus we see that even people who are hardened with greed can on occasion act against the dictates of cold reason.

Since there was no help for it, all of Risuké's possessions were sold and the proceeds offered to his parish temple. This was an unexpected stroke of luck for the priests, who, instead of using the money for memorial services, went up to Kyoto and spent it on disporting themselves with young actors, thus making Risuké's wealth a source of joy to the teahouses of the Eastern Hills. *783*

Strange to relate, even after Risuké was dead, his form wandered about the shops of the wholesale dealers, demanding the debts that were due to him from past years. The merchants, who knew full well that he had died, were terrified to see this apparition, and all of them repaid him, weighing the silver properly and taking care not to give him short measure. These things were bruited abroad and Risuké's dwelling came to be known as the Ghost House. Even when it was offered free, no one would accept it, and it was allowed to go to rack and ruin.

When we take note of all this, we see that certain practices must be eschewed, however profitable they may be. To pawn worthless objects with no intention of redeeming them, to deal in various forms of counterfeit, to trick a girl into marriage in order to lay hands on her dowry, to borrow Mass money from temples and to

Clutching his precious money-bags, the mad tea dealer rushes about his room in a death dance while his horror-stricken servants arm themselves with sticks. Strings of copper coins and packets of gold and silver lie scattered on the floor. At the right a Buddhist priest sits with the agitated maidservants. In the garden on the left is the type of storehouse *(kura)* after which the book is named.

avoid repayment by going into bankruptcy, to join a gang of gamblers, to sell worthless mines by means of trickery, to force people
784 into buying ginseng against their will, to arrange for a man to commit fornication with a married woman and then to blackmail him with the threat of exposure, to sell stolen dogs, to receive money for looking after babies and then to let them starve to death,
785 to pluck the hair from the heads of drowned people and sell it—all these may be means to make a living; but for him who indulges in such brutish ways, it were better that he had never enjoyed the small chance of having been born into this world in human form.

Nothing that he does seems wicked to him who is already tainted with evil. But, when we look at these various shameful ways of making money, we perceive that only he who earns his living by proper means can really be called a human being. The life of man may be a dream; yet it lasts some fifty years, and whatever honest work we may choose in this world, we shall surely find it.

RECKONINGS THAT CARRY MEN THROUGH
THE WORLD

AT THE YEAR'S END A SINGLE DAY
IS WORTH A THOUSAND POUNDS OF GOLD

For an eclipse of the sun to fall on the morning of New Year's Day is a rare event indeed, but it happened sixty-nine years ago and again   *786* in the Year of the Monkey under the ninth sign of the calendar,   *787* that is, in the fifth year of Genroku. Since the Gio calendar was first introduced into our country in the fourth year of Empress Jito's   *788* reign, new calendars have frequently come into use, but they are all alike in being founded on the eclipses of the sun and moon, and no one can dispute their accuracy. Having made our way through the entire year from the opening line of New Year's Day, we reach the final passage, which is New Year's Eve. On this day people are   *789* all in a flurry of activity as they prepare for the New Year's celebrations, and no one has time for singing *joruri* or ditties.

Things are especially busy in the poorer parts of the town where people live crowded in their hovels. Here everything seems to come together on the same day; the men and women bustle about the place, some of them quarrelling, others doing the final laundry for the year, still others patching up the frames of their plastered walls. Yet, though they are all hard at work preparing for the New Year, none of them can possibly afford to enjoy a piece of rice cake or a   *790* dried sardine. When we compare these folk with those who live in more prosperous state, their lives seem wretched and pitiful indeed.

In one poor part of the town there was a row of half a dozen tenement huts. One might well wonder how these people were going to tide themselves over the New Year's holidays. Yet none of them seemed worried about managing their expenses; for each family was depending on putting some object in pawn. According to their normal practice, they had paid their rent that day. All credit sales were suspended during the holidays; such household necessaries as they might require—rice, bean-paste, vinegar, soy sauce, salt and

791 oil—could all be bought with ready cash. Now they knew that they could rest at ease: no bill collector would intrude into their houses, carrying his account book and dunning them for payment, as happened on the other seasonal days of payment; there was no need for the poor people to be frightened, or to make apologies to

792 anyone. "There are pleasures in poverty" is an ancient saying, and these are no empty words.

When we look about us in the world, we see that people who are in far less straitened circumstances than those who inhabit these

793 huts often fail to pay their bills. Such people are no better than day-time thieves who have managed to insinuate themselves into the world of honest men. All too many people live prodigally during the year, buying everything on credit and failing to make their monthly accounting; and it is not surprising that, when the final day of payment comes, such people should be unable to settle their bills. Compared to them, the poor people in the tenements, who live from hand to mouth and whose daily expenses are but trifling, do not require so much as a petty-cash book, and they manage to end the year without too much anxiety.

Yet we cannot help pitying them as they prepare to get through the New Year holidays by pawning their few possessions. One of the families pawned an umbrella, a cotton gin and a tea kettle, and for these three items was able to borrow one *mommé* of silver. In the house next door the mother had to give up the sash that she wore every day and in its place use a piece of twisted-paper string; to-gether with the sash, this family pawned one man's cotton ker-chief, one small nest of boxes without a lid, a weaver's reed big

794 enough for three hundred warp-threads, a one-*go* and a five-*go*

measure box, five porcelain Minatoyaki dishes, one mounted   *795*
image of Buddha for hanging on the wall, together with various
Buddhist altar fittings; and for all these twenty-three items they
received just one *mommé* six *fun*. Thus they saw in the New Year.

Another neighbour was an entertainer. Until then he had spe-   *796*
cialized in the Kowaka Dances, but during New Year's he was go-
ing to change to the Daikoku dance. Having decided that he could   *797*
manage with just a five-copper mask and a paper hammer, he
pawned his ceremonial headgear, his ceremonial robe and his wide
trouser skirt for two *mommé* seven *fun* and thus contrived to spend
the holidays at his ease.

In the next-door house lived a peevish, impecunious *ronin*. He   *798*
had long since sold the last of his armour and his caparison, and had
spent the proceeds to support himself and his wife. Later he had
taken to fashioning "bream fishers" with his pocket knife, using   *799*
horse-tail hairs for the lines; but these toys were no longer in fash-
ion, and on the day in question the *ronin* found himself at his wit's   *800*
end. He cudgelled his brains for a scheme that might tide him over
New Year's Eve, and finally decided to have his wife go to the
pawnbroker's with an old scabbard of his that had been lacquered
with imitation gold-dust.

When the wife of the *ronin* handed the scabbard to the pawn-
broker, he examined it briefly and threw it back at her.

"And how do you expect me to use such an object?" he said.

At this the lady's colour changed abruptly. "How dare you
throw people's valuable property about like that and damage it?"
she said. "If you won't take it for pawn, you should say so and be
done with it. And then you have the effrontery to suggest that it's
useless! It was in this scabbard that my father sheathed the long-
handled sword with which he performed such great feats of valour
at the battle of Ishida Jibu no Sho. Having no son, he bequeathed it   *801*
to me. At the time of my marriage, while I was still living prosper-

ously, I had the scabbard carried before me in a special travelling box when I proceeded to my husband's house as his bride. And now to be told that this is a useless object! It's a disgrace to my ancestors. I may be a woman, but I still have a sense of honour, and I value that honour more than my life."

Then, with a cry of "Have at you!" she pounced on the pawnbroker. The latter was much troubled and did his best to apologize, but the lady was not to be pacified. Meanwhile several neighbours had gathered in the shop. Seeing what was afoot, one of them whispered to the pawnbroker, "You'd better settle with her before she lets that *ronin* husband of hers hear about this. He's a real bloodsucker!" The pawnbroker took this advice and gave the woman

802 three hundred coppers and three *sho* of unpolished rice.

How times change! This woman's father had once enjoyed a

803 stipend of six thousand bushels of rice a year, and she herself had been brought up in the greatest luxury. Yet, having come to her present state of poverty, she had sunk to extorting money from people by unfair means. It is pitiful indeed when we think of it; but

804 it also shows that people do not die simply from being poor.

Having settled the matter, the pawnbroker gave the woman the three hundred coppers and the three *sho* of rice.

805 "But we shan't be able to use this unpolished rice at home tomorrow," said the wife of the *ronin*.

"Fortunately," said the pawnbroker, "I have a hulling mortar in my shop."

He lent her the mortar, and, after the rice had been pounded, saw

806 that she returned home. Here, indeed, was a case of losing three hundred coppers at a touch!

The neighbour of the *ronin* was a woman in her thirties, who had lost her husband some years before. She had no son on whom she could count for support and lived entirely by herself. This woman deliberately made herself inconspicuous by cutting her hair short and wearing plain clothes. Yet she did not give up all her past vanity, and she was far from shabby. Each day she busied herself twisting strands of Nara hemp, pretending that this was a mere pastime, though in fact it was her means of livelihood.

As soon as the Twelfth Moon began, she started to make all the proper arrangements for the New Year holidays: she laid in a few months' supply of firewood; then she bought one medium-sized yellowtail, five small sea bream and two cod, and hung them on her fishhooks; finally she provided herself with an entirely new set of special chopsticks for the New Year's soup, as well as lacquered chopsticks, lacquered Kinokuni bowls and even new lids for the pots. As her New Year's presents she sent the landlord one small tunny, a pair of little sandals with silk cords for his daughter and a pair of socks embossed with silk for his wife; then she presented all the families in the tenements with New Year's rice cakes, to each of which she added a pinch of burdock; and thus she contrived to see in the New Year according to established convention. Since none of the neighbours had guessed the way in which she made her living, they could not understand how she managed her household affairs so well.

The hut behind hers was shared by two women. One of them was still young and blessed with reasonably good features, but, to her great dismay, had been unable to find a husband. Each time that she looked in the mirror she would clap her hands with an air of understanding and exclaim, "Ah, to be sure, no man would accept a girl with a face like that!" And so she resigned herself to remaining single.

The other woman had formerly worked as a decoy maid in an inn near the image of Jizo at Seki on the Tokaido. Travellers who were paying secret visits to the Isé Grand Shrine frequently stopped at this inn, bringing along their own provisions of rice. The maid had treated them badly, and her service had come to an end. One of her habits had been to steal the travellers' rice. Instead of having retribution in the next world, she had been punished in her present life; for, after leaving the inn, she became a mendicant pilgrim, who depended on the scanty offerings of rice that people threw into her bowl. She did her best to appear devout, but it was all a case of sham piety and lip service. With her devil's heart disguised by monkish *811* robes, she was indeed a wolf in sheep's clothing. She entirely neglected to practise her devotions, but, because people are ready to *812* pin their faith even on a sardine's head, her black hempen garbs inspired them to give her alms, and she had managed to live off Buddha for the past fifteen years. Each morning she set out on her pilgrimage, stopping every fifty yards or so at places where passers-by might throw rice into her begging bowl. To gather a single *go* of rice she had to stop at twenty such places, and to obtain five *go* meant walking a mile and a half. Unless a person has strong faith, such work will seem hard indeed.

In the course of the previous summer the woman had suffered a sunstroke and been obliged to pawn her clerical robes for one *mommé* eight *fun*. When she recovered, she was hard put to redeem them, and her livelihood had suffered in consequence. Though she displayed no less piety than before in praying for the salvation of passers-by, they were far less ready with their alms: when in the past she had issued forth in her clerical robes, she had managed to collect five *go* of rice, but now that they were pawned, she was lucky if she came home with a mere two *go*. Things were especially bad during the present season. People were all so busy with their own affairs that they even forgot to observe anniversaries of deaths, and *813* this woman was as useless as a Twelfth Moon priest. No alms whatever came her way, and she was constrained to see in the New Year with a mere eight coppers in her purse.

Truly, nowhere does the sorrow of this world show itself more poignantly than in poor lodgings and in pawnshops, and no tender-

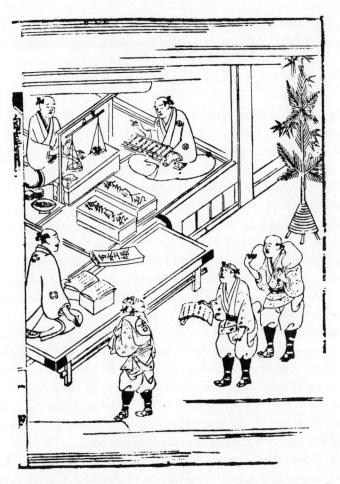

A typical scene at a merchant's house during the year-end period when all outstanding bills must be settled. One clerk works the abacus, another weighs the silver and a third makes entries in the ledger. Three tradesmen have arrived to present their final accounts for the year. At the right stands the gate pine *(kadomatsu)*, a traditional New Year's decoration symbolizing longevity and endurance.

hearted man could ever adopt the broker's trade. The year-end season is full of sad happenings that stir even the outsider's heart.

THE RAT THAT DELIVERED LETTERS

814 The annual Sweeping Day is fixed for the thirteenth day of the Twelfth Moon. There was a man who used to go to his family temple on this day and ask them to give him pieces of bamboo, saying that they were intended for congratulatory gifts and that he would like twelve pieces to match the number of the month. When he had received the pieces of bamboo, however, he did not give them away, but used them for cleaning his house on Sweeping Day; nor did he discard them afterwards, but made them serve for binding *815* the logs on his thatched roof, and bundled the branches together to make a broom. Indeed, this man was so thrifty that he never threw away so much as a speck of dust. In the previous year he had been too busy to have his house cleaned on the thirteenth. Instead he had waited until New Year's Eve and had kept the sweepings as fuel for his annual bath. To heat the water he had even saved the leaves *816,817* from the dumplings of the Fifth Moon and the lotus leaves used at the Bon Festival. What with all these scraps, said he, it should be possible to make a really good fire. Thus he had regard for the most trifling matters. He was forever prying into the household expenses, and was second to none in shrewdly avoiding waste.

The gentleman's mother lived in retirement in a house that she had arranged for herself behind the main dwelling. This old lady displayed an unlimited stinginess, as indeed one might have expected if one knew the son to whom she had given birth. When the time came for her to have her New Year's bath, she brought a single lacquered clog to burn under the bath as fuel. For a while she stood there, while memories of her past returned to her one by one.

"Ay yes," she muttered, "those clogs were in the long chest that

I brought with me when first I came to this house as a bride at the age of seventeen. Since then I wore them through snow and rain, and even after fifty-three years they were as good as new, except for the supports. I had expected to get through my entire life with this single pair. But then, alas, one of the clogs was chewed to pieces by that wretched stray dog and I was left with just one of the pair! What else could I do but consign it to ashes?" After much grumbling in the same vein she finally threw the clog into the furnace.

Then a sad look came to her face, as if some gloomy thought had suddenly engulfed her, and she began to weep profusely.

"Truly," she said, "our days in this world are like a dream! Tomorrow it will be a full year since that other misfortune overtook me. But oh, how grievous it is to think of it!"

While she stood there wailing, the local doctor entered the bathhouse. "Whatever trouble you may have, madam," said he on seeing her, "pray cease your lamentations, for we are now at the auspicious season of the year's end! Can it be that someone you hold dear has died at the New Year?"

"I may be lacking in good sense," replied the old lady, "but rest assured that I should not be grieving like this if it were merely a matter of someone dying! What afflicts me is of a more serious nature. Last year on New Year's Day my younger sister came to visit me from Sakai and brought along a small packet of money as her New Year's present. You can imagine my delight at this gift! I placed it on the holy shelf facing in the lucky direction, yet that very night it was stolen. It could only have been taken by someone who really knew his way about the house.

"I addressed every manner of prayer to the various Gods, but all to no avail. Then I had recourse to a mountain priest. On hearing my story he told me that if the sacred paper strips above his altar began to move and if the light in his lantern gradually died down, it would mean that I should attain my heart's desire and find the

818
819

243

money within a week. He then launched into his prayers, and in the midst of this the paper strips did indeed begin to move and the lantern started to grow dim. Such things, I felt sure, could not belong to this degenerate world of ours, but must be miraculous signs vouchsafed by the Gods and the Buddhas. It was a gratifying omen 820 indeed, and I gave the priest a donation of one hundred and twenty coppers.

"Thereafter I waited for the full seven days, but still there was no sign of my lost packet. I mentioned the matter to an acquaintance 821 of mine and was told that I had simply been throwing good money after bad. It appeared that the man whom I had consulted was one of those rascals who have recently come to be known as the "foxy mountain priests." These men fit out their altars with all manner of hocus-pocus devices. They can even make white paper dolls perform the Tosa invocation dance! This used to be one of the great 822 tricks of Matsuda, the conjurer, but nowadays people have become too clever by far and they take this sort of thing for granted. Gullible as I was, I had been deceived by a simple ruse that anyone else would have known about.

"To make the paper strips move, you see, he had fitted a bowl of water into the altar-stand to which the strips are attached, and had 823 thrown into it a live loach. Then, as he fiercely rubbed his rosary till the beads rattled, and as he recited his prayers turning now to the east, now to the west, he would occasionally strike the altar with the iron club and the priestly staff that he carried. Startled, the loach would begin to swim round in the bowl, thus shaking the stem and making the paper strips move about—much to the amazement of anyone who did not know the trick. As for the light dying down in the lamp, the priest had simply installed a sand glass in the stand, so that the oil might gradually drip out. When I heard this, I realized that I had let myself in for a further loss, on top of the one I had already suffered. In all my life I have never before lost so much as a single copper, and now the year is drawing to an end and still I haven't found that money. This will truly be an anxious holiday for me with all my accounts awry! Alas, what pleasure can I now have in anything?"

Thus the old lady voiced her grievances and wept loudly, little caring how she might be damaging the reputation of the household. Hearing her, the attendants lost all their holiday cheer, and each of them prayed silently to the Gods: "Oh, that she may find that money of hers! It is grievous that we should thus be suspected of thievery."

They had almost finished the sweeping and had searched everywhere, even in the attic, when on a beam in the main house one of the servants discovered a packet wrapped in Sugihara paper. Examination disclosed that this was without doubt that New Year's money for which the old lady had been searching.

"Things will always turn up sooner or later if they haven't been stolen," he said, handing the packet to the old lady. "Yet those rats are really hateful creatures, aren't they, madam, to have played such a trick on you?"

The old lady, however, refused to accept this explanation.

"I've never heard of a rat who could carry something all that way," she shouted, beating her fist on the straw-matted floor. "It must have been one of those black-headed rats that did it. From now on I shall be on my guard!"

The doctor, who was just getting out of the bath, heard her and said, "But, madam, there have been cases in olden times too of rats doing this sort of thing. In the reign of our thirty-seventh sovereign, Emperor Kotoku, on the last day of the Twelfth Moon in the first year of the Taika Era, when His Imperial Majesty was pleased to move his capital and place of residence from Okamoto in the province of Yamato to Toyosaki in Naniwa Nagara, a rat from Yamato also moved his lodgings to Naniwa. This rat, you will be

824

825
826
827

245

amused to hear, brought along all sorts of household objects to fit out his new quarters. Among these were a piece of old material to conceal the entrance of his nest, a paper coverlet to hide himself from kites, an amulet case that might save him from discovery by cats, a sharp stake to block the path of weasels, a prop with which he might open rat traps, a piece of wood for extinguishing oil lamps, a block to help him drag dried bonito into his nest, a strip of dried sea ear to use at his own wedding, the head of a small dried sardine and even a straw wrapper that people use to carry rice when they go to pay their respects at Kumano. All these sundry objects the rat managed to carry in his mouth for a two days' journey. So you see, madam, it is not at all impossible that a rat should have moved your money the short distance from where you live to the main house."

The old lady was not convinced by his words, even though he had cited the ancient chronicles. "It all sounds very clever," she said, "but I never believe anything that I have not seen with my own eyes."

The doctor was at a loss, but after a while he thought of a plan and sent someone to fetch the rat trainer Tobei, who had himself been the pupil of Nagasaki Mizuémon. Presently the trainer arrived with one of his rats.

"This rat," he explained, "can understand what people tell him and can do all sorts of tricks. He'll even deliver a love letter if one of your clerks asks him to."

At these words the rat took a letter between its teeth and, after looking about in all directions, ran over to one of the onlookers and stuck it into the kimono sleeve. Next, someone threw a copper at the rat, saying, "Go and buy a rice cake with this!" The rat picked up the coin, ran off to a nearby shop and duly returned with a rice cake in its mouth.

"Well, well, madam," said the doctor. "Will you concede the point now?"

"To be sure," said the old lady, "I am now prepared to believe that a rat could in fact have carried off my packet of money. Truly, I should never have imagined that it was possible! The fact remains that, since I was unlucky enough to shelter a thieving rat, I have lost the interest that I would have received from that money if it had not been left there idle all year long. My son, in whose house the money lay, must certainly repay me for my loss."

Having made her claim, the old lady calculated the interest for the year at fifteen percent and received full payment on New Year's Eve.

"Now I shall be able to afford a real New Year's!" she said, and retired to her solitude for the night.

NOT EVEN ONE'S GATEPOST IS SECURE IN THIS FLEETING, FLEECING WORLD 832

Custom is a great curer of fear in this world. At the entrance to the gay quarters of Shimabara is a narrow field known as the Shujaku Path, which figures in the words of many a ditty. In the autumn, when the crops began to ripen, they used to put a scarecrow in this field to chase away the birds. They fitted an old sedge hat on its head and attached a bamboo stick to the body. The kites and the crows, however, were thoroughly accustomed to seeing large 833 branded sedge hats like this, and assumed that the scarecrow was simply another pleasure-seeker who was visiting the gay quarters on his own. Accordingly, they were not in the least frightened; in 834 time they came to perch on the sedge hat itself and to make sport with the scarecrow, pretending that it was a real denizen of the world.

In much the same way people who have been in debt for many years no longer find the bill collector such a formidable creature, although as a rule there is nothing in this world so frightening. Once

247

835 they are accustomed to his visitations they do not bother even to leave their house on New Year's Eve in order to avoid him.

It was one such inveterate debtor who on a certain New Year's Eve confronted the bill collector in the following terms: "There has never been a single case since ancient times of a man having his head chopped off for not paying his debts. Now, it isn't that I have funds put aside and am refusing to disburse them. I'd like to settle my debts, you know, but I simply don't have the means. If I had *836* things my own way, money would start growing on those trees *837* this minute. Yet no doubt it is a true saying that 'We must sow before we can reap.' "

With these words the man spread an old mat under a tree in his garden and sat down there in the sun. He then set to whetting the *838* blade of a carving knife and also a pair of iron chopsticks.

"You observe," he said to the bill collectors, "that I have taken special pains in sharpening this knife. I can assure you that it isn't *839* in order to carve up some dried sardines. This knife that you see in my hand may well serve to kill myself! For there's no knowing what lurks in the human heart, and if I should be offended by your importunity, I may suddenly get angry. I am no longer young —already fifty-five, in fact—and I do not cling any more to this *840* life of mine. If one of those bloated money-bags from the centre of the city were by ill chance fated to have an early death, I call the great guardian God of Inari Shrine to be my witness that, if only that man would first pay off my debts, I should not hesitate to cut open my own stomach and die in his place!"

841 So saying, he brandished the carving knife and a foxlike look came on his face. At that moment a garden fowl came chirping in his direction.

"Ah, this bird can precede me on my journey to death!" said the man, and seizing the fowl, he severed its slender neck.

The bill collectors were astounded at this. "We shall have a hard time catching out someone who will go to such lengths as that," they said and left the house. As they passed through the kitchen, they stopped in front of the great kettle, and one of them said, "No doubt this is his wife's destiny, but truly one cannot help pitying the woman who is married to such a short-tempered fellow!"

Thus the man was able to rid himself of the bill collectors without so much as a word of apology. This is a common ruse for warding off one's creditors, but truly it is a knavish way to settle one's debts for the season!

Now among this group of bill collectors there was a young apprentice who worked for a timberman in Horikawa. He was only *842* about eighteen, and still had his side forelock. Yet, though he had *843* a weak, womanly look, he was, in fact, a stout-hearted young man. He paid no attention while the master of the house was carrying out his ruse of threatening violence; instead, he sat down on the bamboo veranda, took out his rosary from the sleeve of his kimono and audibly began to invoke the sacred name of Buddha as he fingered *844* bead after bead. When his fellow bill collectors had left, and everything was quiet, he went up to the master of the house and said, "Well, so much for our little farce! Now if you will kindly let me have the money that you owe my shop, I can go home."

Hearing this, the master said, "When men in their prime have forborne and left me in peace, why should a mere stripling like you remain behind alone? And how dare you assume that knowing tone and refer to other people's actions as a farce?"

"Well," answered the apprentice, "I really don't see why at the height of this busy season you should have to stage a mock suicide. *845* But this discussion is leading us nowhere. Whatever happens, I'm not leaving without that money."

"Without what?"

"The money."

"And who, may I ask, is going to get that money out of me?"

"Who? I can tell you that easily enough. Getting money out of people is my speciality. It's I who've been chosen from among all my fellows to visit the houses were they're having trouble in collecting payment. There are twenty-seven houses in all. Here, look at this account book! You see, I've already collected from the other twenty-six. Now this is the only house left. And I can assure you that I shan't be leaving empty-handed. Until you've settled your bill, all this timber that you used when you repaired your house belongs to our shop. Well, if you aren't going to pay up, I'd better take it all back with me."

So saying, he produced a great mallet and began by demolishing the gatepost.

The master of the house ran up to him. "I'm not going to allow that, young fellow!" he shouted.

"Come, come, sir," said the apprentice, "all this blustering of yours is a bit out of date. You don't seem to have grasped the modern way of doing things. This is how we collect debts these days—by knocking down the gateposts!"

The young man spoke with nonchalance and continued his hammering; whereat the house owner, seeing that there was no help for it, made his apologies and paid his debt in full.

"Now that I've been paid," said the apprentice, "there's really no more for me to say. Yet I can't help being struck by the old-fashioned way in which you tried to force your point. You obviously know how to pick a quarrel when it suits your purpose, but you went about it all the wrong way. This is what you ought to do.

"First you give your wife careful instructions, and from about noon on the last day of the year, you engage in a pre-arranged marital brawl. Your wife changes into her street clothes. 'All right, I'm leaving this house!' she shouts, so that everyone can hear. 'But don't think you're going to get off scot-free! There'll be plenty of blood flowing as a result of this. Do you understand? This won't be any trifling matter, I can tell you! You still want me to get out, do you? Very well, I'll leave, all right! I'll leave this very minute. I'll show you!'

"When your wife has finished, you turn to the bill collector and say, 'I should give anything to be able to settle these debts of mine, so that I might be well spoken of hereafter. After all, man is mor- 846 tal, fame immortal. But now there's no help for it. It's all up with me this very month—nay, this very day! Alas, alas!' With these words you pick up some useless scraps of paper, making the bill collector believe that they are documents of great importance, and you start tearing them up one by one and throwing them away. However hard-hearted he may be, he won't stay long when he sees all this."

"Well, well, I've never heard of that trick before," replied the other. "Thanks to this advice, my wife and I will see our way through the New Year. Won't we, my dear?" he asked, turning to his wife. Then, once more addressing the apprentice, he said, "You may be young in years, but you are my senior when it comes to good sense. That advice of yours will get me through New Year's. And since this is indeed the holiday season, let us drink to each other's health!"

So saying, the master gave orders for the garden fowl to be plucked and made into a broth; and he did not let the apprentice go home before he had regaled him with sakè. When the young man had left, the master said to his wife, "There's no need for us to wait until next year to try that trick. Each New Year's Eve, as 847 soon as it gets dark, those wretched bill collectors come pestering me for payment."

Without any further ado they simulated a marital quarrel and thus they managed to ward off their creditors. Thereafter they be-came well known for their domestic jars, and in due course their home acquired the name of "the brawling house of Omiyadori." 848

THE MAN WHO TURNED INTO GOLD
COINS WHILE HE SLEPT

"Do not forget about your business even while you sleep"—such were the words of a man of great wealth. Certain it is that people dream about what is on their minds. Now, among the many sad and happy dreams that we can have, none is more wretched than that of finding money on the ground. For who drops money nowadays? People value money no less than their own lives, and they seek it with the greatest devotion. Even in a place where great throngs have just been attending a memorial service, even on the day following the Festival of Temma, we may be sure that no one has dropped so much as a single copper. No, money is not to be obtained unless we work for it.

There was a certain poor man who had neglected his own business, and whose dream it now was to become a man of wealth at one fell swoop. This man bore constantly in his mind the recollection of the mountain of unwrapped coins that he had once seen in Edo through the window of a moneychanger's shop in Suruga-machi.

"Oh," thought he, "if only I could have a pile of money like that for myself this New Year's!"

As he lay there on his paper bedding, his only thought was that the coins which he had seen in the shop resting on a strip of shammy leather were not inferior in bulk to his own form. It was dawn on the thirtieth day of the Twelfth Moon. The man's wife woke up, and for some time lay worrying about how she and her husband would manage to get through that day and about all the difficulties that they were bound to have. When she happened to look towards where the early morning light was streaming in, she was astounded to see a heap of gold *koban* lying on the floor.

"What's this? What's this?" she cried delightedly. "It can only be that Heaven has come to our rescue. Wake up, my dear! Wake up!"

"What's wrong?" said her husband, waking from his dream. But no sooner had he spoken the words than the coins disappeared without a trace.

"Oh, alas!" moaned his wife, and she told him what had happened.

"I see," he said. "I was so utterly absorbed in that money which I once saw in Edo that for a time I myself turned into those very coins and appeared to you in that form. Alas, rather than continue in our present wretched state, I should be ready to forfeit my salvation in the next world! Yes, I would willingly strike the bell in Sayo- 850 no-Nakayama and descend into the Hell of Everlasting Torments, if only it meant that we could manage in this present life. For though this world is a paradise for rich people, for poor folk like us, who do not even have a handful of firewood to burn under our cauldron, 851 it is a very hell. Alack-a-day, this year ends sadly indeed!"

As he spoke, evil thoughts formed in his mind and his spirit was transformed. He dozed off for a while and, as he lay there, dreamed that black-and-white hellhounds had come to fetch him with a great clatter of their chariot. 852

His wife was now plunged into even greater sorrow. Finally, she turned to her husband and spoke as follows: "No one in this world ever lives to be a hundred. Therefore it is foolish to have extrav- 853 agant hopes for one's future. So long as we do not alter in our affection towards each other, we shall have a chance to celebrate New Year's happily at some future time. I know that, out of consideration for me, you do not like the idea of my going to work outside; yet both of us, and our baby, too, are rapidly being overtaken by hunger and thirst. I have no choice but to go and work for the sake of our little girl. Fortunately, there is an opening for me just now.

I pray you look after our child and bring her up carefully. This will be a great consolation to me in the future. Nothing can be crueler than to abandon one's child. I beg you take good care of her."

So saying, she shed bitter tears, and her husband, too, was overcome with grief. Unable to make any reply, he turned aside and firmly shut his eyes. At that moment a woman agent from the environs of Sumizomé entered the room, accompanied by an old lady in her sixties.

"Since you have nice full breasts," began the agent, "they are prepared to give you the entire payment of eighty-five silver *mommé* in advance, as I explained yesterday. They'll even provide you with changes of clothes for all four seasons. You can consider yourself lucky, you know. The great giant of a cook whom they employ, and who besides her kitchen work weaves the material for their wadded cotton clothes, is only paid thirty-two *mommé* for the half-period. You can thank those breasts of yours for the good offer they are making you. And if by any chance you don't want the job, I have another suitable candidate in mind—a woman who lives in the north of Kyomachi. It all has to be settled today, and I can't give you any more time to make up your mind."

"Whatever I may undertake," said the wife, "it is simply in order to save our lives. I shall do my best to take good care of their baby. I realize what a precious charge this is, and can only hope that I may be adequate to the task. In any case, I am most anxious to take service as you suggest."

When the agent heard this, she did not bother to address the husband, but immediately replied, "Well then, let's leave for their house as quickly as possible." She borrowed an inkstone from the people in the neighbouring room, indited a contract for a one-year period and paid the agreed money in full.

"It makes no difference," she then said, "if we settle our accounts now or later. So let's do it at once! This is the normal rate." Without a moment's delay, she took the parcel of money, on which was written, "Thirty-seven silver coins, eighty-five *mommé* in weight," and weighed out exactly eight and a half *mommé* as her commission. 858 859

"Well, nurse," said the agent, as she prepared to lead the wife away, "you needn't worry about making any preparations. You can come just as you are."

The husband was now in tears, and the wife's face was flushed.

"Goodbye, Oman," she said to her baby, "Mother's going to her new master now. She'll come and visit you in the New Year."

She made some request of the neighbours and once more burst into tears.

"Don't worry," said the agent reassuringly, "a child can grow up 860 without its parents! And even if you try to kill them, people don't die unless they're fated to. Goodbye to you, sir."

With this brief statement, she left the room, together with the old lady who had accompanied her, and the wife. The old lady, who had been pondering over the ways of the world, glanced back and said, "My little grandchild is in the same pitiful state as this poor baby. It is indeed cruel when a child is weaned from its mother's breast!"

"Well," said the agent, "money is the real enemy. If the baby's 861 going to die—well, it'll just die. That's all there is to it!" Thus she spoke, not caring that the mother heard her words, and then she led the way out of the house.

Soon it was the evening of the last day of the year. Now truly did life seem irksome to the husband. He cast his mind back upon the past and recalled how he had received a good inheritance, but, being unversed in keeping accounts, had lost everything and been obliged to leave Edo. It was only thanks to his wife that he had even been able to live here in Fushimi. 862

"Alas," he thought, "even if the only way we could afford to celebrate was by sharing some lucky tea, it would still have been a 863

255

happy New Year's so long as we could have seen it in together!"

Glancing at the shelf, he was touched to notice two special pairs of chopsticks that his wife had bought in preparation for the holidays.

"This year we'll only need one pair," he said, and, having broken two of the chopsticks, he used them for fuel in the kitchen stove.

Soon it grew dark. Since the baby had not stopped crying for some time, the woman from next door visited the room. She mixed some 864 *jio* syrup with rice powder, boiled it and showed the husband how to feed the baby through a bamboo pipe.

"It may be my imagination," she said, "but it looks to me as if the baby's face has already got thinner, even though your wife's only been gone one day."

"Well, it can't be helped, can it?" said the husband, and he petulantly threw the fire irons on the floor.

"I really feel sorry for you," said the woman. "Your wife's lucky, though. The master of the house where she's working likes to employ pretty women. Besides, she looks very much like his own wife who died recently. She's got exactly the same elegant figure from behind."

The husband did not even wait for her to finish.

865 "The money that they paid her is still intact," he said. "After what you've just told me I realize that I must have her back, even if it means complete disaster."

So saying, he rushed out of the house and returned with his wife. And together they spent a tearful New Year's.

"The Law of Buddha provides a household" is an old saying, but   867
it is still true today.

Every year on the evening of the Setsubun Festival sermons in
praise of Heitaro are delivered in all the temples of the Shinshu
Sect. Though they do not differ in content from year to year, the
stories of Heitaro's life are so admirable that young and old, men
and women, all flock to the temples to hear them.

It happened one year that the Setsubun Festival fell on New   868
Year's Eve. That night both bill collectors and exorcists were visit-   869
ing people's houses, and the tinkling of the weighing scales mingled
with the rattle of dried beans—in such an alarming fashion, indeed,   870
that one might have imagined that a devil had been tied up in the   871
darkness.

In a certain Shinshu temple they beat the drums, lit the sacred
taper before the Buddha and waited for the arrival of the faithful.
Yet by the time that the first bell sounded, no more than three   872
people had appeared. The priest finished reading the scriptures,
and, having pondered for some time over the state of the world,
he addressed the three people as follows: "Well, since on this day
Setsubun has fallen on the fixed holiday of the year, it seems as if   873
everyone was too busy to come to the temple. Yet there must be
many an old woman who has left her affairs to her children and
who has ample spare time. Surely even on a day like this such folk
can't be too busy to visit their temple! If the boat of Buddhism were   874
to arrive for them, I doubt whether they would say that they were
too busy to step aboard. How dull-witted and base they are, these
foolish people!

"Well, there is no point in preaching in praise of Lord Heitaro
to just the three of you. Simply because this is a Buddhist temple

we aren't absolved from keeping our accounts like everyone else. With so few of you present we shan't even be able to pay for the oil in the sacred lamp. To deliver my sermon under such circumstances would be a mere waste. I had better return your offerings and let you go home.

"But first I shall say one thing. That you three should have visited the temple tonight, when all the others were too engrossed in the details of their daily life, means that you are ten million times blessed. This can truly be called piety! The Lord Buddha will see to it that you have not brought yourselves here at this busy time in vain. No, he will record your deeds in his great golden ledger and will not fail to keep a reckoning for you in the future world. Do not for a moment believe that the Buddha will forsake you! He places compassion before all else and there is no deceit in him. Have faith, my children!"

Hearing this, an old woman, who was one of the three visitors, began weeping. "Father," she said, "your gracious words have shamed me to the very bottom of my heart. It was not out of piety that I came here this evening. That only son of mine has been neglecting his work and the bill collectors have been after him for 875 some time. Usually at the seasonal time of payment he manages to put them off with some trumped-up story, but at this particular season he could find no way to escape his duty. He therefore said to me, 'Go to the temple, Mother! After you have left I shall start lamenting loudly, saying that I cannot find you. I shall go from one neighbour to another asking after you. I shall spend the entire night searching high and low with drums and bells, and thus I shall manage to see my way through New Year's Eve without settling 876 any of my debts. I know this is an old sort of trick, but I don't think that anyone else has ever thought of spending New Year's Eve going about calling, "Mother, Mother where are you?" That's my own invention!' And so I came here in accordance with his plan.

"I know, Father, that we are fated to undergo misfortunes in this world and that none of it can be helped. Yet I feel most guilty at having put all our neighbours to such unexpected trouble." So saying, she burst into lamentations.

Next, one of the other visitors said, "Truly, nothing in this world is so uncertain as a man's fate. I myself was born in Isé and do not have a single relation in these parts. I used to be employed by a priest who was attached to the Grand Shrine and who went about Osaka collecting contributions from the faithful. It was while serving as his porter that I had a chance of seeing how prosperous things are in this part of the country. It seemed to me that, whatever work one might choose, this would be an easy place to make a living and to support a small family. As luck would have it, while I was on my way through Yamato, I happened to meet a widow whose husband had owned a shop dealing in small wares. He had left her with a baby who was one year old. The mother was fair-skinned and of sturdy build. I married into the family, thinking that we could work together for our living, and confidently relying on that child of hers for the future. Yet, since I did not know the tricks of the trade, within half a year I had lost the little money that I had started with.

"One day at the beginning of this Twelfth Moon I was sitting at home racking my brains as to how to improve our conditions when I heard my wife, who was dandling the baby in her arms, speaking to him thus: 'You have two good ears, my little fellow, so listen carefully to what I say! Your real daddy was a small man, but he was clever, let me tell you! He even cooked the rice, which is a woman's work, and he used to let me sleep peacefully from evening until morning, while he sat up all night making straw

877

878

sandals. He didn't wear the sandals himself, mind you, but sold them and used the money to buy wadded cotton clothes for his wife and baby at New Year's. Even this bluish-yellow kimono that I am wearing now is a relic of those days. No one can ever take the place of someone who's been really close to you. Yes, cry, my little baby, cry! I know how you miss your daddy!'

"To have married into one's wife's family as I had is a pitiful state indeed, and things were really unbearable for me. Yet there was no help for it and I continued as I was. Then one day I remembered that I still had a little money owing to me in my home village. I decided that I would go and collect it, so that we might have sufficient funds to see our way through the New Year holidays which were approaching. I went all the way back to my home in Isé. But it was to no avail. All the people who owed me money had left and I had to return empty-handed.

"I reached home just before supper this evening. To my surprise I found that New Year's rice cakes had been pounded, that firewood had been laid in and that the tray for the Gods had been prettily decorated with silver fern. I could not imagine how my wife had managed all this, but, when I saw it, I was greatly heartened. 'The world was no such cheerless place,' I thought, seeing how splendidly my wife had arranged everything in my absence. If there 879 was a God who threw one down, there was always another who picked one up.

" 'I'm safely home!' I called.

"My wife treated me with more than usual warmth. First she gave me some hot water to wash my feet. Then without any delay 880 she put a salad of salted sardines on one plate and a dish of boiled sardines on another, and placed the tray before me with a good grace. I picked up my chopsticks and was about to begin eating when my wife said, 'Did you bring that money back from Isé?' I told her about my bad luck, but she would not even let me finish.

" 'How dare you come back empty-handed?' she cried. 'This
to of rice that I've cooked was bought on credit. I contracted to pay
for it by the end of the Second Moon and had to register my own
person as security for the debt. I borrowed it at the rate of ninety-
five *mommé* for a single *koku,* let me tell you! When forty *mommé*
is the normal price for a *koku* of rice, imagine having to borrow
at the rate of ninety-five! It's all your fault, you blockhead! It's
thanks to you that I've suffered this fate! What did you bring
with you when you came into this house? One loincloth—that's
all! No, you don't stand to lose anything, do you? Well, it's grow-
ing dark outside. Get out of this house while you can still find your
way!'

"So saying, she snatched away the tray from which I had just
started eating and chased me out of the house. The neighbours had
observed the commotion and now gathered round me. 'It's hard
for you,' they said, 'but that's what comes from marrying into
your wife's family. To be thrown out this way is the natural fate of
a man who marries like that. Still, you'll find another good berth
for yourself.' With these words they sped me on my way.

"I was too unhappy even to cry. Tomorrow I shall be going back
once more to my home village. But for the present I have nowhere
to spend the night. That's why I came to the temple, even though
I belong to the Lotus Sect." So he completed his touching but at
the same time comic, confession.

The third visitor laughed loudly and said, "It's not so easy for
me to tell my story. If I'd stayed at home tonight, the bill collectors
would have been bothering the life out of me. There's not a soul
in the world who'd lend me as much as ten coppers. I wanted to
drink some sakè tonight and I was cold. I thought of one reckless
scheme after another, but still I couldn't find any good way to get
through New Year's. But then I hit on a really foul scheme. I
knew that crowds of people would be gathering at the Shinshu

temples tonight to hear the sermons about Heitaro, and so I decided
885 that I'd steal a few pairs of straw or leather sandals and sell them to
buy myself some sakè. But I found that all the temples—not only
886 this one—were deserted tonight, and so it's been hard for me to
pluck out the Buddha's eye." The man finished his story in tears.

"Well, well," said the priest, clapping his hands, "poverty is in-
deed the source of many an evil scheme! Truly the Floating World
887 is a sad place that you, who are all born with the possibility of
salvation, should have been afflicted with such wicked desires!"

While the priest sat there, sunk in earnest contemplation of the
realities of human life, a woman rushed into the temple in a state
of great agitation.

"Father, Father," she cried, "my niece has just given birth safely
to her baby! I came here at once to tell you."

Hot on her heels, a man ran into the temple, saying, "The
cabinet maker has just had a quarrel with one of the bill collectors
and he's gone and hanged himself. They're having the funeral after
midnight. I'm sorry to trouble you, Father, but please come to the
place of cremation."

Amidst all this hubbub a man came from the tailor's and said,
"Someone's filched those white padded clothes you gave us for
sewing, Father. We're trying to trace the goods, but if we don't
recover them, we'll pay you compensation. You won't lose by
this, Father."

Then someone appeared from one of the neighbouring houses.
"Our well has become blocked all of a sudden," he said. "May we
888 have your permission, Father, to use the temple well during the
first five days of the New Year?"

After that it turned out that the only son in the family of one
of the main parishioners of the temple had been spending too much
889 of his father's money. He had been treated harshly and forced to
leave his home town. However, the young man's mother had

arranged for him to go to the temple, and had requested that they look after him there until the fourth day of the New Year. This, too, the priest could not very well refuse.

And so it is that, inasmuch as he lives in this same Floating World as all of us, even a Twelfth Moon priest has little time for contemplation. *890*

APPENDICES

APPENDIX I. SOURCES

1. Five Women Who Chose Love (see also Introduction, p. 25).

Book 1: The Tale of Seijūrō from Himéji, the Town of
the Lovely Damsel

Book 3: The Almanac Maker's Tale in the Middle Part

Book 5: The Tale of Gengobei, the Mountain of Love

Kōshoku Gonin Onna was published in Osaka in the Second Moon of 1686.
It consisted of five quarto volumes with illustrations by Yoshida Hambei.
A subsequent edition appeared in 1720 under the title *Tōsei Onna Katagi*
(The Character of Modern Women). The present translation is based on the
modern reprint contained in Volume II of *Teihon Saikaku Zenshū (Standard*
Edition of Saikaku's Complete Works), Tokyo, 1949, pp. 113–222.

The book consists of five tales, each of which is in turn divided into five
chapters. There are various theories concerning the origins of this quinary
division. According to Professor Yamaguchi, it is based on the five-act divi-
sion of classical *Nō* drama; Professor Teruoka, however, considers that it
derives from the five acts of the *jōruri* dramatic ballad, at which Saikaku
had tried his hand in the preceding year.[1] The rather artificial division of each
tale into five chapters helps to account for the irrelevancies and prolixities
that occasionally mar the construction of *Kōshoku Gonin Onna*.

Each of the five tales takes place in a different part of Japan and the re-
spective localities are prominently indicated on the title page. In this sense the
book belongs to the tradition of Saikaku's "provincial stories" *(shokoku-*
banashi), in which he recorded events that had occurred in various parts of
the country.[2] The geographical arrangement of the tales is clearly intended to
be symmetrical: the three middle stories (Books 2, 3, 4) take place in the
Three Cities (Osaka, Kyoto, Edo), while the two outside stories (Books 1,

[1] Teruoka Yasutaka: *Kōshoku Gonin Onna Hyōshaku*, p. 222.

[2] *Ibid.*, p. 227. Saikaku's two main *shokoku-banashi* collections were published within
one year of *Kōshoku Gonin Onna* (1685 and 1687).

5) are set in the less familiar provinces of Harima and Satsuma respectively.[3] There is a corresponding symmetry on the temporal plane; the middle stories are based on events that occurred within four years of the book's publication, whereas the outside stories refer to relatively remote events of about a quarter of a century before.[4]

Although the five tales are structurally independent, they are held together by a common theme, namely, the effect of romantic love on different young women belonging to the townsman (and, in one case, to the peasant) class. Saikaku's previous kōshoku works had been set in the rather insulated world of the gay quarters, but in Kōshoku Gonin Onna he turns to ordinary bourgeois society. In each case the main characters are confronted with a dilemma between conforming to the social code and "choosing love."

Each of the books is named after the man in question, but the main focus is on the heroines. The five women differ in many respects, but they all share a bold, assertive character, which inspires them to take a very positive attitude to the demands of kōshoku. This character may seem rather surprising when we remember, first, that each of them was still in her early teens (Onatsu, Osan and Oman were only fifteen years old) and, secondly, that they lived in a man's society based on complete inequality of the sexes and on a tradition of feminine submissiveness. As the revised title of the work indicates, however, these were the "modern women" of their time. When faced with the choice between conformity and love, they do not hesitate to take the initiative and to lead the action, in full knowledge of the gruesome consequences involved in violating the social code.[5] In every story but the last their decision results in tragedy. As his heroines move ineluctably towards their unpleasant deaths, it is clear that Saikaku sympathizes with them and also with their unfortunate lovers, though he never condones the ill-advised deeds of fornication or adultery that have led to their downfall.

The five tales were all inspired by actual events that were well known in Saikaku's time. These events had captured the popular imagination and had already been recorded, with numerous elaborations and variations, in earlier

---

[3] Teihon Saikaku Zenshū, Vol. II, pp. 17-18.

[4] Loc. cit. The events took place in the following years: Bk. 1—c. 1660, Bk. 2—1685, Bk. 3—1683 or 1684, Bk. 4—1682, Bk. 5—1663.

[5] For a few examples in which the women, rather than the men, take the initiative at a crucial moment, see pp. 87 and 114 of the translation.

ballads and dramatic works. Professor Noma stresses the influence of the *utazaimon* ballads on the plot, structure and general conception of *Kōshoku Gonin Onna*. He particularly refers to the three ballads dealing with the events described in Books 1, 3 and 4. Unfortunately, we know very little about these ballads and it is by no means certain that they antedate Saikaku's work.

Although Saikaku no doubt took much of his material both from the historical events and from ballads and other records that are no longer extant, the important thing to remember is that, like Chikamatsu (and Shakespeare), he moulded this material freely to suit his own artistic purposes. This will emerge from a comparison between Saikaku's and Chikamatsu's treatments of the same stories (pp. 271–2 below). Furthermore, even when the general plots are derivative, the characterization, details and even most of the incidents are Saikaku's own. Such events as Onatsu's retirement to a convent (Book 1), Moemon's clandestine visit to the capital (Book 3) and Gengobei's lavish reception by Oman's parents (Book 5), to mention only three out of scores of possible examples, do not occur in any of the other accounts. It is clear that Saikaku used the traditional plots simply as a springboard for telling his own stories.

The tale of Onatsu and Seijūrō (Book 1) was inspired by events that occurred in Himeji in about 1660. The tragedy of these two lovers was a popular theme for well over a hundred years and was used by numerous writers both before and after Saikaku.[6] The earliest extant reference occurs in a popular song, the *Seijūrō-bushi*, which, according to Professor Teruoka, reflects the widespread sympathy that existed for the ill-fated couple. This song is quoted not only in Saikaku's version (p. 74), but in the *utazaimon* ballad *(Onatsu Seijūrō)* and in Chikamatsu's play on the subject. Among full-length treatments of the story it would appear that Saikaku's is the oldest that survives.[7] At the time when he wrote, however, there were other ballads and plays on the subject which are no longer extant. The *Matsudaira Yamato no Kami Nikki (Diary of Lord Matsudaira of Yamato)*, for example, refers in an entry under the Fourth Moon of 1664 to the fact that a play *(kyōgen)* about Onatsu and Seijūrō was enjoying popularity at the Kanzaburō Theatre in Edo.[8] Among subsequent

[6] A very successful *shosagoto* (dance drama) on the subject was written in 1914 and performed by the great Kabuki actor, Baiko VI, who took the part of Onatsu.

[7] This is based on the assumption that the extant *utazaimon* ballad postdates Saikaku's work.

[8] See text note 74.

versions of the story are those contained in *Midarehagi Sambonyari (Three Stories of Adultery as Revenge)*, an *ukiyo-zōshi* by Nishizawa Ippū published in 1718, and in Chikamatsu's drama, *Gojūnenki Uta-Nembutsu (Prayer-Song Commemorating the Fiftieth Anniversary*, i.e. of Seijūrō's death), published in 1709. Saikaku's account of the event is closest to that presented by Nishizawa and differs widely from those in the *utazaimon* ballad and in Chikamatsu's play.

Without entering into the moot question of which version is closest to the actual events, we may briefly examine Chikamatsu's use of the same story, since this will provide a useful comparison between the approaches of the two writers and will show how they both elaborated on what may originally have been a very simple story of elopement and capture.[9] In Chikamatsu's version, which is evidently based on the *utazaimon* ballad, Onatsu, the heroine, is the daughter of a courtesan from Murotsu. Her father, unaware that she is in love with his handsome clerk, Seijūrō, has with great difficulty succeeded in arranging an advantageous marriage for her; shortly before the wedding, another clerk steals her trousseau and dowry and informs the father that Seijūrō has done this in order to prevent the marriage; the father is livid and dismisses Seijūrō; that night Seijūrō breaks into the building to stab the treacherous clerk, but he mistakenly kills another person; for this he is arrested and executed. Saikaku's story, as will be seen, lacks many of the dramatic elements (the villain, the mistaken stabbing, etc.) used by Chikamatsu. On the whole it is more prosaic, more realistic and probably closer to the actual events. As Professor Teruoka points out, however, the discrepancies between the two versions are not merely a matter of the different demands of drama and prose fiction, but relate to the underlying themes that the respective authors had in mind. Chikamatsu lay great stress on the theme of disloyalty. In one of the climatic speeches Onatsu's father reviles the girl for having deceived him by her liaison with his clerk; he reminds her that her mother was a courtesan and that, despite this social handicap, he has succeeded in arranging a good marriage for her; all the baser, then, her ingratitude in having allowed the demands of her romantic nature to precede the duty of filial obedience. Onatsu stands condemned for wantonness and immorality, both of which, it is implied, are inherited from her mother. Saikaku, on the other hand, makes no such judgements. In his version the elder brother (who takes the

---

[9] The following material is based on Teruoka, *op. cit.*, pp. 35–7.

place of the father as Onatsu's guardian) has hardly any role at all. Saikaku's interest lies in the practical consequences of the conflict between romantic love *(kōshoku)* and the impersonal social code. Seijūrō meets his doom not because of the fortuitous circumstance of having stabbed the wrong person, but because he and his mistress have chosen love in a rigidly stratified society that makes no allowance for human weakness.

Book 3 is derived from far more recent events. The execution of Osan and Moemon took place in 1683 or 1684, only a couple of years before Saikaku's book was written. Here again Saikaku's version differs considerably from that contained in the *utazaimon* ballad and in Chikamatsu's puppet play on the same subject, *Daikyōji Mukashi-goyomi* (1715). The story as it actually occurred seems to have been fairly simple.[10] While Osan's husband, the almanac maker, was absent in Edo, the maidservant, Tama, acted as an intermediary to arrange a love affair between her mistress and the clerk, Moemon; Osan became pregnant and when the result of her infidelity could no longer be concealed she fled to Tamba with Moemon; the fugitives were soon discovered, brought back to Kyoto and executed at Awataguchi, together with the maid. Both Saikaku and Chikamatsu elaborate considerably on this basic plot. The mistaken seduction (p. 86) was evidently Saikaku's invention. Chikamatsu has a similar scene in the first act of his play: Osan, realizing that her husband has been visiting the maid Tama at night, decides that she will teach him a lesson; she changes places with the maid and prepares to upbraid her unfaithful husband when he joins her in bed; meanwhile the clerk, Mohei, who is under obligation to the maid and who knows that she is in love with him, steals to her bedroom, intending finally to gratify her desires; he is, instead, received by Osan, who, believing that it is her husband, responds warmly to his advances. In Chikamatsu's version the outcome is entirely fortuitous, whereas in Saikaku's account the trouble has its roots in Osan's own nature.[11] Another striking difference between the two versions is that in Chikamatsu's play the lovers are spared from execution at the very last moment, owing to the intercession of a powerful priest.

In Book 5 we return to events that were relatively distant in both time and place. The love-suicide of Gengobei and Oman took place in 1663 in the remote and inaccessible province of Satsuma. By Saikaku's time the details

[10] Teruoka, *op. cit.,* p. 130.
[11] This point is elaborated by Teruoka, *op. cit.,* pp. 130–1.

of the story had become thoroughly blurred and here he adapts his source even more freely than usual. The only extant record prior to *Kōshoku Gonin Onna* is a popular song, the *Gengobei-bushi*. This is quoted in Bashō's *Kai-ōi* (1672), in Saikaku's version (p. 117) and in Chikamatsu's play *Satsuma Uta (The Song of Satsuma)* (1704).

From the song we know that the original story ended in a double suicide. This immediately raises the question of why Saikaku should have disregarded his source and given his version a rather unconvincing happy ending. Professor Teruoka suggests several reasons for Saikaku's deliberate departure from his usual realism.[12] First, he appears to have disapproved thoroughly of the double-suicide convention, which appealed so greatly to Chikamatsu and to the romantic taste of the time. There is only one double suicide in all Saikaku's work and in that passage Saikaku strongly voices his opposition to the custom. Secondly, Saikaku may have been influenced by the common convention of giving happy endings to the fifth *dan* of *jōruri* plays. Again, the greater part of Saikaku's life had been spent as a *haikai* poet and it was conventional to end a series of *haikai* with an *ageku;* regardless of the nature of the preceding verses, the content of the *ageku* was invariably peaceful or auspicious and generally it was concerned with spring. Similarly, despite the tragic tone of the earlier stories, Saikaku closes *Kōshoku Gonin Onna* on a deliberately sanguine note. Finally, we should remember that Saikaku was a popular writer and that in the Edo Period, no less than now, the public wanted happy endings. As a rule Saikaku would not allow these demands to interfere with the realism of his account or with the consistency of his theme. Occasionally, however, he will truckle to his readers by relieving the gloom of his tragic works with a relatively cheerful ending.[13]

In Books 1-4 of *Five Women Who Chose Love* Saikaku makes no effort to mitigate the tragedy that results from choosing love in a harsh feudal society. The heroines and heroes invariably receive the punishments that they have prepared for themselves. Then, in order not to sate his readers with the horrid images of the execution grounds, he ends Book 5 by describing Gengobei wallowing merrily in his new-found wealth; and, as if to emphasize the unreality of this conclusion, Saikaku gives a list of the legendary objects that the hero has acquired from his wife's parents.

[12] *Op. cit.,* pp. 205-6.
[13] We find another striking example of this in *Twenty Breaches of Filial Piety in This Land. The Life of an Amorous Woman* also ends on an unexpectedly serene note.

2. *The Life of an Amorous Woman* (see also Introduction, pp. 25–6)

Kōshoku Ichidai Onna was published in Osaka in the Sixth Moon of 1686. It consisted of six quarto volumes, each divided into four chapters. The illustrations were by Yoshida Hambei. The modern reprint on which the present translation is based appears in Volume II of the *Standard Edition of Saikaku's Complete Works*, pp. 223–373.

Certain stylistic elements of the book, especially in the opening and closing chapters, are clearly derived from *Yu Hsien K'u*, the famous T'ang Period novel by Chang Wen-ch'eng, and from *Chiu Hsiang Shih*, Su Tung-po's collection of Buddhist poems. The actual form, however, belongs to a tradition of Japanese mediaeval confessional literature, exemplified by works like *Sannin Hōshi (Three Priests)*. A number of seventeenth-century *kana-zōshi* books, such as *Shichinin Bikuni (Seven Nuns)* (1635), used this confessional *(zange)* type of writing. The most direct literary influence on Saikaku's book seems to have been a three-part work of the "courtesan-critique" genre that appeared in 1677 with the titles *Takitsuke (Kindlings)*, *Moekui (Half-Burnt Fuel)* and *Keshizumi (Charcoal Cinders)*. *Charcoal Cinders* deals with an old lady who was formerly a high-ranking courtesan in the Shimabara, but who has now become a nun and has retired to a mountain cell, where she regales her visitors with tales of her palmy days in the gay quarters. As will be seen, this is precisely the form that Saikaku uses in *The Life of an Amorous Woman*. These sources, however, only provided Saikaku with a bare framework. The substance of his book, the characters and the events, are entirely his own.

The twenty-four chapters of *The Life of an Amorous Woman* are independent units, each told in the first person and describing some episode in the love-life of the heroine. "Ichidai Onna," whose real name we never learn, was born into a good family. Her career started auspiciously in the service of a court lady, but from the outset her erotic nature was to be her undoing. Already at the age of ten she falls "prey to wanton feelings" (p. 124), and two years later she is dismissed from court for having been involved in a love affair. Soon afterwards, she is given a chance to make a respectable marriage, but she is unable to restrain herself from seducing her prospective father-in-law. All hope for a normal life disappears when her parents fall into financial difficulties and sell her to a house in the Shimabara. From then on she is obliged to make her own way in the world, and the subsequent books describe the numerous professions that she attempts.

The action takes place in various parts of the country, though mostly in Kyoto, Osaka and Edo. She serves as a courtesan in each of the three top ranks, then as a bonze's mistress, a teacher of calligraphy, a parlourmaid, a seamstress, a singing nun, a teahouse attendant, a bathhouse girl; later, having sunk to the depths, she becomes a private prostitute, a procuress and a common streetwalker. One interest of the book lies precisely in its realistic depiction of the various occupations that were open to unattached women in the second half of the seventeenth century.

The main interest, however, is in Saikaku's study of his heroine's nature and of how it leads her to disaster. Despite her physical attractions, she is too proud and wilful to succeed for long in the gay quarters; at the same time her passionate temperament will not allow her to remain in any respectable occupation. Occasionally she has periods of remorse and nostalgic longings for a more tranquil form of life; but her efforts to reform are always bedevilled by her violent amorous cravings. The utter downfall that is described in the last two chapters is not the result of any fortuitous circumstances, but the ineluctable outcome of her own character.

The *kōshoku* that inspires the heroine differs completely from the romantic love described in Saikaku's previous book, *Five Women Who Chose Love,* and also from the sanguine rakishness of *The Life of a Man Who Lived for Love.* It is a restless and insatiable search for physical satisfaction. In this book Saikaku gives a remarkably convincing picture of the murky aspects that love can assume when it has become a mere physical appetite unrelieved by emotion. The single-minded, lustful characters that move through the pages of *Kōshoku Ichidai Onna* are almost entirely devoid of romantic feelings. The heroine has not the slightest fondness for most of the innumerable men to whom she gives her body, and they have none for her. In *The Woman's Secret Manual of Etiquette,* for example, her attitude to the young paramour whom she prostrates with her sexual demands is far closer to hatred than to love. *Kōshoku,* when stripped of its tender connotations, can become a burning erethism akin to madness—and, indeed, at one stage the heroine does go mad and roams about the town, singing love songs and repeating the classical demand of the nymphomaniac (p. 164).

Despite its psychological accuracy, Saikaku's account of his heroine is certainly not an attempt at clinical description. His interest is in the human tragedy inherent in *kōshoku* when it is completely separated from romantic love. *Kōshoku Ichidai Otoko* and *Kōshoku Gonin Onna* had both been affirmations of the joys of physical love, but here the stress is on its limitations. Lust without tenderness is shown to be both unhappy and sordid—"the mutual embrace of stinking bones," as Saikaku says, quoting the Chinese poet (p. 192). Furthermore, when love is merely a matter of physical gratification, it is inevitably frustrated by the advance of age and by the accompanying decay of the flesh. This theme, which is stressed in the closing chapters of *The Life of an Amorous Woman,* is entirely absent from the first book of the *kōshoku* cycle, *The Life of a Man Who Lived for Love,* where the hero, Yonosuke, sets off merrily at the age of sixty, to continue his rakish indulgence in the island of women. Yonosuke cannot imagine that his amorous activities will ever pall; but the old lady who sits alone in her cave is fully resigned to the fact that physical decay has made the world of *kōshoku* meaningless for her. It is a significant aspect of Saikaku's realism that he should have ended his *kōshokubon* cycle on this unromantic and sobering note.

The strongly Buddhist tone of the closing pages does not imply that the heroine's resignation is motivated by feelings of piety. The temple scene (pp. 203–8) is introduced not so much for its religious associations as to provide a setting for the five hundred Arhats who so effectively help to recall the heroine's amorous past. Both Saikaku and the heroine are realists enough to know that, if only she had retained her youth and beauty, no amount of piety would have brought her to a desolate mountain cave. She has become a nun simply because the *kōshoku* that ruled her life has proved bankrupt and because the world (as she tells her visitors) has become irksome to her.

3. *The Eternal Storehouse of Japan* (See also Introduction, p. 27)

Book 1, Chapter 2: The Wind That Destroyed the Fan Maker's Shop in the Second Generation

Book 2, Chapter 3: The Daikoku Who Wore Ready Wit in His Sedge Hat

Book 4, Chapter 4: The Ten Virtues of Tea That All Disappeared at Once

Nippon Eitaigura was published in Osaka in the First Moon of 1688, with the subtitle of *Ōfuku Shinchōja Kyō (New Lessons from the Lives of Wealthy Men);* thereafter it appeared in numerous reprintings in Osaka, Edo and Kyoto. It consisted of six quarto volumes, each containing five stories, and was illustrated by Yoshida Hambei. The present translation uses the modern reprint contained in Volume VII of the *Standard Edition of Saikaku's Complete Works,* Tokyo, 1950, pp. 17–175.

In choosing the subtitle for this work, Saikaku clearly had in mind the *Chōja Kyō (Lessons from the Lives of Wealthy Men),* a collection of practical guides for the emergent merchant class, which had been circulated in handwritten form about one century earlier, and which had first been printed in 1627. Part of Saikaku's purpose was to provide his merchant readers with a more up-to-date type of guide that would take into account the new economic conditions produced by the development of mercantile capitalism during the course of the century.[14]

The stories and characters in *Nippon Eitaigura* are, however, based entirely on Saikaku's own observation of his fellow-townsmen. Living in the great commercial city of Osaka, he had ample opportunity to observe the various ways in which tradesmen could amass fortunes and also the circumstances that could lead them to squander the money for which they or their fathers

[14] *Teihon Saikaku Zenshū,* Vol. VII, p. 8.

had struggled so fiercely. Of the thirty stories in the collection, sixteen are concerned mainly with financial success and fourteen with failure. All the stories, however, deal with men who at one time or another have possessed considerable wealth.

In the closing sentences of his final story, Saikaku explains the meaning of the title and the purpose of his book:

> These stories [of wealthy men] have been handed down to us and are here inscribed in the Great Ledger of Japan, so that they may be of use to men who read them in times to come. We have put all these records in order and have consigned them to the Eternal Storehouse; our land, too, enjoys order and peace in this auspicious reign.[15]

The primary aim, then, is didactic and utilitarian. By giving numerous examples of prosperity and decline, Saikaku provides his townsmen-readers with practical advice as to how they should conduct their lives.

The acquisition of money was the guiding principle for the townsmen, and Saikaku supports this principle in the strongest terms: "Though we cannot take it with us when we die, money is the one thing that is essential in the present world."[16] Money, as it appears in *Nippon Eitaigura,* is no elusive commodity, but something that can be acquired in large quantity by anyone endowed with a reasonable amount of intelligence and energy. Nor is it necessary to use dishonest means in its pursuit; indeed, all sharp practices must be strongly condemned. "The life of a man may be a dream, yet it lasts some fifty years, and whatever honest work we may choose in this world, we shall surely find it."[17]

Inasmuch as the honest acquisition of wealth is the townsman's main aim in life, poverty must be regarded as a sort of illness. It is an illness, however, that can be cured by hard work, thrift, care of one's health and the other ingredients of the "millionaire pills" (Introduction, p. 33). Equally, it can be induced or aggravated by falling in love with a courtesan, becoming devoted to the tea ceremony, studying military arts in disregard of one's townsman status, drinking at dinnertime, investing in mines, associating with priests or actors and in countless other ways.[18]

[15] *Op. cit.,* p. 175. *(Osamaru* [order] is a pivot word.)
[16] *Op. cit.,* p. 77. See also the opening sentence of Bk. 1, Chap. 2, p. 211 of translation.
[17] P. 232 of translation.
[18] *Op. cit.,* pp. 73-4.

On the whole it would appear that Saikaku's practical advice on how to avoid losing one's money was considerably more useful than the methods he describes for making it. In both cases, however, his stress was on the personal qualities that one should develop or restrain, rather than on any specific techniques of business. In writing *Nippon Eitaigura,* the first and most popular of his townsman cycle, Saikaku was not trying to produce a mere textbook. In contrast with the authors of the *Chōja Kyō,* whose only purpose was to provide practical guidance, Saikaku was first and foremost a creative writer. He was, as we have seen, fascinated with money ("Nothing in this world," he writes, "is as interesting as money."[19]) and with the various effects that it could have on people. The contemporary success of the book derived largely from its instructive content. The interest for most modern readers, however, certainly does not lie in the didactic elements of *Nippon Eitaigura,* but in the realistic evocation of the rich merchants of the time, in the lively humour (especially when depicting misers) and in the vivid accounts of how men will struggle feverishly for money—and then spend no less energy in wasting it.

4. *Reckonings That Carry Men through the World* (see also Introduction, p. 29)

Book 1, Chapter 2: The Ancient Scabbard
Chapter 4: The Rat That Delivered Letters
Book 2, Chapter 4: Not Even One's Gatepost Is Secure in This Fleeting, Fleecing World
Book 3, Chapter 3: The Man Who Turned into Gold Coins While He Slept
Book 5, Chapter 3: Lord Heitarō

Seken Munesanyō, the last of Saikaku's works to appear during his lifetime, was published in Osaka in the First Moon of 1692, with the subtitle of *Ōmisoka Ichinichi Senkin (At the Year's End a Single Day Is Worth a Thousand Pounds of Gold).* It consisted of five quarto volumes, each containing four stories. The illustrations are by Makieshi Genzaburō, a pupil of the Hambei School. The present translation is based on the modern reprint in Volume VII of the *Standard Edition of Saikaku's Complete Works,* Tokyo, pp. 179–298.

[19] *Op. cit.,* p. 8.

The general subject of *Seken Munesanyō* is the same as that of *Nippon Eitai-gura,* namely, the economic life of the townsmen. The approach and the theme, however, are entirely different.[20] A brief comparison of these two representative *chōnin* works will throw considerable light on the nature of *Seken Munesanyō.*

In *Nippon Eitaigura* Saikaku's emphasis was on the various ways of making or of conserving wealth. The characters in *Seken Munesanyō* set their sights far lower; they are concerned not with wealth but merely with solvency. Most of the stories deal with the shifts used by the poor townsmen to survive economically during that most crucial period of the year—the last days of the Twelfth Moon, when "a single day is worth a thousand pounds of gold."

In Saikaku's time almost all transactions among townsmen were done on credit. Bills were payable during the various holiday periods, but final settlement could normally be postponed until the end of the year. In order to start the new year properly, it was essential to clear all one's debts by the last day. During this period the bill collectors (a rough and rather callous breed of men) were out in full force, and life for the indigent townsman could become a veritable Hell. By setting all his stories during the critical year-end period, Saikaku was able to concentrate on the dark and tragic side of the townsman's existence. "The year-end season," as he writes, "is full of sad happenings that stir even the outsider's heart."[21]

In *Nippon Eitaigura,* too, the year-end often figures as a background; but in *Seken Munesanyō* it occupies the very centre of the stage. For this reason, it is significant that, unlike the characters in *Nippon Eitaigura,* those in the later work are as a rule anonymous, being simply designated by their status— "the master," "the retired mistress," "the wife," "the son," "the bill collector," "the clerk," "the poor man," etc.[22] Most of the stories contain numerous characters, and the action is dominated not so much by any one of these characters as by the pervasive fact of the year's end and its drastic significance for the poorer members of the townsman class. Although several of the characters emerge vividly from these stories (the miserly old woman in *The Rat That Delivered Letters,* for example, and the *rōnin's* shrewish wife in *The Ancient Scabbard),* the emphasis is usually on the anonymous group rather

[20] Hisamatsu Senichi in *Kokubungaku,* Vol. II, No. 6 (1957), p. 5.
[21] P. 242 of translation.
[22] *Teihon Saikaku Zenshū,* Vol. VII, p. 10.

than on the individual protagonist. This, again, represents an important difference from *Nippon Eitaigura,* where each of the stories centres about a single character.

Japanese critics have a great fondness for the pair of words *sekkyokuteki* (positive, optimistic) and *shōkyokuteki* (negative, pessimistic). In discussing Saikaku's *kōshoku* works, for instance, they will frequently contrast the *sekkyokuteki* approach of *Kōshoku Ichidai Otoko* with the *shōkyokuteki* approach of *Kōshoku Ichidai Onna.* Similarly, *Nippon Eitaigura* is described as showing the "positive" aspects of townsman life, as opposed to *Seken Munesanyō,* which concentrates on the "negative" side. This difference in approach between the townsman works is exemplified by the treatment of the dynamic force that is common to them both—money. The money theme in *Seken Munesanyō* is presented in a sad, gloomy light. Money is no longer viewed as a delightful commodity, the desire for which can spur men to great feats of energy; rather, it is "the real enemy," the source of endless worry and despair.[23]

The quadripartite hierarchy of the Tokugawa Period and the social chasm that separated the *bushi* (warriors) from the *heimin* (commoners) must not obscure the great stratifications that existed within each of the classes. So far as the *chōnin* were concerned, stratification was based almost entirely on money. *Nippon Eitaigura,* as we have seen, dealt mainly with the upper-class townsmen, the *bungen* and *chōja* who had at one time or another in their lives either inherited or amassed great fortunes. Most of the characters in *Seken Munesanyō,* however, are the middle and lower townsmen, who have never possessed any wealth and who must struggle unremittingly if they are not to sink into the abyss of misery that is described in such stories as *The Man Who Turned into Gold Coins While He Slept.* Saikaku provides the only realistic account in existence of the lives of what may be described as the *"lumpen-townsmen,"* the economic misfits and failures of his time. "Though this world is a paradise for rich people," says one of the representative characters in *Seken Munesanyō,* "for poor folk like us, who do not even have a handful of firewood to burn under our cauldron, it is a very hell."[24]

In his earlier work Saikaku had implicitly accepted the idea that it was possible for any energetic or intelligent man, however low-born or isolated

---

[23] E.g., p. 255 of translation.
[24] P. 253 of translation.

he might be, not only to "cure himself" of poverty, but to amass considerable wealth by his own honest labours. In *Seken Munesanyō,* however, he seems to have realized that the economic realities of the time were often far less rosy than this idea suggested, and that there were many cases of townsmen who were so utterly sunk in poverty that they could never extricate themselves from it, however hard they might work. In such cases poverty became hopeless and permanent; it was no longer a spur that encouraged men to greater efforts, but a source of increasing misery for the family and "of many an evil scheme."[25]

This concentration on the more pathetic sides of townsman life might well have led to the type of sentimentality that we find in such chroniclers of Victorian poverty as George Gissing or Thomas Hood. Saikaku, however, is saved from this by the vividness of his narrative and by the wry humour with which he describes his characters as they struggle for a few extra pieces of silver or concoct one new ruse after another in a desperate effort to get over the last crucial days of the year.

[25] P. 262 of translation.

APPENDIX II. MONEY IN SAIKAKU'S TIME

In about 1601, shortly after his victory in the Battle of Sekigahara, Tokugawa Ieyasu established a national system of gold and silver currency, the first of its kind in Japan. Iemitsu, the third Tokugawa Shogun, added a new indigenous form of copper currency (the *Kanei-tsūhō*) in 1636, thus inaugurating the so-called "triple-coinage system" *(sanka-seido)*. The currency remained unchanged until the recoinage of 1695, two years after Saikaku's death. Of the three forms of coinage, copper was circulated throughout the country, gold was mainly used in Edo, whereas silver was mainly used in the Kyoto-Osaka-Sakai area of western Japan. Gold and silver mints *(kinza and ginza)* were under the direct control of the government; the silver mint was moved to Edo in 1612 and gave its name to the present Ginza district in Tokyo.

Gold: There were three forms of gold coin. The largest was the *ōban* (or *bankin*), a rounded oblong coin weighing approximately 44 *momme*.[1] The *ōban* was not in general circulation and was mainly used when making presentations to the Shogun, to the various *daimyō* or to temples. It was officially equivalent in value to 10 *koban* (see below), but in Saikaku's time it was actually exchanged at the rate of about 8 *koban*.

The *koban* was an oval coin weighing 1 *ryō*, or approximately 4.8 *momme*. One hundred *koban* were known as a "bundle" and 1,000 *koban* as a "box." The *ichibu-koban* was a rectangular coin worth exactly one-quarter of a *koban* and weighing about 1.2 *momme*.

Silver: Whereas gold coins were more or less fixed in value, silver coins

---

[1]Weights: 10 *rin*=1 *fun*
  10 *fun*=1 *momme*=58 Tr. grains
  1000 *momme*=1 *kan*=8.27 lbs. avdp.

had to be weighed each time to determine their exact worth. They were counted by weight rather than by pieces. There were two types. The *chōgin* were oval coins weighing about 43 *momme;* approximately 230 *chōgin* constituted 10 *kamme (kan)* of silver and were called a "box." The *mame-ita-gin* (also known as *kodama-gin,* or *kotsubu,* "little drops") were small round coins weighing anything from 1 *momme* to 5 *momme.*

Copper: There was only one form of copper coin in Saikaku's time, namely, the *Kanei-tsūhō,* a round piece with a square hole in the centre. The coppers *(zeni* or *ichimonsen)* were strung together in lots of 100 or 1,000. One thousand coppers weighed about 1 *kan* and were known as 1 *kammon.* It was normal to string 96 coppers together *(kurokusen)* and to count them as being worth 100; similarly, 960 coppers were counted as being equivalent in value to 1,000. This resulted from the fact that the rate of exchange between the *Kanei-tsūhō* and the Chinese copper coins known as *Eiraku-tsūhō,* which had circulated until 1636, was officially fixed at 96:100.

Exchange: In 1609 an order of the government fixed the gold-silver-copper rate of exchange at 1 gold *ryō*=50 silver *momme*=4 copper *kammon.* There was no official banking system, however, and money-changing was carried out by the merchants at a fluctuating rate. At the time when Saikaku wrote the works translated in this volume the actual rate of exchange was 1 gold *ryō*=60 silver *momme*=4 copper *kammon.*

Equivalents: Since Saikaku obviously attached such importance to monetary details (see Introduction, pp. 34–5), a special effort has been made in the present translation to give meaningful equivalents in the notes to the money mentioned in the text. The usual method for computing equivalents is based on the price of rice. This, of course, has many drawbacks, partly because of the frequent fluctuations in rice prices, partly because in the Tokugawa Period rice prices tended to be much lower in relation to other commodities than they are at present. It serves, however, to give a general idea of money equivalents. In 1681, 1 *koku* (4.96 bushels) of rice was worth about 77 *momme* of silver; in 1684, it had fallen to 40 *momme;* in 1691, it fluctuated between 41 and 53 *momme.* In 1952, 1 *koku* of rice cost 8,500 *yen;* in 1956, it had risen to 10,900 *yen* and in 1958, the official price for rationed rice was 12,200 *yen.* In determining the following approximate equivalents I have used the rice prices for 1684 and for 1956; for rates of exchange I have used 1 gold *ryō*= 60 silver *momme*=4 copper *kammon,* and 1,000 *yen*=£1=$2.80.

1 gold *ryō*	=¥ 16,350	=£ 16.7.0	= $ 45.75
1 *ichibu-koban*	=¥ 4,087.50	=£ 4.1.9	= $ 11.35
1 silver *momme*	=¥ 272.50	=£ 0.5.6	= $ 0.75
1 silver *kamme*	=¥272,500	=£272.10.0	=$763.00
1 copper *kammon*	=¥ 4,087.50	=£ 4.1.9	= $ 11.35
1 copper *monsen*	=¥ .04	= 1d.	= $ 0.01

As the current price of rice continues to go up, these modern equivalents of Edo currency will, of course, have to be increased.

APPENDIX III. THE HIERARCHY OF COURTESANS

Courtesans had flourished in Japan since ancient times and the institution is even mentioned in the eighth-century anthology of poems, the *Manyō-shū*. Until the end of the eighteenth century, they usually operated on an individual basis and without any legal restrictions regarding their area of activities. The first "licensed quarters" *(yūri)* were established in the Rokujō district of Kyoto in 1589 under Hideyoshi. The Tokugawa policy of centralization and systematic control encouraged the establishment of such quarters in most of the large towns. By Saikaku's time the traditional system of "scattered prostitution" *(sanshō)* had given way to one of "centralized prostitution" *(shūshō)*.

In 1679 there were over one hundred licensed quarters in Japan. Although they differed in the details of their organization, they were all modelled on the Shimabara district of Kyoto. The Shimabara courtesans were divided into two main classes, the *age-jorō* and the *mise-jorō*. The *age-jorō* were professional entertainers, often endowed with considerable elegance and culture (see Introduction, p. 9). Although they were at the same time prostitutes, high-ranking *age-jorō* were in a position to turn down unwelcome customers; frequently their services would be monopolized by a single customer for a year or more. The *age-jorō* lived in the house of their employers *(kutsuwa* or *yūjoya)* and were summoned to the nearby "houses of assignation" *(ageya)* to entertain their customers. In contrast, the *mise-jorō* (also known as *hashi-jorō* or *tsubone-jorō)* were common prostitutes, who either plied their trade in the "houses" *(mise)* where they lived, or who were summoned to outside "teahouses" *(chaya)*. The institution of *geisha* did not exist in Saikaku's time (note 20); it owes its origins, however, to that of the *age-jorō*.

Both classes of courtesans were elaborately stratified. The girl's rank was determined by her appearance, her cultural attainments, her seniority in the district and, most important of all, her ability to please customers. Recruitment, promotion, demotion and dismissal provided for a good degree of

285

mobility. The hierarchy of *age-joro* had become clearly defined by the middle of the seventeenth century. At the summit were the *tayū*, the aristocrats of the gay quarters, who were characterized by their "spirit" and "pride" *(iki* and *hari)*, and by the respect that was accorded to them in the microcosmic world that they inhabited. *Tayū* were to be found in only five districts, viz. Shimabara (Kyoto), Shinmachi (Osaka), Yoshiwara (Edo), Maruyama (Nagasaki) and Kanayama (Sado Island). As befitted their elevated position, they were extremely rare. Among the 983 courtesans employed in Shinmachi in 1688, for example, there were only 17 *tayū*.

Below the *tayū* came the *tenjin (tenshoku)*. The third rank consisted of the *kakoi*, the *hanya*, the *hikifune-joro* and the *taiko-joro*. The *hanya* (half nights) differed from the *kakoi* in that they could be hired either by the day or by the night. The *hikifune-joro* (boat-drawing courtesans) and the *taiko-joro* (drum-playing courtesans) had the same rank as the *kakoi;* their services did not, however, extend to the bedchamber, but were limited to the "parlour" *(zashiki)*, where they assisted the *tayū* in entertaining guests with music, wine, dancing, etc. In addition, there were apprentice courtesans, known as *kaburo (kamuro)*, who were invariably in attendance on the *tayū* and the *tenjin;* they are the origin of the modern *maiko* of Kyoto.

The Yoshiwara hierarchy of *age-joro* differed in certain particulars from that of Shimabara. The three principal grades were *tayū* (later known as *oiran)*, *kōshi* and *tsubone*. The services of the *tsubone* (like those of the *hanya* in Kyoto) were divided into a day period and a night period. There was also a fourth grade known as *sancha*. These were originally private prostitutes and bathhouse girls who had flourished on an independent basis after the Yoshiwara district had been destroyed in the great fire of 1657; in 1665 the government had ordered them to give up their private practice and to enter the rebuilt Yoshiwara. The *sancha* entirely lacked the elegance of their superiors in the hierarchy, and were in fact closer to common *mise-joro*.

Detailed information on the organization, customs and etiquette of the various districts was set forth in the numerous *yūjo-hyōbanki* (see Introduction, p. 13). These practical manuals also gave the name of each girl in the quarter, together with her rank, her physical attributes, her cultural attainments, etc. In 1678, when the institution had become firmly established, a very interesting work, known as the *Shikidō Ōkagami (The Great Mirror of the Way of Love)*, was published in Edo; this was a sort of encyclopaedia giving details on the gay quarters throughout the land.

The principal basis for the hierarchy of courtesans was the varying cost of their services. The cost differed from town to town (being highest in the Yoshiwara), but was uniform for any class of courtesan within the same quarter. There were no distinctions in nomenclature for the *mise-jorō* and their hierarchy was determined entirely by price. The following chart shows the basic cost of hiring the various classes of courtesans in eight different districts. It is based on material contained in the *Shokoku Irozato Annai (Guide to the Pleasure Quarters in Different Provinces)* (1688) and on Saikaku's own work, notably *The Great Mirror of Beauties* (1684). Prices are given in *momme* of silver; figures separated by a colon refer to courtesans whose services could be divided between a day period and a night period.

	AGE-JORŌ				MISE-JORŌ (classes)			
	tayū	tenjin, kōshi	kakoi, hikifune-jorō, etc.	sancha	1st	2nd	3rd	4th
Yoshiwara (Edo)	74	52	25 : 25	15–20	5	4	3	1.5
Shimabara (Kyoto)	58	30	18, 9 : 9		3	2	1	0.5
Shinmachi (Osaka)	46	30	17		3	2	1	0.5
Maruyama (Nagasaki)	30	20	8 : 8			2	1	
Kanayama (Sado)	35	25	15 : 15			3	2	
Chimori (Sakai)		23–8	17		2	1	0.6	0.4
Kitsuji (Nara)			15, 9 : 9			1	0.5	
Shumokucho (Fushimi)			18, 9 : 9			1	0.5	

As will be seen, the price range within a single district was considerable. In Shimabara, for example, the "fee" *(agedai)* of a *tayū* was 58 *momme*. Since she was always attended by a *hikifune-jorō* (at 18 *momme*), the basic cost of her services was 76 *momme*. This compared with 18 *momme* for a *kakoi* and half a *momme* for a low-ranking *mise-jorō*. Translating these figures into modern Western equivalents (App. 11), we find a range extending from $58 (£21), through $14 (£5), to a mere 40 cents (3 s).

The actual cost of consorting with *tayū* was, however, far greater than these figures would suggest. In *The Great Mirror of Beauties* Saikaku with characteristic thoroughness itemizes the expense of a customer's first visit to a Kyoto *tayū*. When the basic fee and all the numerous tips to attendants are included, we arrive at the rather substantial sum of 551 *momme*, approximately $420 (£150).

Furthermore, it was normal for the fashionable townsman to keep a high-ranking courtesan for his own entertainment during at least one twelve-month period. In the same book Saikaku calculates that at the most economical rate possible this luxury cost no less than 29 *kamme* of silver, the equivalent of about $22,100 (£7,900). Saikaku frequently warned his townsman readers about the danger of dissipating their fortunes in the gay quarters. *The Life of a Man Who Lived for Love* sets forth the minimum amounts of invested capital that a man should have in order to permit himself the pleasure of frequenting various classes of courtesans. For a *tayū* one needed at least 500 *kamme* ($381,500; £136,250), for a *tenjin* 200 *kamme* ($152,600; £54,500) and for a *kakoi* 50 *kamme* ($38,150, £13,625).

Not infrequently the pleasures of the gay quarters proved to be ruinous. Thus the millionaire hero of *The Wind That Destroyed the Fan Maker's Shop in the Second Generation* (pp. 211–16) having suddenly discovered the charms of the Floating World, succeeded in spending the equivalent of about $1,500,000 (£550,000), in the course of four or five years and ended his days as a beggar. It is worthwhile noting that the passage of time has not made the pleasures of the "flower and willow world" appreciably cheaper. The company of a fashionable *geisha* nowadays can be almost as ruinous as that of a *tayū* in Saikaku's time. The first night with a popular Shimbashi *geisha* costs well over $280 (£100).

SELECTED BIBLIOGRAPHY

TEXTS

Originals or copies of block-printed texts

Kōshoku Gonin Onna, offset photo reproduction in 1 volume and reduced size, ed. Yoshida Kōichi, Koten Bunko, Tokyo, 1956.

Kōshoku Ichidai Onna, full-size reproduction in 6 volumes and full size, ed. Aikaku Shoin, Tokyo, 1927.

Nippon Eitaigura and *Seken Munesanyō,* original block-printed texts (1st editions), published in Osaka in 1688 and 1692, respectively, and belonging to the translator's library.

Modern reprints

Saikaku Meisaku Shū (Collection of Saikaku's Masterpieces), expurgated 2-vol. edition of Saikaku's works, Nihon Meicho Zenshū Kankō Kai, Tokyo, 1929.

Teihon Saikaku Zenshū (Standard Edition of Saikaku's Complete Works), ed. Ebara Taizō, Teruoka Yasutaka, Noma Kōshin, Chūō Kōron Sha, Tokyo, Vol. II, 1949; Vol. VII, 1950.

CRITICAL WORKS, COMMENTARIES AND PARAPHRASES

General

Noma Kōshin: *Saikaku Nempu Kōshō (A Chronological Study of Saikaku),* Chūō Kōron Sha, Tokyo, 1952.

Takano Tatsuyuki: *Edo Bungaku Shi (A History of Edo Literature),* Vol. I, Tōkyō Dō, Tokyo, 1952.

Teruoka Yasutaka: *Kinsei Haiku (Modern Haiku),* Gakuto Sha, Tokyo, 1952.

——: *Saikaku,* published in the series, "Nihon Koten Kanshō Tokuhon," Sōgen Sha, Tokyo, 1956.

——: *Saikaku Hyōron to Kenkyū (Saikaku Criticism and Research)*, 2 vols., Chūō Kōron Sha, Tokyo, 1948, 1950.

Yamaguchi Takeshi: *Edo Bungaku Kenkyū (A Study of Edo Literature)*, Tōkyō Dō, Tokyo, 1933.

Dealing with specific works

Asō Isoji: *Saikaku Zenshū (Complete Works of Saikaku)*, Vol. II, including translation into modern Japanese of *Kōshoku Gonin Onna* and *Kōshoku Ichidai Onna*, Kawade Shobō, Tokyo, 1952.

Ichiba Naojirō: *Seken Munesanyō Zenshaku (Complete Interpretation of "Reckonings That Carry Men through the World")*, Bunsendō Shobō, Tokyo, 1934.

Ōyabu Toranosuke: *Nippon Eitaigura Shinkō (A New Commentary on "The Eternal Storehouse of Japan")*, Hakutei Sha, Tokyo, 1937.

Teruoka Yasutaka: *Kōshoku Gonin Onna Hyōshaku (Commentary on "Five Women Who Chose Love")*, Meiji Shoin, Tokyo, 1953.

Yoshii Isamu: *Kōshoku Ichidai Onna*, Kadokawa Shoten, Tokyo, 1952.

TRANSLATIONS INTO ENGLISH

Bary, W. T. de: *Five Women Who Loved Love* (trans. of *Kōshoku Gonin Onna*), Tuttle, Tokyo, 1956.

Hibbett, Howard: *The Floating World in Japanese Fiction* (trans. from *Kōshoku Ichidai Onna*), Oxford University Press, London, 1959.

Huggins, H. and Osamu Shimizu: *Intimate Tales of Old Japan* (includes trans. from *Saikaku Shokoku-banashi*), Tokyo, 1929.

Lane, Richard: "The Umbrella Oracle" (trans. from *Saikaku Shokoku-banashi*), pp. 354–6 of *Anthology of Japanese Literature* (Keene, Donald [ed.], New York, 1955).

——: "Two Samurai Tales: Romance and Realism in Old Japan" (trans. from *Saikaku Shokoku-banashi*), *The Atlantic Monthly*, Jan. 1955.

——: "Three Stories from Saikaku" (trans. from *Saikaku Shokoku-banashi*, *Zoku Tsurezure* and *Saikaku Oki-miyage*), *Japan Quarterly*, Jan.-Mar. 1958.

Mizuno Sōji: *The Way to Wealth* (trans. from *Nippon Eitaigura*), Tokyo, 1955.

Rahder, J.: "Saikaku's 'Life of a Voluptuous Woman,' Second Book" (trans. from *Kōshoku Ichidai Onna*), *Acta Orientalia*, XIII, 4, Leiden, 1934.

G. W. Sargent: "The Tycoon of All Tenants" (trans. from *Nippon Eitaigura*), pp. 357–62 of *Anthology of Japanese Literature*, op. cit.

———: *The Japanese Family Storehouse* (trans. of *Nippon Eitaigura,* Cambridge University Press, London, 1959.

Satō Ken: *Quaint Stories of Samurai* (trans. from *Nanshoku Ōkagami, Budō Denraiki, Buke Giri Monogatari* and *Yorozu no Fumi Hōgu*), Paris (private distribution), 1928.

NOTE: For detailed bibliographies see Teruoka: *Saikaku* (cited above), pp. 245–54, and Teruoka: "Saikaku Kenkyū Bunken Sōran" ("Bibliographical Synopsis of Saikaku Studies") in *Kokubungaku,* Vol. II, No. 6 (1957), pp. 104–18.

NOTES

1. *Himéji, the Town of the Lovely Damsel* (Sugata Himeji). *Hime* is used here in a double sense: as the first character of the town Himeji, and in its original meaning of "damsel" or "princess." Saikaku's titles, subtitles and chapter endings frequently contain double (sometimes triple) meanings and puns *(kakekotoba)* for which the Japanese language is particularly well suited.

2. *Love Is Darkness* . . . (Koi wa yami . . .) Proverb signifying that love infatuates (cf. "Love is blind").

. . . *the Land of Love* (yoru wo hiru no kuni). Lit., "the land which makes night into noon," i.e., the gay quarters. The free, rapid association of ideas and images was an outstanding characteristic of the *haikai*. The present 8-word title, for example, contains 3 linked ideas: (i) love is darkness *(koi wa yami)*, i.e., love can make one throw reason to the wind, (ii) the darkness of night lends itself to the mysteries of love *(koi wa yami-yoru)*, (iii) there is a land (viz., the gay quarters) that makes night as bright as day *(yoru-wo-hiru no kuni)*. Between (ii) and (iii) we see a typical instance of the stylistic device known as *shiritori* (lit., "taking the rear or buttocks") in which the last word of one clause serves at the same time as the first word of the succeeding clause.

The influence of *haikai* poetry on Saikaku's prose style is especially evident in the titles and in the opening and closing passages of his books (see also notes 4 and 75 below).

3. *Murotsu.* Town in Harima Province, present-day Hyōgo Prefecture (capital Kōbe); in Edo Period, a principal port for Inland Sea traffic, famous for its gay quarters.

4. *waves . . . ships . . . treasure* (takarabune no namimakura, etc.). There is an allusion here to the old custom of placing an engraving of the treasure ship *(takarabune)* of the Seven Gods of Luck under one's pillow on New Year's Eve to ensure good dreams. *Namimakura* (wave pillow) also has the meaning of sea voyage or of sleeping on board ship, with the further

suggestion that the treasure ships themselves are using the waves as pillows. This opening sentence contains a typical *haikai*-type chain of interrelated images and "pivot words" *(kakekotoba)*.

5. *the hero of old* (mukashi otoko). This refers to Ariwara no Narihira (825–880), grandson of the Emperor Heijō and one of the Six Poetical Geniuses *(Rokkasen)* of the Heian Period. Famous for his good looks and for the number of his love affairs, he is generally identified with the hero of the great classic Ise Monogatari *(The Tales of Ise);* he has also been credited with authorship of this work.

6. *piled up to the very ceiling* (chitsuka ni tsumori). Lit., "piled up one thousand hand-breadths." It was customary for courtesans to send their customers written pledges of fidelity *(seishi),* which, however, no man of the world would take at their face value. The sending of fingernails, toenails or hair was a similar convention.

7. *the most jealous of women* (rinki fukaki onna mo). Reference to the *Tsurezuregusa (Gleanings from My Leisure Hours,* c. 1330): " . . . a rope woven from the locks of women's hair will bind a very elephant."

8. *River of the Three Ways* (Sanzu no Kawa). A Buddhist Styx, near whose banks a devilish old hag used to revile passing sinners and rob them of their clothes.

9. *Korai Bridge* (Kōrai Hashi). Bridge in the Eastern Ward of Ōsaka and the site of many old-clothes dealers.

10. *Storehouse of the Floating World* (ukiyo-gura). *Ukiyo* (floating world) was the conventional image used by writers, both lay and clerical, to convey the transitoriness of present life; in Saikaku's time it also suggested the fugitive pleasures of the demimonde; hence *ukiyo-e,* the genre paintings. By further extension, *ukiyo* meant "fashionable," "up-to-date," as in *ukiyo-motoyui* (fashionable type of paper cord for tying the hair). It also had the sense of "depraved" as in *ukiyo-dera* (the temple of a depraved priest).

11. *publicly disowned* (kandōchō ni tsukete). This refers to the posting by one's father of an official act of disownment, as opposed to private disinheritance *(naishō-kandō).* In a society such as that of Tokugawa Japan, in which status depended almost entirely on one's family connexions, disownment was far more than a matter of losing one's inheritance and indeed represented the greatest of disasters for the individual.

12. *a girl of pleasure* (jorō). Generic term including the entire gamut of professional women, from the most exalted courtesan *(tayū)* whose nightly hire was the equivalent of about $58 (£21), to the meanest strumpet *(hashi-jorō)*, who might cost a mere 40 cents (3 s).

13. *a lantern on a moonlit night* (tsukiyo ni chōchin). Proverbial expression for extravagance.

14. *drum-holders* (taikomochi). In the Edo Period professional male entertainers, corresponding (very roughly) to European jesters, buffoons or "allowed fools"; they would accompany customers on drinking expeditions to the gay quarters, where they often had the role of elegant panders. They would frequently supervise the entertainment at fashionable parties and had considerable influence over the courtesans. In more recent times the word *taikomochi* came to mean "flatterer" or "sycophant." A few rather elderly *taikomochi* still exist in Kyōto and in the Yoshiwara district of Tōkyō, but they are sufficiently rare to have been classified officially as National Treasures *(kokuhō)* and no more are being trained.

15. *aged procuresses* (yarite). Elderly women who supervised and attended courtesans. It was their function both to procure customers for their charges and to repel the attentions of unsuitable would-be customers.

16. *ceremonial tea* (kadocha). Tea offered to passers-by on the first day of the Seventh Moon (of the lunar calendar) in commemoration of the deceased.

17. *the Sacred Bonfire* (okuribi). This was lit on the 16th day of the Seventh Moon at the end of the Urabon (Buddhist festival for the dead, Sanskrit: *Ullambana)* to speed the departing spirits on their return to the yonder world. Seijūrō and his friends were practising what might be compared to a "black Mass." The tooth sticks *(yōji)* were large tasselled implements used for brushing one's teeth. *The Holy Shelf* (Sonryō no tana), lit., "shelf for the spirits of the dead," was customarily set up during the Urabon before the tablet of the deceased; on it were offered gourds, aubergines, lotus leaves and the like.

18. *"Isle of Nakedness"* (Hadakajima). Island appearing on maps of Chinese origin circulating in Saikaku's time. Other odd islands were the Isle of Pygmies, Women's Island, etc. Seijūrō's only interest in the island was in its name, which provided a convenient pretext for having the girls undress in supposed imitation of its inhabitants.

19. *her kimono* (katabira). The *katabira* is a hemp garment worn in warm weather.

20. *a courtesan named Yoshizaki* (Yoshizaki to ieru kakoi-jorō). The *kakoi* ranked third (after *tayū* and *tenjin*) in the hierarchy of *age-jorō* (high-class courtesans) in Kyōto and Ōsaka. In a town like Murotsu where there were no *tayū* or *tenjin*, the *kakoi* occupied the highest rank. In Shimabara (Kyōto) the *kakoi*'s fee was 18 *momme* of silver (equivalent to about $14; £5); originally the fee was 15 *momme* and Saikaku here writes the word *kakoi* with the characters for "fifteen." The *age-jorō*, a number of whom normally lived together in the house of their employer, were called out to entertain guests in various *ageya* (houses of assignation), as opposed to the far less dignified *mise-jorō*, who plied their trade in the houses *(mise)* where they lived. In this sense the *age-jorō* belonged more to the category of professional entertainer than to that of mere prostitute, the latter class being represented by *mise-jorō, yaha-tsu* (streetwalkers), etc. In Saikaku's time, the term *geisha* was not used in its modern sense (it referred to any person, male or female, whose profession was based on artistic accomplishment), nor was there any real equivalent to the present-day *geisha* institution. Even the most exalted and artistically accomplished *tayū* could be hired by the night for sexual purposes, although it is true that she might on occasion turn down a client if he was too displeasing, a luxury which her less elevated colleagues could ill afford.

21. *The Goddess Benzai* (Benzaiten). A typically sophisticated pun pounced on by the jaded group to discomfit the girl. The word for macula *(namazu)* is homonymous with that for catfish, an animal with a rather mottled appearance. According to legend (referred to in *haikai* of the Teitoku School and therefore familiar in fashionable company), a catfish had acted as messenger for the Goddess Benzai (Saravasti). This Goddess, one of the Seven Lucky Gods (Shichifukujin), was regarded as a paradigm of beauty—hence the irony of the pun. It was customary for people suffering from vitiligo *(namazu)* to offer images to the Goddess on which a catfish *(namazu)* was painted in white, the characteristic colour of the disease—so strong was the influence of puns on people's thinking.

22. *A man stripped stark naked* . . . (otoko wa hadaka hyakkan). Proverb. One *kammon* of copper was equivalent in value to about one-quarter *koban* of gold; accordingly, 100 *kammon* corresponded to about $1,150 (£410) in present-day values.

23. *the house* (ageya). High-class house of assignation (see note 20 above) to which the top-ranking courtesans (i.e., *tayū, tenjin* and *kakoi*) were summoned to entertain customers.

24. *one cup in each hand* (ryō no te ni temmoku futatsu). The servant served the cups perfunctorily with her hands instead of using a tray in the proper manner.

25. *gold in his purse* (ichibu-koban). Lit., "a gold piece." Rectangular gold coin worth one-quarter of a *koban*, i.e., about $11 (£4) in present values.

26. *attachments to the world* (yo ni nagori ari). Reflexion of the Buddhist notion that one cannot free oneself by death so long as one has unfulfilled obligations or longings in the present world. In Minakawa's case these obligations (attachments) probably involved repaying her debt to her employer by continuing her work as a courtesan.

27. *now is the time* (sasa ima ja). As usual in *Kōshoku Gonin Onna*, the woman takes the initiative at the moment of crisis. Minakawa's reason for leaving the room after pretending to abandon Seijūrō was that she feared that they were being overheard. Her ruse was designed to put the brothel-keepers off their guard. It also gave her a chance to change into the white clothes traditional for suicide.

28. *her employer's house* (oyakata no moto). Being an *age-jorō* (note 20 above), she did not, like the lowly *mise-jorō*, live in the house where she practised her trade, but was called to the various *ageya* as her services were required.

29 *eighteen years of age* (sono toshi wa jūku). The age, however, at which Buddha is said to have taken his vows.

30. *the town of Himéji*. One of the main ports on the Inland Sea, some 35 miles west of modern Kōbe and 15 miles east of Murotsu; site of the famous castle built by Akamatsu no Sadanori in the 14th century.

31. *of the greatest fastidiousness* (otoko no irogonomite). *Irogonomu* is the Japanese *(kun)* reading of the compound usually pronounced *kōshoku*, which appears in so many of Saikaku's titles. The word has a wide range of meanings whose emphasis varies not only with the historical periods, but within Saikaku's work itself. Thus, in the classical Heian Period, the main significance of *kōshoku* was "sensitive," "discerning" *(aware wo shiru)*. In *Kōshoku Ichidai Otoko, kōshoku* has primarily the sense of dandyism, epicureanism or hedonism;

notes: 32-37

in *Kōshoku Ichidai Onna,* the emphasis is frankly on sexual lust or amorousness. In the present book its main significance is a girl's romantic love for a man, which leads her to defy feudal convention, family obligations, propriety and the entire tradition of feminine submissiveness. Clearly Saikaku's different uses of the word *kōshoku (irogonomi)* overlap and mutually influence each other; however, the emphasis of the meaning varies distinctly, depending on the central theme of the respective books. In the present passage the implication is that, if Onatsu had been the conventional type of girl who accepted the first man whom her family proposed as husband, she would in all likelihood already have been betrothed, as the normal age for a girl to be married in this period was between 14 and 15.

32. *in the capital itself* (miyako ni mo). I.e., Kyōto, the reputed centre of Japanese beauties in Saikaku's time.

33. *that famed courtesan of Shimabara* (Shimabara ni . . . tayū). Shimabara was the pleasure quarter of Kyōto. The courtesan in question was a *tayū* (see note 20 above), renowned in later years for her great beauty. High-ranking courtesans all had their own crests and these were familiar to the habitués of the gay quarters.

34. *too wide for my taste* (haba no hirosa wo utateshi). A wide *obi* was the mark of a dandy and a libertine; Seijūrō had abandoned such interests. Kame (the maid) was a *nakai,* a rank of domestic servant intermediate between *koshimoto* and *gejo.* In order to suggest their relative ranks, the latter will occasionally be translated "parlourmaid" and "scullery maid" respectively; *nakai* will be given as "housemaid." As a rule the *koshimoto* would serve the family of the house, the *nakai* was responsible for guests and customers, and the *gejo* worked in the kitchen. The most important differences between these ranks, however, were those of status and salary.

35. *relics of the young man's past adventures* (mukashi no fumi nagori arite). It was a custom among the more romantically inclined young blades to sew up the love letters they had received in their *obi* or kimono as souvenirs of past joys.

36. *"Master Kiyo"* (Kiyo-sama). An affectionate diminutive for Seijūrō.

37. *the Feast of the Dead nor the New Year's celebrations* (Bon mo Shōgatsu mo wakimaezu). Reference to the proverbial saying, *"Bon to Shōgatsu ga*

297

issho ni kita yō," i.e., as if the Bon Festival (in midsummer) and New Year's were to come together. This is normally used to suggest an extremely busy time, as though one had to prepare for the two great celebrations at once. It can also be used to denote one happy thing coming on the heels of another. Saikaku, however, uses it to describe the absent-minded state into which Onatsu had been plunged by her love.

38. *The parlourmaid* (koshimoto). A higher rank of domestic servant than the illiterate maid *(nakai)* mentioned previously (see note 34 above).

39. *my mouth is small . . .* (kuchi chiisaku). A small mouth and curly hair were among the conventional signs of a sexually passionate woman, in both cases (according to Professor Teruoka) because of physiological analogy.

40. *the flames of fleshly lust* (shini). One of the Three Evils *(Sandoku)*, the others being greed and querulousness.

41. *while there is life, there is hope* (inochi wa monodane). Reference to the proverb, *inochi atte no monodane* ("in life lies the seed of all things," i.e., so long as one is alive, anything is possible). Here again we find a *haikai*-type succession of images: *monodane* (the *seed* of all things) . . . *koigusa (blades* of love) . . . *nabikiaeru* (can sway together, i.e., like blades of grass in the wind).

42. *Onoé.* Village near Kakogawa (between Kōbe and Himeji) noted for the beauty of its cherry blossoms.

43. *demon fox* (Osakabe-gitsune). Demon foxes, such as the one who was believed to inhabit the top of Himeji Castle, were noted for bewitching people.

44. *who in his dreams became a butterfly* (yume wo kochō). Chuang Chou, who after his famous dream was not sure whether it was he who had dreamed that he was a butterfly or a butterfly who had dreamed it was Chuang Chou. Chuang Chou and his butterfly dream were already well known in 10th-century Japan and had captured the fancy of many writers, including Murasaki Shikibu.

45. *with much rejoicing* (ikizue nagaku tanoshimi). Lit., "their staffs being long, they rejoiced . . . " *Ikizue* (staff), however, is here merely used as a *makura-kotoba* ("pillow word" or conventional epithet) to support *nagaku* (long, at length, much), in reference to the staffs used by palanquin bearers. Such stock epithets are scattered throughout Saikaku's writing.

46. *pantomime dancers* (Dai-kagura). A group of itinerant performers specializing in the lion dance and other items deriving from the Great Pantomimic Dances *(Dai-kagura)* at the Ise Shrine.

47. *Outside the company of courtesans* (machi-nyōbō wa mata arumajiki). *Machi-nyōbō* (town ladies) refers to women other than professional courtesans. The implication is that normally only the latter, thoroughly experienced as they were in the ways of gallantry, would have recognized in the present situation an opportunity to consummate a relationship with a man.

48. *gasping with passion* (hanaiki sewashiku). Lit., "breathing hard through the nose"—one of many conventional literary images to suggest intense sexual excitement.

49. *busy at his loincloth* (fundoshi ugokashi). A Peeping Tom, frequently engaged in onanism, was a conventional component in erotic art of the time.

50. *hiding one's head while revealing one's buttocks* (kashira kakushite ya shiri to ka ya). Reference to the proverb, *"Kashira kakushite shiri kakusazu,"* which roughly corresponds to the idea of burying one's head like an ostrich.

51. *already Onatsu's gait . . .* (haya Onatsu koshitsuki hirataku narinu). *Hirataku* here has the sense of being free, relaxed or easy—the result of Onatsu's recent encounter.

52. *there was no turning back* (norikakatta fune). Lit., "a boat which one has boarded." Reference to the proverb, *"Norikakatta fune de ushiro e wa hikarenai,"* signifying that one has crossed one's Rubicon. Here it is also used for its nautical connotation as an "associate word" *(engo)* in relation with "the harbour" and with "year waves" *(toshi-nami)*. The use of *engo* was a stylistic conceit much favoured by Saikaku. In most cases *engo* are untranslatable without considerable distortion.

53. *Shikamazu.* Harbour on the Inland Sea serving Himeji.

54. *the area of the capital* (Kamigata). Specifically, the area comprising Kyō-to and Ōsaka.

55. *"Ten men—ten provinces"* (Jūnin yoreba tōkuni). Proverbial expression to denote multiplicity of provenance.

56. *the Gods at Sumiyoshi* (Sumiyoshi-sama). Guardian deities of sea voyages.

57. *seven coppers* (shichimon). One copper *(ichimonsen)* was equivalent to

about one penny (or four *yen)* in present-day values. The passengers were therefore charged a little over 7 cents (6 d.) each.

58. *Kōzu.* Area *(chō)* in the South Ward of Ōsaka.

59. *the Mount Myoshin Shrine at Murotsu* (Muro no Myōshin). More commonly known as Kamo Jinja. In one of the early versions of the Onatsu-Seijūrō story (the *utazaimon* ballad) Onatsu is said to be the daughter of a courtesan of Murotsu. This may be the reason that she sends her petition to a temple in Murotsu rather than in Himeji. Also there is the fact that Seijūrō came from Murotsu.

60. *the Great Shrine of Izumo* (Izumo no Ō-yashiro). In the Tenth Moon the Gods from all over the land congregated at the Great Shrine of Izumo and there arranged all matters pertaining to matchmaking. In every part of Japan but Izumo this month was accordingly known as *Kannazuki* (the Godless Month); in Izumo it was known as *Kami-arizuki* (the Month with Gods).

61. *elder brother's wishes* (oya-ani shidai). Onatsu's parents were dead and her elder brother, the proprietor of Tajima-ya, had assumed the legal and moral authority over her which her father would normally have had.

62. *so fastidious in love* (iro wo konomite). (See note 31 above). The oracle's statement epitomizes the theme of the present book, which is concerned with the destiny of those who, because of love, choose to violate social convention and to disregard family authority.

63. *seven hundred gold* koban (koban nanahyakuryō). A *koban* was an oval gold coin, weighing exactly 1 *ryō* or 4.8 *momme* (i.e., 278.4 Troy grains). In present-day values (based on the price of rice) it was worth about ¥16,350 or $46 (£16.7.0). The sum in question here was therefore equivalent to about $32,025, (£11,450).

64. *he met his end* (sono mi wo ushinaikeru). Seijūrō was liable to execution on 3 separate counts. The Tokugawa legal code (as laid down in the *Genroku Gohōshiki* and the *Osadamegaki Hyakkajō)* provided for the capital punishment of anyone who (i) had illicit intercourse with his master's daughter, (ii) abducted his master's daughter, (iii) absconded with a sum of 10 *ryō* or more (about $460 [£165] in present-day values).

65. *the Sixth Moon* (Roku Gatsu). I.e., according to the Lunar Calendar.

The First Moon and the New Year's celebrations began on about February 15 and marked the beginning of spring. Summer began at the beginning of the Fourth Moon (about May 15), autumn in the Seventh Moon (about August 15) and winter in the Tenth Moon (about November 15). It should be remembered that in premodern Japanese literature the phases of the moon have a particular significance, since the new month invariably began with the new moon and full moon came on the 15th day. By mentioning, for example, that the moon is 17 days old (p. 96) Saikaku gives the exact date.

66. *The Seven Hundred Gold Pieces* . . . (inochi no uchi no Nanahyaku-ryō no kane). Lit., "the seven hundred *ryō* of money in the period of life." A typically elliptical chapter heading.

67. *To know nothing* . . . (nanigoto mo shiranu ga Hotoke). Reference to the proverb, *Shiranu ga Hotoke,* lit., "not to know is to be [like] Buddha." Cf. "Ignorance is bliss."

68. . . . *kill Onatsu too!"* (. . . Onatsu mo korose). Well-known popular ballad *(hayari-uta)* of the time. Saikaku occasionally quotes ballads and catches which, rather anachronistically, refer to the recent doings of the characters themselves. Though it did not take long for such events to be recorded in plays and ballads, it seems unlikely that the characters involved would have become part of popular tradition while their stories were still unfolding.

69. *"Yahan ha ha!"* Meaningless rhythmic syllables *(hyōshi-kotoba)* used in folk songs. *"That man who passes there . . .":* another popular ballad.

70. *having washed clean the blood* (chi wo susuki). Beheading was the normal form of execution. The bodies of executed criminals were usually left where they had fallen as a gruesome warning to other potential lawbreakers. The authorities did not allow tombstones to be erected in memory of executed criminals. His friends therefore built a simple mound.

71. *her dagger* (mamori-wakizashi). Short sword carried by women for self-defence. A Buddhist ceremony *(hōji)* was normally held 100 days after a person's death.

72. *the summer period of retirement* (gechū). Ninety-day period of retirement, from the middle of the Fourth Moon to the middle of the Seventh Moon, devoted to religious meditation and to ascetic practices, such as making one's hand into a torch by burning oil on the palm, and also to reading and copying

the Sutras. "The Great Sutra" *(Daikyō)* normally referred to the *Muryōju-kyō* (Aparamitāyas Sutra) of the Jōdo Sect.

73. *Princess Chujo* (Chūjō-hime). (753-781) Daughter of Fujiwara no Toyonari, the Minister of the Right. She took the tonsure in the sixth month of her 15th year and became an illustrious nun, who, among other things, is reported to have embroidered the famous Jōdo Mandala tapestry. Onatsu becomes a nun at exactly the same age. (Note that Seijūrō took his vows at the same age as Buddha.)

74. *in the area of the capital* (Kamigata). (See note 54 above). The Matsudaira Diary, in an entry for the Fourth Moon of 1664, speaks of the Seijūrō Ballad *(bushi)* as being very popular in Edo and having been made into a Kabuki play. From this we may judge that it must have been current in the Kyōto area some time before, probably only a year or two after the actual historical events in question (1660-1).

75. *no more certain than a bubble* (utakata no awa-re naru yo ya). The closing sentence consists of another untranslatable complex of paronomasia, associate words, pivot words, etc. The central image is that of the New River, which refers to the Anji Canal in Ōsaka, opened the year before this book was written (1685). This becomes the "river of love," referring *back* to the phrase, "their names had floated" *(na wo nagashikeru)* and *forward* to the boat. The boat, in turn, belongs to the popular ballad, "Let us build a little boat and set Onatsu in it. To fair Seijūrō we'll give the oars!" Like the New River, the love between Onatsu and Seijūrō is new, i.e., a breach of feudal conventions. Finally, *aware* (sad, poor) contains a pun on the word *awa* (bubble).

76. *in the Middle Part* (chūdan ni miru). The almanac was divided into three parts and this story about the almanac maker's wife is in the middle part of the present book. The middle part of the almanac also contained a section on people's fortunes and there is a vague suggestion here of ill-omen.

77. *Inspection* (sekimori). Lit., "barrier keeper." This word was also used in the sense of appraising the respective charms of passing women, like the barrier keeper who inspects the credentials of passing travellers. The display of various types of feminine beauty and the critical comments of male observers were a literary convention going back at least as far as *Utsubo Mono-gatari* (953-84) and represented notably in the "Amayo no Shinasadame" ("Judgements on a Rainy Night") in Book 2 of *The Tale of Genji*. The form

had already been tried with some success by Saikaku in *Kōshoku Nidai Otoko* (1684), when a group of young men give their views on the women who pass by, but never with the painstaking detail and attention to physiognomy displayed in the present chapter. It is further worth noting that in the earlier book Saikaku's young blades come to the conclusion that the only real beauties are courtesans, whereas in the present work, in which the heroines all belong to the *bourgeoisie,* the young men find that beauty exists among ladies of the middle class and even among working women. (Teruoka: *Kōshoku Gonin Onna Hyōshaku,* p. 98.)

78. *second year of Tenna* (Tenna ninen). 1682. The actual events on which this story is based occurred in 1683 or 1684.

79. *New Year's Writing* (kissho). Traditional practice of calligraphy on New Year's Day, still observed under the name of *kakizome.* Traditionally, fresh spring water is used for preparing the ink.

80. *men first lie with women* (hime-hajime). There are various theories as to the original meaning of this term, but, according to popular belief, it refers to the tradition that the second day of the First Moon marked the beginning of conjugal relations for the year. The first day had a quasi-religious nature; it was devoted to various celebrations, whose ritual purity would be marred if sexual intercourse were to take place during that time.

81. *the wagtail* (koi-shiri-dori). Lit., the "love-knowing-bird." Its peculiar name derives from the legend in the *Nihonshoki* (A.D. 720) that a wagtail taught the ways of love to the Gods Izanagi and Izanami, the progenitors of Amaterasu-Ōmikami (the Sun Goddess).

82. *Almanac Maker* (Daikyōji). Head of the guild specializing in the mounting of religious paintings, etc.; he also each year published the official almanac for the court and received a yearly stipend from the Shōgun. Later, by a typical process of debasement, the word came to signify a paper hanger.

83. *eyebrows, delicately shaped like a new moon* (katsura no mayu). Lit., "Judas-tree eyebrows." According to Chinese legend, Judas trees *(katsura)* grew on the moon. Hence "Judas-tree eyebrows," in conjunction with the reference to the crescent float, implies slender, delicately curved eyebrows shaped like a new moon.

84. *crescent float* (tsukiboko). Famous festival car pulled through the streets of Kyōto at the time of the Gion Parade in the Sixth Moon (nowadays July

10-28. The float *(hoko)* is a kind of ornamental tower, with a tall mast in the centre, placed on four massive wooden wheels and elaborately decorated. The one referred to by Saikaku had a new-moon motif. Others were shaped like mountains; hence the preceding "mountain of love" *(nasake no yama)*. There were originally 66 floats in all.

85. *Muromachi-dori.* Street in Kyōto famous for its many drapers. Muromachi was a quarter in Kyōto where the Ashikaga Shōguns had established themselves, and which gave its name to the Muromachi Period (1392-1573).

86. *the Eastern Hills* (Higashiyama). Mt. Higashi, situated in the southeast of Kyōto. Yasui was the site of a temple which was famous for the surrounding wistaria.

87. *Billowing out like clouds of purple* (mura-saki no kumo). Typical pivot word: *mura-saki* = (i) purple, (ii) bloom in profusion.

88. *Four Heavenly Kings* (Shitennō). Reference to the Four Buddhist Kings of Heaven, one for each direction of the compass, who keep the world safe from attacks by demons. By extension, any group of four men who excel in some particular field, in the present case, libertinage.

89. *Morokoshi* . . . Names of famous *tayū* who flourished variously in the years 1660-85. Shimabara was the famous licensed quarter of Kyōto, corresponding to Yoshiwara in Edo and Shinmachi in Ōsaka. *Tayū* existed in only 5 places in Japan, namely, Shimabara, Yoshiwara, Shinmachi, Maruyama (Nagasaki) and Kanayama (Sado Island).

90. *Shijogawara.* Area in Kyōto containing seven of the best-known Kabuki theatres. The gentlemen whose names appear were Kabuki actors of the time (c. 1670-90), well known for taking the parts of women *(onnagata)*. The theatre in Saikaku's time was a centre of paederasty.

91. *after the theatre had finished* (shibai-sugi). By official order the Kabuki theatre opened at half past seven in the morning, so that it would finish at about five o'clock in the afternoon. No evening performances were permitted.

92. *teahouse* (mizu-chaya). Lit., "water teahouse." These were genuine teahouses, as opposed to the *iro-chaya* (love teahouses), where women were offered as well as the more usual refreshments.

93. *the bonze Yoshida* (Yoshida no hōshi). Yoshida Kenkō (1283-1350),

famous poet and court official who became a Buddhist monk in 1324. The passage quoted here is taken from his *Tsurezuregusa* (note 7 above) and reads in full: "To sit alone in the lamplight with a book spread out before you, and hold intimate converse with men of unseen generations—such is a pleasure beyond compare." Trans. by G. B. Sansom in *Transactions of the Asiatic Society of Japan*, Vol. XXXVII, p. 17. Well-known passages from classical literature are still frequently used to decorate material, pottery, etc.

94. *nun* (bikuni). Nuns, known as *togaoi bikuni* (blame-bearing nuns), frequently attended girls of good family when they went out, in order to act as chaperones and particularly to take responsibility for any errors that their charges might commit.

95. *her teeth were blackened and her eyebrows shaved* (kane tsukete mayu nashi). Marks of married women. It was traditional for all married women to blacken their teeth. Courtesans also blackened their teeth on the theory that they were married to their customers even though only for one night (cf. the expression *ichiya-zuma*, "one-night wife," to describe a courtesan). Women shaved their eyebrows on the birth of their first child. The original reason for these practices was presumably to make married women less attractive to other men and therefore more likely to remain faithful. The prevalence of caries may have been a further reason for tooth-blackening.

96. *the design of many sparrows* (hyakuba-suzume no kiritsuke). A type of appliqué, very fashionable at the time, made by cutting out designs from one piece of material and sewing them on the surface of another.

97. *lacquered sedge hat* (nuri-gasa). *Kasa* (originally, "umbrella") was a type of large headgear of wickerwork or sedge used by men and women of all classes for walking and travelling. There were several varieties, such as *ami-gasa, suge-gasa, Kichiya-gasa, nuri-gasa*. Apart from protecting the wearer from the elements, certain types of *kasa* could be pulled over the face to preserve his anonymity (cf. note 120 below).

98. *that nurse of hers* (sono toki no daki-uba). The nurse probably dropped her when she was a child or in some way allowed her to be injured.

99. *leather-soled socks* (kawatabi). Fashionable during the early part of the century, but already out of date in Saikaku's time.

100. *food for smoke* (kefuri no tane). The normal phrase is *omoi no tane*

(food for thought), but in view of the girl's occupation, *omoi* is changed to *kemuri* (smoke). A typical conceit.

Tobacco was introduced by the Portuguese in about 1590 and attained immense popularity in Japan during the 17th century.

101. *informal crest* (kakushimon). Crest of sailboats, etc., worn on informal occasions in place of one's official family crest. (Not, as some commentaries suggest, a "hidden crest" sewn on the lining.)

102. *knotted in front* (mae ni musubite). The fashion of knotting the *obi* in front is said to have started in the middle of the 17th century among teahouse girls in the Gion area of Kyōto and later to have been adopted by courtesans and other women of fashion.

103. *a Shimada coiffure, so shaped that it fell down in the back* (nage-Shimada). An extremely fashionable style at the time. The Shimada was one of the main forms of hair style, normally worn by unmarried women between the ages of about 17 and 30, and also by courtesans; there are numerous varieties of Shimada (e.g., nage-Shimada, sage-Shimada, taka-Shimada.). It was worn by teahouse girls in Shimada on the Tōkaidō and became popular in the 1680s.

104. *Kichiya-style sedge hat* (Kichiya-gasa). Named after Uemura Kichiya, a Kyōto actor who flourished from about 1660 to 1680 and who was famous for taking women's roles *(onnagata)*. Like many such actors he frequently set feminine fashions.

105. *soft-footed gait, her hips voluptuously swaying* (nukiashi chū-bineri). Suggestive style of walking favoured by courtesans and copied by other fashionable women.

106. *forelock* (maegami). The forelock or frontlet worn by boys until celebrating the ceremony of assuming manhood *(gembuku)* at the age of about 15. Until 1652 young Kabuki actors *(wakashu)* continued to wear the forelock and this was one of the main aspects of their charms so far as male admirers were concerned; in that year the government, alarmed at the incidence of male immorality in the theatre, ordered actors to shave their heads like other men. A forelock continued to be the distinguishing mark of homosexuals (see p. 102 of translation).

107. *"for those who had not seen the blossoms"* (minu hito no tame). Ref-

erence to the poem of Hitomaru in the *Shūishū* anthology (early 11th century):

Tago no ura no	I shall go
Soko sae niou	Holding high a spray of wistaria that sways
Fujinami wo	like waves,
Kazashite yukamu	A spray whose scent may reach
Minu hito no tame	To the very depths of Tago Bay—
	For those who have not seen the blossoms.

(The poet, who has been out to view the wistaria, is bringing back a spray to show those who have not been able to go and see the blossoms.)

Here and in the following notes the italicized words are those quoted by Saikaku.

108. *the Present-Day Komachi* (Ima Komachi). Reference to Ono no Komachi, one of the Six Poetical Geniuses (Rokkasen) in the 9th century, whose work is contained in the *Kokinshū* anthology (905). Komachi was famous for her beauty. Having been the mistress of the Emperor Nimmyō, she is reported to have turned down all other men and to have died a pauper. Her life, like that of the Present-Day Komachi, the heroine of this book, ended tragically.

109. *"colour of the flowers"* . . . *a singular wantonness of spirit.* (hana no iro . . . itazura-mono). Reference to Komachi's poem in the *Kokinshū*:

Hana no iro wa	The colour of the flowers
Utsurinikeri na	Alas, all faded away!
Itazura ni	While aimlessly
Waga mi yo ni furu	The long rains
Nagame-seshi ma ni	Pour down outside.

The key words in this famous poem all have double meanings:
Hana no iro = (i) colour of the flowers, (ii) a woman's beauty
yo = (i) world outside, (ii) relations between a man and a woman
furu = (i) to rain, (ii) to spend the time
nagame = (i) long rains, (ii) to gaze, linger
The poem can therefore also be read to mean as follows, and this is clearly the sense in which Saikaku has quoted it:

My beauty
Alas, all faded away!
While vainly

I spend my time
Lingering in thoughts of him I love.

Saikaku is also playing on the multiple meaning of the word *itazura*, which
in the Heian Period was used (as in the poem) in the sense of "idle," "fruit-
less," "aimless," "vain," but which later came to have the additional mean-
ing of "lewd," "wanton," "immoral." There is the further suggestion that
the rich sensuousness of feminine fashion and beauty such as is displayed in
this introductory chapter *(hana no iro)* might easily lead to wanton behaviour
by women *(itazura)*.

110. *"like a floating weed"* (ukikusa). Reference to Komachi's poem in
the *Kokinshū:*

Wabinureba	So forlorn I am
Mi wo ukikusa no	That my body is like a floating weed
Ne wo taete	Unmoored from the roots that once secured it.
Sasou mizu araba	Were water here to tempt me
Inamu to zo omou	I should float with it for sure.

"Floating weed" is a conventional image to suggest a precarious, uprooted
or (as in this case) emotionally unattached existence.

111. *"fragile loveliness"* (obotsukanaki sama). Reference to a passage in the
Tsurezuregusa: "The purity of the yellow rose, the fragile loveliness of the
wistaria—these are among the things that I am loath to leave."

112. *the Glib Arranger* (Shaberi no Naru). *Naru* was a name used in refer-
ence to people who arranged marriages and employment *(nakōdo)*. The word
is here used as a pun on the verb *naru* (i.e., *shaberi ga naru* = to be fluent in
speech). Professional go-betweens of this type normally received 10 per cent
of the dowry.

113. *above Karasumaru* (Karasumaru noboru-chō). One of the streets lead-
ing "up," that is, in the direction of the Imperial Palace.

114. *two-handled keg of* sakè (tanomi-daru). *Sake*-keg customarily sent by
the man to his future wife's home to confirm their betrothal. *Tanomi* is here
used in a double sense: (i) he *requested* the go-between to arrange the match
(fukaku tanomi), (ii) he sent a *betrothal keg (tanomi-daru)*.

115. *His suit having been favourably answered* (negai shubi shite). I.e., by the
girl's father giving his assent to the Glib Arranger.

116. *head is the seat of God . . . hair upon his head* (shōjiki kōbe). Refer-

ence to the proverb, *Shōjiki no kōbe ni kami yadoru* ("The honest man's head is the seat of God"). Play on the word *kōbe* (head).

117. *giving his brow a narrow look* (hitai chiisaku). It was customary for men of fashion to pluck out their front hair carefully, thus giving themselves a high forehead.

118. *barely more than seven inches* (gosun ni tarazu). The fashionable width for men at the time was 10–12 inches.

119. *the Ceremony of Boyhood* (kamioki shite). Ceremony performed at the age of 2; from this time on, the baby's hair was allowed to grow long.

120. *donned a sedge hat* (amigasa wo kaburazu). A customer entering the Shimabara pleasure quarter was expected to rent a sedge hat at one of the tea-houses situated outside the Tamba Entrance; he would wear this on the street so as to avoid recognition. "To don a sedge hat" was therefore a euphemism for "to visit the gay quarters." For *kasa*, see note 97 above.

121. *cauterization* (kyū). Burning the down from dried leaves of a plant (Japanese *mogusa* = English "moxa") on the skin was a traditional treatment in both China and Japan for a variety of ailments and is still quite widely used. It was also a common punishment for children.

122. *the parlourmaid Rin* (koshimoto no Rin). See note 34 above.

123. *Také*. Common name *(tsūshō)* commonly used for a maid and often transmitted from one to the next in the same household. It had no relation to the servant's real name.

124. *the final application of salt* (shio-yaihi). At the end of the cauterization, salt was placed on the treated area and a final quantity of the moxa burned over it; this was to prevent inflammation.

125. *Kyushichi*. Common name *(tsūshō)* for menservants.

126. *the days flowed by* (hikazu furu shigure). *Furu* is used as a pun: (i) the days *passed*, (ii) the rains *poured down*. "Flowed" conveys the general ambiguity.

127. *season of winter rains and deception* (shigure mo itsuwari). Reference to the poem of Fujiwara no Teika (Sadaie) in the *Zokushūishū* anthology (c. 1276):

Itsuwari no	This is indeed a world
Naki yo narikeri	Without deception.

Kannazuki   From whose Truth may they proceed—
Ta ga makoto yori   These winter rains
Shiguresomekemu   In the Godless Month?

(For Godless Month, see note 60 above.) The poet here comments on the unvarying regularity of the seasons; specifically he refers to the Tenth Moon, which is always marked by early winter showers *(shigure)*. Even when the Gods are absent the rains do not fail to start on the appointed date. Whose power *(ta ga makoto)*, he asks, is responsible for this complete reliability *(itsuwari no naki yo)* of the natural world? There was a fixed association between deception *(itsuwari)* and the early winter showers of the Godless Month *(shigure);* the Tenth Moon was sometimes known as the Deceitful Month *(itsuwari no tsuki)*. See also note 217 below.

128. *in the kitchen* (niwa). Accurately speaking, the unfloored part *(doma)* of the kitchen.

129. *the Vigil* (Kagemachi). Lucky days were selected on the First, Fifth and Ninth Moon and vigil was kept until moonrise on the preceding nights. People usually kept themselves awake by playing games of one kind or another.

130. *the seven bells* (nanatsu no kane). The seventh watch began at 4 A.M. and ended at 6 A.M.

131. *loincloth* (shita-obi). The present-day *fundoshi,* still widely worn by Japanese men.

132. *to her surprise* (odorokareshi). Osan had clearly been asleep during the entire encounter—a notable departure from Saikaku's usual realism. The text allows no possibility of her having feigned sleep during the seduction.

133. *her sash too was undone* (obi wa hodokete). The *obi* (sash) is the most crucial part of a woman's attire and came to have a highly suggestive meaning in Japanese literature, especially drama. The voluntary untying of the sash suggested that the woman was ready to accept a man's advances; it was customary for lovers to undo each other's sashes. In the present context the undone sash is positive proof to Osan that her honour has been compromised.

134. *paper handkerchiefs* (hanagami). Paper handkerchiefs were used for blowing the nose, wiping the face and other purposes. They almost invariably figure in descriptions of erotic scenes and are a standard adjunct of the so-called Spring Pictures, the success of the amorous encounter being in propor-

tion to the number of such handkerchiefs depicted. *Wake mo naki* is used as a *kakekotoba* meaning (i) *scattered* (in reference to the paper handkerchiefs), (ii) *amorous, sexual* (in reference to the seduction).

135. *throw away my life* (mi wo sute). Adultery, especially with one's husband's servant, was a capital offence (cf. note 64 above).

136. *the paths of Hades* (Shide no tabiji). Shide no Yama, a steep mountain in the Buddhist Hades, over which dead people journeyed.

137. *"the horse he once had rid" for her whom he now "so dearly craved"* (norikakattaru uma . . . kimi wo omoeba). Reference to the poem of Hitomaru in the *Shūishū* anthology (late 10th century):

Yamanashi no	In the village of Kohata
Kohata no sato ni	In Yamanashi
Uma wa aredo	I have a horse.
Kachiyori zo kuru	Yet now I come on foot
Kimi wo omoeba	To you whom I so dearly crave.

Saikaku uses the "horse" of the poem in reference to Rin, with the suggestion that Moemon has discarded the latter in favour of his new mistress. In addition, *norikakattaru uma* is a pun on *norikakattaru fune* (note 52 above) and carries the usual suggestion that, having set about their affair, there can be no turning back.

138. *The Lake That Took People In* (Hito wo Hametaru Ushio). Pun on the verb *hameru*: (i) to plunge, throw into, (ii) to deceive, ensnare. The lake in question is Biwa-ko outside Kyōto.

139. *recorded in* The Tale of Genji (Genji ni mo kakinokoseshi). There is, in fact, no such passage in *The Tale of Genji*. Saikaku may have found the spurious quotation in the *Shinyūki* (1643), and he himself had already cited it in his *Kōshoku Nidai Otoko* (1684) as coming from the volume in *Genji* entitled *Kashiwagi*.

140. *the Ceremony of Exhibiting the Holy Image* (Ishiyama-dera no Kaichō). The Ishiyama Temple outside Kyōto is the place where, according to tradition, Murasaki Shikibu began writing *The Tale of Genji;* the supposed quotation from *The Tale of Genji* (note 139) serves, by a typical process of association, to introduce the temple. The Holy Image was that of Kannon, the Buddhist Goddess of Mercy (Avalokitésvara), and the ceremony in question took place in the Third Moon of 1676.

141. *"people leaving the capital and others returning"* (yuku mo kaeru mo). Reference to the poem of Semimaru in the 10th-century anthology, *Gosenshū*:

Kore ya kono	Lo, the meeting barrier of Ōsaka
Yuku mo kaeru mo	Where people part from each other,
Wakarete wa	Some leaving the capital and others return-
Shiru mo shiranu mo	ing!
Au-saka no Seki	Here pass people who know each other,
	And here also pass strangers.

Ōsaka here has a double meaning: the first part is written with the character for *au* meaning "to meet." The word can by extension mean "to have a love affair" and the poem as quoted by Saikaku carries the suggestion that everyone must at some time or other cross the barrier of love, just as all people entering or leaving the capital must pass the Ōsaka Barrier: Osan and Moemon are no exceptions.

142. *the Long Bridge of Seta* (Seta no Nagahashi). The famous double bridge originally built in the 8th century. The following passage is known as a *michiyuki*. This was a literary device, especially favoured by writers of ballads *(jōruri)*, in which a travel through the country was described with punning references to various places visited, the names of the places being related to the thoughts or emotions of the characters.

143. *Mount Toko* (Toko no Yama). The word has a triple meaning: (i) *Mount Toko* (written with the characters for "bird" and "dragon"), a place of many poetical associations *(uta-makura)* situated to the east of Hikone near Kyōto, (ii) *toko*—bed, nuptial couch, etc., (iii) *toko no yama*—the backstage room in the Edo theatre used for arranging the headdress of the Kabuki actors, whence the reference to Osan's hair.

144. *pillow* (makura). "Headrest" is certainly a more accurate translation of *makura,* which is a hard wooden stand. "Pillow" is, however, preferred in the present translation, since it can convey the same erotic images as the Japanese word.

145. *Kagami Mountain* (Kagami no Yama). Lit., "Mirror Mountain," another well-known *uta-makura.*

146. *Cape Wani* (Wani no Misaki). Lit., "Crocodile Cape," a promontory north of Katada. There is an implied reference to the proverb, *wani no kuchi*

wo nogareru ("to escape from a dragon's mouth," i.e., from a precarious situation).

147. *Katada.* North of Ōtsu on the lake. The first character in the name suggests "hard," "difficult," i.e., like the lovers' fate.

148. *Mount Nagara* (Nagara-yama). Mountain west of Ōtsu in the same range as Mt. Hiei. The name is placed in punning juxtaposition with the verb *nagaraeru* (to live long), i.e., Would that the name of Live-Long Mountain might be an omen of our own longevity!

149. *Fuji of the Capital* (Miyako no Fuji). I.e., Mount Hiei northeast of Kyō-to, the site of the great Tendai Sect monastery. There are two consecutive quotations here:
(i) *from Ise Monogatari:*
Sono yama wa koko ni tatoete wa Hiei no Yama wo *hatachi* bakari kasane *taran hodo shite* ("If one were to describe yon mountain [i.e., Fuji] to people from these parts [i.e. Kyōto], one should say it is as though one were to pile up twenty Mount Hieis one on top of the other.") This is a piece of poetic license; Mount Fuji is in fact less than five times as high as Mount Hiei.

Saikaku here refers to Osan's age, which was not yet 20 in the Japanese reckoning: the girl realizes that, just as the snows on Mount Hiei will presently melt, her own life will soon end before she even reaches the age of 20.
(ii) from the Nō play, *Shiga:*

Yuki naraba	If there be snow,
Ikutabi sode wo	I call to mind how I crossed the mountains
Harawamashi	in Shiga
Hana no fubuki no	And time after time brushed aside
Shiga no yamagoshi	The blizzards of cherry blossoms
	That settled on my sleeves.

In the present text Saikaku changes the image to the very conventional one of wetting one's sleeves with tears *(sode wo nurashi).*

150. *Shiga.* Site of Emperor Tenchi's palace in the 7th century. The place fell into disuse as a result of the Jinshin Rebellion and was much lamented by poets as a symbol of past glory. Used here as an *engo* in connexion with the quotation from *Shiga* (note 149 above).

151. *lanterns of the Dragon God* (Ryūtō). The phosphorescence that occa-

sionally shines like lanterns in the water was, according to ancient legend, caused by the Dragon God. Here, however, Saikaku refers to the lanterns lit outside Shintō Shrines in the evenings, "lanterns of the Dragon God" having become a more or less conventional phrase.

152. *in this box* (hasamibako ni). Lacquered travelling box carried at the end of a pole.

153. *five hundred gold* koban (kinsu gohyakuryō). (See note 63 above.) The equivalent of about $22,900 (£8,175) in present-day values.

154. *the Floating World* (ukiyo). See note 10 above.

155. *Seki-no-Izumi-no-Kami*. Belonged to the second generation of an illustrious line of sword makers originating in the 15th century. Saikaku here seems to contradict himself, as he mentions earlier that Moemon took little interest in the appearance of his sword.

156. *Rock Leaps* (iwatobi). Exhibition diving from steep cliffs performed for sightseers.

157. *the attendants* (minamina). Servants who had accompanied them from Kyōto on their expedition to the Ishiyama Temple, and who of course knew nothing of the plot.

158. *invoking the Sacred Name of Buddha* (Nembutsu no koe). Three-word prayer taught by the Amida sects since the 10th century. By simply repeating the words, *Namu Amida Butsu* (Hail Amitabha Buddha), the believer might, according to Genshin and his followers, be born into Amida's Western Paradise.

159. *Gold Pieces* (koban). See note 63 above.

160. *those who fly across the hills to Tamba* (Tamba-goe no mi). It was traditional for people in Kyōto who had suffered such disasters as disinheritance or bankruptcy to escape to the Province of Tamba (north of Kyōto). To leave Kyōto under such circumstances became known as "flying across the hills to Tamba."

161. *all else had been cast out in its favour* (tamashii ni rembo irikawari). Lit., "her soul had gone and lust had entered in its place."

162. *a sheaf of cedar leaves* (sugiori). A bundle of cedar leaves bound into a ring was the sign of a *sake* shop; cf. the vintner's bush in European countries.

163. *bean drums* (kaburi-taiko). Also known as *mame-taiko*: flat toy drums

with hard beans attached to each end on a thread, so that they made a noise when shaken.

164. *an umbrella to a cat* (neko ni karakasa). I.e., pearls before swine. The more usual expression is "a gold coin to a cat" *(neko ni koban)* but, since the man had in fact been given a gold coin, this would hardly have served as a simile.

165. *two hundred gold* koban. The equivalent of about $9,150, (£3,270.)

166. *my very flesh and blood* (nokanu naka). Lit.,, "a fast or inseparable connexion." Marriage between first cousins was considered quite auspicious.

167. *"Strike while the iron's hot!"* (Zen wa isoge). Proverb, lit. "Hasten good things."

168. *the Fiery Horse* (Hinoe-Muma). It was widely believed that women born in the year of the Fiery Horse (one of the 60 recurrent combinations in the Chinese Zodiac) would kill their husbands. The belief persists today in certain regions. Osan clearly hopes that this piece of information will put Zetarō off the marriage. His reply is a crude attempt at humour, as neither the Cat nor the Wolf figure in the Zodiac.

169. *blue lizards* (ao-tokage). Known to be poisonous and often fatal if eaten.

170. *since we're related* (shinrui). See note 166 above.

171. *the Tango Way* (Tangoji). On the Japan Sea and comprising the northwestern part of the mountainous Tamba Province.

172. *the Monju Temple* (Monjudō). Temple in honour of Mañjuśrî, the Bodhisattva of wisdom and intellect.

173. *abandon the ways of the Floating World* (ukiyo no sugata wo yamete). I.e., become a nun.

174. *love between men* (shūdō). A rather irreverent pun on the Bodhisattva's name. In Japanese, Mañjuśrî is read *Monjushiri;* the pun is on *shiri* (buttocks, bottom) and refers, of course, to paederasty.

175. *Hashidaté* (Hashidachi). "The Bridge of Heaven," most commonly known as Ama-no-Hashidate, one of the Three Scenic Wonders of Japan (the other two being Miyajima and Matsushima), is a great sandbar some 200 feet wide that projects about 2 miles into the Bay of Miyazu (Japan Sea). On

it stand groves of pine trees which have been bent into fantastic shapes by the wind. The Monju Temple was on the coast directly opposite the tip of the sandbar.

176. *"a dog's dung in the darkness"* (kuragari no inu no kuso). Proverbial expression used in reference to a person who takes advantage of the fact that no one has noticed his lapse to hide it from the world. Just so, a man who accidentally steps on some dog's excrement while walking at night hides the fact from his companions for fear of being ridiculed.

177. *the uncertain wind* (mujō no kaze). Reference to the proverb, *Mujō no kaze wa toki wo erabanu*, lit., "the uncertain wind does not choose a time," i.e. "death keeps no calendar."

178. *"useless journey to the capital"* (muyō no Kyō-nobori). Proverbial expression for extravagance.

179. *double image of the moon* (kage futatsu no tsuki). The Hirosawa Pond in the western outskirts of Kyōto was famous from olden times for reflecting a double image of the moon.

180. *eighty mommé of silver* (gin hachijū-me). 0.66 lbs. avdp. About $60 (£22), in present-day values, 1 *momme* of silver being equivalent to about 270 present-day *yen*.

181. *the Third Avenue* (Sanjō). Kyōto has 9 numbered avenues running parallel from east to west, the First Avenue being at the level of the Imperial Palace and the Ninth Avenue at the southern extremity of the city.

182. *the Begging Proxies* (daimachi). It was a custom on the 17th, 23rd, and 27th nights of the month to pray to the Gods while waiting for the moonrise *(tsukimachi)*. Cf. *Kagemachi*, (note 129 above). Rather than actually going to the temples or shrines themselves, people would often pay special beggars to go as proxies for them. This was a simple way of avoiding the vigil while making sure that the Gods received one's prayers.

Twelve coppers (equivalent of about 15 cents [1 s.]) was the standard cost of the sacred taper *(tōmyō)* offered to the gods. The *daimachi* (Begging Proxy) in this case evidently came from Atago Shrine on the summit of Mt. Atago (west of Kyōto), a famous seat of mountaineering ascetics.

183. *drama* (kyōgen-zukushi). Type of Kabuki fashionable at the time, in which actual domestic events were treated in a traditional style. Fujita Ko-

heiji was a well-known actor in the Kyōto-Ōsaka area; he died in about 1698. Until about 1660 plays had been written in one act; thereafter they began to have several acts, as in the case of the present play.

184. *as though one foot were dangling . . .* (jigoku no ue no issoku-tobi). Proverbial expression. Cf. "sleeping on a volcano."

185. *Chrysanthemum Festival* (Kiku no Sekku). Ninth day of the Ninth Moon. One of the Five Annual Festivals (Gosekku), which comprised (i) the Day of Man (Jinjitsu), 7th day of the First Moon, (ii) the Doll, Peach or Girl Festival (Hinamatsuri), 3rd day of the Third Moon, (iii) the Boy Festival or Festival of Flags (Tango no Sekku), 5th day of the Fifth Moon, (iv) the Festival of the Weaver or Stars (Tanabata Matsuri), 7th day of the Seventh Moon, and (v) the Festival of the Chrysanthemums (Kiku no Sekku), 9th day of the Ninth Moon. These were the 5 main feasts of the year, but in addition there were innumerable minor local festivals.

186. *together with the girl* (onna mo onaji). This was the girl for whom Osan had written the love letter that had led to all the complications. In the actual events on which Saikaku's story is based her name appears to have been Tama and she evidently acted as an effective intermediary for the two lovers; it is interesting to note that Saikaku here accidentally refers to her as Tama instead of Rin. Osan and Moemon were liable to execution according to the law which provided for death in cases of adultery between a man and his master's wife. Also, they had absconded with 500 *ryō* of gold, the theft of more than 10 *ryō* being a capital crime. Persons accessory to criminal adultery, that is, go-betweens, were also liable to capital punishment. Awataguchi was the site of the execution grounds in the east of the city at the terminal point of the Tōkaidō highway. According to one of the more detailed sources, the three culprits were led through the streets as a public warning; the two lovers were crucified and the maid decapitated, her head being then exposed to public view. Tokugawa law was especially ruthless in cases such as this in which the master-servant relationship had been violated and the husband made to suffer humiliation at the hands of his inferior.

187. *as the morning dew on the grass* (tsuyugusa to narinu). A standard image for death on the gallows.

188. *pale-blue silk* (asagi no kosode). It was customary for women to wear pale blue or white for executions or suicides (cf. note 27 above).

189. *the ballads* (hayari-uta). See note 68 above.

190. *shaved his hair . . . his topknot short* (ushiro-sagari ni . . . kamisaki mijikaku). Old-fashioned style of dressing a man's hair used in remote parts of the country like Satsuma.

191. *a custom of these parts* (kuni-fūzoku). Normally long swords would only be carried by *samurai,* but in Satsuma (Southern Kyūshū), with its strong military traditions, even a scion of a merchant family could carry one with impunity. Satsuma was also noted for the prevalence of paederasty, which, as in ancient Sparta, was one aspect of the military tradition.

192. *a flower endowed with the gift of human speech* (hana no mono iu). Reference to the Emperor Hsüan Tsung's description of his concubine Yang Kuei Fei, the great Chinese beauty of the 8th century, as "a flower who understands words."
Kaigo no hana ("word-understanding flower") had become a conventional epithet for great beauties.

193. *my dewlike life* (romei). Standard image for life's evanescence.

194. *the spirits of the dead return* (naki hito no kuru). Eve of the 13th day of the Seventh Moon, part of the Urabon (note 17 above).

195. *the square lantern* (orikakedōrō). Special form of square paper lantern fashioned of bent bamboo and used during the Urabon rites.

196. *sutras for the dead* (Tanagyō). Sutras recited before the Holy Shelf during the Urabon in honour of the spirits of the dead.

197. *the sacred bonfires* (mukaibi). Bonfires of reeds lit on the night of the 13th day of the Seventh Moon to welcome the spirits of the dead (cf. the *okuribi,* note 17 above).

198. *the bill collectors* (kakegoi). New Year's Eve and the 14th day of the Seventh Moon (Bonzen) were the two main days in the year for the settlement of debts.

199. *the Bon dances* (Bon-odori). Country dances performed to the music of flutes and drums outside shrines, temples, etc. during the Urabon Festival (13th to 16th days of the Seventh Moon). Although theoretically in honour of the dead, the dances came to be of a very secular nature and the songs usually consisted of love ballads. The O-Bon dances are sometimes quite lewd in spirit and may be thought to have been originally associated with the

Midsummer Festival (the 15th of the month is Chūgen or Midyear Day), rather than with any religious rites.

200. *Mount Koya* (Kōya-san). Mountain in Nara Prefecture east of Wakayama. It is celebrated for the monastery on its summit, founded in A.D. 816 by Kōbō Daishi (744–835), the great exponent of Shingon Buddhism. Even today more than a million pilgrims visit Mount Kōya annually; it is the site of a Buddhist university.

201. *the Poem Month* (Fumizuki). So named from the fact that the Festival of the Weaver (Tanabata Matsuri) takes place in the Seventh Moon. During this festival, poems are written in dedication to the two stars that dwell on opposite sides of the Milky Way, the Herdsman (Altair) and the Weaver (Vega).

202. *a gilded guard* (kintsuba). Favoured by young Kabuki actors and very fashionable at the time.

203. *a whisk style* (chasen). Informal style of tying the queue into a bunch, standing straight out at the back with a tuft at the end, and resembling the split-bamboo whisk used in preparing ground tea *(matcha)*.

204. *various sorts of birds* (samazama no koe). These were all rare fowl. *Hatsugan:* tame pheasant from Southern China with white feathers and black markings. *Karabato:* Nanking bird, a type of pigeon. *Kinkei:* golden pheasant.

205. *"a thousand nights"* (chiyo tomo). Reference to the *Ise Monogatari* (Ch. XXII):

Aki no yo no	Even if I were to make
Chiyo wo hitoyo ni	This autumn night
Naseri *tomo*	Into a thousand nights,
Kotoba nokorite	Many a sweet word would yet remain unsaid
Tori wa nakinan	When the cock's crow announced the break of day.

206. *the Governor* (Daikan). Top official in territories under the direct control of the Tokugawa Government. He had the duties of magistrate, tax collector, etc. In the present context it probably refers to the top official under the *daimyō* of the province.

207. *to the capital* (Miyako ni). I.e., begrudging his present journey to Kōya

(in the direction of Kyōto), which was separating him from his new para-mour.

208. *the sacred mountain of Saint Kobo* (Kōbō no mi-yama). See note 200 above.

209. *Flowers Scattered from Both Hands* (Ryō no Te ni Chiru Hana). Ref-erence to the proverbial saying, *Ryōte ni hana*, "a flower in each hand," i.e. to be doubly favoured, as in the case of a man sitting between two pretty women. In this case Saikaku refers to the spirits of Gengobei's two pretty boys, which appear in the present chapter and which scatter at the appearance of a girl, Oman.

210. *marry her and take her name* (irie). The modern word for a man who marries into his wife's family and takes her surname is *muko*. This form of adoption is a normal Japanese system aimed at preserving the family name and lineage when there are only daughters in the family.

211. *the mourning period* (sanjūgonichi). The normal mourning period is 49 days, but these fickle women cannot even wait 35 days before resuming their coquetry.

212. *uncrested silk garment* (mumon no kosode). Plain kimono worn for mourning.

213. *the sleeves are slightly short* (sukoshi sode no chiisaki). The woman regrets that the sleeves were out of fashion, even though henceforth she has no intention of wearing the garment.

214. *Hama of Satsuma* (Satsuma-gata no Hama no Machi). The present Hama-chō in the city of Kagoshima at the southwestern tip of Japan. The *Ryūkyū-ya* (Okinawa Shop) was one of the many merchant houses in Kagoshima that carried cn an indirect trade with China (mainly Fukien) by way of Okinawa. Direct trade relations with China were officially restricted to Nagasaki, but since Okinawa was in a tributary relationship both to the Manchus and to the *daimyō* of Satsuma Province, Kagoshima merchants (like Oman's father) were able to make vast profits (note 245 below) by importing Chinese goods via Okinawa.

215. *even the moon in its mid-month glory* (izayoi no tsuki). Play on the word *izayoi*, which refers both to Oman's age (16 in the Japanese count) and to the full beauty of the 16-day-old moon.

216. *"set forth up the Mountain of Love"* (Koi no yama irisomeshi). Quotation from the love poem in the 13th-century *Shinchokusenshū* anthology:

Koi no yama	From the moment that I set forth
Shigeki ozasa no	On the Mountain of Love
Tsuyu wakete	And made my way
Irosomuru yori	Through the dense dew-laden bamboo grass
Nururu sode kana	How moist have my sleeves become!

Note that Gengobei is described in the title (p. 100 above) as the Mountain of Love.

Concerning "wet sleeves," see note 149 above.

217. *deceptions of the Godless Month* (Kannazuki itsuwari). Allusion to Teika's poem cited in note 127 above. Again the reference is to trickery in the Tenth Moon, in this case to Oman's disguising herself as a paederast. For all her male appearance, her heart was that of a woman and she could not help being frightened at the dangers of the mountain journey.

218. *only the pine trees* (matsu yori noka ni wa nakute). A conventional pun on the word *matsu* (i) pine tree, (ii) to wait, which, with almost equal conventionality, is translated by "pine." I.e. (i) there was nothing but the *pine trees,* (ii) there was nothing for her but *to wait.*

219. *hard for her to read* (monji mo miegataku). Presumably Oman was reading the book on paederasty in order to prepare for her coming adventure. Japanese commentators have not been able to identify this particular work. Its title contains a play of words on *matsuyoi* (i) waiting for one's lover, (ii) the night of the 14th when one waits for the full moon.

220. *To know nothing . . .* (shiranu ga Hotoke). (See note 67 above). In typical *haikai* style the last word of the proverb (Buddha) is linked with the subject of the following clause; this is another example of *shiritori* (note 2 above). Buddhist priests were normally not allowed to have relations with women, but Gengobei's ignorance of his visitor's true sex excuses him.

221. *ay, and my body, too . . .* (nisei made no chigiri). Allusion to the saying, *fūfu wa nisei,* "The conjugal tie lasts for two existences." Oman, being a woman, gives a vow of complete womanly submission to her future husband.

222. *to pant with passion* (ikizukai araku). See note 48 above.

223. *his bag* (hanagami-ire). Silk or leather bag for carrying paper handker-chiefs, medicine, ear picks, money, etc.

224. *that root called mandioc* (nerigi to iu mono). The root of the manihot plant, which was used, especially by paederasts, evidently as a lubricant.

225. *Gengobei is not alone* (Gengobei ni kagirazu). Saikaku's style here is at its most elliptical and it has seemed necessary to add a few phrases to clarify the train of thought. A literal translation would be, "Capricious piety is not limited to Gengobei. All must (likely) be so. When we consider, even Buddha may have stepped one foot into a not-odious pitfall." I.e., Gengobei retired to his hermitage, not because of any genuine religious convictions, but be-cause of a mere whim resulting from wordly sorrows. This form of motiva-tion, however, is not limited to Gengobei, but is common to all men. Those who have taken up a religious life, therefore, are by no means free from worldly lust, and even Buddha himself may have slipped. "A trap whose depths are far from unpleasing" *(iya naranu otoshiana)* contains a rather lubri-cous double meaning. It refers to (i) the trick that Oman played on Gengo-bei to ensnare him, (ii) Oman's private parts that Gengobei penetrated with such pleasure.

226. *his former name* (Gengobei to na ni kaerite). It was customary to give up one's name on taking priestly vows.

227. *plum calendar* (baireki). In the mountains, where there are no proper calendars, people tell the seasons by the blooming and scattering of the blos-soms. The plum trees blossom in the First Moon and signify the beginning of spring.

228. *no longer lived on maigre diet* (shōjin no Shōgatsu wo yamete). Those who had taken religious vows especially abstained from animal food during the First Moon.

229. *tinkling of the scales* (tembin no hibiki). I.e., the tinkling sound of the little metal mallet *(kozuchi)* as it struck the pivot of the weighing scales to set the beam of the balance in motion. The scales were used for weighing silver coins, whose weight, unlike that of gold pieces, was not standard. Money brokers *(ryōgaeya)* dealt in exchanging gold and silver; they were among the most prosperous merchants of the period.

230. *close upon seventy-five hundredweight of silver* (oyoso sen-kamme). One *kan* (1,000 *momme*) of silver was equivalent in Saikaku's time to about 16.7

ryō of gold (see note 63 above), or, in present-day values, to about ¥272,500. Gengobei was therefore rumoured to have spent in 8 years the equivalent of some $763,000, (£273,000).

231. *went and became a priest* (sute-bōzu ni narikeru). In Saikaku's time, the phrase *sute-bōzu* (abandoning priest) had come to be used derogatively of someone who took the vows not primarily from religious motives, but to escape practical difficulties (cf. note 225 above).

232. *the third day of the Third Moon* (Sangatsu mikka). Date of the Doll Festival (Hinamatsuri), also known as the Peach Festival, when all homes in which there were girl children displayed their dolls and family heirlooms and indulged in numerous traditional festivities, such as those mentioned here.

233. *tray for the Gods* (Kami no oshiki). Square tray, made by bending shingles of wood into shape, used for making offerings of food to the Gods.

234. *a bondman to love* (koi no yakko). *Yakko* here has a double meaning: (i) bondman or slave, as in the proverbial phrase, *koi no yakko* (a slave to love), (ii) a general type of role in the Kabuki theatre, known as *tanzen* or *roppō*, in which the actor was dressed as a *samurai's* bondman or villain *(yakko)* and performed in bold, chivalrous style.

235. *Arashi Sanémon.* 1635-90. Well-known Kabuki actor in Ōsaka, specializing in the *roppō* style. *Arashi* (Storm) was his stage name and referred to the nature of his dramatic style.

236. *Yakkono, Yakkono.* Rhythmic words *(hyōshi-kotoba)* used in the song (cf. note 69).

237. *Gengobei, Gengobei, whither are you bound?* (Gengobei doko e yuku). These are the words of a popular ballad of the period, the *Gengobei-bushi,* in which the penniless condition of a certain gentleman named Gengobei is humorously described. The song was quoted 14 years earlier (1672) by the poet Bashō in his *Kai-ōi,* and Saikaku appears to have taken his lines from there. For the anachronism involved in Gengobei's singing about himself as though he were already a well-known figure, see note 68 above.

238. *three-penny scabbard* (saya ga sammon). See note 57 above.

239. *rough voice* (arakenaki koe). I.e., the robust, bombastic voice favoured by *aragoto* and *yakko*-style actors. Here it is used as a *kakekotoba* on the final word in the song *(arakezuri* in Bashō's version).

240. *Cloth Bleaching posture dances* (sarashinuno no kyōgen-kigyo). *Sarashinuno* are a type of singing and dancing in which the performer carries a long piece of cloth in both hands and, while dancing, goes through the motions of washing the cloth and bleaching it in the sun.

Kyōgen-kigyo (lit., "dramatic flourishes") corresponded approximately to the *shosagoto* (dance plays), an essential aspect of the Kabuki repertoire, which are performed either as interludes or as essential parts of the plays themselves. In the present context Saikaku is also referring to the folk song, quoted in the *Sanka Chōchūka* collection, in which a girl called Oman is described actually bleaching cloth:

Looking down from the high hills
Into the valley below
I see Oman—how pretty she is—
Busy bleaching cloth.

241. *lose all sense of shame* (hajiraezu). Both Gengobei and Oman had given up their positions for the sake of love and had now sunk to the undignified status of being strolling players.

242. *the wistaria's purple blossoms* . . . (murasaki no fuji no hana). Here we have another web of puns, pillow words, etc., in which almost every word is used in two or more senses. Thus *shioreyuku* = (i) to fade, wither, (ii) to come to ruin, sink in fortune; *murasaki* = (i) purple, (ii) a conventional pillow word used in conjunction with *yukari; yukari* = (i) eucalyptus, (ii) relation, acquaintance, friend.

243. *Storehouse Opening* (Kurabiraki). Annual ceremony of inspection or stock-taking performed during the First Moon.

244. *Two Hundred Great Gold Pieces* (Bankin Nihyaku-mai). A *bankin,* more commonly known as an *ōban,* was the most valuable coin in Saikaku's time, being theoretically worth 10 *koban* (note 63 above). It was not in general circulation, however, and its actual value at the time was a little under 8 *ryō* of gold. (In 1725 its value was fixed at 7.2 *ryō*). If we take its value to be 7.8 *ryō,* the 130,000 *ōban* in the boxes were equivalent in present-day values to about $46,400,000, (£16,600,000.)

245. *one thousand gold* koban (koban senryō). (See note 63 above.) 800,000 gold *koban* would correspond to about $36,600,000 (£13,000,000). Oman's parents therefore possessed in gold coins alone close to $84,000,000

(£30,000,000)—a goodly sum even for the wealthy merchants of Saikaku's time.

246. *ten*-kan *boxes of silver* (gin jikkamme-ire no hako). For the value of a *kamme* of silver, see note 230 above. 10 *kamme* of silver consisted of about 230 silver coins *(chōgin)* weighing approximately 43 *momme* (a little over 5 oz. avdp.) each, and were counted as one box *(hako)*. A box therefore corresponded to about $7,630 (£2,725) in present-day values.

247. *a fearful groaning* (umeki koto susamaji). To groan from great riches was a standard expression, corresponding to the English "rolling in money." In Saikaku's description the money itself starts groaning, as though being pressed down by its own great weight.

248. *the Ox and Tiger* (ushi-tora). The northeast corner of the storehouse; this was the unlucky corner according to ancient Chinese beliefs. The Ox (Ushi) is connected with the previous reference to "groaning," a typical *haikai*-type conceit.

249. *rectangular gold pieces* (ichibu). These are *ichibu-koban* (note 25 above).

250. *the outside storehouse* (niwagura). Lit., "garden storehouse," as opposed to the *uchigura,* the indoor storehouse or safe, where gold and other valuables were kept (e.g., p. 73 above). Normally the outside storehouse was used for stacking bales of rice, etc., but so immense was the wealth of Oman's parents that they used it for the overflow of their treasures.

251. *granulated sharkskin* (tsukazame). Used for making sword hilts.

252. *that Lu Sheng used before his wondrous dream* (Kantan no komekachi-gine). Reference to the famous story of Lu Sheng in Han Tan in the Chinese province of Chao, who, while preparing a dish of millet, was offered a magic pillow which permitted him to rise in the world and obtain immense wealth; he awoke, however, to find that it had all been a dream—so short a one, in fact, that his millet was not yet cooked. Oman's parents numbered among their treasures the pestle that Lu Sheng had used to prepare his millet.

253. *Urashima's*. The legendary fisherman-hero and Japanese Rip van Winkle. Urashima's box in the legend is a sort of Pandora's Box which, when opened, turns him instantly into an old man. Parodying the legend, Saikaku makes the magic box a container for a common carving knife.

254. *the God of Riches and Longevity* (Fukurokuju). A long-headed, bearded deity and, like Benzai, one of the Seven Lucky Gods (Shichifukujin). By

introducing the razor Saikaku facetiously suggests that the God was in the habit of trimming his beard.

255. *the Guardian God of Treasure* (Tamonten). Usually known as Bishamonten (Vaisravana in Sanskrit), one of the Four Heavenly Kings (note 88 above) and also one of the Seven Lucky Gods. He guarded against attacks from the North and for this purpose was armed with a javelin.

256. *the God of Wealth* (Daikoku). Still another of the Seven Lucky Gods. Corresponds to the Indian Mahakala. Regarded as the patron God of merchants, he is depicted as a smiling figure seated on a bale of rice with a sack over his shoulders and a little mallet in his hand. The winnow is Saikaku's invention.

257. *God Ebisu* (Ebisu-dono). Said to be the son of Daikoku, he is the God of Honest Dealing and Commerce and also the God of Food; one of the Seven Lucky Gods. He is depicted with a fishing rod in his right hand and a sea bream in his left; he wears a tall black hat of stiff cloth or lacquered paper *(kazaori-eboshi)*. The petty-cash book is Saikaku's disrespectful addition.

258. *the treasures of the world in full array* (yo ni aru hodo no bampō). The items beginning with the mermaid are all of an imaginary nature and belong to the same realm of extravagant fantasy as the immense gold wealth in the coffers of Oman's parents. It is noteworthy that in this book, the only one in *Kōshoku Gonin Onna* to have a happy ending, Saikaku should have brought things to a close on a note of deliberate unreality.

259. *buy up all the great courtesans* (tayū nokorazu ukete). For *tayū,* see note 12 above. *Ukeru* means "to ransom," "to redeem," i.e., to pay off the debts of the courtesans so that they might become exclusively his own mistresses. *Edo, Kyōto* and *Ōsaka*—see note 89 above.

260. *invest money in the theatres* (shibai kanemoto shite sutete). Backing plays was already a costly and venturesome affair; its attraction for Gengobei, however, was not mainly artistic (see note 90 above).

261. *so the ancients say* (kojin mo ieri). Reference to the Chinese poem in the 30-volume *Wen Hsün* anthology (Chou Dynasty):
A beauty with snow-white teeth and eyebrows fine as a silkworm's thread
Is an axe
That cuts off a man's very life.

262. *the Day of Man* (Hito no Hi). More commonly called Jinjitsu. Seventh day of the First Moon, one of the Five Annual Festivals (Gosekku) (see note 185 above); on this day rice gruel was eaten boiled with seven special herbs.

263. *Mumézu River* (Mumezu-kawa). Mumezu (Umezu) is, in fact, the name of a village in the south-western outskirts of Kyōto. The river here is the Katsura River, which flows through Umezu. Saikaku changes the name to Mumezu (Plum-Cove) River in order to refer to the plum blossoms.

264. *"Spring is here!"* (Haru wa ima zo to). See note 65 above concerning the seasons under the lunar calendar.

265. *the pledging liquid* (keisui). The Japanese *(kun)* reading of this elegant euphemism would be *chigiri no mizu,* i.e., the liquid with which a man makes his amorous pledge. *Chigiri* (vow, pledge, troth) is frequently used in a sexual sense (cf. note 221).

266. *knotted in front* (mae ni musubite). See note 102 above.

267. *"The Cell of Love"* (Kōshoku-An). See note 31 above concerning the central significance of the word *kōshoku.*

268. *the plum calendar* (baireki). See note 227 above.

269. *koto.* Ancient harplike instrument.

270. *wanton doings* (itazura). (See note 109 above). The remainder of *Kō-shoku Ichidai Onna* consists of the old lady's story; there is no return to the original setting. It is to be remarked that Saikaku does not have his heroine speak in a specifically feminine style of Japanese. The way in which she passes desultorily from one topic to another and indulges in digressions does, however, remind us that it is an old woman speaking.

271. *the cloistered Emperor Hanazono the Second* (Go-Hanazono-In) (reg. 1428–64). The 102nd Emperor of Japan. A cloistered Emperor was one who had taken religious vows and theoretically retired but who in fact usually wielded greater power than the reigning Emperor himself.

272. *a Shimada coiffure . . . so shaped that it fell down at the back* (nage-Shimada). See note 103 above.

273. *a hidden paper cord after the fashion of the time* (kakushi-musubi no ukiyo-motoyui). This was a dark cord, invisible against the woman's black

hair; the usual paper cords were conspicuous and decorative. For *ukiyo*, see note 10 above.

274. *Court Dyeing* (Gosho-zome). The dyeing of silk was said to have started in about the Kanei Era (1624-43) from a fashion adopted in the court of the Empress Dowager. This was the court where the heroine served.

275. *kemari* (mari). An ancient form of football, played with a ball of deerhide and popular in court circles (see page 164 above). The aim was to keep the ball in the air within a special area.

276. *a soldier of the Guards* (eji). Guards attached to the Palace and to other official buildings in the capital on a rotation basis; as part of their duties, they lit watch fires at night.

277. *Yoshida Shrine* (Yoshida no Mi-yashiro). The shrine in eastern Kyōto where the myriad (Shintō) Gods of all Japan are worshipped.

278. *"emerged into the light"* (araware). Reference to the poem in the 12th-century *Senzaishū* anthology:

Asaborake	At dawn
Uji no kawagiri	As the mist on Uji River
Taedae ni	Clears away
Araware wataru	They emerge into the light—
Zeze no ajirogi	The weir stakes in the rapids.

Uji River, famous as the setting for the last part of *Genji Monogatari*, runs some miles to the east of Kyōto. Its weirs *(ajiro)* figure frequently in classical literature. Like the weir stakes emerging in the light of dawn, the heroine's illicit love was discovered one morning.

279. *In punishment* (korashimekeru ni). Punishment for having illicit intercourse with a man of lower rank (cf. notes 64, 186 above). *Uji Bridge* (Uji-bashi) is near the present village of Uji, a popular resort southeast of Kyōto. This is where the heroine's parents lived.

280. *In former times* (kodai wa). The present passage is particularly elliptical, and it has seemed necessary to eke it out with a transitional sentence (viz. "To be sure, young girls have changed greatly"). The general sense here is as follows: the speaker was amused at the fact that people were surprised at her precocity; to be sure, what seemed precocious some forty years before would nowadays be quite commonplace, since children now grew up very much faster; in other words, the heroine was precocious by the social

standards of the early part of the 17th century rather than by present standards.

281. *the go-between* (nakōdo). The go-between who had arranged the marriage (cf. note 112 above) would come to conduct the bride to her husband's home. The modern type of girl is described as impatiently awaiting her arrival.

282. *coming-of-age* (gembuku). See note 106 above.

283. *Rapids of the Yellow Rose* (Yamabuki no Seze). We have here a typical coda of puns, pivot words, etc. The Rapids of the Yellow Rose was a famous place of poetical associations *(uta-makura)* on the Uji River; its exact whereabouts, however, are unknown. Uji River occurs in the earlier image (note 278 above) and hence the Rapids of the Yellow Rose here refers to the heroine's first love affair. It is also used as an image in conjunction with flower bud *(tsubomi)*.

. . . *purify myself by dwelling here* (sumu mo yoshinashi). Pun on the word *sumu*—(i) to purify, (ii) to live.

284. *Maiden Dance* (Bugyoku). Dance performed by young girls to the beat of the tabor, as described in the present chapter.

285. *the Upper City and the Lower City* (Kamigyō to Shimogyō). The Upper City was the aristocratic part of Kyōto lying north of the Third Avenue (note 181 above); the Lower City was the busy commercial section to the south.

286. *the blue "colour of the flowers"* . . . (hana no iro). There is a reference here to a poem of Ono no Komachi ("The colour of the flowers, Alas, all faded away! . . ." note 109 above). This in turn points the way to the Komachi Dances *(Komachi-odori)*. These are the so-called *Shichiseki-odori*, dances performed from the beginning of the Tanabata Festival (note 201 above) until the end of the Seventh Moon; they are danced by maidens of 13 and 14 to the beat of round hand drums.

Summer robes (yukata) are the unlined cotton garments still widely worn by both men and women during the hot summer months; by the Seventh Moon (i.e. the middle of August), the hue of the *yukata* would have begun to fade.

287. *agémaki style* (agemaki). Children's style of wearing the top knot parted to both sides and bent round into a hoop on top of the head.

288. *the Fourth Avenue* (Shijō-dōri). See note 181 above.

289. *The hand that beats the drum* (hitotsu utsu te mo). The speaker, being a weary old woman, occasionally tends, as we have seen, to jump from one subject to another without any effort at transition. Since Saikaku's style is at the best of times extremely laconic, it has sometimes seemed necessary in the present translation to interpolate a transitional clause or sentence (such as "Now, to play the tabor well is no mean art"), without of course changing the sense of the original.

290. *the Manji Period* (Manji nenjū). 1658–60.

291. *the Province of Suruga* (Suruga no kuni). Part of present-day Shizuoka Prefecture (west of Tōkyō).

292. *Music of the Eight Parts* (hachinin no yaku). Such multiple performances became very popular during the Manji-Kambun period (the 1660s) under the name of *Hachinin-Gei*. This involved the performance by a single singer or player of eight different musical parts.

a paper net (shichō). Normally used as a protection against mosquitoes.

293. *Women's Kabuki* (Onna-Kabuki). Form of Kabuki in which only women acted. It was popular in the early part of the Edo period, but was banned in 1629 on the grounds that it conduced to immorality. The *bugyoku* differed from it in that there was no established theatre and the performers were in the nature of strolling players.

294. *the great lords* (uetsukata). I.e., *daimyō,* the great lords of the feudal domains, holding fiefs of not less than 10,000 *koku* of rice a year (the equivalent in present-day money values of approximately $280,000 [£100,000]).

295. *plaited to the left* (hidari-nawa). The sash was normally plaited to the right, but it became fashionable in the mid-17th century to plait it to the left.

296. *medicine box* (inrō). Oval lacquer box suspended from the sash and elaborately decorated; it was originally designed for carrying one's seal and seal ink, but in the Tokugawa Period was used for pills, powders and other medicines.

297. *like a lad's* (wakashu no gotoku). See note 106 above.

298. *warriors* (saburai-shu). I.e., *samurai* or *bushi,* hereditary warriors who were either in the service of a *daimyō* or served as guards in the Imperial

Palace. They had the privilege, not enjoyed by merchants and their other technical inferiors, of carrying two swords.

299. *the Eastern Hills* (Higashiyama). (See note 86 above). There were several fashionable restaurants and teahouses in this area.

300. *one rectangular gold piece* (kin ikkaku). Another word for *ichibu-koban,* the equivalent of about $11 (£4). (See note 249 above).

301. *the young apprentices employed in the pleasure houses of Naniwa* (Naniwa no irozato no kaburo). *Naniwa*—old name for Ōsaka. The gay quarter *(iro-zato)* of Ōsaka was Shinmachi (note 89 above). The young apprentices in question (called *kaburo)* were employed in the brothels and other houses of pleasure to entertain visitors, pour their *sake,* etc.; they themselves normally became courtesans when they reached the proper age.

302. *my employer's house* (oyakata). See note 28 above.

303. *some noisy airs* (sawagi no uchi ni). In this way they would avoid being overheard in their amorous pursuits by the other members of the household. The girls who performed *bugyoku* were originally entertainers or artists rather than prostitutes, but, as usual in such cases, the distinction lapsed before long.

304. maiko. Lit., "dancing girls." Young girls working as apprentice entertainers in Kyōto. In later days they were trained to become *geisha* (see note 20 above) and their present role is that of apprentice *geisha.* The maiko were theoretically virgins, but this rule was, as we can judge, frequently disregarded. On the whole, it may be said that the distinction between entertainer and prostitute was even more tenuous in Saikaku's time than now.

305. *one piece of silver coin* (gin ichimai). I.e., 1 silver *chōgin* (note 246 above); this weighed approximately 43 *momme* (5 oz.) and was worth about $34 (£12), in present-day currency.

306. *the West Country* (Saikoku-gata). Region comprising Shikoku, Chūgoku and Kyūshū.

307. *Kawaramachi.* Road running parallel to the Kamo River on the west side.

308. *the warm season* (suzumi no koro yori). Lit., "from the season when one enjoys the evening cool."

309. *not especially ill* (sanomi kusuri hodo no on-kishoku ni mo arazu). Lit., "not ill to the point of taking medicine."

310. *Takasé River* (Takase-gawa). An artificial tributary of the Kamo River, running east from Nijō through Fushimi to the Yodo River, and used for transporting merchandise to and from the capital.

311. *couch between them* (futari no naka ni nesasarete). That is, had her *futon* (quilted bedclothes) spread out on the floor between theirs.

312. *Provincial Lord* (Kokushu). The highest class of *daimyō* in pre-Restoration Japan. He enjoyed a revenue of at least 300,000 *koku* of rice a year (about 1.5 million bushels, the approximate equivalent in present-day money values of about $8,400,000 [£3,000,000]).

313. *In the auspicious days of this Reign.* See note 314 below.

314. *the winds that blow through the pine trees* (matsu no kaze). Reference to the song from Zeami's Nō play, *Takasago*: "Ah this happy reign, in which the whole land rejoices in peace and no winds disturb the branches!" Saikaku here introduces "pines" *(matsu)* in reference to the famous twin pines in the play at Takasago and Sumiyoshi. Zeami's original reads, *eda wo narasazu* (does not disturb the branches); Saikaku substitutes *Edo* (the Bakufu capital) for *eda,* thus paying passing respect to the Tokugawa Government for maintaining peace in the land.

315. *serving in the Eastern provinces* (Tōhoku-zume no toshi aru). That is, resident in Edo according to the Tokugawa Government's rule prescribing "alternate attendance" *(sankin-kōtai)* at the Shōgun's Court for all important *daimyō*. According to this rule, the *daimyō* was compelled to spend several months in Edo yearly and, when he returned to his fief, he was obliged to leave his wife and family behind as unofficial hostages. All this was part of the policy of preventing any possible anti-Tokugawa uprising by the great feudal lords.

316. *housekeeper* (o-tsubone). Lady in charge of the domestic maids in great feudal households.

317. *once they were bedewed with rain* (hitosame no nure ni). Metaphor for being exposed to physical love.

318. *Izumo . . . Oki Islands* (Yakumo-Takkoku . . . Jima no Oki no Kuni). Both are situated in present-day Shimane Prefecture on the Sea of Japan. For Izumo, see note 60 above; the Oki Archipelago lies some 45 nautical miles north of Izumo.

319. *the game of* go (gi). Complicated game played on a board with 361

intersections (19 square); it was introduced from China in the 8th century.

320. *the art of incense* (kōdō). Ancient aristocratic pastime, which was already well developed by the time of *Genji Monogatari* (10th century). Incense-burning gatherings *(takimono-awase)* were held at court and the guests would identify and judge various blends of incense.

321. *Emperor—he who was the second son of an Emperor* (ni no Miya-Shinnō). This can only refer to Emperor Daigo the Second (reg. 1318-39) (the second son of Emperor Uda the Second [reg. 1274-87]), who was deposed by Ashikaga hegemony; he spent some time on the Oki Archipelago, although he was never actually exiled there. The famous Imperial exile to these islands was the Cloistered Emperor Toba the Second (reg. 1193-7); in 1219 he attempted to overthrow the Hōjō Regency and to restore the Emperor's actual power, but he was defeated and banished to the Oki Islands, where he died in 1239. It seems probable that the speaker (if not Saikaku himself) is confusing the two events.

322. *an aged retainer* (oku-yokome). Retainer in charge of a *daimyō*'s household affairs.

323. *glasses* (megane). Glasses are believed to have been introduced into Japan by the Dutch at the beginning of the 17th century. There are contemporary references to the glasses of Ieyasu, the first Tokugawa Shōgun (1541-1616).

324. *octopus* (tako). Octopus, being of a rather rubbery consistency, had been excluded from his menu.

325. *knightly estate* (bushi). See note 298 above.

326. *ceremonial dress* (hakama kataginu). The *hakama* is the ancient ceremonial trouser skirt of stiff silk which is worn (chiefly by men and boys) over the kimono and tied about the waist; the *kataginu* is the sleeveless robe or cape originally worn only in aristocratic circles, but in Saikaku's time also worn by merchants, especially on formal occasions. The *hakama* is still occasionally used for formal wear.

327. *household keys* (ginjō wo azukarikeru). The household retainer, among his other duties, had that of keeping the locks of the house.

328. *up to Kyoto* (nobosaruru). One travelled *up* to the capital even though it might lie to the south (cf. the up-train from the north of Scotland to London).

329. *a stone Buddha before a cat* (neko ni ishibotoke). Variant of *neko ni ko-ban* (note 164 above), i.e. "pearls before swine." It is used here because of the subsequent reference to Buddha.

330. *the Heavenly City* (Jakkō no Miyako). Reference to Jakkō Jōdo, a term for the Buddhist Paradise; in the present context, Kyōto. See note 329 above.

331. *elegant draper's shop* (gofukusho). Draper purveying to the *daimyō* and the court nobility. Muromachi refers to Muromachi-dori (note 85 above).

332. *retired master and mistress of this house* (go-inkyo-fūfu). It was customary for the head of a household to shave his head and retire voluntarily after reaching a certain age; he would bequeath his position to his eldest son and himself become an ordinary member of the family. Sometimes he would make religious vows and retire to a monastery. In other cases he would remain in the house or in a detached building with his wife, enjoying the less onerous life that resulted from his abdication of family responsibility. In such cases he was often well advised to provide himself with substantial retirement funds *(inkyo-kane)*, so as not to be dependent on his children. Frequently, however, the real authority remained in his hands, and in any case he would normally be consulted on all important family and business matters, even though he no longer held nominal responsibility. (The system persisted in a modified form until 1947, when the entire basis of the traditional family system was altered by statute.)

333. *four features* (omote-dōgu no yotsu). I.e., eyes, ears, nose and mouth.

334. *her mouth small* (kuchi chiisaku). See note 39 above.

335. *scarcely eight inches in length* (hachimon sambu). One *mon* was the diameter of the standard copper coin *(ichimonsen)* and remains the normal unit for measuring sizes of Japanese socks *(tabi)* and hence the length of feet. One *mon* (which was divided into 8 *bu)* corresponds to 0.96 inches. Small feet, in Japan as in China, were a mark of aristocratic beauty.

336. *big toes were bent back* (oyayubi sotte). This was a mark of elegance (as can be judged from studying prints of the *ukiyoe* school); in particular, it suggested a woman of passionate temperament.

337. *The trunk of her body* (dōai). A long trunk was thought to be a great asset for a woman, whereas the length or beauty of her legs was not con-

sidered important. This is to be explained, on the one hand, by the concealing nature of the kimono, and on the other, by the emphasis on *seated* beauty. For a woman dressed in a kimono and seated in the Japanese fashion, a long trunk would be an asset, whereas the appearance of her legs would be of little interest. Similarly, since a woman's breasts were severely constricted by the kimono and the sash, their size or shape was not a significant constituent in her looks, and they are never mentioned as a mark of beauty.

It may be remarked that the reason that Saikaku describes the present painting with such detail is that it turns out to be a close likeness of the heroine of the book. She is, of course, a paradigm of beauty by the standards of the period.

338. *an agent* (hitooki). Intermediary who specialized in placing people in various types of work, and whose function varied from that of pander *(zegen)* to that of employment broker *(kuchiire)*.

339. *one hundred* koban *of gold* (hyaku-ryō). (See note 63 above). Equivalent of about $4,575 (£1,635).

340. *exchanged these into silver coin* (gin ni shite). The rate of exchange at this period was about 60 silver *momme* for 1 gold *ryō*. Ten *momme* (the amount given to the errand woman) weighed 1.32 oz. and was the equivalent of about $7.50 (£2.15.0). This exchange was necessary for the agent, since the smallest gold coin in circulation was the *ichibu-koban* (note 25 above), the equivalent of about $11 (£4).

341. *twenty* mommé *of silver* (gin nijū-me). The equivalent of about $15 (£5.10.0).

342. *one piece of silver coin* (gin ichimai). (See note 305 above.) Equivalent of about $32 (£12).

343. *substitute-parent* (torioya). See note 344 below.

344. *a son and heir* (wakadono nado). A man who had not succeeded in having a son by his legal wife would frequently make inquiries through the intermediary of an agent *(hitooki)* about finding a suitable concubine *(mekake)*. The role of concubine was legally recognized during the Tokugawa Period, and there was no lack of candidates for such posts, especially when a wealthy *daimyō* was involved. If the girl was of humble parentage, she would obtain a "substitute-parent" *(torioya)* in order to raise her social posi-

tion; this was purely for the sake of form, not in order to delude her prospective master about her actual status. After the audience *(memie)* the girl, if she had proved to be satisfactory, would be installed as an official concubine. Should she give birth to a son, she would be presented with an allowance of rice *(fuchimai)* (rice being the standard medium of exchange for all except the merchant class), and part of this allowance would be paid to the "substitute-parent" for his role in having made the match possible.

345. *six fun* (rokufun). There are 10 *fun* to 1 *momme*. One *fun* was therefore equivalent to about 7 cents (6 d.). Accordingly, the total cost of the interview was about $19 (£6.15.0.) in present-day values (rental of clothes $15.25 [£5.9.0]; palanquin $2.65 [19 s.]; attendants $1 [7 s.]).

346. *Shimabara and Shijōgawara* (Shimabara Shijōgawara). The centres of female and paederastic pleasure, respectively (see notes 89–90 above).

347. *bald-pated drum-holders* (taikomochi no bōzu). Lit., "drum-holder priests"); the "drum-holders" *(taikomochi)* (see note 14 above) customarily had their heads shaved like the clergy. Well-to-do gentlemen also used to shave their heads after they had reached a certain age and officially retired from active life (note 332 above). The merchants would therefore confuse the girls by making them believe that the dissolute panders in their company were in fact affluent gentlemen from the provinces, who might be looking for suitable concubines to take along when they left the capital.

348. *the proprietor* (teishu). I.e., of the teahouse or other establishment where they had summoned the girls, in order, ostensibly, to select an official concubine. The girls were thus being tricked into the role of common prostitute.

349. *pillow* (makura). See note 144 above.

350. *two small pieces of gold* (kinsu niho). I.e., 2 *ichibu-koban,* equivalent of about $22.50 (£8) (see note 25 above).

351. *futile work indeed* (zehi mo naki koto). She had received a fee equivalent to only about $22.50 (£8), though she might have spent almost $20 (£7) on her own preparations (note 345 above).

352. *noblewoman of the provinces* (kuni-jorō). Also known as *kuni-gozen;* euphemism for a *daimyō*'s concubine. So called because she was free to accompany him to his fief, whereas his official wife was normally obliged to remain in Edo (note 315).

353. *the great journey* (harubaru). A distance of about 370 miles over mountainous country along the old Tōkaidō highway. The journey was normally done in 53 stages. By modern express train it takes less than 7 hours.

354. *Musashi*. West of Edo; contained in present-day Saitama and Kanagawa Prefectures and Tōkyō Metropolis. Asakusa is now a part of Tōkyō, best known for its garish amusement quarter.

355. *a second Yoshino . . . from Cathay* (Kara no Yoshino). Yoshino is a small mountain town south of Ōsaka, long famous for its cherry blossoms. China is here regarded as a sort of earthly Elysium, and a Chinese Yoshino must therefore contain cherry blossoms of the most fantastic beauty. This is, of course, simply a poetic turn of phrase suggesting that the heroine lived in the greatest splendour.

356. *Sakai-cho*. Site of Edo theatre in Nihonbashi Ward.

357. *that other thing* (sono koto). I.e., physical lust.

358. *the scent of a loincloth* (fundoshi no nioi mo). I.e., have no carnal knowledge of men (see note 131 above).

359. *Hishikawa* (Hishigawa). I.e., a painting or print of the school of Hishikawa Moronobu (d. 1694), the first of the great *ukiyoe* painters. The *ukiyoe* painters frequently began their careers by producing works of an erotic nature, partly in order to make money and partly because the artistic depiction of erotic scenes was considered to be an excellent form of training in draughtsmanship. Most of the great *ukiyoe* artists, including Moronobu, Harunobu and Utamaro, have left numerous works of this type, called *shunga* (spring pictures). A similar tradition exists among writers and in certain cases has continued until modern times.

360. *my heel* (ashi no kibisu). The feat may seem somewhat less startling when the reader remembers the traditional Japanese sitting posture and the suppleness that results from it.

361. *cold and insensible tools* (itazura-gokoro mo naki). Lit., "I bent the heel of my foot and the middle finger of my hand, which do not have a wanton spirit. . . ."

362. *jealousy* (rinki). Women of breeding were supposed not only not to show this emotion, but actually to be devoid of it. As the heroine points out,

however, this absence of jealousy, noble though it may be, may itself facilitate various infidelities by the husband.

363. *invigorating herbs* (jiōgan). A form of aphrodisiac whose chief ingredient was the reddish-yellow *jiō (saohime)* plant (cf. note 224 above).

364. *Kiyomizu Temple* (Kiyomizu). Famous temple standing on a hill in the eastern part of the city. Built in 789 by Tamura no Maro, the famous hero who conquered the Ainu, it was founded in 805 and devoted to the Eleven-Faced Kannon. The present structures were built in 1633 by the 3rd Shōgun, Iemitsu. The 2-storeyed West Gate (Saimon) is the principal gateway.

365. *"Bitter is the Floating World . . ."* (Tsuraki wa ukiyo . . .). This appears to belong to a class of mournful refrain, having 4 lines of 7 syllables each, that was popular in the gay quarters from about 1620 to 1670, that is, many years before the main events of the present story. For "Floating World," see note 10; for the dew image, note 193.

366. *at the Sixth Avenue* (Rokujō ni). In 1602 the licensed quarter was moved from Yanagi-machi to Muromachi at the Sixth Avenue (note 181); in 1641 it was established at Shimabara (note 20), northwest of the Nishi Honganji (Temple).

367. *the great courtesans* (tayū). (See note 12 above.) "High (-ranking)," "top (-ranking)" or "great" courtesan in the text will invariably refer to *tayū*.

368. *Katsuragi the Second* (nochi no Katsuragi). In accordance with the standard Japanese system of preserving the same names in a profession, the *tayū* would frequently bequeath their names to their successors, even though they might not be related, so that the latter might benefit from their prestige. *Katsuragi* was originally the name of one of the great clans, and had later been adopted in the gay quarters.

369. *Kambayashi*. Famous house of assignation *(ageya)* in the Shimabara district.

370. *fifty gold* koban (gojū-ryō). The equivalent of about $2,300 (£820). (See note 63 above).

371. *employer* (oyakata). See note 28 above.

372. *Moon Capital* (Tsuki no Miyako). "Moon" is used here (i) as a conventional epithet *(engo)* in relation with Kyōto, (ii) to imply that the hero-

ine's beauty, now that she has reached the age of 16 (Japanese count), is fully developed like that of the 16-day-old moon (cf. note 215 above).

373. *the floating trade* (nagare no kotowaza). Euphemism for prostitution; the image is the same as in *ukiyo*. See note 10 above.

374. *apprentice* (kaburo). See note 301 above.

375. *"midway starter"* (tsukidashi). *Tsukidashi,* as used in the present context, were girls who became courtesans without having gone through the apprenticeship of being *kaburo.*

376. *wooden support* (komakura). Lit., "little pillow," a thin strip of wood normally used to prepare and raise the Shimada coiffure. Courtesans, with their very luxuriant hair, did not need to raise their Shimada artificially by inserting a support of this kind.

377. *a floating walk* (uke-ayumi). Coquettish style of walking affected by courtesans. The woman would walk slowly along the street, her body turned slightly aside, and her feet moving as though she were kicking up something with the tips of her toes. For "soft-footed gait" *(nukiashi),* see note 105 above. This passage describes a courtesan's different styles of walking from the point when she leaves for the house of assignation until she returns home.

378. *the house of assignation* (yadoya). Same as *ageya* (note 20 above).

379. *town drum-holder* (machi no taiko). This refers to an amateur *taiko-mochi* from outside the gay quarters, as opposed to those professional *taiko-mochi* who lived within the Shimabara area. Both kinds accompanied customers on their visits to houses of assignation and played a central role in the world of courtesans by recommending them to potential clients or, alternatively, by pointing out their defects. It was important, therefore, for these women to be on the best of terms with the *taikomochi,* and we are here given an example of an effort to cultivate good relations.

380. *strikes him smartly on the back* (pisshari pon to tataki). Standard coquettish gesture favoured by Japanese women.

381. *throw it at him* (kore wo uchitsukete). For a Japanese woman to throw some light object (a ball of paper, a match, etc.) playfully at a man is another coquettish gesture (cf. note 380 above) and is supposed to indicate that she is interested in him.

382. *day of payment* (mombi). The established days on which the courtesan was expected to receive a customer; if no man came for her, she was obliged to pay the fee (which he would normally have given to the proprietor of the establishment) out of her own pocket. This, of course, was considered a great humiliation for the girl in question, apart from the financial loss involved.

383. *personal offerings* (miagari). Payment by a courtesan to the proprietor of the fee that would normally be paid for her services. This was done on occasions when the girl preferred to rest and to reimburse the proprietor for the money which she would otherwise have earned; or again, when she was receiving a man to whom she was emotionally attached and preferred to pay the proprietor herself, rather than to have her lover do so; or, as in the present case, when no customer came on the appointed day of payment.

384. *employer's* (naigi no). This refers to the madam to whom the girl has been sold, and who is now highly disgruntled as a result of the latter's failure to obtain a customer on the day of payment.

385. *to heat the water* (gyōzui tore). Courtesans always washed themselves thoroughly with hot water on returning from their visits to houses of assignation *(ageya)*. Thus this girl prepares to wash herself even though she has had no customer. Perhaps she hopes to delude the other inmates of the house into thinking that she has really had an encounter. She is not too sure of herself, however, and addresses the maid softly *(kogoe natte)*, instead of in the imperious manner customary for high-ranking courtesans.

386. *an inexperienced man who has only dabbled in these paths* (shirōto-sui). Lit., "an amateur dandy."

387. *gasping with excitement* (hanaiki, . . . sewashiku). See note 48 above.

388. *seat of honour* (jōza). I.e., the chief guest at the tea ceremony *(cha no yu)*, who first receives the tea bowl from the host and who leads the other guests in the various traditional formalities. For a sophisticated courtesan to dazzle a tyro with her verbal coruscations is as foolish as to choose someone who knows nothing about the tea ceremony for the role of chief guest.

389. *Since he has chosen from the beginning . . .* (kashira ni). What follows is clearly a description of the heroine's own behaviour on such an occasion. As becomes clear later in the narrative, she was in the habit of treating tyros

and other uncongenial customers with the greatest disdain; this, in fact, was the origin of her downfall.

390. *does not undo her sash* (obi wo mo tokazu). See note 133 above.

391. *paper handkerchiefs* (hanagami). See note 134 above.

392. *Festival of the Ninth Moon* (Kugatsu no sekku). I.e., the Chrysanthe-mum Festival (note 185); this was one of the fixed days of payment *(mombi)* in the Shimabara, when courtesans were obliged to receive customers. The unsuccessful customer is, as a last resource, trying to win her favours by suggesting that he will visit her on this day. She, however, rebuffs his heavy-handed overtures.

393. *a whisk* (chasen). Loose, informal hair style (note 203 above), such as would be adopted by a man who has become thoroughly dishevelled after a successful night in the gay quarters.

394. *with young actors* (yarō-gurui). I.e., consort with professional catamites from the theatre (note 90 above). The term *yarō* originally referred to the type of close-cropped hairstyle that the government obliged young actors to adopt in order to reduce their homosexual attractions (cf. note 106 above).

395. *undo her sash* (obi toke). The standard euphemism (note 133).

396. *strikes him on the back* (senaka wo tatakite). See note 380 above.

397. *A woman of the floating trade* (nagare no mi). I.e., courtesan (note 373 above).

398. *Habutaé . . . Ryumon . . . Hachijo. Habutae*—thin, undyed silk; *Ryū-mon*—thick, lustreless silk used for making sashes; *Hachijō*—plain silk fabric woven in various colours on Hachijō Island south of Tōkyō.

399. *tobacco* (tabako). One of the few words of European provenance (in this case, Portuguese) occurring in Saikaku's writings (see note 100 above).

400. *Hosho paper . . . Nobé paper* (Hōsho . . . Nobe). *Nobe* was one type of *Hōsho,* the latter being thick Japanese hand-made paper, originally used for important government documents. The dandy in question here uses it to wipe his face after a few puffs of tobacco. He is, of course, kneeling on the floor in the Japanese fashion; hence, "by his knees" *(hiza chikaku).*

401. *assistant courtesan* (hikifune-jorō). Lit., "tow-boat courtesan." The *hikifune-jorō* were of the same rank as the *kakoi* (note 20 above) and their fee

was the same; they accompanied the *tayū* to the house of assignation *(ageya)* and helped to entertain the guests.

402. *drum courtesan* (taiko-jorō). Courtesan who helped to entertain a *tayū*'s guests by playing the samisen, singing, etc. Her rank and fee were the same as that of a *kakoi*.

403. *Kaga Air* (Kaga-bushi). Ballad especially popular during the 1660s.

404. *jester* (massha). Lit., "subordinate shrine," another word for "drum-holder" *(taikomochi)*, (note 14 above). The derivation of the word *massha* is based on a pun: the jester bears the same general relationship to his customer *(daijin)* as does the subordinate shrine to the main shrine *(daijin)*. *Daijin* means (i) a seeker of riotous pleasure, (ii) Great Shrine. (The second component of the word is written with different characters.)

405. *The Seaweed Gatherer* (Mekari). Nō play by Zenchiku (1405–68). The supporting actor or deutaroginist in a Nō play is known as the *waki;* he is second in importance and usually acts as a foil to the main character, the *shite*. Takayasu belonged to a famous family of *waki* actors that lasted until the Meiji Period. The dandy is making a show of his artistic discrimination by preferring a lesser-known actor to the established master.

406. *Chief Councillor* (Dainagon). One of the high court officials in Kyō-to. Since real power had long since passed out of the hands of the court, these aristocratic officials concentrated on ceremonial functions and also on the preservation of classical learning and artistic forms. A Chief Councillor would therefore be an appropriate person to consult about the authorship of an old verse. By mentioning that he has done so, the dandy not only makes further show of his artistic interests, but suggests that he is familiar with court circles, and is also something of a scholar.

407. *Ariwara no Motokata*. Heian poet and grandson of Narihira (note 5 above). He is the author of the first poem in the *Kokinshū* anthology.

408. *the gay quarters of Edo* (Edo no iromachi). I.e., Yoshiwara (note 89 above).

409. *Kano School* (Kanō no fude). Famous academic school of painting that flourished in the Momoyama and Edo Periods. Its most famous representatives were Eitoku (1543–90), Sanraku (1559–1635) and Tanyū (1602–74), the last of whom was invited by the Tokugawa Bakufu to leave Kyōto and reside in Edo, so that he might help to transport the Kanō art to the new

centre. Tanyū's descendants became official painters to the Shōgunate and held this position until the restoration.

410. *her bamboo crest* (sasa no maru no jōmon). See note 33 above.

411. *one rectangular piece of gold* (kinsu ichibu). I.e., 1 *ichibu-koban* (note 25 above). In other words, each little crab that Chitose ate cost the equivalent of about $11 (£4). There were numerous stories in Saikaku's time of this type of extravagance.

412. *Nokaze.* The woman's name literally means "wind in the fields." There is a pun on the verb *shimiru*, which means (i) to pierce, penetrate (as the wind), (ii) to be impressed, smitten, infatuated.

413. *twenty-five pounds of silver* (gin san-kamme). The equivalent of about $2,300 (£820) (see note 230 above). This enormous cost resulted from the laborious workmanship required to burn a small hole in the exact centre of each of the thousands of slightly raised spots on the dappled material.

414. *Nisan.* Lit., "two-three"; the total was "five," or *go* in Japanese and the man's real name was probably something beginning with *go*, like Go-hei or Gorobei. (An approximate English equivalent would be to call oneself "Tutu" if one's name happened to be Fortescu.) Such playful pseudonyms were frequently sported by ingenious habitués of the gay quarters.

415. *Nagasaki House* (Nagasaki-ya). One of the well-known houses in the Shinmachi gay quarters (note 89 above).

416. *private courtesan* (agezume ni seshi). Nisan paid a sufficient sum to Dewa's employer so that he might visit her daily if so desired, and so that no one else might be allowed to enjoy her favours. This was a normal procedure for wealthy men if they had some favourite courtesan, and the system carries over into the present-day *geisha* institution.

417. *During one gloomy autumn* (aki no sabishiki). *Sabishiki* refers back to *aki* (i.e., "gloomy," "sad") and forward to *jorō* (i.e., "not in demand," "not having any customers"). Nisan paid these unfortunate courtesans out of kindness and not with the aim of enjoying their favours.
Kuken-cho: a centre of houses of assignation in Shinmachi.

418. *Surely Heaven will someday punish . . .* (Ten mo itsu zo wa togame-tamawan). A conventional condemnation of bourgeois extravagance of the type that the Tokugawa authorities used to issue (with little effect) in the form fo sumptuary edicts.

419. *a Worldly Temple* (Seken-dera). I.e., a temple inhabited by one or more depraved priests. The normal word is *namagusa-dera,* lit., "a temple smelling of fish and meat" (note 429 below).

420. *opens up her sleeves* (mata akete). It was customary for a woman, when reaching the autumn of her 18th year, whether or not she was married, to sew up the sides of her long hanging sleeves. If, as in the case of the heroine, a woman wished to give people the impression that she was a maiden, it was therefore necessary to unsew her sleeves.

421. *Female T'ieh Kai* (Onna Tekkai). Tekkai is the legendary Chinese wizard, T'ieh Kai, whose spirit was lodged in the body of a beggar who had died of starvation; T'ieh Kai accordingly limped and was dressed in rags. To show how utterly his spirit was liberated from earthly trammels, he used to blow out of his mouth small figures of himself. A woman who, having lost her innocence, tried to return once more to her maiden state was regarded as puffing forth, as it were, a smaller image of her present self, and hence was compared to T'ieh Kai. The heroine, being of small build, found it relatively easy, despite all her experiences of the past years, to give the impression of being a young girl.

422. *"noonday of Buddhism"* (Buppō no hiru). Proverbial expression referring to the flourishing period of Buddhism. Here, of course, it is used ironically in conjunction with the remark that follows.

423. *temple pages* (otera-goshō). Young boys attending priests and frequently kept for paederastic purposes.

424. *put on a man's loincloth . . . could resemble* (kaku). Pun on the word *kaku* = (i) to wear, (ii) thus. Homosexuality was tacitly condoned in many of the temples; hence the heroine disguises herself as a young boy. The depraved priest is, of course, not deceived by the disguise, which has been adopted to delude outsiders.

425. *of narrow width* (hosoki). Hitherto she had worn the very wide *obi* favoured by courtesans (p. 138 of translation).

426. *a specially painted beard* (tsukuri-hige). Young male attendants used to paint beards on their faces with charcoal to give themselves a dashing air.

427. *unattached warrior* (rōnin-shu). The *rōnin* were masterless *samurai,* who usually made a living by undertaking to perform daring exploits and

other special jobs; they also frequently served as teachers in the private *tera-koya* schools. It is estimated that in Saikaku's time there were almost half a million *rōnin* in Japan.

428. *he firmly shut his mouth* (kuchi fusagu). By the nature of his remark the priest has unintentionally betrayed that he is aware of the true sex of his visitor; he accordingly lapses into embarrassed silence.

429. *the aroma of fish and meat* (namagusaki kaze). Buddhist vows, of course, forbade the consumption of fish or meat, but depraved priests did not observe this any more strictly than they did their vows against fornication; hence they were normally referred to as *namagusa-bōzu* ("priests smelling of fish and meat").

430. *two rectangular gold pieces* (kinsu nibu). I.e., about $22 (£8) (see note 25 above), less than half of what she had received in her days as a *tayū*.

431. *temples of all the eight sects* (hasshū). The 6 Nara Sects and the 2 Kyōto Sects, viz., Kegon, Ritsu, Hossō, Sanron, Jōjitsu, Kusha, Tendai and Shingon. (It may be noted that these did not include the Jōdo Sect, with which Saikaku himself was mainly associated.)

this one religion (kono ishū). I.e., sexual indulgence.

slash his rosary (juzu kiru). I.e., break his religious vows.

Saikaku's usual disrespect for the Buddhist priesthood of the time reaches a climax of expression in the present chapter.

432. *twenty-five pounds of silver* (gin san-kamme). Equivalent to about $2,300 (£820).

433. *Temple of the Floating World* (ukiyo-dera). Another expression for *seken-dera* (note 419 above).

434. *Six Days of Fasting* (Rokusai). I.e., the 8th, 14th, 15th, 23rd, 29th and 30th of each month. In the Edo Period, by a curious transformation, these became the days of licence.

435. *dressed in short coats* (haori ni nashi). Doctors and priests had their heads shaved, but priests normally did not wear *haori*. By donning *haori* (short coats) the depraved priests could pretend to be doctors and thus freely visit the disreputable quarters of the city.

436. *death watch* (taiya). Priest's visit to a parishioner's house to recite the scriptures on the night after the death of someone in the household; cremation took place on the following night.

437. *gather the ashes* (haiyose). I.e., collect the urn of ashes (after cremation) for burial in the temple precincts.

438. *the gong and cymbals* (dora nyōhachi). The various Buddhist trappings normally had an uncomfortable association with death.

439. *Ishichiyo*. Lit., "Rock of a Thousand Ages." There is a certain irony in the priest's choice of this auspicious name.

440. *could enter no action against me* (kuji ni wa narazu). The rupture of a contract of service was normally actionable, but the priest was in no position to call attention to his irregular way of life.

441. *Etiquette* (Shorei). There were two main schools of etiquette in the Edo Period: the Ise School, which had its main following in Kyōto and to the west, and the Ogasawara School in Edo and the east. Both schools had been established during the Muromachi Period (1392–1573); the latter was current among merchant-class families.

442. *to flutter through the sky on the same wing* (hiyoku-renri). This metaphor refers to the classical image (deriving originally from Po Chü-i) in which two lovers are compared to a pair of birds that fly together sharing the same wing and to two trees that grow together with their branches intertwined.

443. *my hair was curly . . .* (kami no chijimite . . .) All the standard marks of an erotic woman (see notes 39 and 336 above).

444. *a roll . . . half a piece* (hitobiki . . . handan). A roll *(hiki)* is 20–25 yards in length; a piece *(tan)* is half a *hiki*.

445. *panting with excitement* (hanaiki sewashiku). The standard euphemism (note 48 above).

446. *"You until a hundred!"* (Sonata hyaku made). Facetious reference to the folk song:

> You until a hundred
> I till ninety-nine—
> Let us live together
> Till our heads are hoary with age!

447. *Sun-Flower Month* (Uzuki). I.e., the Fourth Moon, beginning about May 15. Named after the *utsugi* (deutzia), a type of Japanese sun-flower.

448. *Clothes-Changing* (Koromo-gae). On the first day of the Fourth

346

Moon (the official beginning of summer) it was customary to change from padded winter clothes into ordinary lined kimono. The changes of season are much more rigidly respected in Japan than in the West, by people, if not by Nature.

449. *Townsman's* (Chōnin). In this case the tradesman class, which was theoretically at the bottom of the feudal hierarchy, but which in effect, because of its economic power, steadily gained ascendancy during the Tokugawa Period as the real influence of the military class declined. The characters in Saikaku's books belong overwhelmingly to this class, as did the author.

450. *Parlourmaid* (Koshimoto). See note 34 above.

451. *great summer heat of nineteen days* (Jūku-doyō). The period of the "great summer heat" *(doyō)* normally lasts for 18 days, but in certain years one day was dropped from the calendar as being unlucky, and the period was consequently spread over 19 calendar days. In such years the heat was reputed to be especially severe.

Almost the entire first half of this chapter consists of an old woman's desultory recollections and has little logical connexion with the story in the second half. The train of thought, however, is clear: first there is the description of the funeral procession; then the speaker remembers the beautiful wife of the man who has died; this leads to the question of whether a man should marry beautiful women, followed by a discussion on the disadvantages of marriage in general; it is then observed that men marry despite these disadvantages in order to escape loneliness; the heroine too wished to escape loneliness and therefore took employ with a merchant family. This circuitous form of introduction is to be found in many of Saikaku's works and reveals the influence of *haikai* linked verse, which involves a free flow of associated ideas.

452. *ceremonial dress* (hakama kataginu). See note 326 above.

453. *Three-Foot Goblin* (Sanjakubō no Tengu-banashi). In the year 1685 a priest in Akibayama in the province of Tōtomi (present-day Shizuoka Prefecture) had deluded the ignorant people of his parish by instituting the worship of a creature known as the Great Three-Foot Goblin (Sanshaku Daitengu); he was executed for his malfeasance.

Tengu are mythical forest dwellers equipped with wings and enormous noses; they are ruled by the Great Goblin (Daitengu), a moustachioed creature with a grey beard.

Tengu-banashi usually refers to a boasting story.

454. *the oddest garbs* (. . . kiru mo okashi). This passage describes the various incongruous combinations of clothing worn by men who, being mere tenants (rather than householders), are not accustomed to formal dress. The first man is wearing both a summer and a winter garment at the same time; the second has a pair of formal Japanese socks *(tabi)*, but not the short sword *(wakizashi)* that should always be worn on such occasions; the third combines a thin handwoven garment with a padded coat *(haori)*. The general effect is something like that produced by a Westerner wearing, for example, a bowler hat with morning coat or a pair of heavy walking shoes with a dinner jacket.

455. *trousers* (hakama). See note 326 above.

456. *whale oil . . . picture puzzles* (kujira-abura . . . hanjimono). Whale oil was a cheap, malodorous oil used mainly by poor people for lighting their lamps; picture puzzles *(hanjimono)* were a form of rebus especially popular among townsmen at the time.

457. *road that goes up* (noboru-chō). See note 113 above.

458. *heavy paper* (karakami). Lit., "Chinese paper." Heavy Japanese-style paper used for covering sliding doors.

459. *Jinta of the Gion* (Gion Jinta). This appears to have been a well-known agent *(hitooki)* of the time (note 338 above). The Gion district lies on the east of the Kamo River (Kyōto) between the Second and Third Avenues; it is the present centre of the *geisha* district in Kyōto.

For "go-between" *(nakōdo)*, see note 112 above.

460. *Matsushima*. One of the Three Scenic Wonders of Japan (note 175 above), situated on the sea some 13 miles northeast of Sendai. Its name (Pine Islands) is taken from the hundreds of pine-clad islets that magnificently dot the bay. *Matsuyama Point* (Sue no Matsuyama), the next part of the coast line after Matsushima, is a place of poetic associations *(uta-makura)*. *Shiogama* is a town 7 miles south of Matsushima; it has a shrine famous for its cherry trees. *Mount Kinka* (Kinkazan) is on an island at the southern tip of the Oshika Peninsula, directly opposite Matsushima; it also is an *uta-makura*. *Nagane* is

a famous rock off Kinkazan Island; it is used here as a pun with the meaning of "oversleep" *(naga-ne)*. Oshima (Male Island) is a very impressive island in Matsushima with abrupt cliffs.

461. *game of Six Musashi* (Mutsu-Musashi). A variant of the ancient *Jūroku-Musashi* (Sixteen Musashi) game. In these games, the "parent stone" starts in the centre of the board and competes against a number of "children stones," which start at various points on the circumference. If the "parent stone" moves into a position between two "children stones," it captures them; alternatively, two "children stones" capture the "parent stone" if they can surround it.

462. *the seashore* (ura). Pun on *ura* = (i) seacoast, (ii) heart. The fact that Naniwa (Ōsaka) is on the sea, and the capital (Kyōto) lies inland and surrounded by hills is the basis of this rather banal illustration of the idea that "variety's the very spice of life," which in turn leads to the idea that familiarity breeds contempt.

463. *Yoshino*. (See note 355). The narrator went into the depths of the mountains beyond the village of Yoshino and its famous cherry blossoms.

464. *not a soul was to be seen* (aware shiru hito mizariki). Lit., "I saw no one who knew the pathos *(aware)* of life." *Aware,* however, carries no more of its original force than does "soul" in the English phrase.

465. *the Regular Entry* (Jun no Mineiri). It was customary for mountain ascetics *(shugenja, yamabushi)* to climb the Omine Range of the Yamato Alps (Kii Peninsula) each year between the Fourth and Ninth Moons and to engage in ascetic practices. Normally they would climb the mountains from the south side (Kumano) in the spring; this was called the Regular Entry of the Peak. In the autumn they would climb from the other direction (Yoshino) and it was called the Opposite Entry of the Peak (Gyaku no Mineiri).

466. *elegant draper's* (gofukusho). See note 331 above.

467. *women of middle age* (chūjo). Fourteen to 15 was the normal age for a girl to be married; after about 18 a woman was considered to be middle-aged; old age started at about 30.

468. *putting up and laying down the bedclothes* (nedōgu no age-oroshi). Japanese bedding *(futon)* has to be spread on the floor each evening and put away in cupboards each morning; it is extremely bulky and not too easy for a young girl to manage single-handed.

469. *tie my sash in the back* (ushiro-obi). The style of tying the sash in front had become so well established in the world of fashion (note 102) that to tie it in the back was almost considered to be a mark of rusticity.

470. *"the wild monkey from the treetops"* (Kozue no Kizaru). Because she appeared so *farouche*.

471. *Hail, merciful Buddha!* (Namu Amida Butsu). See note 158 above.

472. *the Twenty-Eighth Day* (nijūhachi-nichi). The 28th day of the Eleventh Moon was the day of the Memorial Service for Shinran (Hōonkō). Shinran Shōnin (1173–1262) was the founder of the Shinshū Sect of Buddhism, which was especially popular among merchant families in the Edo Period and which is now largest sect in Japan.

473. *the altar* (Butsudan). I.e., the Buddhist family altar, on which are placed the Memorial Tablets *(ihai)* inscribed with the posthumous names of deceased members of the family.

474. *his ceremonial robe* (kataginu). Worn on special occasions by members of the Shinshū Sect and others (see note 326).

475. *the Holy Writings* (O-Fumisama). The writings given by Rennyo to his followers; in them he set forth, in the simple form of letters, the essentials of the Shinshū doctrines. They form the basic scripture of the Ōtani Branch of the Shinshū Sect. Rennyo (1415–99) was the 8th Patriarch of the West Honganji, the great Kyōto temple which is still the headquarters of Shinshū.

476. *front* (omote). The front of the house, that is, the shop, as opposed to the residential quarters. An alternative interpretation of the heroine's remark *("Omote no kirai wa naki mono")* is given by Yoshii Isamu. According to his ingenious theory, the front *(omote)* has two separate meanings: (i) the West Honganji (Temple), the headquarters of the Shinshū Sect (i.e., "Surely no one can object to the religion of Shinshū Buddhism"), (ii) the love of women. In (ii) the word *omote* (front) has a physiological connotation. This is the type of *double entendre* that the heroine would have enjoyed since her days as a high-ranking courtesan; also it follows satisfactorily from her previous remark. The difficulty is that *omote* was not normally used in Saikaku's time to describe the West Honganji (Temple), and that the heroine's remark would (if this interpretation were accepted) be impossibly obscure.

477. *untie my sash* (obi toki). See note 133 above.

478. *crane-and-tortoise* (tsurukame). Symbols of longevity, frequently used for decorative purposes.

479. *did not give a fig's end* (shiri ni kikase). The Japanese expression is rather more vulgar—lit., "caused my buttocks to hear her orders."

480. *mountain priest* (yamabushi). Itinerant priests, who wandered about the mountainous hinterland and elsewhere in search of religious experience, and who indulged in exorcism and other such practices. They were originally adherents of the eclectic Jugendō Sect, but many of them had become mere charlatans.

481. *tooth sticks* (yōji). If a woman wished to give special effect to her curses, she would blacken her teeth and insert various objects, such as iron nails and tooth sticks (note 17 above), into her mouth.

482. *Komachi Dance* (odori Komachi). Presumably a song from one of the famous Nō plays, like *Sotoba Komachi* or *Kayoi Komachi,* in which the protagonist is the 9th-century poetess Ono no Komachi. (From the context it appears fairly clear that the heroine did not dance the *Shichiseki-odori* [note 286 above], which also are known as Komachi Dances.) Komachi (note 108 above) was famed for her beauty and for her amorous interests: she was reputed to have fallen on evil days towards the end of her life. In *Sotoba Komachi* the ghost of Ono no Komachi appears before two priests in the form of an old beggar woman and, having first worsted them in a religious argument, re-enacts a love adventure from her former life. She performs a dance in the course of which she is possessed by the spirit of one of her former unrequited lovers. Saikaku's heroine, in her state of nymphomaniac dementia, sings only the words of the love story. She carries a dance-fan *(mai-ōgi)* of the type that is always used in Nō plays.

483. *archway of the Inari Shrine* (Inari no torii). This was the Fukakusa Inari, a shrine dedicated to the rice deity and situated in Fushimi (eastern Kyōto).

484. Kemari (shukiku). See note 275 above.

485. *Front Service* (Omote-zukai). Official title of one type of female attendant in a *daimyō's* household. She was in charge of communications between the "front" *(omote)* and the "interior" *(oku)* of the household. The "front" referred to that part of the household which centred about the *daimyō* himself; the "interior" referred to the women's quarters and the wife's domain (whence the word *oku-sama* for "wife").

486. *great lord* (on-kata). I.e., a *daimyō* (note 294 above).

487. *villa in Asakusa* (Asakusa no on-shitayakata). A detached residence, separated from the *daimyō*'s main manor (see note 354 above).

488. *Kirishima azaleas* (Kirishima no tsutsuji). Type of azalea from Kirishima in Kagoshima (Kyūshū).

489. *crimson; crimson* (kurenai). Typical stylistic device, characteristic of *haikai* poetry, in which a single word is used to link two clauses and is common to both.

490. kemari *shoes* (kutsu). The character indicates the special type of leather shoe used in playing *kemari*.

trousers (hakama). See note 326 above.

hedge (marugaki). Bamboo hedge surrounding the field where *kemari* was played.

Cherry-Piling and Mountain-Crossing (Sakuragasane Yamagoshi). Special plays used in *kemari*.

491. *Yang Kuei Fei* (Yōkihi). See note 192 above.

492. *Crown Prince Shotoku* (Shōtoku Taishi). 572–621. Second son of the Emperor Yōmei. After the accession of his aunt, the Empress Suiko, he became Regent and exercised the real power in the state. Shōtoku Taishi is best known for his propagation of Buddhism. His father is said to have invented the game of *kemari* for the young man's amusement.

493. *flippant, servile* (keihaku). The word *keihaku* contains both ideas; in Japanese there is not felt to be any incompatibility between them.

494. *shaking her head the while and joggling her knees* (kashira wo furi hiza wo yurugase). Standard marks of nervous servility or desire to please a superior. Cf. the expression *bimbō-yusuri*, lit., "poor man's shakes."

495. *Jealousy Meeting* (Rinki-kō). Informal gatherings of wives during which each woman in turn would revile her unfaithful husband, his mistresses, etc. This peculiar manner of venting jealous resentment was in vogue during the early part of the 17th century and derived from the strongly established convention that prohibited women from expressing their jealousy more directly (cf. note 362 above). Although male infidelity was considered normal and wifely demonstrations of jealousy were taboo, women felt the need to express their resentment in some way. The present chapter describes

a special type of Jealousy Meeting in which the women's pent-up jealousy is directed against a scapegoat in the form of a doll.

496. *Chinese tassel* (karafusa). "Chinese," as usual, connotes "elegant," "superior," "expensive," etc. (cf. note 355 above).

497. *to court disaster* (wazawai maneku). According to Yoshii, this simply involves the idea that a woman's beauty brings happiness and that ugliness brings unhappiness. The correct explanation, however, appears to be that given by Teruoka and Asō: Saikaku is here referring to the legend about the tutelary God of Katsuragi, who had been assigned the task of constructing a stone bridge between two mountains, but who, because of his appalling ugliness, was ashamed to work in the daylight; as a punishment for working only at night, he was bound by a spell. The story is contained in the ancient *Fusō Ryakki* chronicle. This ties in with the reference to the *Shūishū* poem (note 498 below).

498. *"even a night pledge"* (yoru no chigiri mo). Reference to the poem in the 10th-century anthology, *Shūishū*, of which a fairly literal translation would be:

> Even the night pledge
> Of the stone bridge
> Has had to end.
> How forlorn he is in the light of day—
> The God of Katsuragi.

This poem refers to the legend about the ugly god of Katsuragi (note 497 above). "Night pledge" *(yoru no chigiri)*, however, has a double meaning: (i) pledge to work at night (like the god of Katsuragi), (ii) amorous intercourse at night *(chigiri, like nuregoto, itazura, jiyū ni naru, kataru, wake tateru,* etc., being one of the numerous euphemisms for this activity). According to meaning (ii), the poem is a lament at the ending of a night of love at the appearance of daylight. Saikaku's use of *yoru no chigiri* in the present context refers to "love at night"; at the same time it is connected with the earlier reference to the God of Katsuragi.

499. *Tochi.* In present-day Nara Prefecture.

500. *Kasuga Shrine* (Kasuga). Famous Nara shrine founded in 768, when Nara was still the capital of Japan, by Fujiwara no Nagate, as the tutelary shrine of the Fujiwara family. It consists of 4 small shrines painted in vermil-

ion and built in the ancient style of architecture known as Kasuga. They are surrounded by woods.

501. *my eyebrows were itching* (mayune kakinureba). Itching eyebrows were supposed to be a sign that one's lover would visit one shortly.

502. *Akashi.* Twelve miles west of present-day Kōbe. Famous as the site of Hikaru Genji's exile in *Genji Monogatari.*

503. *married into the family and took her name* (irie). See note 210 above.

504. *year of the Fiery Horse* (Hinoe-Muma). See note 168 above.

505. *Kuwana.* Fourteen miles west of Nagoya in present-day Mie Prefecture. One of the 53 stages on the Tōkaidō highway from Kyōto to Edo.

506. *as virgin as on the day when she was born* (kinyōbō nite). No man had been willing to marry such a jealous girl.

507. *far too much good sense* (ki wo tōshisugite). The lady realizes that her failure to find a husband was due to her own excessive jealousy. Now she is jealous of the doll precisely because of its supposed lack of jealousy. The doll, not being cursed with a jealous nature, would have been able to obtain a husband where she had failed.

508. *a bolster* (naga-makura). More accurately, "long headrest" (cf. note 144 above).

509. *middle residence* (on-naka-yashiki). Separate residence of the *daimyō,* apart from both his main house and the women's quarters.

510. *my mistress* (kokujo). Lit., "woman from the Province" (cf. note 352 above).

511. *take the vows* (shukke ni mo naru). Because she felt so disgusted at the behaviour of her own sex.

512. *Paper Spring Cord* (hane-motoyui). For "paper cord" see note 273 above. The *hane-motoyui* had wire inserted, so that the ends of the cord would stand up.

513. *pairs of shining mirrors* (masukagami no futa-omote). One to view the front, and the other to view the back, of the hair.

514. *Low Shimada* (Sage-Shimada). Shimada with the chignon so tied as to lie flat (opposite of Taka-Shimada).

515. *Hyogo style . . . Five-Stage style* (Hyōgo-mage . . . Godan-mage). The former was a very elaborate style popularized by the courtesans of Hyōgo in the early part of the 17th century. The latter is unknown, but presumably involved tying the hair in five different levels or stages. Both had gone out of fashion by the middle of the century, although Hyōgo-mage wigs continue to be used in Kabuki.

516. *width of their sleeves* (sodeguchi hiroku). See note 34 above.

517. *swaying their hips loosely and kicking out their feet* (suegoshi kedashi no dōchu). Courtesan's suggestive style of walking (cf. note 377 above).

518. *mouth is large* (kuchi no ōki naru). See note 39 above.

519. *the nine points* (kokono-tokoro). The 9 elements of feminine attraction, viz., feet, hands, eyes, mouth, head, spirit *(ki)*, standing posture, seductive air and voice (cf. notes 333 and 337 above).

520. *eighty* mommé *of silver a year* (hachijū-me). About $60 (£22) (see note 180 above). This was less than one-twelfth of what she had received as a priest's concubine (note 432) and approximately the same as the amount that a *tayū* and her attendant courtesan would receive for a single night's entertainment. Respectability offered little financial reward for women.

521. *second day of the Clothes-Lining Month* (Kisaragi futsuka). The Clothes-Lining Month was the Second Moon of the lunar calendar (beginning on about March 15); it was so called because clothes were given a special lining as a protection against the cold winds. Periods of domestic and other service customarily began on the second day of this month.

522. *audience* (memie). See note 344 above.

523. *Wight of the Ten Strands* (Tosuji-Emon). A scornful term for people with a scant growth of hair. "Wight" *(Emon* = orig. "Guard") was a standard suffix used for purposes of personification.

524. *fully figured* (ji nashi). Lit., "with no ground." Material on which the spaces between the patterns are fully decorated with gold or silver foil; the general effect is that of lamé.

525. koto. See note 269 above.

526. *Empress Koken* (Kōken Tennō). Reigned 749–57. This is a popular, but incorrect, belief. The first Imperial edicts concerning the making of

women's clothes were in fact issued in the years 719 and 730 during the reigns of the Empress Genshō and the Emperor Shōmu respectively.

527. *the land of Yamato* (Wakoku). Yamato corresponds roughly to present-day Nara Prefecture. In a broader sense it refers (as here) to all Japan.

528. *Abé tea . . . Tsuruya bean-jam buns* (Abecha . . . Tsuruya ga manjū). The tea came from Abe County in present-day Shizuoka Prefecture. Tsuruya bean-jam buns *(manjū)* were a speciality of Edo, the main shop for them being in Asakusa. The present chapter is set in Edo.

529. *the cloudless moon could sink behind the hills without troubling our spirits.* (kokoro ni kakaru yama no te no tsuki mo kumori naku). Reference to the poem in the *Fūgashū* anthology (compiled under the ex-Emperor Hanazono in 1346):

Izuru tomo	Now that I no longer care about the moon
Iru tomo	Whether it comes out
Tsuki wo omowaneba	Or disappears from sight,
Kokoro ni kakaru	I am not troubled in my heart
Yama no ha mo nashi	By the mountain's edge.

The poem is inspired by the Buddhist notion of Nirvana: a man who no longer cares even about the beauty of the moon has indeed begun to free himself from the trammels of worldly illusions. Such a man is, of course, not troubled about the mountain's edge *(yama no ha)* beyond which the moon disappears. Saikaku changes *yama no ha* to *yama no te,* the residential area for warriors, thus vaguely adding the suggestion that the heroine was now also free from caring about such worldly phenomena as *samurai.*

530. *Eternity, Bliss, Real Self and Purity* (Jōrakugajō). The four "virtues" of Buddhahood, involving the triumph over creation and destruction, life and death, egoism and the desire of the flesh, respectively. So far as the heroine was concerned, it was the last of these that had the greatest significance.

531. *in the lining* (uragata ni). Japanese clothes have to be entirely resewn each time that they are cleaned, a process that takes place at least once a year. The young man had evidently hidden his erotic picture in the lining of his under-kimono and forgotten to remove it when sending his clothes to the seamstress (cf. notes 35, 359 above).

532. *her toes bent back* (yubisaki kagame). A standard detail in such pictures

356

is that the woman's toes are bent back as a sign of erotic tension (cf. note 336 above).

533. *desire for a man* (tonogokoro). Pure physical desire without the slightest emotional concomitant.

534. *repeat their tender vows time after time* (chigiri no hodo naku). *Chigiri* ("tender vows") is a euphemism (cf. note 265 above).

535. *constrained them to take early leave of this Floating World* (nagaki ukiyo wo mijikaku miseshi). Lit., "showed them the long Floating World as short," i.e., shortened their lives by making them indulge in excess (e.g., p. 157 above).

536. *even if their husbands left them* (en-naki wakare ni). Lit., "a parting without karma," i.e., a parting not caused by the death of one of the partners (as opposed to *mujō no wakare*). That widows should remain faithful to their dead husbands' memory was admirable enough, but that women whose husbands had left them should do so was for the heroine a mark of the greatest moral distinction and made her realize what a wanton she herself had become.

537. *my single* go *of rice* (ichigō-meshi). Women of the rank of *gejo* (note 34 above) customarily received 1 *gō* of rice (a little under one-third of a pint) three times a day, if they were employed by members of the warrior class (note 344 above). This was considered the normal amount of rice to give low-ranking servants. (It is, incidentally, quite a reasonable quantity by present-day standards.)

538. *hair water* (bimmizu). Water used for keeping the hair in order. It was prepared by steeping the *sanekazura* (a type of vine) in water.

539. *long-houses* (nagaya). Long, single-storeyed buildings situated within the precincts of the *daimyō's* mansion and used to house his retainers. By the usual process of depreciation *nagaya* has come to mean "tenement house."

540. *Shiba fish* (Shiba-sakana). Assorted fish landed at Shibaura, the Edo fish market.

541. *plain dark-blue clothes* (kon no dainashi). Tight-sleeved costume of plain dark-blue material worn by lackeys, footmen, etc.

542. *Waterfall of Otowa* (Otowa no Taki). Waterfall below one of the cliffs under the Kiyomizu Temple in Kyōto (note 364 above). The faithful are in the habit of offering prayers by the waterfall to the God Fudō-Myō-ō.

357

543. *the thought impressed itself . . . make an abyss* (omoi no fuchi to narite). *Fuchi* (pool, abyss) is used in a double sense: (i) "I was impressed with the thought" *(omoi no fuchi to narite)*, (ii) "he could make an abyss in the solid earth" *(chi no horuru . . . fuchi)*.

544. *the Kyoto battlefield of Shimabara* (miyako no Shimabara-jin). "Shimabara" here involves a double meaning with a rather risqué connotation. It refers (i) to the Christian Rebellion of Shimabara in 1637 (which ended in the massacre of the insurgents at the hands of the Government forces and in the virtual suppression of Christianity in Japan for the remainder of the Tokugawa Period), (ii) to the gay quarters in Kyōto (note 89 above).

545. *I could no longer stand it* (kono koto tsunorite). I.e., the idea of wasted amorous opportunities.

546. *Hongo.* Area in the Bunkyō Ward of Tōkyō (Edo); site of the present Tōkyō University.

547. *for that one thing alone* (sore bakari ni). I.e., for the satisfaction of her lustful desires (cf. note 357 above).

548. *Motomachi.* Area in Nihonbashi (Edo), famous for its drapers and chemists. It is one of the principal shopping areas in modern Tōkyō.

549. *Echigo-ya.* Opened in Motomachi in 1673; it later acquired the name of Mitsukoshi and developed into the present famous department store of that name.

550. *I have given up my service* (rōnin no mi to nari). Lit., "have become a *rōnin*" (note 427 above).

551. *ukogi.* Alaliacea.

552. *eighth day of the Ninth Moon* (Kugatsu yōka). I.e., the eve of the Chrysanthemum Festival (note 185 above) and one of the days fixed for the settlement of bills, debts, etc.

553. *the tier box* (kakesuzuri). Inkstone cases, arranged in tiers (with each case fitting into the one below it) and fitted with drawers in which to place bills, small change, etc. The austere, conscientious and miserly clerk or merchant who falls prey to the calls of Eros is a stock figure in Saikaku's works.

554. *proprietor in Kyoto* (Kyō no danna). The main office of the Echigo-ya

was in Kyōto; the proprietor was one of the founders of the Mitsui line, which in the Meiji Era was to become the leading *zaibatsu* concern in Japan.

555. *a white rat* (shiro-nezumi). Standard epithet applied to a faithful old clerk. The expression derives from the fact that the God of Wealth, Daikoku, is depicted with small white rats (see note 256 above).

556. *Kyuroku.* Popular name *(tsūshō)* for young menservants (cf. note 125 above).

557. *his box* (hasamibako). See note 152 above.

558. *a small silver coin* (komagane). Small bean-shaped coin (usually known as a *mame-ita-gin*), which was minted during the entire Edo Period. Its weight varied from about 1 to about 5 *momme* of silver. The coin in the text was therefore worth about $4 (30 s.) in present values.

559. *one rectangular gold piece* (ichibu). See note 25 above.

560. *would not serve for binding buttocks* (shiri wo musubanu). Proverbial expression denoting laxity, in this case of a moral nature.

561. *He Who Looked for Future Splendour* (Eyō Negau Otoko). Lit., "The Man Who Desired Luxury." The title here is even more enigmatic than in most of Saikaku's chapters and it has seemed necessary to eke it out with the word "future." The reference is to the final sentence in the chapter.

562. *the Autumn Change* (aki no degawari). The 5th day of the Ninth Moon was one of the established days on which terms of service started or ended (cf. 2nd day of the Second Moon, note 521 above). *Aki* is a standard *kakekotoba*—(i) autumn, (ii) become bored *(akiru)*.

563. *Sakai.* Ancient trading port some 8 miles south of Ōsaka. It specialized in the China silk trade and went into a decline after the ban on foreign trade in 1635. (Since 1945 it has become an important industrial city.)

564. *six* fun (rokufun). See note 345 above.

565. *—as I understood it—a certain retired gentleman* (nanigashi-tono no go-inkyo to ka ya). (See note 332 above). The sex of the person is not specified and the heroine assumes that it must be a man. The omission of personal pronouns in Japanese makes such confusion far more likely than in English; it also poses an almost insoluble translation problem in a case like this when the confusion is a fundamental aspect of the story.

566. *putting up and laying down the bedclothes* (yoru no dōgu no age-oroshi). See note 468 above.

567. *"no devils in this world"* (seken ni oni wa nashi). Reference to the proverb, "You may cross the world, yet you will never find a devil," that is, kind people are to be met wherever one may go. (Like many such saws, however, it is balanced by one that points in an opposite direction, namely, "When you see a stranger, think of him as a thief" [*Hito wo mitara dorobō to omoe*].)

568. *the mistress* (uchikata). I.e., the retired mistress (note 332 above), whose husband the heroine assumed that she would be serving.

569. *she belongs to the Lotus Sect* . . . (Hokkeshū nareba). I.e., the Nichiren Sect, founded by the patriot-priest Nichiren (1222–82) and basing its religious doctrines on the Saddharma Pundarika (Sutra of the Lotus of Truth). Nichiren and his followers were noted for their intolerance of other established Buddhist sects, including the various Amida sects, for whom the invocation of the Sacred Name *(Nembutsu,* note 158 above) was the basic essential for salvation. The present advice might therefore be very roughly compared to warning a maid who is about to take service with a strictly Protestant family not to recite her *Ave Marias* in the mistress' presence.

570. *wife of the young master in the main house* (omote no oku). Omote is here used in opposition to the separate building in which the retired mistress *(go-inkyo)* lived.

571. *don't you give a fig's end* (shiri ni kikashitamae). See note 479 above.

572. *red rice* . . . *Tenshu rice from Banshu* (akagome . . . Banshū no Tenshumai). Cheapest and most expensive types of rice, respectively.

573. *in the devil's corner* (kimonkado). I.e., at the northeast corner of the intersection of two streets (cf. note 248 above).

574. *Sumiyoshi Festival* (Sumiyoshi no Matsuri). Annual festival held at the Sumiyoshi Shrine on the 30th day of the Sixth Moon. The Sumiyoshi Shrine is an ancient shrine in Ōsaka dedicated to 4 deities, 3 of whom are guardians of sea voyages (cf. note 56 above).

575. *the Harbour* (Minato). Eastern part of the city of Sakai. The reference to wistaria-viewing is obscure, since there are no well-known wistaria in this area.

576. *retirement funds* (inkyo-kane). See note 332 above.

577. *though the spirit may be willing enough, the flesh is weak* (nani wo iutemo kokoro bakari). Lit., "whatever [the person] may say, it is only the spirit."

578. *the middle door* (nakado). Sliding door separating the shop from the kitchen of the residential part of the house.

579. *"tread the salt" of these shores* (kono ura no shio wo mo funda). I.e., put up with the disadvantages of this service. Reference to the *haikai* in the *Kefukugusa* anthology (1638):

Tabi tatete	Lo, having set out on my journey
Yuki no shio fumu	I make my way along the mountain path
Yamaji ka na	Treading the salt-like snow!

"To tread snow" became an expression meaning "to undergo a hard experience." Here Saikaku adds "shore" *(ura)* because the heroine's hardship involves remaining in the seaport of Sakai.

580. *Mystery Women Who Sing Ditties* (Kouta no Denju-Onna). For "mystery women" see note 581 below. "Ditties" *(kouta)* were sung by courtesans of all ranks, usually to the accompaniment of the samisen, for the entertainment of their customers.

581. *a call-bird . . .* (yobukodori). The opening sentences consist of a web of riddles, puns and literary allusions of the type much favoured by Saikaku and his contemporaries. A "mystery woman" *(denju-onna)* refers to a common bathhouse courtesan, whose fee was 6 *momme* of silver (about $4.50 [32 s.]) a night. Saikaku here suggests a derivation for her peculiar name. To summon or call a woman is *onna wo yobu* (cf. the modern American "call girl"). The word *yobukodori* is related to this by its first element, *yobu* (to call, summon). Now the *yobukodori* (call-child-bird) is one of the three mysterious "birds" of the *Kokinshū* poetic anthology. (The *Kokinshū* contains various words, known as *Kokin-denju*, concerning whose meaning there are numerous arcane traditions or mysteries.) The usual meaning of *yobukodori* is "cuckoo," but, according to one tradition, its real meaning is "monkey." Saikaku thus relates the bathhouse women who are "called" for 6 *momme* a night to the *yobukodori* and thereby to the arcane traditions or mysteries of the *Kokinshū*: hence the name *denju-onna* (mystery woman).

"Perplexed" (obotsukanakute). Refers to a poem in the *Kokinshū* concerning the *yobukodori*.

Ochi-kochi no	Lo, how perplexed sounds the cuckoo
Tazuki mo shiranu	As he calls out
Yamanaka ni	Helpless and forlorn
Obotsukanakumo	In the mountain's depths,
Yobukodori ka na	Not knowing whether he should go here or there!

Bath attendants are known as "monkeys" (furoya-mono wo saru to iu). Because they scratch dirt off bodies. There is also a reference here to the tradition (mentioned above) that *yobukodori* originally meant "monkey." Thus the derivations of the two names for a bathhouse courtesan (viz., "mystery woman" and "monkey") are both ingeniously, though spuriously, related to the arcane traditions contained in the *Kokinshū*.

582. *with the chignon bound in the back* (oshisagete). A fashionable style at the time (cf. *nage-Shimada* note 103 above).

583. *Once the evening begins* (kuregata yori). In Saikaku's time bathhouses were used during the daytime for bathing, but in the evening for making secret rendezvous with the female bathhouse attendants *(agariba no onna* or *yuna)* who worked there.

584. *sleeves are always short* (yuki mijika ni). In order not to wet them while they are washing their customers.

585. *bathcloth* (furoshiki). Large cloth or towel on which people sat and rested after their bath. After about 1740, *furoshiki* were used (as at present) for wrapping things, and lost their original meaning.

586. *so that others in the room can overhear her words* (hoka no hito kiku hodo ni). She expects that the customer will enjoy having other people overhear her flattering suggestion that he is a fashionable man of the world who is likely to be visiting the theatre or the gay quarters on his way home. The type of man described in this chapter is precisely one who cannot afford such expensive diversions and who instead resorts to common bathhouse attendants. The naïve customer, however, takes the woman's flattery seriously and produces a letter that he pretends to have received from some high-ranking courtesan.

587. *his bag* (hanagami-ire). See note 223 above.

588. *Ogino . . . Shiga*. These 21 women were all actual courtesans in the

Shinmachi district of Ōsaka (note 89 above), where the present chapter is set. Such lists, which occur quite frequently in Saikaku's works, would have been interesting for those of his readers who were habitués of the gay quarters.

589. *the strumpet Yoshino* (hashitsubone no Yoshino). *Hashi-tsubone* was one of the terms used for the low-ranking prostitutes *(mise-jorō)*, who lived in the houses where they carried on their trade (note 20 above). These women, who were also called *hashi-jorō*, *tsubone-jorō* or *hashi-keisei*, were divided into 4 classes and their fee varied from half a *momme* to 3 *momme* of silver a night (about 50 cents [3 s.] to $2.50 [17 s.]). (The lowest-ranking of the *age-jorō*, by comparison, received 18 *momme* a night.) So far from being able to recognize the writing of a high-ranking *tayū*, the simple bathhouse girl was not even familiar with that of a humble *hashi-tsubone*. The present Yoshino should not be confused with the famous Kyōto *tayū* of that name.

590. *scent of aloeswood before a dog* (inu ni kyara). One of the numerous proverbial expressions that are equivalent to the biblical "pearls before swine" (cf. notes 164, 329 above).

591. *the crested comb of some high or medium courtesan* (tayū tenjin no mongushi). The *tenjin* (or *tenshoku*) was a medium courtesan who ranked between the *tayū* and the *kakoi* (note 20 above). Her fee in Shimabara was 30 *momme* a night (compared with the *tayū's* 58 *momme* and the *kakoi's* 18 *momme*).

592. *unaccompanied* (tomo wo tsurezaru). It was customary for townsmen *(chōnin)* to be accompanied by a manservant *(genan)* when they set out for the bathhouse or elsewhere. The ostensible purpose of this attendant was to carry his master's sandals (cf. pp. 148-9 above). Young men, however, were usually unable to afford such a servant.

593. *an infusion* (chirashi). A mixture of fennel and other aromatic herbs that is made into a powder and infused in hot water.

594. *Yuzen.* Miyazaki Yūzen, a popular 17th-century painter in Kyōto.

595. *the final bath* (shimai-buro). I.e., take a bath after all the customers have used it.

596. *Kyuroku.* See note 556 above.

597. *three layers of clothes* (kiru mono mitsu). To wear several layers of

clothes was a mark of elegance. This plebeian girl in her rented clothes is giving herself airs.

598. *will you, dear?* (kore konata). The girl's language is familiar and un-ceremonious, totally different from that of a proper courtesan.

599. *her* sakè *cup aslant* (sakazuki wo asō mochi). Lit., "to hold it lightly." This is a form of feminine modesty especially affected by courtesans and present-day *geisha*. When the customer is pouring *sake* for the woman, she will hold her cup at an angle so that she will only have to drink a small amount of the intoxicating liquid. The common bathhouse girl is here de-scribed as aping the manners of refined courtesans. In the same way, she chooses the light refreshments, such as pepper skins, rather than the more solid fare.

600. *sea bream from the Front . . . spiked mackerel from the Bon Festival* (mae no tai . . . Bon no sashisaba). Sea bream caught in the Naruo Sea in front of (that is, off the coast of) Nishinomiya, a few miles west of Ōsaka. They were supposed to be a delicacy. "Spiked mackerel" *(sashisaba)* con-sisted of two slices of salted mackerel spiked on a stick; it was normally eaten at the time of the Bon Festival in the Seventh Moon. When a man from Ōsaka, who is accustomed to such delicacies as sea bream from the Front, goes to the mountainous hinterland of Kumano, he may even in the Ninth Moon be given salted mackerel, which in more urbane circles would only be eaten during the Bon Festival. Yet he can adapt himself to his primitive surroundings and even enjoy this humble fare. Just so, a man who consorts with a common bathhouse girl must forbear from comparing her with the more refined courtesans to whom he may be accustomed and should enjoy her as she is.

601. *the filth of evil passions* (bonnō no aka). *Bonnō* is the Buddhist term re-ferring to carnal desire, evil passions, etc. It here echoes the previous reference to the Buddhist Bon Festival. Diverting oneself with a bathhouse girl (as opposed to indulging in more serious entertainment with a real courtesan) should be regarded as simply being an easy way to rid oneself of impure passions *(Bonnō)* just as one goes to the bathhouse to wash the dirt from one's body.

602. *the new canal* (kawabori). This is the Ajikawa in Ōsaka, on which work was started in the Second Moon of the year 1684.

603. *Perhaps it is merely his fancy* (omoinashi ka). Despite the sultriness of the night, he imagines that her limbs are cold from so much exposure to water during her daytime work at the bathhouse.

604. *Carnal pleasure between man and woman* . . . (nannyo no inraku). Reference to the poem of the Sung dynasty essayist and poet Su Tung-p'o (1063–1101) contained in *Chiu Hsiang Shih*:

A woman adorns her fair skin with powder, reddens her lips, blackens her eyebrows.

[Yet] carnal pleasure between man and woman is but the mutual embrace of stinking bones.

605. *defile the water of my heart* (kokoro no mizu wo nigoshinu). A quotation from *Hotoke no Hara*, the Nō play of Zeami: "Clear the impurity in the water of my heart."

606. *waves of age* (oi no nami). Standard image for an old person's wrinkles (cf. p. 152 above). Here, of course, it is used in imagistic connection with the "sea of love."

Settsu (Tsu no kuni) was the province in which Naniwa (Ōsaka) was situated.

607. *procuress* (yarite). See note 15 above.

608. *employers* (oyakata). (See note 28 above). The procuress *(yarite)* was paid a fee by the employer *(oyakata)* to train the courtesan. It was considered a rather unseemly occupation.

609. *two rectangular gold pieces in advance* (nikaku). I.e., about $22 (£8) in present-day terms. It was normal for a customer to give fairly substantial tips to the various people who attended his favourite courtesan, including the procuress. These payments were virtually obligatory on the seasonal days of payment *(sekki)*, notably at New Year's and at the time of the O-Bon holiday. The heroine, having herself been a high-ranking courtesan, was especially severe in her treatment of the girls over whom she had charge. She would, for instance, scold them when they had secretly met their special paramours. (Such meetings were always frowned on by the employers, even when the proper fee was paid, since they tended to lead to emotional complications.) The customers therefore tried to mitigate the harshness of her behaviour towards their favourite courtesans by paying her in advance of the fixed days.

610. *Six Coppers for the Way* (rokudōsen). Six *mon* (about 7 cents [6 d.]) was the sum normally thrown into the coffin of a dead person so that he could pay his way across the Stygian *Sanzu no Kawa* (note 8 above).

611. *Tamazukuri*. Suburb of Ōsaka, south of the great castle.

612. *a hat in the form of a lotus leaf* (hasu no hagasa wo kitaru yō). In her gloomy vision the heroine saw the embryos of all the children she had failed to bear (cf. p. 162 above). What looked like a lotus-leaf hat was the placentae of these unborn children.

613. *carry me!* (owaryo). The words are spoken in the children's dialect of western Japan. Japanese children are normally carried on their mothers' backs until the age of about 3.

614. *Wada*. Wada Yoshimori (1147-1213), a famous warlord of the Kamakura Period, was reputed to have had a family of 93 children.

615. *the room next to mine* (kabedonari). The heroine's lodging house was evidently of the flimsiest possible construction and it was easy not only to hear but to see what was happening in the neighbouring rooms.

616. *pints of* sakè (konakara-zake). The measure is equivalent to 2.5 *gō,* or approximately 0.8 pints.

617. *informal crests* (kakushimon). See note 101 above.

618. *hidden paper cords* (shinobi-motoyui). Same as *kakushi-motoyui* (note 273 above).

619. *bound Shimada* (hikishime-Shimada). Also known as *shimetsuke-Shimada,* normally formed by tying two paper cords at half the hair's length.

620. *Takénaga* (nagahira-gami). Type of thick Japanese-style paper (cf. *hōsho,* note 400 above).

621. *refabricated paper handkerchiefs* (sukikaeshi no hanagami). *Hanagami* made from waste paper and therefore of the cheapest available quality.

622. *headbands* (hachimaki). Wrapped round the forehead to absorb perspiration and to show that the wearer is bent on some vigorous action and will brook no interference.

cheek towels (hō-kaburi). Worn over the face as a disguise.

623. *matting* (gozamushiro). The young pimps-*cum*-bodyguards *(gifu)* brought these mats for the women to spread on the ground when they found

a customer. This was the lowest form of prostitution in the Tokugawa period and was normally practised out-of-doors or in such improvised shelters as deserted huts or work sheds.

624. *rain capes* (kappa). Another word of Portuguese origin (cf. note 399 above). The clasps were made of horn and were fashioned into the proper shape by hand.

625. *had to embellish herself* (iro tsukurite). The husband had his wife eke out their meager income by engaging in prostitution, while he accompanied her as a tout. This was a fairly common recourse adopted by poor people of the time. A more drastic method was to sell one's wife outright to a house in the gay quarters.

626. *poured some salt into hot water* (sayu ni shio irete). This was regarded as a potent restorative.

627. *by rough calculation* (menoko-zanyō). I.e., calculation by the eye, as opposed to abacus, etc.

628. *five coppers . . . out of each ten* (jūmon de gomon). (See note 57 above.) Ten *mon* (about 10 cents [10 d.]) was the standard fee for common street-walkers in Saikaku's time. The touts kept 50 percent as their own share.

629. *paper handkerchiefs* (hanagami). (See note 134 above). She had to use her own *hanagami* and thus incurred a loss.

630. *Temma*. The old vegetable market in Ōsaka. *Farmers' boats* (hyakushō-bune). Boats in which farmers transported their vegetables from the province of Kawachi down the river to Ōsaka.

631. *not yet so much as shaved the sides of his forelock* (kado sae iranu maega-mi). Some time before cutting off the forelock (note 106 above), it was nor-mal to shave it at the sides; this was known as the "half forelock" or the "side forelock." This young man, however, was so rustic and naïve that he had not yet even taken this preliminary step towards manhood.

632. *made the waves of the river our pillow* (onozukara namimakura). See p. 88 above for the same image; also note 4.

633. *pilgrims' inn* (junrei-yado). Lodging house for pilgrims. It was one of the cheapest types of inns and would only be visited by the meanest harlots.

634. *ceremony of invoking the Sacred Name* (Nembutsu-kō). See note 158 above.

635. *pressed three fingers of each hand* (mitsuyubi wo tsukite). To lay down the three middle fingers of each hand is a ceremonious gesture.

636. *Thirty-Three Holy Places* (sanjūsansho). The 33 holy places in the west of Japan that were dedicated to Kannon, the Goddess of Mercy (note 140 above).

637. *suitable gage for ten coppers* (jūmon ni Kagagasa ichigai). Reference to the proverb, "To accept a wattle hat as a gage for one hundred *kamme* of silver" *(hyakkan no kata ni amigasa ichigai)*, that is, to accept something of ridiculously small value as a pledge for the repayment of a substantial debt. In this case the sum which the woman considers that the men owe her is only ten coppers (note 628 above) and the sedge hat is a very adequate substitute.

638. *middle-ranking courtesans* (tenshoku). See note 591 above.

639. soka. Lowest form of strumpet in western Japan during the Tokugawa Period; also known as *yahatsu*. In Edo these women were known as *yotaka* (night-hawks).

640. *3 fun* (sampun). A *fun* was equivalent to about 7 cents (6 d.) (see note 345 above). There were 10 *ri* to 1 *fun*; 1 *ri* (or *rin*) was worth about a half-penny.

641. *In your nightdress* (Kimi ga Nemaki). Words from one of the vulgar ditties sung by strumpets in western Japan.

642. *the pimp* (gifu). (See note 623 above). The heroine was too old to sing such a tune properly herself, or indeed to ply the profession that it denoted; hence the title of this chapter.

643. *For a thousand men who see . . .* (meaki sennin). Reference to the proverb, "For a thousand seeing people in the world, there are a thousand blind people" *(yo no naka wa meaki sennin mekura sennin)*, i.e., the world holds as many foolish as wise men.

644. *eight bells . . . then seven* (yatsu nanatsu). 2 A.M. and 4 A.M. respectively (cf. note 130 above).

645. *The Five Hundred Disciples* (Gohyaku Rakan). The 500 followers (Arhat) of Buddha. They themselves are also referred to as Buddhas.

646. *the Daiun Temple, the paradise of this present world* (mokuzen no Jōdo Daiunji). The Daiunji is one of the ancient temples of the Tendai Sect; it is situated in Atago, a few miles to the west of the city. Jōdo is the great 12th-

century Amida sect to which Saikaku himself belonged (note 431 above). Here, however, he is using the word in a more general sense, with the meaning of "land of perfect bliss" or "paradise."

647. *Recitation of the Holy Names* (Butsumyō). Annual Buddhist Mass, held for 3 days following the 19th day of the Twelfth Moon, for the confession of sins, during which the names of the Buddhas are recited.

648. *Chojamachi*. Street in the northern part of Kyōto west of the Imperial Palace. It literally means "Millionaires' Street."

649. *hidden tattoo* (kakushi-bokuro). Tattoo where one would normally not see it, in this case, on the inside of his arm. Tattooing reached the height of its popularity during the Edo Period.

650. *exchanged the tenderest pledges of affection* (mōshikawashi). Another euphemism for sexual activity (cf. note 498 above).

651. *Kamigyo*. Northern part of Kyōto (see p. 126 ff.).

652. *Six Days of Fasting* (Rokusai). See note 434 above.

653. *Shijogawara*. (See note 90 above). The description "who had formerly been an actor in the Shijogawara" would unmistakably imply that the man was a paederast.

654. *teahouse* (chaya). In this case, an *iro-chaya* (note 92 above).

655. *postures* (shosa). I.e., the various pleasures of the bedchamber. The word *shosa* has a theatrical connotation and refers to the fact that the man was an actor.

656. *his days were folded up* (tatamare). *Tatamu* (to fold) is used here in 2 senses: (i) to die (as in "When death hath foulded up thy dayes"), (ii) to fold up a collapsible paper lantern, thus extinguishing the candle of life.

657. *Toribéno*. Ancient cemetery on the western slopes of Higashiyama.

658. *temple wife* (daikoku). Cf. p. 148 ff. above.

659. *some form of consumption* (rōsaikataki). Illness, akin to tuberculosis, and normally contracted as a result of overwork. (The first element, *rō*, means "labour," "work.")

660. *ended in smoke* (kefuri to nari). I.e., had died and been cremated. The phrase is the Japanese equivalent of "dead and buried."

661. *warehouse clerk* (kurayashiki-shu). The *kuraya* (warehouses) were used

for storing rice and other commodities from the various fiefs when they arrived in Ōsaka to be sold.

662. *singing nun* (uta-bikuni). Originally these were nuns who went about chanting the *nembutsu* (note 158). By Saikaku's time they had sunk to the rank of common prostitutes. By disguising themselves as nuns these women were able to circulate freely, visiting private houses, etc., in the pursuit of their profession.

663. *that which the people of this world so greatly prize* (hito no oshimu mono). Viz., money.

664. *manager's fee* (o-ryō no temae). I.e., the manager of the group of singing nuns to which the heroine had belonged. This man, whose role corresponded to that of certain modern *oyabun* (bosses), had to be paid a substantial fee for his "protection." The generous warehouse clerk helped her to pay this fee.

665. *sad floating trade* (ukinagare no koto). For "floating trade" *(nagare no kotowaza)*, see note 373 above. *Uki* is here used with its double sense, viz., (i) "floating," (ii) "sad."

666. *the chariot of fire* (hi no kuruma). Reference to the burning chariot that exists in the Buddhist Hell. It is used by the hellhounds *(gokusotsu)* to carry sinners to their torments.

667. *One's name remains in the world* (Na wa todomatte). Quotation from one of the verses in the *Chiu Hsiang Shih (Poems of the Nine Forms)*, a collection of Buddhist poems by Su Tung-p'o, in which are described, sometimes with gruesome detail, the various forms of a corpse's decomposition. Such works, which were often accompanied by rather unappetizing drawings, were designed to remind people of the evanescence of physical life. (For another quotation from Su Tung-p'o, see note 604 above.)

668. *release the ship of the Sacred Law . . . reach the other shore* (tomozuna wo tokisutete . . . kano kishi ni). Reference to a line in Zeami's Nō play *Sanemori:* "the ship of the Sacred Law in which we may cross to the land beyond."

669. *evil passions* (Bonnō). See note 601 above.

670. *that pond* (kore naru ike). I.e., the famous Hirosawa Pond at the foot of Mt. Narutaki to the west of Kyōto (note 179 above). Suicide, far from

being a mortal sin, is viewed as a type of liberation from the trammels of earthly desire. It does not, however, represent true salvation, which can only be reached by achieving enlightenment *(satori)*. The course that the heroine adopts is therefore a more worthy one from a religious point of view.

671. *invoking the Sacred Name* (Nembutsu). See note 158 above.

672. *a single woman* (ichidai onna). In the title of the book *ichidai* is used in the sense of "lifetime," "whole life." Here, however, it refers to the fact that the heroine is absolutely alone in the world, having neither husband nor children. For this reason she could speak quite openly of her life, without fear of bringing dishonour on anyone else.

673. *what people like having in their houses* (ie ni aritaki). Quotation from *Tsurezuregusa:* "The trees people like having in their houses are the pine and the cherry." The opening sentence of Saikaku's chapter announces the spirit of the entire book.

674. *garden storehouse* (niwagura). This was the out-of-door storehouse in which rice and other bulky commodities were kept (cf. the indoor storehouse [*uchigura*], p. 73 above).

675. *bought up* (kaioki). That is, bought at a cheap price and stored in expectation of a rise in the market.

676. *the joys of Kiken Castle* (Kikenjō no tanoshimi). Heavenly castle inhabited by Śakra Devānām Indra (Taishakuten), the Guardian God of Buddhism. There is a reference here to the passage in Zeami's play, *Kantan:* "Lo, this prospect is such that one can but bethink oneself of the joys of Kiken Castle."

677. *Bridge of the Fourth Avenue . . .* (Shijō no hashi wo . . .). If one crossed this bridge going east, one came to the teahouse area of Gion (note 459 above); if one went west from Ōmiyadōri towards Tambaguchi, one crossed the Shimabara district (note 33 above). In other words, this man refrained from visiting either of the two main pleasure quarters in the city.

678. *priests from the surrounding hills* (shosan no shukke). The main Kyōto temples were situated on the surrounding hills and mountains. This gentleman avoided consorting with priests and was therefore not obliged to give alms to their temples.

679. ronin. For the more usual meaning of *rōnin* ("unattached warrior"),

see note 427 above. Here it is used in a more general sense to refer to men who have no definite occupation and who live by their wits. The friendship of such men was liable to be a costly business.

680. *No songs* (koutai). Short extracts from *Nō* recitations.

681. *in a natural voice* (jigoe ni shite). That is, not in the resonant, declamatory tone normal for songs of this type. He sang to distract himself and not for the pleasure of others.

682. *one hundred and fifty hundredweight of silver* (nisen-kamme). (See note 230 above). Equivalent of about $1,526,000 (£545,000) in present-day values.

683. *a strickle* (masukaki). Short bamboo stick used for levelling the rice or other cereals placed in a *masu*. (The *masu* is a boxlike instrument of various sizes used for measuring commodities in bulk.) The age of 87 (88 in the old Japanese count) was known as the "rice age" *(beiju)*, and it was customary to ask people who had attained this age to carve a levelling stick for one: this was considered to augur well for one's own longevity.

684. *autumn rains* (shigure). (See note 127 above). The autumn rains began in the Tenth Moon (i.e., in the middle of November).

685. *a man of great wealth* (chōja). There were two principal grades of rich merchants in the Edo Period: a man with a fortune of 500 *kamme* of silver or more was known as a *bungen;* if one had more than 1,000 *kamme,* one became, as in the present instance, a *chōja.* (The approximate equivalents are $380,800 [£136,000] and $761,600 [£272,000] and the terms will be translated as "man of wealth" and "man of great wealth," respectively.)

686. *the seven days* (nanuka). The first 7 days after a person's death are a period of deep mourning, during which numerous Buddhist ceremonies are carried out. The full mourning period lasts for 49 days (note 211), but this mercenary young man opens the shop for business on the 8th day.

687. *another twenty-two years* (ima nijūninen). The mistake is Saikaku's and is one of the several indications of the speed at which he must often have been writing (cf. note 186 above). The correct figure, of course, is "twelve."

688. *a full hundred* (chōbyaku). The copper coins used in the Edo Period *(ichimonsen)* had a hole in the centre (like the present-day 5-*yen* pieces). It was normal to string 96 together, and these were counted as being worth the same as 100 copper coins; similarly 960 copper coins strung together were worth 1,000 coppers or *ichikammon.* The term "a full hundred" *(chōbyaku)*

was used when, instead of the usual 96 coppers, there were in fact 100. Here the money-conscious young man uses it in reference to his father's age.

689. *Imperial Botanical Gardens* (Go-yakuen). Garden in which were grown medicinal herbs for use in the Imperial Palace. It was situated in Takagamine in the northern suburbs of the city (west of the Daitoku Temple).

690. *offertory rice* (tokimai). Rice offered to a temple at times of fasting, purification, etc.

691. *Nisan*. See note 414 above.

692. "The Five Great Bodhisattvas" (Godairiki Bosatsu). Standard inscription written on letters to ensure their safe delivery; later it simply came to indicate that the letter was important. The custom is believed to have started from the fact that these characters were written on the boxes *(harai-bako)* containing the sprigs of the sacred *tamagushi* tree that were sent to various parts of the country from the Grand Shrine of Ise.

693. *some great nobleman* (go-kugeshu). The name Hanakawa in no way smacks of nobility, but the hero of this story is utterly ignorant both of aristocratic circles and of the demimonde.

694. *strumpet* (tsubone-jorō). See note 589 above.

695. *Sugihara paper* (Sugihara hongo). Type of Japanese-style Hōsho paper originally produced in the province of Harima.

696. *one rectangular gold piece* (ichibu hitotsu). (See note 25 above). Worth about $11 (£4).

697. *upper scale of his weighing machine* (hakari no uwame). Scale on the upper part of the instrument, used for determining the weight of small objects.

698. *one* mommé *and two* fun (ichimomme nifun). An *ichibu-koban* was worth one quarter of a *koban*. A *koban* weighed 4.8 *momme* (note 63 above), and 1.2 was therefore the correct weight for the coin in the letter.

699. *the season for requests* (jibungara no gomushin). Since this was the anniversary of the old father's death (which occurred in about the Tenth Moon), it can be inferred that the New Year's season was approaching. It was usual for customers to give tips at this time to their favourite courtesans, etc. (note 609 above), and the girls depended on these to pay off their debts.

700. *spring stipend* (harugirimai). Lit., "spring-exchange-rice." *Samurai*

were paid their rice allowance 3 times a year: spring (in the Second Moon), summer (in the Fifth Moon) and winter (in the Tenth Moon). The rice allowance was fixed, but the actual amount of money that this rice represented depended on the current rate of exchange; the *samurai* were therefore greatly affected by market fluctuations.

701. *two* mommé *out of this* (kono uchi ni-momme). That is, two *momme* of silver. In 1684 the rate of exchange had been fixed at 1 gold *ryō* = 60 silver *momme* (note 340 above). One *ichibu-koban* (note 698 above) was therefore worth 15 silver *momme*. Nisan was in effect instructing the girl to change the gold coin that he had sent her into silver and to keep 13 (out of the 15) *momme* for her own use; 13 *momme* were equivalent to about $10 (£3.11.0).

702. *three hundred gold coins* (ichibu sambyaku). Equivalent to about $3,433 (£1,226).

703. *Nokazé of the Ozakaya* (Ōzakaya no Nokaze-dono). Nokaze was a famous *tayū* in Kyōto who flourished in the 1680s. For a further example of her success, see p. 146 above. Ōzakaya Tarōbei was an establishment in the Shimabara district where courtesans lived. Such places were known as *yūjoya*, as opposed to the *ageya* (note 20), where they met their customers.

704. *Chrysanthemum Festival* (Kiku no Sekku). See notes 185, 392, 552, 609.

705. *removing his sedge hat* (amigasa nugite). (See note 120 above). It was customary to rent a hat at the teahouse, even though one might be wearing one's own hat on arrival. The fan maker is utterly ignorant of the etiquette that governs the gay quarters and not only fails to rent a hat, but doffs his own.

706. *passed in front of the teahouses* (chaya no mae wo yukisugite). Customers visiting the Shimabara normally stopped at one of the teahouses and were escorted from there to whichever house of assignation they might wish to visit. The fan maker once more displays his naïveté.

707. *the Present-Day Morokoshi of the Ichimonjiya* (Ichimonjiya no Ima-Morokoshi). The Ichimonjiya Shichirōbei was one of the most famous *yūjoya* (note 703) in the Shimabara. Morokoshi was a *tayū* attached to this house in the late 1680s. She was given the epithet "present-day" to distinguish her from a predecessor of the same name (p. 77 above).

708. *blue curtains* (aonoren). Blue shop curtains denoted an establishment

for *mise-jorō* (note 589); yellowish-brown curtains denoted a *tayū* establishment.

709. *trollop* (hashi-keisei). See note 589 above. *Two* mommé: equivalent of about $1.50 (11 s).

710. *Fujiya Hikoémon.* One of the *iro-chaya* opposite the main gate of the Shimabara quarter.

711. *nine* mommé *of silver for the day period* (hiru no uchi kyū momme). The courtesan whom he summoned belonged to the rank of *kakoi* (note 20 above). Her full fee was 18 *momme,* but her services could also be divided into a day period and a night period, in which case the charge was 9 *momme* (about $7 [£2.10.0]) per period.

712. *jesters . . . known as the Four Heavenly Kings* (massha Shitennō). (See notes 88 and 404). The 4 men named flourished in Kyōto in the 1670s.

713. *not a speck of dust or ash remained* (chiri mo hai mo naku). Reference to the proverbial expression used to describe financial ruin: "Even the ash in the hearth has disappeared" *(irori no hai mo naku naru).* The image is also connected with the clause that follows.

714. *did not even have the strength to blow the embers of the fire* (hi fuku chikara mo naku). I.e., with a bamboo blow pipe, the Japanese equivalent of a bellows. This, too, is a proverbial expression to describe destitution.

715. *Once in prosperity* (Ichido wa sakae). From Zeami's Nō play, *Kakitsubata:* "Yet it is truly human fate in this world to live once in prosperity, then in adversity."

716. *Kamadaya.* Probably the great Kamadaya shop named in *Teachings about Millionaires (Chōjakyō)* (1627).

717. *Daikoku.* Daikoku refers here to (i) the name of the shop belonging to the hero's father, and hence the hero himself, who, through adversity, became a man of ready wit, (ii) the God of Wealth (note 256 above).
"To wear on one's sedge hat" *(kasa ni kiru)* means to make a proud display of something (cf. "a feather in one's cap"). This also refers to the name given to the hero's shop after he has reinstated himself in the world.

718. *two-storeyed houses . . .* (nikai-zukuri). The opening words of the story are based on one of the texts used for the Daikoku dance. In these texts the various attributes of the God of Wealth are enumerated—e.g., "First, he rests

375

his feet on two bales of rice; secondly, he laughs merrily; thirdly, he makes *sake* . . ." The Daikoku dances were normally performed on auspicious occasions such as New Year's (see note 767 below).

719. *man of wealth* (bungensha). See note 685 above.

720. *Bridge of the Fifth Avenue* (Gojō no Hashi). The bridge was originally a wooden structure; in 1645, it was rebuilt in stone; it was destroyed in the great earthquake of 1662 and once more built in wood.

721. *third plank* (sammaime no ita). A statue of Daikoku carved from the plank of a bridge was supposed to have miraculous virtues. The third plank from the west had special efficacy.

722. *there is profit in faith* (shinjin ni toku ari). The original proverb is *shinjin areba toku ari* ("Where there is faith there is profit"). "Profit" *(toku)* is written with the character that usually means "virtue" and this gives the proverb a certain ambiguity.

723. *twelve hundredweight of silver* (hyakunanajū kamme). (See note 230 above). Equivalent to about $130,000 (£46,000).

724. *the eve of the Seventh Moon* (Shichigatsu-mae). The O-Bon Festival was one of the two main periods in the year (the other being New Year's) when accounts were balanced and bills settled.

725. *one thousand seven hundred hundredweight of silver* (nihyaku-sanjū kamme). About $175,000 (£63,000). His father's fortune was rapidly being depleted (see notes 685, 719).

726. *the matter came to light* (o ga miete). Lit., "showed its tail." There is a reference here to foxes, who were reputed to bewitch people (note 43). For such a fox to show its tail was to reveal its identity (cf. "show the cloven hoof"). There is also a connexion with Inari (note 483), since foxes were supposed to act as messengers for the Inari deities.

727. *town members* (chōshu). Representatives of the five-family company *(gonin-gumi)* to which the old man belonged. All families were organized into such companies and any official dealings with the government, such as disownment, had to be carried out through them.

728. *having submitted a bill of disownment* (kyūri wo kitte). (See note 11 above.) There were two forms of disownment in the Edo Period: (i) private disownment *(naishō-kandō)*, which was a private arrangement within the

376

family, and which could under certain circumstances be revoked, (ii) official disownment *(kōshiki kandō)*, which was carried out by applying to the town officials and publicly posting a bill of disownment. It is the second system that was applied in the present case. The wearing of ceremonial *hakama* by the town members underlined the official nature of the occasion. A person who had thus been disowned was removed from the family register, excluded from the five-family company and expelled from his native town or village. Unless he disowned his son, a father was legally responsible for the latter's debts and misdemeanours. The five-family company, in turn, was responsible for the defaults of its members.

729. *for the East* (azuma no kata e). For Edo. Having been officially disowned, he was automatically proscribed from Kyōto.

730. *to tuck up his clothes* (shirikarage). It was normal to tuck one's clothes into one's loincloth when travelling on foot or engaging in any strenuous outdoor activity.

731. *inflammation of the brain* (kan). A form of meningitis.

732. *people leaving the capital . . . who were strangers* (yuku mo kaeru mo . . . shiru mo shiranu mo). See note 141 above.

733. *sharp needle pedlars* (kokoro no hariya). Reference to the expression, "to have a needle in one's heart" *(kokoro ni hari wo motsu)*, i.e., to be malicious or cunning. The town of Oiwake (between Kyōto and Ōtsu) was well known for the manufacture of needles.

734. *Hatcho.* Street in the city of Ōtsu (on Lake Biwa due east of Kyōto).

735. *five hundred and eighty coppers* (gohyaku-hachijū). Equivalent of about $6.50 (£2.6.0). 580 was a lucky number.

736. *the Long Bridge of Seta* (Seta no Nagahashi). (See note 142 above.) The present passage is another example of the traditional form known as *michiyuki.*

737. *Uba rice cakes* (Uba ga mochi). It is customary to eat rice cakes *(mochi)* at New Year's. *Uba ga mochi* (lit., "old woman's rice cakes") were a speciality of Kusatsu, a small town opposite Ōtsu on Lake Biwa (about 14 miles east of Kyōto). *Kagami-mochi* (mirror rice cakes) were another variety. For Kagami Mountain, see note 145 above.

738. *the God of Poverty* (bimbōgami). Reference to the proverb, "Poverty cannot keep up with diligence" *(kasegu ni oitsuku bimbō nashi)*.

a tottering old man (ashi yowaki oi): *oi* (old man) is used as a pun on the first element of Oiso.

739. *this must be a pleasant place* (. . . mo tanomoshiki). This seemingly gratuitous observation is inspired by the fact that the Fuwa Barrier was traditionally associated in poetry with autumn scenes and the moon, rather than with the spring.

740. *Tokaido.* See note 353 above.

741. *Shinagawa.* Area in the south of Edo and the last of the 53 posting-stages on the Tōkaidō highway from Kyōto.

742. *two kan and three hundred mon of copper* (zeni nikan-sambyaku). (See note 22 above.) Equivalent to about $27 (£9.10.0).

743. *Tokai Temple* (Tōkaiji). Temple in north Shinagawa, built in 1638. It is situated at the end of the Tōkaidō about half a mile from the harbour.

744. *outcasts* (hinin). *Hinin* (lit., "nonhumans") was the name given in the Edo Period to people who did not fit into the *shi-nō-kō-shō* (warrior-farmer-artisan-merchant) classification; together with the Eta pariah class they were regarded as the dregs of society. Occasionally these outcasts were employed as coolies, or were given such unpleasant jobs as guarding convicts and tending the execution grounds. As they had no regular employment, they were frequently dependent on begging, and one common (though not very accurate) translation of *hinin* is, in fact, "beggar." The outcasts in each community were organized under an "outcast leader" *(hiningashira)*, who was responsible for keeping an "official register" *(hininchō)* of the outcasts in his district. A clear-cut hierarchy existed among the outcasts, the main division being between the *yadoari* (lit., "those with a lodging"), who were listed on the outcast register, and the *yadonashi* ("those without a lodging"), whose names did not appear on any register and who therefore had no legal existence whatsoever. The *yadonashi* (in Kyōto, *kojiki*) were like the unfortunate men in this story, customarily clad in a type of rush matting *(komo)*. The "lodging" referred to the fact of being registered, rather than to actually having a place in which to live, a luxury that few of the outcasts enjoyed.

745. *pillows are close to the waves* (namimakura). A further use of the wave-pillow imagery (see note 4 above).

746. *cut off from their families* (suji naki). Reference to the proverb, "a beggar has no family" *(kojiki ni suji nashi)*.

747. *vintner's provision shop* (sakanadana). The character used for *sakana* indicates that this is not a fishmonger's, but a shop specializing in relishes *(sakana)*, like smoked octopus, dried fish and rice biscuits, which were eaten with *sake;* such shops might also sell *sake* itself.

748. *red-tinged brocade* (momiji no nishiki). It was traditional in classical Chinese literature for a man who had prospered in the world to return to his home village dressed in brocade. The phrase "to wear brocade" *(nishiki wo kiru)* became proverbial in Japan and means "to return to one's home town laden with honours." In this case the brocade is described as red-tinged (maple-coloured) because the man's home town of Tatsuta was famous for the red autumnal tinges of its maples.

749. haikai. Seventeen-syllable poems which reached their height in the Edo Period. Nishiyama Sōin (1605-82) was originally an expert in linked verses *(renga);* later he founded one of the important 17th-century schools of *haikai,* known as the Danrin *haikai.* Saikaku himself started his poetic career under this master.

All the teachers mentioned in this passage were prominent practitioners of their respective arts.

750. *under the fan* (ōgi wo uke). *Nō* dancing is invariably performed with a fan.

751. *Ito Genkichi.* 1627-1705, famous teacher of Confucian ethics.

752. *Yatsuhashi Kengo.* 1614-85, founder of the modern style of playing the *koto* (note 269 above); he was blind.

753. *the small flute* (hitoyogiri). Five-holed bamboo instrument, usually about 14 inches long, resembling the ancient recorder. It is thinner and shorter than the *shakuhachi* flute.

754. joruri. Metrical romances sung during the puppet performances and during certain Kabuki plays to the accompaniment of the samisen. They contain both a description of the dramatic action and the speeches of the characters.

755. *Suzuki Heihachi.* 1666-87, actor in western Japan, best known for taking the roles of young boys; he flourished in the 1680s. Concerning the amorous inclinations of actors, see notes 90, 653 above.

756. *both the gay quarters* (ryō-irozato). Those which specialized in feminine and masculine love respectively (cf. notes 89, 90 above).

Drum-holders (taikomochi). See note 14.

757. *the heart-consuming mansion of anguish* (kokoro no moyuru kataku). Buddhist image in which this insecure and agonizing world is compared to a burning mansion.

758. *unregistered beggar* (nakamahazure no monomorai). I.e., a beggar whose name was not listed on the outcast register *(hininchō)* (note 744 above).

759. *Kuruma Zenshichi.* The Kuruma were a hereditary family of outcast leaders *(hiningashira)* established in Edo by edict of the 3rd Shōgun, Tokugawa Hidetada (1616-22). Beggars attached to outcast leaders were normally registered, but this unfortunate man did not even enjoy this privilege.

760. *aunt* (obasama). The aunt was usually the first person approached when it came to attempting a family reconciliation.

761. *people who have money . . .* (kane ga . . .). Reference to the proverb, "Money makes money" *(kane ga kane wo mōkeru).*

762. *Reigan Island* (Reiganjima). Small island in the Kyōbashi area of Edo.

763. *twenty-fifth day of the Third Moon* (sangatsu nijūgonichi). This was one of the main festival days at the Tenjin Shrine. It has been demonstrated by Professor Ōyabu *(Nippon Eitaigura Shinkō,* p. 202) that the hero waited for about 3 weeks before selling the towels, since he had shrewdly estimated that they would fetch a much better price on the day of the festival. (Shinroku had left Kyōto on the 29th day of the Twelfth Moon and reached Edo on the 62nd day of his journey, that is, at the very beginning of the Third Moon.)

764. *Luck to the buyer* (kōte no saiwai). From the proverb, "Luck to the buyer, good fortune to the seller" *(kōte no saiwai, utte no shiawase).*

765. *a man of wealth* (bungen). See note 685 above. The term is used here in a rather loose sense, since 5,000 *koban* of gold was not equivalent in value to 500 *kamme* of silver.

766. *the Sedge-Hat Daikoku* (Kasa-Daikokuya). See note 717 above.

767. *Eighth . . .* (yatsu). The closing words of the story echo the beginning and refer to the texts used for one of the Daikoku dances (note 717):

" . . . eighth, he enlarges his mansion; ninth, he builds warehouses; tenth, he enjoys peace." The Daikoku dances were popular in the Kyōto area in Saikaku's time.

768. *invested his wealth in gold* koban (koban no kaioki). (Cf. note 675 above). The value of *koban* in terms of silver currency fluctuated during most of the Edo Period. Large profits could be made by buying gold when its value was low and selling when the price rose. In general the tendency was for silver to depreciate in value. In 1609, for example, the value of 1 gold *ryō* was fixed at 50 *momme* of silver; by 1684 it had risen to 60 *momme*.

769. *this peaceful and auspicious reign* (osamaritaru miyo). Cf. note 314.

770. *The Ten Virtues of Tea* (cha no jittoku). *Jittoku* refers to (i) the 10 virtues that were attributed to tea (the virtue of veneration for others, the virtue of divine protection by the Buddhas and the Gods, the virtue of filial piety, etc.), and that were incorrectly believed to be contained in the Somashi Sutra; (ii) an ancient form of clothing originally used for ceremonial purposes, but later worn by tea vendors, doctors and others.

771. *Tsuruga*. Situated in present-day Fukui Prefecture and still one of the chief harbours on the Japan Sea coast. It was at one time the principal port for traffic with Korea.

772. *keelage* (uwamai). A type of transit duty assessed on goods being reloaded for sea or river transport; also known as *unjō*.

773. *one great gold piece* (bankin ichimai). (See note 244 above). Equivalent at this time to about $350 (£125).

774. *Yodo River* (Yodo no Kawa). The keelage at this period on the Yodo River (in Ōsaka) was 6 *momme* of silver (about $4.50 [£1.12.0]) per 100 *koku* (about 500 bushels) of rice.

775. *bags* (hanagami-fukuro). Same as *hanagami-ire* (note 223 above).

776. *an honest head* (shōjiki no kōbe). Reference to the proverb, "The honest man's head is the seat of God" (note 116 above).

777. *Ebisu*. The God of Commerce and one of the Seven Lucky Gods (note 257). To get up early and pay one's respects to this God was known as performing *asa-Ebisu* ("morning Ebisu"); early-morning tea was called *asacha no yu*. Risuke combines the two expressions in his street cry and thereby

attracts the custom of passing merchants, who are always interested in some new fancy of this kind, especially when it may involve good luck.

778. *twelve coppers* (jūnimon). Because it was customary to offer 12 incense tapers to the God Ebisu. Twelve coppers (about 15 cents [1 s.]) would normally have been a very large sum to pay for a cup of tea.

779. *desirous of having him for a son-in-law* (koimuko). See note 210 above.

780. *like scarlet streaks* (kurenai no suji). Anguished tears were frequently referred to in literature as "tears of blood" or "scarlet tears."

781. *breaking off the dead branches* (koboku no eda orite). Quotation from Zeami's Nō play, *Tsunemasa*: "The wind blows through the desiccated trees and the clear sky is filled with rain."

782. *the burning mansion* (kataku). See note 757 above.

783. *teahouses of the Eastern Hills* (Higashiyama no chaya). The *iro-chaya* brothels in the Ishigaki and Hachizaka districts of eastern Kyōto, which catered mainly to professional catamites and which had a large clientele among priests.

784. *to arrange for a man to commit fornication . . .* (tsutsumotase). Lit., "causing [a woman] to hold a pipe (tube)." This was a method of extorting money that had its origins in the Yüan Dynasty of China, when it was known as *mei jen chü* ("the beautiful-woman game"). With the connivance of the woman's husband and of the woman herself, the man would arrange for her to commit adultery with some unsuspecting dupe; thereafter he would extort money from the paramour by threatening to expose him to the cuckolded husband.

785. *to pluck the hair* (kami no ochi). Dead people's hair could easily be plucked out by the roots and sold to wig makers; this was one of the more sordid ways in which rogues contrived to make money.

786. *sixty-nine years ago* (rokujūkunen izen). I.e., in 1623. There is, however, no record of an eclipse taking place on New Year's Day of that year. There were solar eclipses on New Year's Day in 1636 and in 1692. The events of this chapter were presumably supposed to occur in the latter year.

787. *in the Year of the Monkey under the ninth sign of the calendar* (mizunoe saru). 1692. *Saru* (monkey) is also used punningly as the first element of *saruhodo* (indeed).

788. *the fourth year of Empress Jitō's reign* (Jitō Tennō yonen). 689. The Giō (I Huang) Calendar was invented in the T'ang dynasty by Chi Ch'un-feng, introduced into Japan in 676 and, according to the *Nihonshoki*, officially adopted in the 11th Moon of the year 689; it remained in force until 763. The calendar in force while Saikaku was writing was the Jōkyō Calendar, adopted in the 10th Moon of 1684. All the calendars were based on observations of the solar and lunar eclipses.

789. *the final passage, which is New Year's Eve* (sue-ichidan no ōmisoka). Reference to the last part of the *jōruri*, which was known as the *sue-ichidan*. The *jōruri* were normally composed of 5 *dan*. For *jōruri* and ditties, see notes 754 and 580.

790. *a piece of rice cake or a dried sardine* (mochi hitotsu gomame ippiki). Traditional New Year's dishes, which these people are too poor to enjoy. They have all the work associated with the New Year's season, but few of the pleasures.

791. *could all be bought with ready cash* (banji tōzagai ni shite). In Edo times, as now, it was customary for householders to make their everyday purchases on credit. In recent times it is becoming customary to settle one's bills monthly, but the traditional system was to pay part of what one owed on the seasonal days of payment *(sekki,* note 609), to settle half of all one's outstanding debts on the O-Bon Festival and to clear one's debts entirely on the last day of the year. Bill collectors visited people's houses on the day before the feast-day. New Year's Eve was therefore the main day of the year for the settlement of debts. The people in the present story were usually too poor to settle their debts properly and they therefore dreaded these visits; the bill collectors, for their part, would barge unceremoniously *(annai nashi ni)* into the poor people's houses. During the period of the New Year's holiday (the first 5 days or so of the year), however, all credit sales were suspended, and people bought such necessities as oil and rice with ready cash. No bill collectors called during these days and poor people enjoyed a respite from the usual dunning.

792. *an ancient saying* (kojin no kotoba). According to the *Teihon Saikaku Zenshū* (Vol. VII, p. 188), this may refer to a passage from the *Analects*.

793. *daytime thieves* (hiru-nusubito). Rogues who were able to mix in ordinary society by assuming an honest front.

794. *five*-go (gogō). 1 *gō* = 0.318 pints.

795. *Minatoyaki dishes* (Minatoyaki no ishizara). Minatoyaki porcelain came from the village of Minato in Ōshima-gun, Izumi Province.

796. *entertainer . . . Kowaka dances* (maimai). The Kowaka dances (Kō-wakamai), which originated in the Muromachi Period (15th–16th centuries), were danced to the beat of a fan without any musical accompaniment. There were some 30 different types of Kōwakamai, most of them concerned with war and love. The dancer invariably wore a ceremonial headgear and robe *(eboshi* and *shitatate)* and a wide-bottomed *hakama* trouser-skirt.

797. *Daikoku dance* (Daikoku mai). For Daikoku, see note 256 above. This dance was performed during the New Year season to the accompaniment of a special Daikoku song (see notes 718, 767). The dancers would copy the appearance of Daikoku, wearing masks and kerchiefs, and go from door to door performing for money. The custom has some points in common with that of Christmas caroling, but it was on the whole a far more secular affair.

798. *impecunious ronin* (kamiko-rōnin). Lit., a *rōnin* so poor that he had to wear paper clothes.

799. *"bream fishers"* (taitsuri). A hook was stuck to the mouth of a small model sea bream and one would try to catch it with a pole to which a piece of thread or a long hair had been attached. Similar to the present-day *saru-tsuri* (monkey-catching toys).

800. *at his wit's end* (kojiri sashitsumarite). Lit., "the tip of his sword was stuck," i.e., he was at an impasse or "stuck in the mud."

801. *the battle of Ishida Jibu no Sho* (Ishida Jibu no Shō Ran). The reference is to the famous general, Ishida Mitsunari (1560–1600), one of the close followers of Toyotomi Hideyoshi, who after the latter's death set himself up against Tokugawa Ieyasu. He was defeated by Ieyasu at Sekigahara (1600) and was executed in Kyōto. The wife of the *rōnin* in the story claims that her father used this scabbard in the great battle of Sekigahara. *(Jibu no Shō* was Ishida Mitsunari's official title.)

802. *three sho* (sanshō). 1 *shō* = 10 *gō* = 3.18 pints.

803. *six thousand bushels of rice* (sennihyaku-koku). The equivalent of approximately $36,400 (£13,000).

804. *people do not die simply from being poor* (hin nite wa shinarenu). Be-

cause they always find some way to obtain money, even if it means drastically lowering their standards as in the case of the wife of the *rōnin*.

805. *we shan't be able to use . . .* (yō ni tatanu). It would be impossible to have the rice pounded during the New Year holidays. By saying this the woman evidently hoped to extort a little more money from the pawnbroker, or at least to obtain the use of his hulling mortar free of charge.

806. *losing three hundred coppers at a touch* (sawari sambyaku). Proverbial expression signifying that in certain cases one is likely to lose money however briefly one may be involved in the affair (lit., "by simply touching it, you lose 300 coppers"). This, of course, describes the pawnbroker's experience with the scabbard.

807. *decoy maid* (deonna). Maids who stood outside inns to attract passing travellers. They usually beckoned to them with the cry of *Ojare* ("Come in!") and these girls were therefore often known as *ojare*. Needless to say, their entertainment of the guests frequently overstepped the more conventional duties of a maid.

808. *the image of Jizo at Seki* (Seki no Jizō). Jizō (Ksitigarbha) is the Bodhisattva who is regarded *inter alia* as the guardian deity of children. Seki was the 7th stage on the Tōkaidō going from Kyōto towards Edo.

809. *secret visits to the Isé Grand Shrine* (nukemairi). It was a popular custom in the Edo Period for servants and young people to make pilgrimages to the Grand Shrine at Ise without informing their masters or parents. The latter were expected to countenance such expeditions, though in fact the pilgrimages were often undertaken as a pretext for some very secular aim such as meeting a lover.

810. *their own provisions of rice* (kichintomari). It was possible in the poorer class of inn *(kichinyado)* to bring along one's own rice; the traveller was then charged only for the fuel used to boil it.

811. *a wolf in sheep's clothing* (ōkami ni koromo). Proverbial expression, literally meaning "clothes on a wolf."

812. *even on a sardine's head* (iwashi no atama mo shinjin kara). Proverb signifying that credulous and pious people are ready to believe that even so worthless an object as a sardine's head can have divine or miraculous powers. The phrase is similar in meaning but lacks the favourable connotation of "Faith will move a mountain." In the present case the reference is to the

credulity of simple-minded people who will give alms to a dishonest and utterly irreligious maidservant merely because she wears sacerdotal robes.

813. *Twelfth Moon priest* (shiwasu-bōzu). Proverbial expression used to describe someone who is useless and superfluous. In the last month of the year people are so busy with preparations for the year-end and New Year celebrations, as well as with settling their accounts, that they have no time for any priest who may come calling. Money and traditional celebrations clearly took precedence over Buddhism for most merchants of the period.

814. *annual Sweeping Day* (mainen susuharai). Lit., "the soot-sweeping." This was a sort of compulsory spring-cleaning that was supposed to be carried out on the 13th day of the Twelfth Moon in every residence in Edo, including the Shōgun's castle. The custom has survived in a very modified way.

815. *thatched roof* (torifukiyane). A type of roof that was thatched with thin chips of wood; the thatch was pressed down with stones and logs, which were bound together with strips of bamboo.

816. *dumplings of the Fifth Moon* (gogatsu no chimaki). These were the dumplings eaten on the Tango (Boys') Festival on the 5th day of the Fifth Moon. They were wrapped in various sorts of leaves, depending on the region. The cheese-paring son did not even throw away the husks from 7-month-old dumplings, but saved them to use as fuel.

817. *lotus leaves used at the Bon Festival* (Bon no hasu no ha). Offerings placed on the holy shelf during the Bon season were laid on lotus leaves (cf. p. 103 above).

818. *mountain priest* (yamabushi). See note 480 above.

819. *sacred paper strips* (gohei). Pendant pieces of paper that are suspended at Shintō shrines, outside houses, etc., when one is addressing some particular prayer to the Gods. They form part of the ancient indigenous cult of Japan and are supposed to confer special sanctity on the place where they are hung.

820. *one hundred and twenty coppers* (hyaku nijū). Equivalent to about $1.50 (10 s.). Twelve coppers was the normal donation, but the old lady was so delighted at the omen that she violated her usual rules of economy and gave ten times that amount.

821. *throwing good money after bad* (nusubito ni oi). The well-known proverbial expression is *nusubito ni oisen* (lit., "to give money to the thief [who

386

has stolen from one]"). The phrase is used in much the same wide sense as the English "throwing good money after bad."

822. *Matsuda.* Well-known expert in legerdemain and magical tricks who flourished in Edo and Sakai in the 1660s.

823. *as he fiercely rubbed his rosary . . . now to the west* (juzu sarasara to . . . saibō ni). "As he fiercely rubbed his rosary . . ." is a quotation from Kojirō's *Nō* play, *Funa Benkei.*

"Now to the east, now to the west" is taken from an incantation of the Shingon Sect which the mountain priest evidently used in his prayers.

824. *black-headed rats* (atama no kuroi nezumi). "Black-headed rat" is a standard phrase referring to a pilfering servant.

825. *Emperor Kotoku* (Kōtoku Tennō). Reigned 645-54. It was in this reign that the great Taika Reform was enacted (646). According to the present count, Kōtoku was the 36th (not the 37th) Emperor. In Saikaku's time, however, Empress Jingū (201-69) was counted as the 15th sovereign, and as a result the numbers of all the subsequent Emperors and Empresses were one greater than in the modern count.

826. *first year of the Taika Era* (Taika gannen). 645.

827. *Okamoto.* Capital established by Emperor Jomei in 630. Prior to 710, when the first permanent capital was erected in Nara, it had been customary for the Imperial Palace to be rebuilt in some new site at the beginning of each new reign.

828. *to use at his own wedding* (yomeiri). There were numerous stories in Saikaku's time about the weddings of mice and rats. (It may be noted that *yome-ga-kimi* is another word for "rat.")

829. *pay their respects at Kumano* (Kumano-mairi). I.e., visiting the Three Great Shrines of Kumano in the Kii Peninsula (note 465).

830. *cited the ancient chronicles* (nendaiki wo hikite). Specifically, Volume XXV of the *Nihonshoki,* which records the Imperial move to Toyosaki. The details about the rat, however, are Saikaku's.

831. *Nagasaki Mizuémon.* Famous trainer of small animals who flourished in Edo in the 1680s and 1690s.

832. *Fleeting, Fleecing World* (Kari no Yo). The title is based on a pun. Kari = (i) temporary, evanescent, fleeting, (ii) debts. The story tells about

how at New Year's people with debts are in danger of being fleeced of their possessions. In order to convey the spirit of the original pun it has seemed permissible to substitute "fleecing" for "debts" in the translation.

833. *large branded sedge hats* (yakiin no ōamigasa). The sedge hats rented by visitors to the gay quarters (notes 120 and 705) were branded with the name of the teahouse to which they belonged.

834. *on his own* (tomo nashi). See note 592 above.

835. *to leave their house on New Year's Eve* (ōmisoka ni mo dechigawazu). See note 791 above.

836. *money would start growing on those trees* (kane no naru ki). Proverbial expression (lit., "trees on which money grows") suggesting the way in which money can multiply itself indefinitely by accumulating interest (cf. the corresponding English expression, "to think that money grows on trees," which has the opposite implication).

837. *'We must sow before we can reap'* (makanu tane wa haenu). Proverb, lit., "a seed that is not sown will not grow."

838. *iron chopsticks* (manabashi). Used in cooking fish and fowl.

839. *dried sardines* (gomame). See note 790 above.

840. *centre of the city* (nakagyō). Area including Karasumaru and Muromachi, inhabited by wealthy money-changers, drapers, dyers, etc.

841. *a foxlike look came on his face* (kitsune no manako shite). See note 726 for connexion of foxes with the Inari Shrine.

842. *Horikawa.* Area in Kyōto in which there were many lumber merchants.

843. *side forelock* (sumi-maegami). See note 631 above.

844. *invoke the sacred name of Buddha* (Shōmyō tonaete). That is, he repeated the Nembutsu (note 158 above).

845. *mock suicide* (shini-tengō). The word *tengō* (trick, joke) belongs to the West Japan dialect. The verbal exchanges in the present story derive much of their pungency from the use of dialect.

846. *man is mortal, fame immortal* (hito wa ichidai na wa matsudai). Proverb, lit., "Man for one generation, his name for generations to come." The person in the story implies that in view of his wife's bloodthirsty threats he has a rather short life expectancy.

847. *as soon as it gets dark* (yoru fukete kara). The bill collectors normally called first at houses where they were confident of obtaining payment without too much trouble; they left refractory customers, like the man in the present story, to the end. Accordingly this man was accustomed from past years to having bill collectors visit him late in the evening, and he prepared to confront them with his newly discovered ruse.

848. *Omiyadori.* This is the street on which the customer lived; it runs through Kyōto from north to south, west of the Imperial Palace.

849. *Festival of Temma* (Temma Matsuri). Shintō festival held in Ōsaka on the 25th day of the Sixth Moon. It was customary to travel by boat from Naniwa Bridge to Ebisu Island, and the Festival of Temma was therefore also known as the Boat Festival.

850. *strike the bell . . . Everlasting Torments* (muken no kane wo tsukite). According to an ancient tradition, the person who struck this bell would enjoy prosperity in the present world, but would in exchange be condemned after his death to the Hell of Everlasting Torments *(muken-jigoku)* while his descendants would become beggars. This particular Hell corresponds to the Sanskrit Avici; it was the lowest of the Eight Great Hells and was reserved for egregious sinners, who were subjected to torture by fire. Sayo-no-Naka-yama is a slope near Kanaya in Ōmi Province (present-day Shiga Prefecture); it figures frequently in classical poetry. The bell in question was believed to be in the Kannon Temple near Sayo-no-Nakayama. This rather Faustian legend was well known in the Edo Period; it clearly appealed to Saikaku and he refers to it several times in his writing.

851. *our cauldron* (kama). Implied reference to "Hell's cauldron" *(jigoku no kama)*, one of the places of torment in the after-life.

852. *their chariot* (kuruma). See note 666 above.

853. *it is foolish* (oroka nari). People do not live long enough to realize their hopes or prayers for windfalls. The wife's attitude is one of down-to-earth realism, in contrast with the husband's state of raving excitement.

854. *accompanied by an old lady* (babasama wo tsuredachi). The old lady is the grandmother of the child to whom the wife in the story is to act as wet-nurse. The real mother has evidently died, or for some other reason become unable to nurse her child.

855. *nice full breasts* (chifukuro mo yoi). Her breasts were still full from feeding her own child.

856. *eighty-five silver* mommé (hachijūgo momme). About $65 (£23). This was to be her salary for one year (cf. note 520 above).

857. *the half-period* (hanki). The full-period *(ichinen-ikki)* was for a year; the half-period *(hannen-hanki)* was the basis on which the lower-ranking servants were usually paid, and lasted either from the Third to the Ninth Moon or from the Ninth to the Third Moon. The cook was, therefore, being paid at an annual rate of about $48 (£17).

858. *Thirty-seven silver coins, eighty-five* mommé *in weight* (hachijūgo-momme kazu sanjūnana). The *mame-ita-gin* (note 558) varied in weight from about 1 to 5 *momme* (0.13 to 0.66 oz.) Their value could only be determined by weighing.

859. *eight and a half* mommé (hachimomme gofun). The standard agent's fee was exactly 10 percent.

860. *a child can grow up without its parents* (oya wa nakeredo ko wa sodatsu). Proverbial saying. (The more usual form is *Oya wa nakutomo ko wa sodatsu.)*

861. *money is the real enemy* (kane ga kataki). Proverbial saying (cf. "Money is the root of all evil").

862. *Fushimi*. District to the east of Kyōto.

863. *lucky tea* (daibuku). Tea brewed on the morning of New Year's Day with freshly drawn water. A pickled plum was immersed in the tea before it was drunk.

864. *jio syrup* (jiōsen). Syrup made from the roots of the *jiō* plant. It was considered to have an invigorative effect (see note 363).

865. *"The money that they paid her is still intact"* (saizen no gin wa sono mama). He intends to repay the 85-*momme* advance to his wife's new employers, even if it means that he and his family will starve as a result.

866. *Lord Heitaro* (Heitarō-dono). Heitarō was the popular name for Shimbutsu, a disciple of Shinran Shōnin (note 472). He was converted to the Shinshū Sect during the time that Shinran was travelling in the province of Hitachi (northeastern Japan). Heitarō died in 1261; numerous miraculous deeds were ascribed to him. During the Edo Period it was customary on the night of the Setsubun (the festival that marks the eve of the beginning of

spring) for believers in Shinshū to congregate at their temples and to listen to sermons in praise of Heitarō. Stories about him appeared in *The Life of Heitarō (Heitarō Ichidaiki)* and similar books.

867. *"The Law of Buddha provides a household"* (setai Buppō). One of the many disrespectful saws about the Buddhist church that were current in Saikaku's time. The full saying was "The Law of Buddha provides a household, invoking the Sacred Name fills one's stomach" *(setai Buppō hara Nembutsu)*. That is to say, religious devotion is not always inspired by purely spiritual motives (cf. "rice Christians").

868. *the Setsubun Festival fell on New Year's Eve* (ōmisoka ni setsubun arite). The Setsubun Festival is now fixed on February 4, but it used to be a movable holiday. The most recent year before 1692 (the date of *Seken Munesanyō)* in which Setsubun coincided with New Year's was 1662.

869. *exorcists* (yakuharai). In Saikaku's time there were in effect a class of beggars who used to go from house to house during the Setsubun Festival, ostensibly to drive out evil spirits by means of various exorcist spells, but actually to collect alms. According to the *Kiyū Shōran* (1830), the custom originated in the idea that bad luck was something that people wanted to throw onto the street, just as they threw out scraps of food and worthless objects for beggars. The exorcists went round like garbage collectors, picking up scraps of bad luck as it were, and were paid for their pains. Bill collectors and the tinkling of the scales (for weighing silver coins) were, of course, associated with New Year's; exorcists and bean-throwing belonged to the Setsubun Festival.

870. *the rattle of dried beans* (mame utsu oto). It is customary on the evening of the Setsubun Festival to have a bean-throwing ceremony *(mamemaki)*. Handfuls of dried beans *(oniyai no mame)* are scattered by the head of the household or by the eldest son, to the old cry of *Fuku wa uchi, oni wa soto* ("In with good luck, out with the devils!"). This ancient ceremony, which is supposed to drive out evil spirits, is performed in the various parts of the house and also in shrines and temples. It is still practised annually on February 4.

871. *a devil had been tied up in the darkness* (kuragari ni oni tsunagu). Proverbial expression used to evoke a weird or eerie atmosphere such as would exist if one found oneself in some dark place where a devil had been tied up and one was in danger of bumping into him at any moment.

872. *the first bell* (shoya no kane). About 8 P.M.

873. *the fixed holiday of the year* (ichinenjū no sadame naru). New Year's (as opposed to the movable Setsubun Festival).

874. *the boat of Buddhism* (Hotoke no omukaibune). The boat of the great Buddhist vow in which human beings are carried to safety (cf. note 668 above for the same Buddhist boat imagery).

875. *seasonal time of payment* (sekki-sekki). See note 791 above.

876. *I know this is an old sort of trick* (furui koto nagara). To avoid settling one's debts by pretending to be faced with some personal crisis was a standard ruse with numerous variations (cf. pp. 250–1 above).

877. *a priest who was attached to the Grand Shrine* . . . (danna-mawari no tayūdono). *Tayū* was the common name for the *goshi*, a special type of priest attached to the Grand Shrine of Ise. It was his duty to visit supporters of the Ise Shrine in various parts of the country (in this case, Ōsaka) and to collect contributions from them. In return he would transmit their personal prayers to the Gods at Ise, and also used to give believers special paper amulets *(taima)* from the Grand Shrine.

878. *I married into the family* (irimuko shite). See note 210 above.

879. *If there was a God who threw one down* . . . (hikiaguru kami mo arite). Reference to the proverb, *sutsuru kami areba hikiaguru kami ari.* ("God never shuts one door but he opens another.")

880. *salad of salted sardines* . . . (iwashi-namasu . . .). Standard dishes served during the Setsubun Festival.

881. *to.* One *to* = 0.1 *koku* = half a bushel.

882. *register my own person as security* (warera ga mi wo tegata ni kakiirete). It was possible, though illegal, to put oneself as security for the repayment of a debt. If the debt was not settled on the stipulated date, one was obliged to take service as a domestic servant or as a common labourer.

883. *when forty mommé is the normal price* (seken wa yonjū-me). In 1684 the price of rice was 40 *mommé* per *koku*; in 1691, it fluctuated between 41 and 53 *mommé*. By buying 1 *to* of rice on credit at the rate of 95 *mommé* per *koku,* she had therefore incurred a loss of about 112 per cent, and an actual loss of 5.5 *mommé* (about $4 [30 s.]). This represented the interest accruing during the two months' period of the loan. Extremely high rates of interest were common at this time.

884. *even though I belong to the Lotus Sect* (Hokkeshū naredomo). (See note 569 above). Adherents of the Nichiren Sect would not normally attend services at the temple of one of the Amida sects like Shinshū.

885. *straw or leather sandals* (zōri sekida). All footwear was removed before entering a temple.

886. *to pluck out the Buddha's eye* (Hotoke no me wo nuku). Proverbial expression meaning to act profanely for motives of greed.

887. *you, who are all born with the possibility of salvation* (Buttai naredomo). Lit., "you are all Buddha-natures." The priest's words are based on the belief, expressed in the Nehan (Nirvana) Sutra and elsewhere, that all living creatures have a predisposition towards becoming Buddhas.

888. *the first five days of the New Year* (Shōgatsu gokanichi). This was a holiday period and it was hard to have work done (cf. *sanganichi,* the first three days of the New Year).

889. *forced to leave his home town* (tokoro wo tachinoku). He had presumably been disowned (note 728 above).

890. *a Twelfth Moon priest* (shiwasu-bōzu). See note 813.

NOTE: The following general entries appear in the Index: clothing, coiffure, coins, courtesans, laws, proverbial expressions, quotations and literary references, stylistic devices.